Malise Ruthven is the author of *Islam: A Very Short Introduction*; *Islam in the World*; *The Divine Supermarket: Shopping for God in America*; and *A Satanic Affair: Salman Rushdie and the Wrath of Islam*. A former writer and editor with the BBC's External Services, he has taught and lectured widely in Britain and the United States on religion and the Middle East. He has written for the *Times Literary Supplement* and the *Guardian*, among other publications, and is currently a visiting professor at the University of California, San Diego.

A FURY FOR GOD

The Islamist Attack on America

———————

MALISE RUTHVEN

Granta Books
London · New York

Granta Publications, 2/3 Hanover Yard, Noel Road, London N1 8BE

First published in Great Britain by Granta Books 2002

A CIP catalogue record for this book
is available from the British Library.

1 3 5 7 9 10 8 6 4 2

ISBN 1 86207 540 9

Typeset by M Rules

Printed and bound in Great Britain by Mackays of Chatham PLC

In memory of my father,
Patrick Hore-Ruthven (1913–1942),
who died in the jihad against fascism

And we are here as on a darkling plain
Swept with confused alarms of struggle and flight,
Where ignorant armies clash by night

MATTHEW ARNOLD

CONTENTS

Preface   XI

Glossary   XV

1   September 11th   1
2   Jihad   44
3   The Aesthetics of Martyrdom   72
4   A Fury for God   99
5   Cultural Schizophrenia   134
6   The Seeds of Terror   169
7   Jihad in America   201
8   A Clash of Civilizations?   240

Notes   292
Index   313

PREFACE

This book makes no great claims to originality. Much of the material has already been published elsewhere – in scholarly articles, in newspapers and on the Internet, as well as in other books. Some of this material will already be familiar to readers saturated by media and newspaper coverage of September 11th and its aftermath. Part of it, however, will be known only to specialists. In putting together these two different kinds of material I am hoping that new insights will be forthcoming. For example, most newspaper commentary takes the "Islamic" religious motivations of the terrorists at face value, unaware perhaps that for several decades scholars and specialists have analysed or "deconstructed" the religious and political outlook that informs the Islamist movements. Leading scholars in the field, however, have pointed out that Islamist movements owe much more than they care to admit to ideas imported from the "West" they profess to despise. Other commentators, including leading politicians, have gone to considerable lengths to exculpate the "moderate majority" of Muslims from sympathy with the attacks. While fully endorsing the motives behind such statements – which is to argue that a whole religious tradition cannot be held responsible for abuses or distortions invoked in its name – I cannot accept that the tradition as a whole is somehow blameless. All three Abrahamic monotheisms contain within them justifications for violence that can be exploited for causes that may be denounced as "evil" or "terrorist", as well as for causes often considered admirable, such as patriotism, national resistance or the promotion of human rights.

This book was written in the "heat of the moment", between October 2001 and February 2002. A constant flow of new material became available as I was working on it. In a story in which the factual bases kept shifting, consistency was well nigh impossible. There are bound to be contradictions, while some repetitions are also inevitable. Conceived and executed in haste, the book cannot hope to provide a definitive analysis. At best it is an "interim report", a provisional exploration of some of the forces at work, intellectual and psychological, as well as religious and political, behind the September 11th attacks.

Nearly eight months after the attacks, our knowledge of the details is still very sketchy. On 30 April 2002, following months of investigations involving thousands of agents, as well as the arrest and interrogations of hundreds of Arab and Muslim immigrants, the director of the FBI, Robert Mueller, said there was still no hard evidence revealing how the attacks had been planned and executed. The hijackers left no "paper trails" in the form of mobile phone bills or credit card receipts. They did not use laptops and stored nothing on computer hard drives. The money they received from abroad was sent in small amounts to avoid detection. The only certainty was that the attacks had been a considerable time in the planning – as much as five years, according to FBI officials.

An independent writer can hardly hope to succeed where the FBI has so signally failed. I make no claim to produce factual evidence not already in the public domain. My purpose has been rather to explore the religious, ideological and political background behind the atrocities: the classical doctrine of jihad (holy war) and the influence of the "martyr" Sayyid Qutb (1906–66) on modern Islamist activism; the love–hate relationship between sections of Muslim youth and "the West", and the desperate acts of "self-martyrdom" by which some young Muslims seek to resolve the painful personal conflicts engendered by "cultural schizophrenia"; the axis of oil that ties profligate American consumers to the tribal absolutism of Saudi Arabia; the possibility – unproven – of an "Iraqi connection" with the September 11th attacks; the much discussed "clash of civilizations" between the Islamic and Western worlds.

I could never have completed the project in such a relatively short time without assistance from other people. James Howarth provided valuable help with Arabic and English texts and material on the Internet. James Price and Dr Michelle Spuler also supplied me with useful material during the early stages of the project. Sajidah Ahmad's editorial contribution went beyond the call of duty. Dr Charles Tripp, who read the typescript in draft, made several valuable suggestions, to which I have tried to respond within the constraints of a very tight deadline. None of the above bears any responsibility whatsoever for the tenor of my interpretations or for factual errors. I also received useful help from Steve Bonella, Prunella Bramwell-Davies, Dr Susan Buckley, Gurbir Dhillon, Professor Fawaz Gerges, Tim Hodgkinson, Trevor Mostyn, Elfi Pallis and Benjamin Shaw. My thanks to all of them, and especially to Tiggy for her critical eye and her forbearance; to Neil Belton for his continuing patience and support; and to the staff of the British Library for their efficiency and courtesy.

La Jolla, California, 1 May 2002

GLOSSARY

'abd   servant, slave

'abda   female servant, slave

agal   headrope worn around the *kaffiya* (head-dress); originally rope used for camels

ahl   family, people

ahl al-bait   family of the Prophet

ahl al-kitab   people of the book

ahl al-hadith   people of tradition – those who opposed the Mu'tazalite rationalists

al   family, house (as in Al Sa'ud)

al-   definite article

'alim (pl. *'ulama*)   learned man, religious scholar; though Islam has no priesthood, the *'ulama* are often described as the "guardians" of the religious tradition

Allah   the name for God in Arabic, used by all Muslims and also by Arabic-speaking Christians and Jews; it incorporates the definite article *al-*, giving it a more abstract meaning than the English word God (i.e. "the god" or even "the deity")

Allahu Akbar   "God is Greater!"

amir (pl. *umara'*)   commander; also prince

amirate, emirate   Muslim state ruled by an amir

'anqud (pl. *'anaqid*)   cluster or bunch, as in grapes – a term used

to describe the self-contained cellular structure of the Islamist
movements in Egypt

ard (pl. *aradi*) earth, land

aradi amariyya princely lands

'asabiyya group feeling, "a corporate spirit oriented towards
obtaining and keeping power" (Albert Hourani), a concept
employed in Ibn Khaldun's theory of cyclical renewal

asbab al-nuzul occasions of revelation – a technical term used by
scholars to coordinate passages in the Quran with episodes in
the life of the Prophet Muhammad

asnam (sing. *sanam*) idols

aya (pl. *ayat*) sign or "miracle" from God – a term used for
both the "miracles" of nature and individual verses of the
Quran

bai'a oath of allegiance to a leader

bhakti (Sanskrit) devotion

bin (also *ibn*) son of, often abbreviated to b.

bint daughter of

bled al siba (Morocco) "lands of insolence", where the writ of
the state is weak

burqa the complete covering used by women in some parts of the
Muslim world, notably Afghanistan

caliphate the realm ruled by the Caliph (see *Khalifa*), often syn-
onymous in early Islamic times with *dar al-islam*; also reign or
the period of time that any given Caliph ruled (e.g. the caliphate
of al-Ma'mun)

dar home, abode, sphere

dar al-harb the abode or sphere of war (i.e. non-Islamic lands)

dar al-hijra abode of emigration – a term used for the agricultural settlements established by Ibn Sa'ud in the 1920s

dar al-islam the abode or sphere of Islam

da'wa preaching or missionary activity

dhikr "remembrance" of God – a term applied to rituals performed by different Sufi orders

dhimmi, ahl al-dhimma a protected subject of the Muslim state;
originally applied to Christians and Jews, *dhimmi* status was

extended to Zoroastrians, Hindus and other subjects of the Muslim state

din religion

din al-fitra "natural religion" – a term sometimes applied to Islam by its advocates

diya blood money; composition (i.e. compensation) for murder

dunya world

fard 'ain an individual duty or obligation in Islam

fard kifaya a collective duty or obligation in Islam

fatwa a legal ruling, opinion or advice given by a *mufti*, a qualified legal scholar

fiqh jurisprudence (lit. "understanding" the will of God)

fitna strife, social unrest – a term used for any period of conflict, for example the civil wars in the decades after Muhammad's death in 632

ghadba "fury" or outrage

hadd (pl. *hudud*) "boundaries" or limits – a term used for the moral limits established by God in the Quran; the Islamic laws imposed under martial law by the Pakistani dictator General Zia ul-Haqq were known as the "Hudood Ordinances"

hadith (pl. *ahadith*) tradition, saying or action attributed to the Prophet Muhammad or his contemporaries; these were passed down orally for two or more centuries after Muhammad's death in 632

Hajj the annual pilgrimage to Mecca, one of the five duties or obligations of Islam, which every practising Muslim is expected to perform at least once in his or her lifetime

Hajji one who has performed the Hajj

hakimiyya sovereignty, governance

hakm (pl. *ahkam*) rule

haram sacred, forbidden; also sanctuary, such as in Mecca

al-haramain the two sanctuaries of Mecca and Medina; *bilad al-haramain*, "Lands of the Two Sanctuaries", is a term used by, among others, Osama bin Laden for the Arabian peninsula

Haram al-Sharif the Noble Sanctuary, Jerusalem

harim female part of the household, to which, in traditional

Muslim societies, nonrelated males are not admitted

hijab "veil" worn by some Muslim women, from a Quranic term used for curtain or screen

hijra (sometimes *hegira*) the migration of the Prophet Muhammad and his companions from Mecca to Medina in 622; it came to be used by extension to mean the emigration of Muslims from *dar al-harb* to *dar al-islam* either physically or spiritually

hijri (adj.) appertaining to the Muslim (*hijri*) lunar calendar, which starts in 622, the year of the *hijra*; dates are therefore given as AH, *anno hegirae*, and 2000 CE, for example, was 1421 AH

himaya protection – that is, granted by a superior to a subordinate tribe

ibn (pl. *bin*) son of

i'jaz inimitability; the miraculous quality of the Quran's language

ijtihad effort, endeavour or diligence; most commonly used to denote an individual interpretation of the Quran, or independent judgement in a legal or a theological question

ilhad heresy

iman faith

insan human being, humanity; *al-insan al-kamil* is the perfect man or complete human being – a concept defined by Ibn 'Arabi and thereafter widely used in Sufism

intihar suicide

irhab terrorism

Islam submission or self-surrender to God, the name given to what would become a major world religion

Isma'ili a minority tradition of the Shi'a who follow leaders in the line of Isma'il b. Ja'afar; the Isma'ilis are now divided into two main groupings: the Nizaris, who regard the Aga Khan as their "Living Imam", and the Mustalians or Bohras, whose Imam is in concealment or occultation

istishhad "self-martyrdom" – a term now used for suicide bombings

ittihad unity, union; *muttahid*, united

jahiliyya the period of "ignorance" or paganism prior to the revelation of Islam; used by Islamists as a term of abuse against contemporary rulers or other Muslims considered insufficiently pious or radical

jama'a (pl. *jama'at*)   assembly, association

al-Jama'at al-Islamiya (Ar.)   Islamic associations – a term used for the Islamist groups in Egypt

Jama'at-i-Islami (Urdu)   South Asian Islamist party founded by Abu'l-'Ala Maududi in 1941

jihad   "struggle" – a term used for holy war; the "greater jihad" is sometimes used to refer to the struggle against one's own evil tendencies, while the "lesser jihad" is the physical struggle against one's enemies or the enemies of Islam

jizya   the poll tax paid by *dhimmis*

kafala   sponsorship

kafil   sponsor

kafir, (pl. *kuffar* or *kafirun*)   infidel, nonbeliever in Islam

kata'ib (sing. *katiba*)   battalion, brigade, Phalange (a Lebanese political party); some of the Palestinian suicide bombers wear bandanas proclaiming their membership of *kata'ib al-Qassam*, the al-Qassam Martyrs Brigade

Khalifa   Caliph, politico-religious leader of the community of Muslims after the death of the Prophet Muhammad, God's vice-regent on Earth

khariji (pl. *khawarij*)   Kharijite, seceder – a term applied to the first sectarian dissenters who "went out" (*kharaja*) from the Muslim community; **neo-kharijites** modern sectarians, such as the Takfir wa-l-Hijra (TwH), who have seceded from the main body of the Muslim community to form their own sectarian communities

khuwwa   extraction

kitab (pl. *kutub*)   book

kufr   disbelief in God – a term sometimes employed polemically by Muslims of different persuasions against each other

Mahdi   messianic figure in Islamic eschatology

mahram   people of the opposite sex to whom one is forbidden (that is, to marry)

majlis al-shura   consultative council

mamluk (pl. *mamalik*) "owned" – a term used for the technically slave status of the rulers of Egypt from the thirteenth to the nineteenth centuries

mashura see shura

maslaha public interest

mawlid feast day commemorating birth of saintly person

mihna "inquisition" established under caliphate of al-Ma'mun to enforce Mu'tazilite doctrine

mufti see fatwa

muhajir (pl. *muhajirun, muhajirin* [colloquial]) one who migrates (from evil, or from a non-Muslim state) in emulation of the migration (*hijra*) of the Prophet and his companions from Mecca to Medina in 622, the event which marks the beginning of the Muslim era

mujahid (pl. *mujahidun, mujahidin* [colloquial]) one who struggles or fights for God's cause; a holy warrior

mujtahid a scholar who interprets the Quran using individual reasoning, of *ijtihad*

mukhabarat intelligence services, secret police

mushrik (pl. *mushrikun, mushrikin* [colloquial]) an "associator" or idolator – a term of abuse often levelled at one's religious opponents

Muslim (pl. *Muslimun, Muslimin* [colloquial]) one who professes Islam, or who is born into a Muslim family; nonpractising Muslims are sometimes described as "cultural Muslims"

Muslima a female Muslim

mustashhid a self-martyr – a term used for suicide bombers

mutawwa'in religious police; short term for members of the "committee for upholding the good and forbidding the evil" (*al-amr bi'l-ma'ruf wa'l-nahy an 'al-munkar*), as found in Saudi Arabia and in Afghanistan under the Saudi-sponsored Taliban regime

mu'tazila Mu'tazilites, "those who keep themselves apart", often described as "rationalists", who believed that the Quran was created in time

nafa (pl. *anfas*) self; soul; also spirit, person, being identity

naskh abrogation – a technical term used in Quranic exegesis to designate the abrogation of some Quranic verses by others, or of previous scriptures by the Quran

nikah marriage contract

pir (Urdu, Pers.) a Sufi saint or spiritual master

al-Qaʿida the foundation, the base; the word can also mean model or principle, as in something one should aspire to follow

al-salaf al-salih the "righteous ancestors"; *salafi* and *salafiyya* are now used by Islamist radicals who look to the righteous ancestors for inspiration, but the same term was used by modernists in an earlier period referring to the righteous ancestors in order to find ways of accommodating Islam to contemporary realities

shahada the declaration of faith, one of the five duties or "pillars" of Islam, according to the formula "There is no God but Allah. Muhammad is the messenger of Allah"

shahid a martyr or "witness" for the faith

shaikh elder; religious or tribal leader

Shiʿa party, group, coming to mean the "party" of ʿAli, the Prophet Muhammad's closest male relative, whose supporters believe he was cheated of the caliphate; the Shiʿa became the minority tradition in Islam

Shiʿi a Shiʿite or member of the Shiʿa, the minority tradition

shirk "association" of lesser beings with the deity; polytheism

shura consultation, sometimes used as Quranic justification for democratic institutions

Sufi an Islamic mystic

Sufism the mystical tradition in Islam

sultan holder of authority – a title used by Muslim rulers

sultaniyya authority

sunna custom or practice of the Prophet Muhammad, as transmitted through the corpus of hadiths; the term Sunni is given to the majority tradition in Islam, which is distinguished from the Shiʿa minority

suq (pl. *aswaq*) market

takfir   the declaration that someone is a *kafir* or infidel; excommunication

al-Takfir wa-l-Hijra   "excommunication and migration" – the name given to the Islamist Society of Muslims in Egypt; a group of the same name based in Algeria is on the US State Department's list of proscribed terrorist organizations

taqiyya   "dissimulation" – a term used for the practice of some Shi'a dissidents who concealed their true allegiance to an Imam from the House of 'Ali behind the outward veneer of Sunni conformity

tariq   road

tariqa   "way" – prescribed by a Sufi mystical order

al-tariqa al-mutawasita   the "middle way" of Islam

al-tawassur al-islami   Islamic conception – a term used by Sayyid Qutb

tawhid   divine unity or unicity

thawb   robe or garment worn by men; some Wahhabis wore them short (i.e. above the ankle) in imitation of what they considered to have been the practice of the Prophet Muhammad

'ulama (sing. *'alim*)   the legal scholars of Isalm, "guardians" of the faith

Umma   the world-wide community of Muslims

'Umra   the lesser pilgrimage to the shrine at Mecca which can be performed throughout the year

wafd   delegation – name given to Egypt's first modern nationalist party after Britain prevented the government from sending a delegation to the Paris Peace Conference in 1919

waqf (pl. *awqaf*)   religious foundation or trust

zakat   purifying dues or ritual charity, one of the five "pillars" or duties of Islam

Chapter One

September 11th

The images at first seemed like a disaster movie. The smoke and the flames were billowing out of the twin towers of the World Trade Center, once the world's tallest skyscraper, still, in the age of globalization, the most vivid symbol of America's economic might. It was only when we saw the sequences over and again that the message really came home. Those tiny antlike figures jumping into oblivion were real people, not actors or stuntmen, human beings caught in their final, desperate moments. We saw the towers implode and collapse into a heap of crumbling masonry and twisted metal, the clouds of dust filling streets full of people running or staggering away. These scenes, constantly played and replayed on the screen and in our heads, generated a hypnagogic state lying somewhere between dream and wakeful fantasy. The repetitions, the absence of a musical score, and the familiar, authoritative voices of the newscasters ground them into the part of the brain that experiences the world as real.

As the days passed, a flood of personal narratives, jarred, twisted and severed, invaded our feelings. The message "I love you" left on a husband's answering machine from the wife who was trapped in the burning building; the husband who called from the toilet in one of the doomed planes repeating those same three simple words; the heroism of the passengers on the fourth hijacked plane who fought the terrorists, causing the plane to crash before it could hit its destined target, the White House or Capitol; the banker who struggled down fifty flights of steps from one of the collapsing towers, only to discover that his mother and sister were passengers on one of the hijacked planes.

The terror had come to New York on a bright sunny morning out of a clear blue sky. People having breakfast in the Windows of the World restaurant on the 107th floor of the North Tower could see for forty miles. Below them tens of thousands of people were setting about their tasks at the start of another day in one of the world's largest, and busiest, office complexes. They came from many different backgrounds.

One of the survivors, financial services executive Adam Mayblum, was checking e-mails at 8.47 a.m. when American Airlines flight 11 – a Boeing 767 – hit the North Tower between the 95th and 103rd floors. "The building lurched violently and shook as if it were an earthquake. People screamed. I watched out of my window as the building seemed to move 10 to 20 feet in each direction. Light fixtures and parts of the ceiling collapsed. The kitchen was destroyed. We were certain it was a bomb." Mayblum was lucky: he made it to the bottom down the emergency stairwells.[1] Eric Levine, a trader with Morgan Stanley, was on the 64th floor of the South Tower when the second plane, United Airlines flight 175 – another Boeing 767 – hit the building at about the 80th floor. He was already in the stairwell being evacuated when he heard a huge explosion that "shook the whole building . . . I tried to stand up but the building was still shaking and the lights were flickering on and off . . . then the building began to sink, that's the only way I can describe it. The floor began to lower under your feet and all I could think about was that it would crack open and I would fall hundreds of feet to my death. People began screaming and crying and praying out loud for God to help them. I remember that I began to pray once the floor gave out. Asking God to just let the building stop shaking long enough for me to get out . . . Somewhere along the route between the 44th and 34th floors I lost sight of the little Filipina woman who had been hanging on to my arm for dear life. She was there one moment and gone the next . . . Around the 25th floor we began to smell jet fuel and a lot of it . . . After what seemed like an eternity, but actually took about 40 minutes, we saw our first glimpse of the outside world. People were screaming and running everywhere, emergency vehicles wherever you looked . . . I could not believe what I was seeing. Both buildings were on fire with flames shooting out of them about 100 feet high. Huge plumes of thick black smoke were billowing out of them and when I looked at Tower 2 you could still see the tail end of the jet hanging out of the building. I ran 15 blocks to my apartment where I sat in shock watching the replay of the buildings falling."[2]

There were 115 nationalities among the almost 3,000 confirmed deaths. All walks of life were represented, from the financial traders of companies like Cantor FitzGerald to the janitors who cleaned the offices and scrubbed the toilets. Over the following months their obituaries, accompanied by postage-stamp-sized portraits, would appear in the pages of the *New York Times*. "Here in the democracy of the dead," wrote Harold Evans, "is a marvellous mosaic of a great city, of dreams small and large, of fretful talents and settled routines, of large ambitions and little common decencies, people of all faiths and none."[3] In catastrophic situations such common decencies become acts of heroism: people risked their lives, sometimes died, for courtesies like helping a fat or lame person on the stairs. The heroism of the fire department has passed into legend. One group that suffered badly for its courage was the fire department's "special operations command", the first to appear on the scene, whose job it is to rush into burning buildings when everyone else is pouring out. On the morning of September 11th the group lost 75 members of the more than 300 firefighters who died.[4]

Standing 1,360 feet above street level, 100 feet higher than the Empire State Building, the World Trade Center was an obvious target for terrorist attack. In 1993, Ramzi Yousef (who may have been an Iraqi agent and would later be described as "the world's

most wanted terrorist") and a group of fellow conspirators, most
of them veterans of the CIA-sponsored jihad against the Soviets in
Afghanistan, tried to blow up the building by planting a home-
made bomb in a rented van in one of the basement car parks. Six
people died in the attack, and more than a thousand suffered
injuries. The bomb, containing 1,200 pounds of urea nitrate and
liquid hydrogen, left a crater 200 feet wide and several storeys deep.
At one of the two trials of Yousef in 1996, the FBI agent who
brought him back to America from Pakistan testified that Yousef had
hoped that one of the towers would topple onto the other, killing
tens of thousands of people, to let the Americans know that they
were "at war".[5] Although the bombing caused massive disruption to
New York's financial centre, from the terrorist's point of view the
operation could be rated a failure. The massive steel supports at
the base of the building withstood the blast remarkably well.

For what were in their time the two tallest buildings in the
world, the Twin Towers were unusually light, being built to a novel
design that used the outer walls, made from 240 vertical columns
of toughened steel bound together by horizontal steel trusses, to
support the building's weight. They were among the first high-rise
buildings to use a tube structure rather than the frame structure
used in earlier skyscrapers, and the first to be designed without any
masonry at all. As Minoru Yamasaki, the architect, explained in his
autobiography, "Using the exterior wall meant employing the most
efficient structural system available – the entire building perimeter – as a strong tube to act as the cantilever."[6] The system,
known as Vierendeel trusses, is less expensive than skyscrapers of
conventional design. Yamasaki estimated that the technological
breakthroughs used in his construction enabled his client, the New
York Port Authority, to build the two 110-storey towers for about
the same cost as more conventionally designed 50- or 60-storey
structures.[7] He was especially proud of the way the towers, built to
withstand the tail end of the Caribbean hurricanes that occasionally lash New York, absorbed the motion of the wind. The building
moved "about eight inches over ten seconds in a hundred-mile-an-
hour wind, which is hardly any movement at all". In older

structures in the 60-storey range, movement in heavy wind was so great that the top storeys had to be evacuated. "This has never happened in the Trade Center towers," Yamasaki concluded happily, "and I doubt if it ever will, despite the frequent gusts of strong winds at their upper elevations."[8]

Neither Yamasaki nor anyone else can have reckoned on the impact of two Boeing 767s, each loaded with more than 10,000 gallons of aviation fuel. The North Tower lasted for 103 minutes after the initial impact, the South Tower for only 53 minutes, apparently because the second plane was travelling much faster than the first, well above the manufacturer's safety limits.[9]

Experts are divided over the reasons the towers collapsed. Some blame directly the impact of the planes, which knocked out as many as 40 of the vertical steel columns at the perimeter of each building. The impacts also damaged the steel columns at the core, which prevented people in the impact zones and above from escaping down the stairwells housed in the core. Most of the people who died were trapped above the floors hit by the planes. In the North Tower everyone on or above the 92nd floor perished; everyone on the 91st floor survived, while 20 people on the 83rd died. In the South Tower, about two-thirds of the office workers had reached safety before the second plane crashed into floors 78 to 84.[10] The people we saw jumping to their deaths from the upper floors must have known full well that they were doomed because of the fires and blockages in the stairwells. Eyewitnesses said the roofs of buildings close to the tower were covered with bodies. These unfortunates, who came to be known as "jumpers", made the intelligent choice: instant suicide was preferable to death by burning and suffocation.

Structural engineers who saw the television footage estimated that the buildings absorbed the impact remarkably well, allowing up to 25,000 people on the lower floors to escape. Gordon Masterton, chair of the structural and buildings board of the British Institute of Civil Engineers, said, "I reckon the force of the impact was something like 8,000 to 10,000 tons, like 20 of the biggest trucks colliding with the tower simultaneously. That was probably more than double its design capacity under hurricane winds. Yet the building absorbed it."[11] Many experts saw the explosions and aviation fuel fires as being primarily responsible. Writing in *New Steel Construction* Charles Clifton, a structural engineer at the New Zealand Heavy Engineering Research Association, argued that by penetrating the perimeter frames, the planes would not only have stripped the fire protection off the columns, they would also have shattered many of the internal supporting columns, leaving the rest vulnerable to fire. The fireproofing and sprinkler systems had been designed to protect the building from the type of fire expected in an office building: one fuelled by paper, desks and other office furniture, not by kerosene. Water sprinklers in these circumstances would have been useless. Hydrocarbon fires, which develop much more speedily and reach much higher temperatures than fires fuelled by other materials, are usually fought with chemical foam.

When the planes hit the buildings and exploded, the aluminium in the wreckage would have rapidly heated towards 1,500°C, the temperature at which steel melts. The collapse would have been abetted by the softening of the thin steel trusses, only four centimetres thick, that held up the floors and bound the walls. Once these floor supports had begun to melt, each tower was subjected to a chain reaction with every floor falling onto the one below. The accumulating weight of 110 collapsing floors accelerated to a speed of 250 miles per hour, causing each tower to collapse in about 15 seconds. Fire chiefs and engineers have agreed that the fireproofing of the structure was inadequate. Kafko, a mineral-based fireproofing applied to the steel columns, has been described as "very fragile" and particularly difficult to apply to the floor trusses. Leslie Robertson, the engineer largely responsible for the detailed structural work on the Twin Towers, admitted that although the possibility of a plane crashing into the towers had been built into the design, the explosion of aviation fuel and fire were not fully taken into consideration. Opinions were divided on whether other buildings could have survived an equally ferocious attack. Clifton said that "the very light and open structure probably made the buildings more vulnerable to collapse from the aircraft impact than would have been the case for a heavier structural system".

Paula Hawkins notes that

> ... the terrorists had either done their homework, or were very lucky: they struck the towers at precisely the right height. Had the planes hit the buildings any higher up, it is likely that the weight of the floors above the crash site might not have been sufficient to bring the building down. And lower down on the building, the vertical columns are thicker, and fewer would have been destroyed by the impact.

"It is difficult to draw firm conclusions," she writes after considering the expert evidence. "Had the building been made of a more solid frame structure, it might have collapsed more quickly. But a concrete structure would have been more resistant to fire than the steel tube structure of the towers."[12]

Impact or fire? Luck or design? The questions go to the heart of the New York atrocity and to the response it provoked. The scale of the deaths it caused – initially placed at more than 6,000, though later reduced to half that number – generated an unstoppable political momentum which George W. Bush was able to ride by declaring "war on terrorism". People compared the atrocity to the Japanese attack on Pearl Harbor, the event that brought the United States into the Second World War, to the 55,000 deaths suffered by America in Vietnam or even to the atom bomb attack on the Japanese cities of Hiroshima and Nagasaki in 1945. In fact, the eventual death toll of 3,216, including the passengers and crews of all four jets and the victims of the attack on the Pentagon, is well below that of the victims of several recent massacres, including Hama in Syria in 1982 (where 10,000 to 20,000 Muslim Syrians were slaughtered by the Baathist regime), the Iraqi poison gas attack at Halabja in 1988 (between 6,000 and 8,000 Iraqi Kurds), Srebrenica in 1995 (7,300 Bosnian Muslims) and Mazar-i-Sharif in 1998 (between 5,000 and 8,000 of the Shi'i Hezara minority murdered by the Taliban).[13]

Peter Bergen, a terrorism specialist at the CNN TV network, sees the 1993 attack on the World Trade Center as a "dress rehearsal" for the much more devastating attack that came eight years later.[14] It would certainly appear that the conspirators of September 11th learned from the previous failure – assuming, that is, that they intended to kill more than six people in their second attempt. We do not know if they studied the building's design. What is known, however, is that Mohammed Atta, the man who commanded the operation, had trained as an architect. Moreover he had an aversion to high-rise buildings, which he saw as being alien to Islamic culture. It seems unlikely that men who had carefully studied airline schedules in order to ensure that the planes were fully loaded with aviation fuel would have neglected to examine the structures of the buildings.

Less spectacular, but equally impressive in terms of planning, was the attack on the Pentagon, headquarters of the US Department of Defense. At 9.38 a.m. American Airlines flight 77, a Boeing 757 *en route* from Dulles International airport near Washington, DC, to Los Angeles, crashed into the south-western side of the building killing 189 people, including the 64 passengers and crew aboard the plane. The US military headquarters was built in 1943 out of reinforced concrete to withstand a conventional bombing attack and was less vulnerable than the Manhattan Twin Towers. The plane struck three of the concentrically arranged pentagons or "rings" which house the offices of the world's greatest military power, but compared to the World Trade Center the casualties were light. As in New York, most of the damage was caused by the aviation fluid which exploded on impact, sending sheets of flame through the corridors. The US Defense Secretary, Donald Rumsfeld, the Bush administration's leading "hawk" in the subsequent campaign against al-Qa'ida and the Taliban, escaped unhurt. The plane hit the opposite side of the building from where he happened to be working at the time. The fourth plane to be hijacked that morning, United Airlines flight 93, a Boeing 757 *en route* from Newark to San Francisco, came down at 10.04, 80 miles southeast of Pittsburgh, Pennsylvania, exactly one hour and seventeen minutes after the first plane hit the North Tower. In this case the hijackers did not reckon with the presence of cellular phones: a passenger who spoke to his wife learned of the attack on New York. Recognizing that their plane was aimed at a similar target, possibly the White House or the Capitol, he and some fellow passengers decided to fight the hijackers, causing the plane to crash and losing the lives of the passengers and crew.[15]

The picture that emerged in the days following the attacks was of a ruthless operation carried out with fiendish efficiency, the result of months rather than weeks of meticulous planning. The attacks were impressively coordinated. The hijackers pondered a complex series of airline schedules. They studied the aircraft, and the leaders acquired sufficient expertise as pilots to fly the planes and hit three of the four targets, with devastating accuracy in the case of the Twin Towers. They boarded their chosen flights in carefully worked-out dummy runs, studied the security systems and chose their weapons – simple box cutters or Stanley knives, implements used by any designer or builder or electrician. They were familiar with the scandalously lax security at American airports, where poorly trained screeners, employed by subcontractors, were paid $6 an hour to read the X-ray scanners through which passengers' luggage must pass. They worked out the dispositions of passengers and cabin crews so that when the moment for action arrived, they would be able to overwhelm all opposition. In the three successful attacks this coordination was perfect. Their choice of transcontinental flights – Boston and Washington (Dulles) to Los Angeles, Newark to San Francisco, ensured that the planes were loaded with fuel. Once airborne, the civilian jets became cruise missiles, their autopilots replaced by the steely resolution of the *mustashhid* or suicide martyr's will.

Since there were no survivors from the hijackings, we can only infer what happened from information passed by the FBI to journalists, newspaper investigations after the event, including interviews with people who met the hijackers, passenger manifests, images from one or two security cameras, the records of air traffic control, and the cellular phone calls made by passengers aboard United Airlines flight 93.

The attacks on America had been long in the planning. The first of the hijackers to arrive in the United States seems to have been Nawaq al-Hamzi, a Saudi citizen from Mecca who had spent a year at the al-Faruq training camp established by Osama bin Laden in Afghanistan. In November 1999 – 22 months before the attack – he rented an apartment in San Diego, California, and took flying lessons with another Saudi hijacker, his fellow Meccan Khalid al-Midhar.[16] Both men were on board American Airlines flight 77 when it took off from Dulles International bound for Los Angeles. Nawaq al-Hamzi sat in seat 5F, next to his younger brother Salem. Khalid al-Midhar was a few rows behind, in seat 12B.

Although Nawaq was the first to arrive in the US, the FBI and the media are in agreement that Mohammed Atta, a 33-year-old Egyptian architect and town planner, was in local command of the operation. Atta studied at Harburg Technical University in Hamburg after graduating in architecture at Cairo University. He arrived in Florida in June 2000 with a fellow student at Harburg, 24-year-old Marwan al-Shehi. Al-Shehi and another plotter, Ziad Jarrah, had visited Afghanistan with Atta in 1998 or 1999, where it is assumed that bin Laden and the al-Qa'ida leadership gave the plan their blessing. It was widely reported that Mohammed 'Atef, an al-Qa'ida operative subsequently killed in the bombing of al-Qa'ida bases in Afghanistan, was in overall charge of the operation. Atta and al-Shehi took lessons at the flying school run by Huffman Aviation in Venice, Florida, a company that specializes in training foreign pilots. The two men learned the rudiments of aviation and navigation before receiving hands-on instruction in single-engine planes. The cost of the training was around $1,000 per week, paid for by funds wired from the United Arab Emirates.[17] After the flying lessons, Atta and al-Shehi received two days' training on a Boeing 727 flight simulator at the SimCenter flight school at Opa-Locka airport near Miami at a cost of around $800 per hour. Noticing how they kept apart from other customers, the staff thought they were just "shy foreigners" trying to acquire the skills they needed to obtain jobs as pilots in their home countries.

Harry George, SimCenter's owner, explained that the exposure he gave Atta and al-Shehi on the 727 simulator would have been enough for them to fly the two 767s they hijacked into the North and South Towers of the World Trade Center. The controls and flight deck layouts are similar in order to make it easier for pilots to switch from one to the other. According to George, Atta showed no interest in doing takeoffs and landings on the simulator. "We mostly did turns and a couple of approaches," he told reporters.[18]

It was recalled at the flying school that Atta and al-Shehi were often rude and offhand, and that they indulged in careless, debonair flying. In one remarkable incident, the two men caused near panic on Boxing Day 2000 when the plane they had rented stalled on the runway at Miami International airport while the Christmas traffic was at its height. As darkness fell they simply abandoned the plane on the tarmac, causing a massive jam, and took a $200 taxi ride back to Venice.[19]

Although Atta aroused suspicions locally, no one alerted the security authorities. In January 2001 his tourist visa had expired when he came back from a trip to Spain (where he may have been in touch with other al-Qa'ida cells and ETA, the Basque separatist organization whom the Spanish authorities claim to have been in league with al-Qa'ida), but he managed to convince immigration officials that despite his comparatively advanced age of 33 he was waiting for a student visa. (Astonishingly, new visa extensions for Atta and al-Shehi arrived for them at Huffman Aviation in March 2002, six months into the "war on terrorism".) In April 2001 Atta was pulled over by police while driving without a licence north of Miami. Like many other booked drivers in the land where the motorist rules, he did not bother to show up in court. That same spring he flew to a small airport in the Appalachian Mountains and began asking pointed questions about chemical factories and nuclear power plants: the fellow aviator whom he had questioned joked to a colleague, "Sounds like terrorists."[20]

By midsummer the plot appears to have been in place. Ziad
Jarrah, the third member of the cell Atta had assembled in
Hamburg, arrived together with Ahmad al-Haznawi, a 20-year-old
Saudi from Baljuraishi in the Asir province. A fourth member,
the so-called "twentieth hijacker" Zakarias Moussaoui, a French
citizen of Moroccan origin who had lived in Brixton, London, was
already under arrest in the US on immigration charges. The
immigration authorities had been informed after he had acted
suspiciously at the Pan Am International flight school in Eagan,
Minnesota. Like Atta he had wanted to learn how to fly a
passenger jet at cruising altitude, but not how to take off or land.
He showed no aptitude for flying and refused to divulge his real
name, preferring to use the pseudonym Zuluman Tango Tango.
After his arrest he was found with a French passport, an outdated
visa obtained in Islamabad, and a fake Algerian passport.

Although the FBI had been told by the French authorities that
Moussaoui was a terrorist suspect, no action was taken against him
until after September 11th, when he was seen in his secure unit
cheering the television footage of the destruction of the World
Trade Center. Until then the FBI had been unable to persuade
lawyers at the Justice Department to allow them to search his possessions. When the FBI finally checked his computer they found
information about aerial crop-spraying, prompting concern about
chemical and biological attacks, as well as information that might
have enabled them to forestall the September attacks.[21] The French
intelligence service claimed they had placed Moussaoui under surveillance in 1999 when he made several trips to Pakistan and
Afghanistan. Moussaoui seems to have replaced a fourth member
of the Hamburg cell, Ramzi bin al-Shibh, a Yemeni who had
lodged with Atta in Germany but had failed to obtain a US visa.[22]
Ahmad Ressam, arrested for his part in a plot to attack Los Angeles
International airport during the 1999–2000 millennium celebrations, had begun to cooperate with the FBI before the September
11th attacks but it was not until afterwards that he was asked
about Moussaoui, whom he identified as a militant he had met at
a training camp in Afghanistan.

By September 7th, the hijack teams were in place. Jarrah's team travelled to Newark, New Jersey, where they stayed in the Airport Marriott hotel to prepare the hijacking of United Airlines flight 93; another team, led by a mysterious figure named Hani Hanjur who entered America on a student visa but never took up his studies, was in Maryland, close to Dulles International airport, in preparation for American Airlines flight 97; the teams of Atta and al-Shehi moved to Boston, where some of the junior members are reported to have availed themselves of a prostitute on at least two occasions. According to several accounts, before leaving Florida Atta and al-Shehi had drawn attention to themselves in Shuckums Seafood Bar, where al-Shehi drank several screwdrivers (orange juice and vodka) with an unnamed associate who drank rum and Coke. Atta stood at the other end of the bar drinking cranberry juice, playing games on a video console and leering at a passing waitress who felt he was "undressing her with his eyes".²³ Earlier accounts indicated that it was Atta who drank rum and Coke. This seemingly "unIslamic" behaviour prompted much comment after the September 11th attacks, suggestive of attitudes that were inconsistent with the hijackers' religious motivation. Would "genuine religious fanatics" anticipate the rewards of martyrdom by drinking and whoring prior to their apotheoses? After a dispute about the $48 bill, al-Shehi flashed a wad of notes at the waitress, claiming he was a pilot with American Airlines (a gesture which, given his state of inebriation, suggests an element of wishful thinking). Afterwards Atta and al-Shehi went their separate ways, al-Shehi to join his team in Boston, while Atta, accompanied by a Saudi, 'Abd al-'Aziz al-'Umari, flew to Portland, Maine, where his image was captured on two security cameras, before taking an early flight to Boston in preparation for the hijacking of American Airlines flight 11.

For air traffic control the first sign of trouble came at 8.14 a.m. According to subsequently released recordings, two controllers, one in Boston, the other in Athens, Ohio, agree that the pilot of American Airlines flight 11 is out of contact. "He won't answer you," Athens tells Boston. "He's nordo [no radar], roger. Thanks." Ten minutes later, the voice of one of the hijackers is heard addressing the passengers: "We have some planes. Just stay quiet and you'll be OK. We are returning to the airport. Nobody move, everything will be OK. If you try to make any moves you'll endanger yourself and the airplane. Just stay quiet." At 8.33 a hijacker's voice is heard again. "Nobody move, please, we are going back to the airport. Don't try to make any stupid moves."[24] The pilot of United Airlines flight 175, which crashed into the South Tower, got a message from air traffic control asking him to look out for American Airlines flight 11, to which the pilot responds, "Affirmative: we have him, he looks, uh, about 20, yeah, about 29, 28,000." The controller asks the United Airlines pilot to keep out of the other plane's way. Then at 8.41, just ninety seconds before his plane is taken over, the pilot betrays his unease: "We heard a suspicious transmission on our departure out of Boston. Someone keyed the mic and said: 'Everyone stay in your seats.'" At 8.46 the aircraft's transponder signal stops. Seven minutes later the controller says, "We may have a hijack . . ." The first indication of trouble with American Airlines flight 77, which left Dulles International at 8.20 a.m. came thirty-six minutes after takeoff when a controller was unable to contact the pilot. It crashed into the Pentagon at 9.38, just fifty-one minutes after American Airlines flight 11 hit the North Tower of the World Trade Center.[25]

Of United Airlines flight 93, which crashed in Pennsylvania twenty-six minutes after the attack on the Pentagon, we know rather more. Some of the passengers and some crew, herded into the back of the plane by the hijackers, were in touch with people on the ground. Todd Beamer, an accountant, spoke to a phone operator. He told her that one passenger was dead and that one hijacker claimed to have a bomb. Jeremy Glick, a sales manager, phoned his wife, who confirmed that other planes had been hijacked. Thomas Burnett told his wife, "I know we're all going to die . . . If they're going to run this into the ground, we have to do something . . . I love you, honey." It is thought that these three men and two others, Mark Bingham and Lou Nacke, a weight lifter with a Superman tattoo on his shoulder, took on the hijackers, causing the jet to crash.[26]

The talk of the bomb on United Airlines flight 93 and the earlier transmissions picked up by air traffic control reinforced the FBI's conclusion that not all the hijackers were told they were on a suicide mission. It is possible that as many as 13 out of the 19 had been kept in the dark. Only six suicide notes were discovered. The final letter, urging the martyrs "to crave death" (see below) may not have been read by all of them.

We can only imagine the scenes on board the planes. Did the hijackers force their way into the cockpits shouting "Allahu Akbar!" (God is Greater!)? Did they put on red bandanas before committing their acts of murder and self-sacrifice? Did they behave like the characters in the movies they perversely seemed to imitate: the fanatical Arabs who feature, to the disgust of Muslims living in the West, in many Hollywood movies? Brian Keenan, the Irish writer and lecturer who with John McCarthy, a British TV reporter, endured four and a half years of captivity after being taken hostage by Hizbollah extremists in Lebanon in 1986, was acutely aware of the love–hate symbiosis between the Hizbollah youth and the macho Western stereotypes they loved to hate – a version of what Dickens once called "the attraction of repulsion". In Keenan's narrative:

The young man unresolved in himself chooses, as men have done throughout history, to take up arms against his sea of troubles. He carries his Kalashnikov on his arm, his handgun stuck in the waistband of his trousers, a belt of bullets slung around his shoulders. I have seen so many young men in Beirut thus attired, their weapons hanging from them and glistening in the sun. The guns were symbols of potency. The men were dressed as caricatures of Rambo. Many of them wore a headband tied and knotted at the side above the ear, just as the character in the movie had done. It is a curious paradox that this Rambo figure, this all-American hero, was the stereotype which these young Arab revolutionaries had adopted. They had taken on the cult figure of the Great Satan they so despised and who they claimed was responsible for all

the evil in the world. Emulating Rambo they would reconquer
the world and simultaneously rid themselves of that inade-
quacy which they could never admit.[27]

In the case of the September 11th hijackers, the paradox is even
more compelling, for the stereotype they seemed to emulate was
that of the anti-Muslim, anti-Arab figure manufactured in what
their own demonology would regard as the Jewish-controlled stu-
dios of Hollywood. In *Reel Bad Arabs: How Hollywood Vilifies a
People*, Jack Shaheen exposes what he sees as a major cultural
injustice, namely American cinema's "systematic, pervasive, and
unapologetic degradation and dehumanization of a people".[28]
From his extensive research over two decades Shaheen reaches the
conclusion that "Hollywood has projected Arabs as villains in
more than 900 feature films", from *Imar the Servitor* (1914) to
The Mummy Returns (2001), in which "evil" Arabs "stalk the
screen". "The vast majority of villains are notorious shaikhs, maidens, Egyptians and Palestinians. The rest are devious
dark-complexioned baddies from other Arab countries, such as
Algerians, Iraqis, Jordanians, Lebanese, Libyans, Moroccans,
Syrians, Tunisians and Yemenis . . . Missing from the vast majority
of scenarios are images of ordinary Arab men, women and children, living ordinary lives. Movies fail to project exchanges
between friends, social and family events."[29] "Do not expect,"
Shaheen warns his readers, "to see movie characters patterned
after Arab scholars, those innovative individuals who provided us
with the fundamentals of science, mathematics, medicine, astron-
omy, and botany"; nor will the filmgoer find the Arab seamen who
pioneered revolutionary navigational techniques, enabling them to
cross the oceans. The Arabs who "brought to Indonesia and Spain
a fresh and vigorous religion, new technology, and new knowledge" are very largely absent from Hollywood screens.[30]

Of the numerous films reviewed by Shaheen in his book, one in
particular deserves attention for its almost uncanny prescience.
Executive Decision is a thriller about Islamist terrorists who hijack
a Boeing 747 and are about to bomb New York with canisters of

deadly poison gas until prevented by the all-American hero, played by Kurt Russell. In Britain the film had caused outrage amongst Muslims not just because of its racial stereotyping and anti-Muslim assumptions, but because it was shown on television the very same evening that a nail bomb, thrown by a deranged racist homophobe, had exploded near the mosque in London's Brick Lane, injuring several members of the Bengali community. Leading the cast of villains, all of whom are depicted as dark-skinned Palestinians, is Nagi Hassan, played by David Suchet, best known for his portrayal of Agatha Christie's Hercule Poirot, and as Melmotte in the TV adaptation of Anthony Trollope's *The Way We Live Now*.

In the film, the Palestinians are depicted as ruthless, cruel and fanatical. Chanting "Allahu Akbar", they beat and kill members of the aircrew and several passengers, including a US senator and a blonde stewardess. Their fiendish plot is to unload enough DZ-5 nerve gas to kill virtually the whole population of the Eastern Seaboard – some 40 million people. The link with suicide bombers in Israel–Palestine is made explicitly. In one scene set in London, a Palestinian fanatic enters the Marriott Hotel with the Quran in one hand and a bomb in the other, and blows himself up along with scores of diners. No consideration is given as to why the Arab characters might feel this way. Their posture is one of pure malevolence, a demonic Them erupting into the Panglossian world of nice people like Us.

In Britain the term "Islamophobia" has been coined to include such media stereotyping. A commission headed by Professor Gordon Conway, vice-chancellor of the University of Sussex, describes "Islamophobia" as "a useful shorthand way of referring to dread or hatred of Islam – and therefore to fear or dislike of all or most Muslims".[31] A touchstone for journalists and editors, as the Runnymede Trust Commission argues in its chapter on media coverage, would be to substitute the terms "Islam" and "Muslim" with "Christianity" or "Christian", "Judaism" or "Jew", and to see if the article or passage in question would still pass muster for publication. "Editors may ask themselves: 'Would I print this article or cartoon, or make this juxtaposition of text and illustration, or slant this story in this way, or make this generalisation, if it were about any other topic besides Islam? For example, if it were about a Jewish person or community?'"[32] If Hollywood scripts were subjected to the substitution test, how many of them would ever get made into films?

Shaheen identifies a number of the Islamophobic themes in *Executive Decision*:

> Throughout, devout Islamic practices are equated with terror. Implying the Holy Quran encourages the killing of innocents, the camera reveals a Muslim terrorist's ring displaying the word "Allah". When asked whether mistreating people has anything to do with his "cause" Nagi says, "It says here in the Quran." Before and after killing passengers, Nagi prays. And when he spots several F-14s approaching, Nagi shouts: "It's the sword of Islam . . . sent to deliver a blow to the belly of the infidel." Exclaiming *Allahu Akbar* Nagi boasts to a cohort "We are the true soldiers of Islam."[33]

A Stealth superjet flies under the belly of the 747, enabling Kurt Russell's multi-ethnic squad of special forces soldiers to board it and overcome the crew. After a nailbiting struggle Russell manages to crash-land the jet when all the terrorists have been wiped out.

History does not relate if Mohammed Atta or any of his associates ever saw this film or any of the others listed in Shaheen's compendium. But negative stereotyping, psychology tells us, can all too easily become self-fulfilling. Victims, like the Jewish *marranos* (pigs) reviled in Christian Spain, have a habit of appropriating negative labels, turning them into badges to be worn with pride. The jihad (struggle) against *kufr* (disbelief) which the hijackers and other Islamists espouse is not so much a "war between civilizations" (see Chapter 8) as a struggle waged over contested identities within the individual self. Like the "born-again" Christian who takes Jesus as his "personal saviour" after a lifetime's experience viewed, in retrospect, as "sin", the born-again Muslim's quest is in the first instance private, even narcissistic.

The appetites he indulges in the bars and brothels of Hamburg, the XXX-rated videos he watches in his motel room, the casinos of Las Vegas where he gambles, the alcoholic drinks he consumes and the video games he plays are perceived in that part of the psyche where the Quranic deity resides as transgressive, polluting and Satanic. Islamic law, as applied in most of Egypt or Saudi Arabia before the advent of modern consumer capitalism, protected the Muslim from sin by setting clear boundaries regulating social behaviour. The legal compendia or books of *fiqh* (jurisprudence) distinguished five categories into which all types of human behaviour was organized: obligatory, recommended, indifferent, disapproved of, forbidden. In the modern Islamist discourse the Muslim who questions or transgresses the boundaries established for ever by God risks *kufr* (infidelity or disbelief). *Kufr* is on the increase because in Western cities and even, increasingly, in cities with Muslim majorities the boundaries (*hudud*) "established by God" are everywhere disintegrating. As Jonathan Raban observes, the Islamist websites and magazines aimed at the Muslim diaspora represent the life of the Muslim in the West

> . . . as a hazardous survival exercise in enemy-occupied terri-tory. *Kufr* is an oppression as real as any Middle-Eastern tyranny. In some ways it's even more dangerous to live among the *kuffar* [unbelievers] than in, say, Fahd's Saudi Arabia or Mubarak's Egypt, because the forces of *kufr* are more insidi-ous and omnipresent. The Shaytan [devil] stalks the suburbs, trying to catch the believers off guard.[34]

Loneliness and uncertain identities, sometimes compounded by the sexual misery of desire and repulsion, create dangerous ten-sions in the hearts and souls of young Muslim men living in the West, where they are surrounded by the endless temptations to transgress from the "straight path" decreed by God. Abouhalima, convicted for his part in the 1993 World Trade Center bombing, lived for seventeen years in Germany and the United States – enough time, he told Mark Juergensmeyer, to understand the

"spiritual emptiness" of people "who have no religion".
Juergensmeyer, who interviewed him in prison, relates, "He
finished his point by saying 'the soul, the religion, you know,
that's the thing that's revived the whole life. Secularism' he said,
looking directly at me, 'has none, they have none, you have
none.'"35

Though "spiritual emptiness" may exist anywhere, the particular variants Muslim emigrants perceive in the West may have less to
do with secularization and material prosperity than with problems
of cultural intercourse. In most modern Western societies, spiritu-
ality has long escaped from the "sacred canopy" of religion under
church control, into the broader avenues of theatre, sport, music,
the visual arts. The perception of spiritual emptiness is really a
mark of cultural alienation. The emigrant becomes obsessed with
the materialistic and hedonistic aspects of Western culture because
he does not know how to gain access to its spiritual and aesthetic
goods. How many Islamists plotting the downfall of "Western civilization" are prepared to spend time in art galleries, sports arenas
or concert halls? Judging from the newspaper accounts of the terrorists' movements before the hijackings, most of their time in the
West was spent in cheap tacky cafés, bars, fast-food restaurants,
amusement arcades, even brothels. As Raban acutely remarks:

> A powerful sense of *kufr* helps the believer to live in western
> exile in the necessary state of chronic persecution, from which
> his theology was born, and on which its survival depends . . .
> It also confers a heroic glamour on the everyday alienation
> felt by the immigrant – especially the male immigrant – who
> struggles to keep his head up in a foreign culture . . . Your cor-
> rosive solitude is the measure of your invincible superiority to
> the *kuffar*, in their hellbound ignorance and corruption.36

Many Islamists resemble the Stalinists and Nazis. Their obsession
with "decadence" – whether "Western" "cosmopolitan" or "bourgeois" – makes them blind to the cultural riches of the civilization
they deplore.

Like tourists who refuses to move outside the Club Med compound in Turkey or Tunisia with its familiar foods, states of undress and pleasant social interactions, the Islamists' reluctance to explore the richer potentialities of Western culture is made up of an equal mixture of laziness and wilful ignorance. Only the instrumentalities of Western culture need be mastered: how to operate machinery, mix chemicals, program computers, fly planes (all of them skills that can be deployed, with devastating consequences, in acts of terrorism when anger, frustration and rage have done their work). The philosophical presuppositions behind the technicalities, the condition of epistemological doubt, is spurned, because it threatens the structure of an identity rooted in the received certainties of faith. Unlike the Club Med tourist, however, the immigrant has no privileged enclave beyond the inner recesses of the heart where the perfection of Islam in its purity resides. What is left of Islamic "civilization", the fabric of tradition one finds in the labyrinthine alleys of the Aleppo souks so admired by Atta in his thesis on the Islamic city or the glorious mudbrick streets of old 'Unaida in Saudi Arabia, are everywhere succumbing to the corrosive effects of modernity. But for the Islamist it is not "our" modernity, it is "theirs".

Within a few weeks of September 11th, American bombers were pounding Taliban positions in Afghanistan. President Bush's intelligence officials had identified al-Qa'ida as responsible for the atrocity a few hours after the attack. The information linking bin Laden to the atrocity was sufficient to convince the British government, and, less enthusiastically, its European partners. With active support from Britain, Bush declared "war on terrorism". By the end of 2001 the initial, military phase of the campaign was almost over. With US air support and help from US special forces and the British SAS on the ground, the United States had enabled the Northern Alliance to overthrow the Taliban regime protecting bin Laden and al-Qa'ida. The "Afghan Arabs" and other volunteers who assisted bin Laden were on the run, betrayed by some of their former Taliban allies. A new interim government, under

Hamid Karzai, a kinsman of the exiled monarch, in which most of the competing tribal factions were represented, had been forged in Bonn under US and European auspices. Iran's support of the new government was crucial. A new strategic alliance was developing between the old Cold War enemies, Russia and America.

Other world leaders jumped on the anti-terrorism bandwagon. In Israel, faced with the reluctance or inability of Yasser Arafat, president of the Palestinian Authority, to control suicide bombers and other Hamas militants, prime minister Ariel Sharon used the "war against terror" to destroy what was left of the Oslo peace process and to advance his programme of keeping the illegal Jewish settlements on the West Bank and in Gaza in defiance of UN resolutions. In successive responses to Palestinian acts of terror, he sent his tanks into Palestinian Authority territory incurring barely a whisper of protest from a formerly critical US government. As Isabel Hilton noted, "The war against terrorism has proved a blessing to governments embroiled in long-running conflicts, especially though not exclusively, where the rebels are Muslim."[37] In Nepal the government abandoned negotiations with Maoist insurgents; in India (after an attack on the parliament in New Delhi left twelve dead, including the terrorists) V.K. Maholtra, the spokesman for the Hindu nationalist Bharatiya Janata Party (BJP), the largest party in the governing coalition, demanded a more "proactive and hot-pursuit policy" in Kashmir; in Chechnya, the Russian president Vladimir Putin, once the subject of widespread international criticism for the brutality of his campaign against Muslim separatists, was allowed a free hand to deal with "terrorism" in his own way, far from public scrutiny. In Beijing a Communist Party directive listed "underground gangs", Xinjiang separatists, "splittists" including Tibetans, "unstable social elements" and the Falun Gong religious movement as terrorist "threats" facing the People's Republic.[38] The Algerian, Egyptian, Syrian and Turkish governments joined the campaign with varying degrees of enthusiasm, seizing the opportunity to enlist international support for the suppression of domestic opposition. In Zimbabwe the increasingly dictatorial president Robert Mugabe even used the "war against terrorism" as a stick with which to beat opposition journalists and politicians during the rigged presidential elections of March 2002.

Some of the international ramifications of the atrocity will be explored later in this book, in particular the relations between the Islamic and Western worlds. Here, however, a more immediate question suggests itself: had the number of casualties been significantly lower, would the consequences have been any different? Would the US response, with all the future complications entailed by it, have been less global? Would the international "coalition" against terrorism have held in the face of many fewer casualties than had been sustained, for example, by Spain in its campaign against Basque separatists, or Britain in its struggle with the IRA? Was the result – the loss of three thousand innocent lives – intended by the perpetrators? Or was the outcome partly due to the building's design, an unintended consequence of what really motivated the terrorists, the desire to draw attention to themselves by engaging in the "propaganda of the deed" by attacking a symbol of US economic power? This question will not necessarily produce an unambiguous answer: but there is evidence to suggest that the casualty rate exceeded expectations. The amateur video of a conversation in (probably) Qandahar between bin Laden and an unnamed cleric from Saudi Arabia released by the State Department on 13 November 2001 allows for both possibilities.

According to the official transcript of the tape, bin Laden says this:

> . . . we calculated in advance the number of casualties from the enemy, who would be killed based on the position of the tower. We calculated that the floors that would be hit would be three or four floors. I was the most optimistic of them all . . . Due to my experience in this field, I was thinking that the fire from the gas in the plane would melt the iron [*sic*] structure of the building and collapse the area where the plane hit and all the floors above it only. This is all that we had hoped for . . .[39]

The authenticity of the tape and its provenance have both been challenged. Its release just when the US Green Berets and fighters from the Northern Alliance were closing in on the al-Qaʿida redoubt at Tora Bora seemed suspiciously convenient, given the US government's earlier refusal on security grounds to reveal more than the sketchiest details of the evidence linking bin Laden or al-Qaʿida to the attacks on New York and Washington. The sceptics included the former head of the Pakistani Interservices Intelligence (ISI), General Hamid Gul, an Islamist hard-liner who suggested the figure in the video might be a doppelgänger, a view held by many of bin Laden's supporters in the Muslim world. They considered the Saudi dissident a pious man who would never have countenanced attacks on innocent people. In this view the tape was an outright fake manufactured by the CIA or perhaps by Mossad (Israeli intelligence), to discredit their hero. A more ingenious suggestion was that the video had been "planted" by bin Laden himself to assist the legal defence of detainees held in Western jails by suggesting that the hijackers were unaware of the outcome as they only received their instructions at the last moment, challenging intelligence reports which spoke of "years of preparation, flight schools, dummy runs in private planes, flight coordinates in the terrorists' briefcases".[40]

Even if the casualty rate had been much lower, however, hijacking the planes and flying them into the Twin Towers would still have been seen as an "act of war" rather than a purely criminal act. The US administration's rhetorical response, however, did raise a question that is endemic both in "asymmetrical warfare" and religious terrorism. A week or two after the skybombings Terry Jones, the former member of the Monty Python comedy team, made one of the more memorable remarks about the "war on terrorism" by asking in a radio interview, "Can you wage war against an abstract noun?" The very use of the word "war" in this context made an important concession to the terrorists by elevating them to the status of combatants, rather than treating them as outlaws and criminals. In Northern Ireland the British government had resisted the demands of republican prisoners to be granted political status for precisely this reason. Although the hunger strikes and "dirty protests" eventually led to concessions being made in the prisons, the insistence of successive British and Irish governments on continuing to criminalize terrorism by use of police methods and court proceedings has yielded long-term benefits. In Ireland terrorism has been marginalized, if not yet finally defeated, by solid, if sometimes flawed, police methods. Mao Zedong, one of the most successful revolutionary leaders in history, famously likened the revolutionary communist to a fish: to survive and prosper the revolutionary organism must swim in sympathetic waters. To adapt the metaphor only slightly, terrorism can be likened to a pest or parasite, such as the mosquito, which needs stagnant waters or a swamp to breed in. Drain the swamp, clear the waters, and the threat will be reduced, if not eliminated.

The terrorist attacks on New York may have been planned and funded internationally: attacking the "causes" of terrorism in the stagnant political waters of Palestine or Kashmir, or the fetid swamps represented by "collapsed states" such as Afghanistan or Somalia, might be a long-term strategic imperative, but it would be unlikely to yield immediate results. A cell of three or four determined people could still make a bomb sufficiently powerful to paralyse a city – whether or not they received their training with the CIA.

Demonization of "the other", the reduction of the world to Manichaean dimensions, is the stuff of fundamentalist discourse. The community of the saved, embattled but exclusively possessed of the truth, wages its ceaseless campaign against the "enemies of God" in the certainty of ultimate salvation. Fundamentalism is seen by liberal religionists as a "distortion" or "perversion" of religious truth. In a general sense this may be so, since religions, as we have come to know them, contain a rich and varied mix of what scholars call "cumulative tradition". The cultural residues of religion in ritual, music, art and literature are so impressively variegated, and inspiring, that "anti-religionism", as distinct from atheism, seems absurd. Atheism avoids the charge of absurdity because it addresses a much narrower, philosophical question than religion does: the existence or nonexistence of God. From where most of us stand, as inheritors of religious traditions, whether we describe ourselves as believers or not, fundamentalism may indeed seem a distortion of the tradition. If, however, one cuts away the growth of "cumulative tradition" a very different picture emerges. The "fundamentalist" is the believer who reaches into the core of his tradition, who identifies and returns to the "fundamentals" in order to recover that faith in its pristine form. That faith at its origins *is* Manichaean, involving as it does a radical separation of the world between the saved and the damned, believers and infidels. The men who hit New York and Washington may indeed be the personifications of "evil" or "nihilism" in the minds of the survivors and all who feel for them. But within their own frame of reference they are martyrs for the faith. Since all are now dead, their individual motivations will continue to elude us. But something is knowable about their backgrounds as well as the religious and political passions that fuelled their rage.

The men who performed this operation were not amateurs in the usual sense of the word, nor were they failures or misfits. Their technical proficiency was fuelled by a passion so powerful and resolute that they were more than prepared to embrace the certainty of death. Suicide bombing is not new. In the twentieth century the tactic had spread by imitation. During the Second World War kamikaze pilots expressed their devotion to the Japanese emperor by driving their planes, loaded with bombs, onto the decks of American ships. In Sri Lanka, Hindu Tamil separatists wishing to secede from the Sinhalese–Buddhist majority invented the "human" suicide bomb, creating mayhem and confusion in Colombo and other cities. Tests conducted on the remains of the suicide bomber who assassinated the Indian prime minister Rajiv Gandhi in 1991 revealed the perpetrator to have been a woman who hid her lethal package under her sari. In Lebanon, Shi'ite Muslims belonging to the Hizbollah (Party of God) movement fighting foreign troops in the 1980s used the tactic to great effect. Two trucks loaded with explosives driven by

Lebanese Shi'ites killed 241 US and 58 French marines in almost simultaneous suicide bombings in Beirut in October 1983. Suicide bombings conducted by Shi'ites ceased after Shaikh Muhammad Hussein Fadlallah, spiritual leader of Hizbollah in Lebanon, and other clerics ruled suicide attacks (or "self-martyrdom operations") contrary to Islamic law.[41]

Shaikh Fadlallah's ruling, of course, did not deter Palestinian Muslims belonging to the mainstream Sunni tradition. Both Hamas and Islamic Jihad, the two Islamist groups operating within Israel and the territories occupied in 1967 (some of which came under Palestinian Authority control following the Oslo accords), adopted the tactic in their fight against the Israelis. Shortly before the September 11th attack on America, the newspapers were full of photographs of mutilated and blood-spattered people in the aftermath of a suicide bomb planted in a crowded pizza parlour in Jerusalem. Fifteen people, including several young children and babies, were killed. Many more were suffering from hideous injuries that would stay with them for the rest of their lives. Along with the faces of grieving parents and pictures of the dead families in happier days, there were portraits of the Palestinian suicide bomber, taken from the video released to the news media just after his death. A solemn young man, wearing the obligatory religious beard and a bandana proclaiming his membership of the al-Qassam brigade, stares at the camera with a glazed, other-worldly look. He holds an M16 rifle in one hand. In the other he holds the Quran. His waist is strapped with explosives.

The posthumous video is an essential part of this armoury. Most Palestinian suicide bombers have made videos prior to their attacks in which they justify their actions on religious grounds. The Land of Palestine must be liberated. Jewish settlement must stop, or be reversed. The martyr who sacrifices himself for his people will go straight to heaven where he will live like a prince and rejoice, for eternity, in the arms of gorgeous young female companions. In some of the videos or in televised interviews the siblings and parents of the suicide bombers, far from appearing distraught with grief, express their pride at his sacrifice, and joy at the prospect of eternal felicity in store for him.

The "self-martyrs" (*mustashhidin*) are far from being the victims of *anomie*, the condition of alienation Emile Durkheim associates with suicide. They are not isolated, lonesome individuals, but zealots with community support.

Nevertheless in some of the videos there is also an underlying current of wretchedness and despair. In one of the tapes seen by Juergensmeyer, the volunteer explains that since everyone has to die eventually, one is indeed fortunate to be able to choose one's destiny. There are those who "fall off their donkeys and die" and those "whose donkeys trample them and they die". There are those who are hit by cars and suffer heart attacks and "those who fall off the roofs of their houses and die". "What a difference there is between one death and another!" the volunteer exclaims, evidently implying that he is fortunate to have the opportunity for martyrdom. "Truly there is only one death, so let it be in the path of God."[42]

Most of the suicide bombers in Israel-Palestine are young, idealistic men in their twenties. While clearly religious, they are presumed to be under the influence of terrorist "godfathers" who control the campaign in which they willingly take part and prepare them, like sacrificial lambs, for their final act of self-immolation. Their families receive compensation from charitable funds originating in wealthy Arab states, including Iraq. In the spring of 2002, as the war between Israel and the Palestinians escalated, the compensation Iraq paid to the families of *mustashhidin* was increased from $10,000 to $25,000.[43] The context in which the killer–martyrs operate is highly politicized: a reluctant signatory to the Oslo accords, Israel has consistently refused to implement them in accordance with Palestinian desires, by freezing the construction of some Jewish settlements in the occupied territories and dismantling others. While brutal both for the perpetrators and the victims, the suicide bombing tactic is not irrational.

Though exceptionally well equipped to combat external enemies – thanks in part to the $3 billion annual subsidy it receives from the United States – Israel is extremely vulnerable to attacks from within, from the civilian population. Many Israelis and Arabs resemble each other physically: one suicide bomber even dressed himself up as an Israeli soldier, an ideal disguise in a highly militarized country where a large proportion of the youth is dressed in battle fatigues. Another was able to infiltrate himself into the strictly Orthodox quarter of Meah Sharim in Jerusalem on the Sabbath, disguised as a worshipper. The pervasive presence of the "enemy in our midst" generates a mood of perpetual anxiety in Israel, damaging tourism and discouraging would-be immigrants and adding to the subversive trickle of wealthier, bourgeois emigrants. The bombing of a discotheque in Tel Aviv patronized mainly by teenagers of Russian origin was particularly devastating: it was callous and brutal, but not necessarily irrational. It sent two messages: Israelis cannot be safe anywhere, even in Tel Aviv, the original centre of modern Jewish settlement. Russian teenagers beware! This is not *your* country!

September 11th obviously bore an affinity to these atrocities. As with the suicide bombings, there were no warnings. The motivation appeared religious. The perpetrators combined, in a single act, martyrdom with suicide. The similarities seemed obvious; but so too were the differences. While suicide bombers in Israel–Palestine issued no warnings and made no demands, their actions were implicitly coercive. They put pressure on Israel and its partner in the now-defunct peace process, Yasser Arafat: on the former to relinquish the Jewish settlements, on the latter to avoid making any concessions to superior Israeli power. Implicit in the bombings was the message that they would cease if Palestinian demands were met. If the contested settlements were removed, and Palestine acquired statehood, the Palestinian security forces would be able to end them. In such an eventuality how many parents or siblings would still approve the sacrifice of a beloved son or brother? By contrast with the ruthless, but not necessarily irrational, actions of the terrorist godfathers in Palestine, the attack on New York seemed nihilistic, even apocalyptic. As Paul Bremer, former State Department counter-terrorism coordinator, has argued:

There's no point in addressing the so-called root causes of
bin Laden's despair with us. We are the root causes of his terrorism. He doesn't like America. He doesn't like our society.
He doesn't like what we stand for. He doesn't like our values.
And short of the United States going out of existence, there's
no way to deal with the root cause of his terrorism.[44]

Religious violence differs from violence in the "secular" world by
shifting the plane of action from what is mundane, and hence negotiable, to the arena of cosmic struggle, beyond the political realm.
Targets of religious terror are symbolic as much as strategic. The
attack on the World Trade Center caused massive loss of life, para-
lysed New York for several days and did some $100 billions' worth
of damage. Panic, fear and economic damage, however, could be
achieved just as effectively, with much less risk, by attacking power
stations, or contaminating food and water supplies: witness the disruption caused by the anthrax scare, which on present evidence
appears to have been the work of a disaffected scientist rather than
an Islamist terrorist group. The symbolic target may be functional,
like the World Trade Center, but it also has the added value for the
terrorist of representing something beyond itself. "The towers are
in their own way as American as the Statue of Liberty or the
Washington Monument," wrote Juergensmeyer of the 1993 attack,
"and by assaulting them activists put their mark on a visibly
American symbol."[45]

In a global culture dominated by television, visibility is everything: the image of the second plane hitting the South Tower, the
collapse of the two towers into piles of dust and rubble became not
just events but icons, or perhaps counter-icons that etched themselves into the conscious or unconscious minds of the whole of
humanity. Some American television stations played the sequences
backwards, as if to restore the "innocence" lost on September
11th. A British network briefly set them to music, until the switch-
boards were jammed by protests from furious viewers. At Varanasi
(Benares), the holy city on the Ganges, the attack was celebrated as
a manifestation of the forces of destruction at the festival to the

goddess Durga. In one of the many side-shows devotees had erected a pair of cardboard towers repeatedly hit by a primitive model plane, with an explosion of crackers and lights.[46] When the composer Karlheinz Stockhausen referred to the attacks on the Twin Towers as a "work of art", the outrage he caused led to cancellations of performances of his work, but public indignation does not diminish the force of his observation. In the video age the literalness of the image replaces the density of language. Jean Baudrillard, with typical exaggeration, makes the point that terrorist acts have emerged "less from passion than from the screen: a violence in the nature of the image".[47] Regardless of the presence or absence of passion the collapse of the towers was a resounding media event, a perfect icon of destruction, of hubris punished and arrogance brought low. The symbolism was biblical and Quranic: in the Bible, the people who build the tower of Babel are punished for their presumption; in the Quran the peoples who fail to heed God's messengers are destroyed in a series of cataclysms known in the literature as the "punishment stories".[48]

In their first reaction, before they checked themselves, America's leading fundamentalists responded almost gleefully, like some Muslim Palestinians who were shown on television dancing in the streets. Jerry Falwell, founder of the Moral Majority, blamed "the pagans, and the abortionists, and the feminists, and the gays and the lesbians" for creating an environment which might have "caused God to lift the veil of protection which has allowed no one to attack America on our soil since 1812". Though he partly withdrew these remarks after protests from gay and lesbian groups, his fellow evangelist Pat Robertson, host of the 700 Club programme on which Falwell appeared, thoroughly endorsed them. "We have sinned against Almighty God, at the highest level of our government, we've stuck our finger in Your eye," said Robertson. "The Supreme Court has insulted You over and over again, Lord. They've taken Your Bible away from the schools. They've forbidden little children to pray. They've taken the knowledge of God as best they can . . . out of the public square of America."[49] In New York City itself, a fundamentalist minister called David Wilkerson was quoted as saying the attacks were a warning of greater destruction to come unless New Yorkers repented and abandoned their sinful ways. Hal Lindsay, author of *The Late Great Planet Earth*, a massively best-selling fundamentalist reading of the books of Daniel and of Revelation written in the style of a disaster-movie scenario, announced that the attack really was the beginning of the "end-times" predicted in scripture. "The Battle of America has begun! . . . The decline of the United States has begun . . ." he announced triumphantly, predicting, not for the first time, that the event foreshadowed the coming of Armageddon and the return of Christ as the divine ruler.[50] In America, the world's most religious industrialized country, the apocalyptic dimensions of the attack were immediately understood in terms of motivations and categories not dissimilar to those that inspired the terrorists.

President George W. Bush, catching the public mood, loaded his speeches with religious, end-times language. "Good will prevail against evil." States supporting terrorism or preparing weapons of mass destruction that could be used against America or its allies constituted an "axis of evil" that must be resisted. Terrorism was not so much a problem endemic to modern societies, one that demanded a broad band of common-sense solutions along the spectrum from political engagement to draconian security measures, such as the British government had deployed in Ireland. Rather it was an apocalyptic struggle waged between ultimate "good and evil". The "traditional Manichaean streak" in American diplomacy, in which problems of international relations are viewed as "moral struggles between good and evil",[51] produced disdainful comments from several European leaders. It is the duty of politicians, however, to face challenges and to present their policies in the vernacular. The language of the pulpit is far more pervasive and persuasive in America than in world-weary, sceptical Europe where preachers face empty pews. To judge by his popularity ratings, George W. Bush, who is a cleverer politician than he is sometimes given credit for, was perfectly in tune with public sentiment.

American patriotism has deep biblical, Protestant roots: as Herman Melville famously realized: ". . . we Americans are the peculiar chosen people – the Israel of our time; we bear the ark of the liberties of the world".[52] According to a 1983 Gallup poll, 62 per cent of Americans "have no doubts" that Jesus will return to earth again; 40 per cent accept the Bible as the literal word of God, a style of interpretation that does not preclude updating specifics: the doctrine of biblical inerrancy held by all fundamentalists permits the swords and chariots of scripture to be transmuted into nuclear weapons and aircraft. A 1977 study revealed that at least 8 million Americans are premillennialists, who believe that Christ will return as an earthly ruler after a period of tribulation predicted in scripture, when terrible happenings such as wars, plagues and famines will wreak havoc in the world.[53] Premillennialists welcome such events as signs that "end-times" are approaching. As Reuben Torrey, one of the founders of modern fundamentalism, put it during the 1920s, "the darker the night gets, the lighter my heart gets".[54] Though obsessed with the destiny of the Jews as God's chosen people, premillennialists looked calmly on the Holocaust – a "sad but wholly forseeable instance of God's effort to correct His recalcitrant people, and a foretaste of worse ahead," as Paul Boyer puts it. "It took Hitler to turn the Jews towards Palestine," declares one of the numerous tracts on the subject. "It will take a greater Hitler to turn them towards God."[55] Meanwhile, the modern state of Israel, as the key element in God's final plan for humanity, must be backed to the hilt – in territorial terms, if needs must be, from the Nile to the Euphrates. The impact of these beliefs, held by some 30 million adults, on America's Middle East policies has consistently been underestimated by political analysts, who rarely stray physically, or mentally, beyond the Washington beltway.[56]

For believers predisposed towards finding divine portents in contemporary history or current affairs, such twentieth-century events as the departure of the Turks from Palestine, the Balfour Declaration establishing a national home for the Jews in Palestine, the Nazi persecutions, the founding of Israel in 1948 and its capture of the Old City of Jerusalem in 1967, fulfilled the predictions of scripture. Between 1967 and 1990 there was a real possibility that the Middle East dispute could have erupted into a generalized nuclear conflict: the danger remains with us today.

An essential feature of the premillennial, apocalyptic fundamentalism that characterizes the Protestant tradition in America is its emphasis on personal salvation. The problematic of how a kind and merciful god could preside over such cosmic destructiveness is never fully addressed. With the coming of Christ the "saved" – those millions of Americans, including George W. Bush, who claim to have been born-again, to have "taken Jesus as their personal savior" to use the phrase borrowed from eighteenth-century German pietists – will be "raptured". The unsaved – nominal Christians, non-righteous Jews who persist in refusing to recognize Christ as Messiah, Hindus, Muslims, Confucians, animists, agnostics and the rest of unsaved humanity will perish in a series of dreadful cataclysms described in the Book of Revelation. The underlying morality is personal, almost narcissistic: I am a good "saved" person. I struggle against evil not for the good of humanity, but for my own salvation.

Religious fanaticism is far from being unique to the Western monotheisms: as I write, Hindu fanatics are murdering Muslims in pursuit of an ideal of "purity" that has become politicized, by transference from "caste" to "nation", in a manner that ominously resembles the rise of Nazism in Europe. But the apocalyptic nature of the Western religious imagination makes Western monotheisms (including Islam) peculiarly vulnerable to violent forms of fanaticism. Because the Abrahamic divinity has been exempted from evil, the symbolic images of cosmic struggle over which he presides are particularly susceptible to what might be called the "actualization of eschatology", in other words the enactment of apocalyptic scenarios on the plane of history, in real time, in the real world. Millenarian expectations are built into both the major ideological systems – Marxism-Leninism and Nazism – that fuelled the orgy of destruction Europe inflicted on itself in the mid-twentieth century. Both ideologies are deeply linked to the Judaeo-Christian apocalyptic tradition. Apocalyptic thinking is also central to the Islamic militancy, past and present. Given the cultural legitimacy or weight of authority conveyed by these traditions, only a few small steps are needed for an actor to move from a "religious" – that is, symbolic – understanding of the apocalypse to a historical one in which the divine imperative becomes an order to kill and be killed.

Just over two weeks after the September 11th attack, the FBI released a translation of an Arabic document left behind by Mohammed Atta, generally thought to have been the pilot among the five men who hijacked American Airlines flight 11 from Boston, the Boeing 767 that crashed into the North Tower of the World Trade Center. The agents found it in his luggage, which remained in Boston after failing to make the connection from a flight from Portland, Maine, where he had spent the previous night. A similar text was found in the wreckage of United Airlines flight 93 which crashed in Pennsylvania.

The document, posted on the FBI website and published in translation by the *Washington Post*, has been subjected to a detailed analysis by Kanan Makiya and Hassan Mneimneh.[57] It is a chilling reminder of the way in which sacrifice and violence may be blended in the religious mind: the certainty of death is linked directly to the promise of paradise. The message is profoundly solipsistic: at no point in the document's published excerpts is there any sense of human compassion, beyond concern for the would-be martyr's soul, over the likely consequences of the act. The apocalyptic mind is solipsistic in two respects: the actor who undertakes an apocalyptic mission identifies his action with the will of God; by so doing he leaves to God the moral consequences of his act. There is no hint of justification for the action in the document. It is not a manifesto; nor is it an explanation. The moral and intellectual arguments have been left entirely with God.

The text contains some guidance of a purely practical nature. "[Check] the suitcase, the clothes, the knife, your tools, your ticket . . . your passport, all your papers. Inspect your weapon before you leave." But this is linked directly to the practice of the "righteous predecessors", who "tightened their clothes as they wore them prior to battle. And tighten your shoes well, and wear socks that hold in the shoes and do not slip out of them." By an almost magical association, the practical need for tight shoes (or perhaps trainers), required for the deft footwork the hijacker will need on board the aircraft, is assimilated with the practice of the righteous predecessors or Companions of the Prophet who tightened their armour for battle during Islam's heroic age.

Throughout the text, practical instructions alternate with pious invocations in the manner of a medieval devotional manual. The hijacker must always maintain a positive attitude:

> Forget and force yourself to forget that thing which is called the World; the time for pleasure is gone and the time for reckoning is upon us. So therefore you must use these few remaining hours that you have to seek forgiveness from God. You must be convinced that these few remaining hours that you have are few indeed, and after that you will begin living a life of happiness, a life of eternal paradise. Be optimistic, for the Prophet (Peace Be Upon Him) was always positive. Always repeat or remember the verses whose recitations are desirable before death. Remember that God said, "If Allah helps you, no one can vanquish you. If He forsakes you, who can help you after that? So the believers should put their trust in Allah."[58]

The hijackers are urged on in their endeavour with several other Quranic quotations: for example they are reminded: "Obey Allah and His messenger and do not quarrel amongst yourselves lest you lose heart and your momentum disappear. And be steadfast, for God is with the steadfast."[59] "You were longing for death before you met it. Now you have seen it with your own eyes."[60] The hijackers are urged to keep their minds open and responsive.

> You will enter heaven, you will enter a life of eternity. Remember if you encounter any problem how to get out of it. The believer is always put to the test. You will never enter

paradise unless the greatest trial confronts you. Make absolutely sure of all your possessions ... your bag, your clothes and the knives. And your identity documents and your passport and all your papers. Make absolutely sure that no one is following you and be very watchful that you are very clean and also that your shoes are clean.

Emphasis is placed on ritual purity. Prior to the hijacking the would-be martyrs are urged to "perform the dawn prayer with an open heart" and also told: "don't go until you have performed your ablutions for your prayers. Continue the prayer and when you enter the airplane say: O God open all doors for me [*Allahum aftah li kul al-abwab*]."

In the most sinister of the passages analysed by Makiya and Mneimneh the document tells the hijackers what to do if they encounter resistance: "If God grants any one of you a slaughter, you should perform it as an offering on behalf of your father and mother, for they are owed by you." Makiya and Mneimneh point out that the word used for slaughter – *dhabaha* – rather than the more familiar *qatala*, kill, connects the act of murdering a passenger to the ritual sacrifice of an animal by slitting its throat. *Dhabaha* is what Abraham was prepared to do to his son on God's instructions until the child was replaced with the sheep which is now slaughtered at the 'Id al-Adha, the feast of sacrifice. The thought expressed in the document, say Makiya and Mneimneh, "is that a civilian passenger attempting to resist his hijackers is a gift bestowed by God upon the man chosen to kill him". The sense throughout "is that the would-be martyr is engaged in his action solely to please God. There is no mention of any communal purpose behind his behaviour. In all of the four pages available to us there is not a word or an implication about any wrongs that are being redressed through martyrdom", whether in Palestine, Iraq or Arabia. Martyrdom does not appear in the document as a favour bestowed by God on the warrior for his selfless devotion to the community's defence. It is, rather, "a status to be achieved by the individual warrior and performed as though it were his own private act of worship". The document's author has taken the "shell of a traditional religious conception", replacing its original content with "radically new content which finds its legitimation in the word of God [and] the example of his prophets". This substitution amounts to "a deeply subversive form of political and ideological militancy". "The idea that martyrdom is a pure act of worship, pleasing to God, irrespective of God's specific command, is a terrifying new kind of nihilism."[61]

We shall have occasion to endorse this comment in the following chapters. Islamism is not the same as Islam: it is important to distinguish between the ideology of a small minority and the religion that is practised with varying degrees of enthusiasm by one fifth of humanity. But to distinguish between them does not necessarily mean that they can be separated. Islamism could be described as a strand, or series or threads, within the closely woven fabric of Islamic faith and practice. Generally speaking, Islamists go to the mosque, pray regularly, observe Ramadan and make the Hajj or 'Umra (lesser pilgrimage) as punctiliously as other Muslims, if not more so. What distinguishes them from other Muslims is radicalism, rather than piety. In this respect the word "fundamentalist", adopted from American Protestantism, is a misnomer. With few exceptions (for example, anti-abortion activists who assassinate doctors performing abortions) American fundamentalists are law-abiding, political conservatives who use their voting power – in elections or in local community structures such as school boards – to express their religiously based concerns. Most are biblical literalists insisting, for example, that the account of creation in the Book of Genesis is scientifically true, that Adam and Eve were real people and that Jesus Christ physically rose from the dead.

Many Muslims – indeed the vast majority – share such "fundamentalist" attitudes in so far as they believe the Quran to be the unmediated word of God dictated to Muhammad, without human editing. The Islamists, however, go much further than their American counterparts in defending their literaslist positions. Where American fundamentalists have books they regard as anti-religious removed from publicly funded school libraries, their Islamist counterparts have targeted writers and university professors who dare to challenge their shibboleths. The prominent secular writer Farag Foda was assassinated in June 1992 with the apparent approval, if not connivance, of some of the leading scholars of al-Azhar, the foremost academy of the Sunni religious establishment. An assistant professor of Arabic at Cairo University, Nasr Abu Zaid, was denied promotion because he advocated modern methods of linguistics, including socio-political analysis, in understanding the Quran.

Abu Zaid's case became a *cause célèbre* in Egypt and beyond after his Islamist opponents tried to use court proceedings to have him declared an infidel (*kafir*) which would have resulted in his wife having to divorce him under Shari'a rules prohibiting Muslim women from marrying nonbelievers. Though the court ruled that the issue was outside its jurisdiction, a fatwa (legal opinion) was issued against him. Faced with continued threats against his life, Abu Zaid and his wife chose exile: he now lives and teaches in the Netherlands.

The Abu Zaid affair is highly significant, revealing as it does the intellectual atmosphere that prevailed on the Cairo University campus during the time when Mohammed Atta was an undergraduate. An intrepid scholar and critic, Abu Zaid had taken the job in the Arabic department as a specialist in the Quran and *hadith* (traditions attributed to Muhammad) knowing that a graduate student had previously been dismissed on account of his dissertation: *he* had wanted to study stories in the Quran from the perspective of literary criticism. Abu Zaid's thesis focused on Mu'tazili concepts of figurative speech in Quranic exegesis.

The Mu'tazilites, sometimes known as "rationalists", were a group of Muslim scholars who came under the influence of Greek philosophical thought. They achieved considerable power during the caliphate of al-Ma'mun (813–33) when they established a kind of inquisition, known as the *mihna*, according to which scholars at the caliphal court were obliged to proclaim their adherence to the doctrine that the Quran had been created in time. Emphasizing references to an "Arabic Quran" that occur in the sacred text, they

argued that the decrees embedded in such a text were evidently
subject to time and place, and might possibly be overruled by an
inspired imam or caliph. The attractions of this theory for al-
Ma'mun were clear. Their opponents, who came to be known as the
ahl al-hadith, the People of Tradition, argued that, on the contrary, the Quran was "uncreated" being, as it were, an inseparable
part of the Godhead.

Obviously the decrees of an "uncreated" Quran were eternally
unchangeable: a doctrine that would make the caliph and other
worldly rulers clearly subject to the decrees of "what God sent
down". The Mu'tazilites were eventually overthrown by the *ahl al-
hadith*. They rallied around Ahmad Ibn Hanbal whose refusal to
accept the Mu'tazilite doctrine, despite torture and imprisonment,
made him into a heroic figure for what could be called, anachro-
nistically, the "Islamic religious Right". Islamic modernists tended
to view the defeat of Mu'tazilism in the face of populist pressure as
an underlying reason for Muslim intellectual decline, although it
took centuries to take effect. Abu Zaid's resurrection of this ancient
controversy using modern linguistic methods was indubitably bold,
given the atmosphere on the Cairo University campus. As Abu
Zaid himself explained:

Language is a human invention, in that it reflects social con-
vention regarding the relationship between the sound and the
meaning . . . Language does not refer directly to reality;
instead, reality is conceived, conceptualized, and then symbolized through a system of sounds . . . The Mu'tazilites . . .
drew from the Quranic text on the assumption that it was a
created action and not the eternal verbal utterance of God. In
other words . . . they endeavoured to build a bridge between
the divine word and human reason. That is why they maintained that the divine word was a fact which adjusted itself to
human language in order to ensure the well-being of
mankind. They insisted that language was the product of man
and that the divine word respected the rules and forms of
human language.[62]

Taking the Mu'tazilite approach, Abu Zaid concludes that the Quran is a historical text, subject to "human understanding and interpretation", whereas the language of God, His actual words "exist in a sphere beyond any human knowledge". Because the Quran is a literary text a "socio-historical analysis is needed for its understanding, and a modern linguistic methodology should be applied in interpretation".

In March 1993 the promotions committee at Cairo University voted to deny Abu Zaid tenure on grounds of apostasy, although he has continued to protest that he is neither an apostate nor a heretic, but rather a thinker who works within the frame of Islam. What especially aroused the ire of the authorities was an article he published the previous year which argued that the rhetoric of so-called "moderate" or "institutional" Islam of al-Azhar and similar institutions differed more in style than in content from that of the Islamist opposition and the so-called extremists – the Muslim Brotherhood, the Islamic associations (*al-Jama'at al-Islamiya*) Islamic Jihad and so forth. A crucial part of his argument was that both groups held literalistic views about the Quran and hence on the nature of Islamic law. Both believed that God's law was unalterable and fixed for eternity. Neither accepted the neo-Mu'tazilite view that laws should be reinterpreted and changed in accordance with the changing needs of society.[63]

I have not established the extent of Mohammed Atta's involvement, if any, in the campaign against Abu Zaid. He had already left for Germany when the controversy was at its height. However, conversations he had held with his fellow student at Harburg, Ralph Bodenstein, seem highly significant. "Atta was highly critical of Abu Zaid," Bodenstein recalled. "He insisted that it had been right to declare him an apostate. The Quran was the word of God. It must be taken as it is." When Bodenstein, an Arabist and graduate in Middle East studies, asked why, if the Quran was apparently self-explanatory, scholars had for centuries been filling libraries with works of *tafsir* (commentary), Atta became agitated. "He could not accept that there was more than one way of reading the Quran, one way of being a good Muslim.

He could never concede that there were contradictions or difficulties. To acknowledge a single one would lead to the collapse of
the whole."[64]

I was familiar with this mindset: I had encountered it among
educated Muslims in Britain when investigating the Rushdie affair.
A young biology teacher I met in Bradford had used almost identical words. The Quran was perfect, inviolable, true in the sense
that a scientific manual was true. A single flaw in the text would
call the rest into doubt, just like the faulty fuel seal that caused the
Challenger spacecraft to explode. "The text has gone out of its way
to tell you 'I am beyond corruption'," Anwar had said. "If a single
word has been added or subtracted, the whole edifice collapses!"[65]
Neither Anwar, my Bradford interviewee, nor Atta had received a
"traditional" education in the Islamic sciences, where students
learned to analyse the text philologically, to penetrate its multiple
meanings, to explore the apparent contradictions.

Traditional Islamic science, for example, had to deal with the
problem of "abrogation", according to which some Quranic verses
were superseded by others (see page 49). Muhammad's prophetic
mission had extended for nearly a quarter of a century, from the
first revelations he received in the cave at Mount Hira, near Mecca,
around 610 till shortly before his death in 632. Classical commentators and those who were trained in the "religious sciences" took
care to contextualize the meanings of the sacred text by reference to
what they called the "occasions of revelation" (*asbab al-nuzul*).
Indeed it was in order to grasp more completely the language of
God that the early exegetes made use of the Prophet's hadiths ("traditions"), the secondary body of literature based on the orally
transmitted recollections of Muhammad's contemporaries. The
Quran, the collection of revelations believed to have been received
from God and offered without personal interpolation or editing by
Muhammad while in "prophetic mode", is far from being self-
explanatory. Unlike the story of Jesus in the Gospels, it was never
edited into a coherent narrative. To understand its meanings reference had to be made to the oral records of Muhammad's
contemporaries. During Islam's classical period, the contingent

nature of divine revelation was thoroughly understood. The meaning of each verse in the text had to be explored by reference to all the others containing similar content. Enormous attention was given to philology and grammar. The trained minds in the religious sciences were literary men *par excellence*, experts in the parsing and analysis of language. Little, if any, of this tradition would have been familiar to the architect and town planner Mohammed Atta, or to Osama bin Laden, a structural engineer. For him, as for many students of his ilk, the Quran was "rocket science".

_____

Chapter Two

Jihad

Verily these Turks thought that theirs was the kingdom and
the command was in their hands. They transgressed the command of God's messengers and of His prophets and of him
who commanded them to imitate them. They judged by other
than God's revelation and altered the Shari'a of our master
Muhammad, Messenger of God, and placed the poll tax [*al-
jizya*] on your necks together with the rest of the Muslims . . .
Verily the Turks used to drag away your men and imprison
them in fetters and take captive your women and your children and slay unrighteously the soul under God's protection.
In all this they had no mercy upon the small among you nor
respect for the great among you.

proclamation of the Mahdi, 1882[1]

The ruling [fatwa] to kill the Americans and their allies – civilians and military – is an individual duty for every Muslim
who can do it in any country in which it is possible to do it, in
order to liberate the al-Aqsa Mosque [in Jerusalem] and the
holy mosque [in Mecca] from their grip, and in order for their
armies to move out of all the lands of Islam, defeated and
unable to threaten any Muslim . . . [People] even believe that

this situation is a curse put on them by Allah for not objecting
to the oppressive and illegitimate behaviour and measures of
the ruling regime: ignoring the divine Shari'a law, depriving
people of their legitimate rights; allowing the Americans to
occupy the land of the Two Sanctuaries . . .

fatwa issued by Osama bin Laden and
four other scholars, Afghanistan 1998[2]

Nearly twelve decades separate these two proclamations, and
though the circumstances in which they were issued may seem
different, the underlying message is the same. The first is a proclamation of the Mahdi Muhammad Ahmad, in 1882, raising the
standard of revolt against the Egyptians, nominal subjects of the
Ottoman Sultan and the British who occupied their country. The
same year nearly eight thousand men under Hicks Pasha, a retired
Indian army officer, perished at Shaikhan; the following year
General "Chinese" Gordon, the military hero who suppressed the
Boxer rebellion in China, was sent to avenge Hicks Pasha. Instead
of sticking to his brief, which was to evacuate the garrison of Anglo-
Egyptian troops at the strategic fort of Khartoum near the junction
of the White and Blue Niles, Gordon decided to "smash up" the
Mahdi with Sepoy levies. Isolated by the Mahdist forces, he died a
hero's death on the steps of the governor's house at Khartoum.

An engraving of the picture of Gordon surrounded by dervishes
with spears, now in Leeds Art Gallery, hung in many Victorian
homes. It became an icon for the British Empire, imbuing the
British public with a thirst for revenge. It wasn't until 13 years
later that General Kitchener finally defeated the forces of the
Mahdi's successor, the Khalifa, at the Battle of Omdorman. The
Khalifa was killed. British troops desecrated the Mahdi's tomb,
fragments of which were taken as keepsakes. (One such fragment,
green wood embossed with gilt calligraphy, used to adorn the
dining room of a family friend in Ireland.) All but one of the
Mahdi's offspring were massacred. A posthumous son, 'Abd al-
Rahman (d.1959) supplied the vital link of genetic continuity

between an anti-colonial movement and the modern postcolonial state. The Mahdi's grandson, Sayyid Sadiq al-Mahdi, is an Islamic scholar with degrees from Oxford. He has served two terms as his country's prime minister as well as periods of imprisonment and house arrest. Though his political fortunes would be eclipsed by those of his brother-in-law, the Muslim Brotherhood leader Hasan al-Turabi, descendants of the Mahdi's original followers, named the Ansar after the Prophet Muhammad's "helpers" in the city of al-Madina, are still a substantial presence in the political life of modern Sudan.

The second quotation heading this chapter is from the fatwa against Jews and Crusaders issued by Osama bin Laden with four other Islamic leaders in February 1998. The geographical circumstances, of course, are different. The Mahdi was objecting to the encroachments of the Egyptians, whom he refused to acknowledge as Muslims, referring to them only as "Turks". Under the Khedive Ism'ail, a nominal subject of the Ottoman Sultan, Egypt had endeavoured to extend its rule into the Upper Nile region. As a political–religious movement the Mahdiya, drawing on messianic themes that are latent in all three Abrahamic religious traditions (they are also present in Buddhism, Zoroastrianism and Hinduism), was built around the resistance of the Baqqara, cattle nomads of Arab origin who objected to Egyptian encroachments. Bin Laden and his colleagues were objecting to the presence of US troops in Saudi Arabia, the land of the "Two Sanctuaries" (Mecca and Medina) and to the Israeli occupation of Jerusalem. Despite these obvious differences, the resemblance between the two statements is clear: foreigners are occupying the lands of Islam; nominal Muslims who collaborate with them are not ruling in accordance with the laws "sent down by God".

There are other instructive parallels. After the New York atrocity hundreds of Islamic leaders and scholars united to condemn it as contrary to Islam. For example the Grand Mufti of Saudi Arabia, Shaikh 'Abd al-'Aziz bin 'Abdullah bin Muhammad Al al-Shaikh, stated in a fatwa that the hijackings and the attacks were "nothing but a manifestation of injustice, oppression and tyranny, which the Islamic Shari'a does not sanction or accept, rather it is expressly forbidden and it is amongst the greatest of sins".³ At a conference held in London, Prince El Hassan bin Talal, brother of the late King Hussein of Jordan and former Crown Prince of the kingdom, a direct descendant of the Prophet Muhammad, spoke for many when he stated:

> Such acts of extreme violence, in which innocent men, women and children are both the targets and the pawns, are totally unjustifiable. No religious tradition can or will tolerate such behaviour and all will loudly condemn it . . . All ordinary Muslims stand together in condemning such acts of terror. Contemporary Muslim societies have been largely shaped by the recent legacy of their colonial subjugation. Yet, despite their often grim social reality, ordinary Muslim men, women and children abhor those who would use violence to air their grievances.⁴

At the same conference, Dr S.F. Milani, citing numerous Quranic passages, stated unequivocally that the concept of jihad (meaning "struggle", often translated as "holy war") can never justify Muslims attacking civilian targets. The greater jihad, following the teachings of the Prophet, was the struggle against evil. The lesser jihad, armed struggle, only applied to Muslim self-defence. "Even if a state of war exists between a non-Islamic and a Muslim country, no Muslim is permitted to assault, attack or harm any non-Muslim civilian who does not physically participate in the fighting."⁵ The balance of educated Islamic opinion, reflected in statements throughout the Islamic world, was unequivocal in condemning these atrocities as contrary to the laws of Islam.

Such statements, though well intentioned, do not dispose of a fundamental theological problem. The God of Islam is always merciful and compassionate: the epithets *al-rahman al-rahim* (usually translated as "the Merciful, the Compassionate") cognates of the word for "womb" with its connotations of loving care, are the most widely celebrated of all the divinity's attributes,

since they occur in the invocatory formula that prefixes all but
one of the Quran's 114 suras or chapters. As almost every
account of Islam will explain, the word *Islam* (self-surrender)
derives from the same root as *salam* (peace). In its self-definition
Islam is primarily a "religion of peace". The problem consists not
in the idea of peace as a goal, but in the means deployed to
achieve it. In the Quranic discourse, as in the legal formulations
derived from the Quran and the Prophet's traditions, the very
notion of peace is conditional on acknowledgement of the Islamic
idea of God.

In his recent study of the Quranic teachings on jihad, Reuven
Firestone argues that different verses on war, which are far from
being consistent, reflect arguments within the early Islamic community about the necessity or desirability of fighting. In subsequent
writings "the most often cited verses express a highly ideological
approach to war. They are understood to command unlimited war
against non-Muslims, enjoining the killing of idolators, and refuse
to offer peace until Islam is the hegemonic religion." Some verses
call for an apparently nonmilitant means of propagating the faith:
"Call thou [all mankind] unto thy Sustainer's path with wisdom
and goodly exhortation, and argue with them in the most kindly
manner: for, behold, thy Sustainer knows best as to who strays
from His path, and knows best He as to who are the right-
guided."[6] "Do not argue with the followers of earlier revelation
otherwise than in the most kindly manner."[7] This stress on kind-
ness and tact in propagating the message of Islam is consistent
with the often-cited injunction "There shall be no coercion in matters of faith."[8] Other verses allow fighting for the defence of the
faith. For example in surat al-Hajj:

> Permission to fight is given to those against whom war is
> being wrongfully waged – and, verily, God has indeed the
> power to succour them – those who have been driven from
> their homelands against all right for no other reason than
> their saying "Our Sustainer is God". For, if God had not
> enabled people to defend themselves against one another,

monasteries and churches and synagogues and mosques – in which God's name is abundantly extolled – would surely have been destroyed.[9]

According to the liberal modernist exegesis of Muhammad Asad the implication of this and other verses is unambiguous: "The defence of religious freedom is the foremost cause for which arms may – and indeed must – be taken up or else, as in the concluding phrase of 2:251 'corruption would surely overwhelm the earth'."[10]

Other verses, however, seem to sanction aggressive warfare within established customary limitations: "Fight during the sacred months if you are attacked: for a violation of sanctity is [subject to the law of] just retribution. Thus if anyone commits aggression against you, attack him just as he has attacked you – but remain conscious of God and know that God is with those who are conscious of Him."[11] The latter proviso, according to Asad, makes it clear that combatants "must, when fighting, abstain from all atrocities, including the killing of non-combatants".[12] Another category of verses, however, appears to command unrestricted warfare for the Islamic state or polity: "And when the sacred months are over, kill the polytheists [*mushrikun*] wherever you find them, and take them captive, and beseige them, and lie in wait for them in every stratagem [of war]; but if they repent, establish regular prayers, and pay *zakat*, then open the way for them, for God is the dispenser of mercy."[13] This latter verse, often known as the Sword Verse, is the most widely cited example of Islam's sanguinary admonitions.

Scholars during the formative period of Islamic development attempted to deal with the apparent contradictions between these different injunctions by referring to the "occasions of revelation", *asbab al-nuzul*. Different Quranic passages were matched against what was known about the Prophet's life from the oral sources called *hadith* – traditions or narratives. The meanings or intentions of certain verses were seen in the context of Muhammad's prophetic ministry. Another important exegetical tool was the doctrine of abrogation (*naskh*) (see page 42). The point of departure

was a verse that states: "Any verse [*aya*] which We annul or con-
sign to oblivion We replace [*nansakh*] with a better or similar one.
Dost thou not know that God has the power to will anything?"[14]
Muhammad Asad, a convert to Islam from Judaism, takes issue
with the commentators who saw this passage as allowing for the
abrogation of an earlier Quranic verse by a later one. According to
Asad, the word *aya* in this context only makes sense if translated as
"message", meaning that earlier divine revelations given to Jews
and Christians are superseded by the message of Islam.[15] His
understanding of the passage ultimately flows from the belief that
the Quran, whilst revealed in stages during the Prophet's lifetime,
exists in its entirety as a coherent whole: it is the Word of God in
which contradictions or amendments are impossible. Other references suggested the possibility that Muhammad might forget
revelations sent to him.[16] Given the challenge this would mount to
the very concept of prophethood, "divinely controlled forgetting by
means of which the divine author would determine the final con-
tents of His Book" was the best that could be hoped for.[17] While
the actual text of the Quran remained inviolable, says Firestone:

> an extra-textual hierarchy of versification could be established
> by the *naskh* works, which was done in parallel with the
> *asbab* material on the occasions of revelation. The general
> rule of thumb was to determine which of the inconsistent
> statements on a topic was the latest to have been revealed.
> Because of the accepted view that the revelations were given
> serially in accordance with the specific historical unfolding of
> Muhammad's prophetic career, they were understood to have
> been revealed in response to particular situations faced by the
> Prophet and the Muslim community. According to the stan-
> dard Muslim view, Muhammad was confronted with many
> different and inconstant predicaments during his evolving mis-
> sion as *prophète extraordinaire*. God therefore personally
> guided his apostle by sending Muhammad revelations to help
> him through difficult and uncertain times. Conditions nor-
> malized, however, as the community grew and its organization

became more advanced and secure towards the end of his life. In cases of contradiction, therefore, the earlier revelations were considered to have been given specifically in order to assist with the contingency of the moment, while later revelations were considered to be normative and eternal.[18]

The revelations on warfare are a case in point. The famous Sword Verse (9:5) is stated in some of the specialist works to have replaced as many as one hundred and twenty-four verses.[19] Using the *naskh* and *asbab* methodologies described above, scholars concluded that during the period when Muhammad resided in Mecca, when his community was weak and vulnerable, the Quranic verses were mainly concerned with avoidance of physical conflict. Only after the persecution that resulted in the *hijra* – the migration of Muhammad and his companions to Medina – were Muslims given permission by God to fight in self-defence. As the community continued to grow, "further revelations widened the conditions and narrowed the restrictions under which war could be waged until it was concluded that war against non-Muslims could be waged at virtually any time, without pretext, and in any place".[20]

Firestone, who finds serious problems in the traditional approach, proposes a different reading. The contradictions in the Quranic teachings on war can be understood in their historical context as "signposts along the way of that difficult transitional path" from the old norms of war as practised by the pre-Islamic Arabs of the *jahiliyya* – the "period of ignorance" prior to the coming of Islam – and the form of ideological warfare that developed under Islam.[21] His argument is consistent with that of many other scholars, including Muhammad's British biographer W. Montgomery Watt, who described how the energies of the Arab tribes, previously consumed in internecine conflicts, were redirected outwards under the banner of Islam.

When the disparate tribes of Arabia were consolidated into a single, massive and basically united sociopolitical group, the tremendous energy that had previously been expended in tribal feuds, raids, and attempts at dominating other groups could no longer be released. Most of the pre-Islamic criteria for determining success – honor, manliness, strength, prowess in fighting – would also naturally be suppressed in such a state. This tremendous energy, therefore, needed release, and the only way possible was outward, against the outsider, the nonmember of the now extrakinship affiliation of the Islamic Umma [community]. This release of energy, channeled as it was through new definitions of self and other and through a religious framework of solidarity based on a unifying God and prophet, became the power that drove the holy war enterprise that takes shape in the great Islamic conquest.[22]

In his famous *Muqaddima* – or "Prolegomena" to the History of the World[23] – the important medieval thinker Ibn Khaldun (d.1406) located the Islamic conquests in the wider context of the whole of human history. Basing his knowledge on what might be called the political ecology of his native North Africa, he argued that the earliest form of human society was that of the hardy people of the steppes, deserts and mountains where authority was based on ties of kinship and group cohesion – what he called *'asabiyya*, "solidarity" or "group feeling". A ruler with *'asabiyya* was well placed to found a dynasty, since city folk tended to lack this quality. When dynastic rule was stable and prosperous, city life would flourish. But every dynasty bore in itself the seeds of decline, as rulers degenerated into tyrants, or became corrupted by luxurious living. In due course, power would pass to a new group of men from the margins. Thus, for Ibn Khaldun, the Greeks and Persians had been replaced by the Arabs; and the Arabs, having founded an empire that stretched from Spain to the Indus valley, were in due course replaced by Berbers in the west and Turks in the east.

In this cycle of human movements in West Asia and North Africa, the Arab moment of physical dominance was surprisingly brief. The territories conquered by the handful of nomadic tribes erupting from the Arabian peninsula (the word "Arab" for Ibn

Khaldun and his contemporaries meant "bedouin", and was syn-
onymous with cruelty and barbarism) were much too vast to be
brought under a single administration. Within a generation the
heirs of Muhammad were being torn by factional strife, while in
less than two centuries the power of the caliph was passing to local
commanders and eventually to palace bodyguards – usually
Turkomans from Central Asia whose technically unfree status led
to their eventually being designated as the "owned ones" (*mam-
luks*). But in terms of language, religion and, ultimately,
civilization, the Arabs left a mark that would prove far more
durable than their military achievements, remarkable though these
were. The religion of Islam guaranteed that Arabs would achieve a
cultural dominance far out of proportion to their numbers. Since
Islam was a religion of orthopraxy, in which properly regulated
social behaviour, enshrined in the Shari'a law, counted for more
than theological belief, the common Muslim identity created an
international society which, for all its political uncertainties and
ethnic diversity, was remarkably homogeneous.

As Albert Hourani explained in his magisterial *A History of the
Arab Peoples*,

> The canons of correct behaviour and thought, of learning and
> high skills linked the generations, but they also linked the
> cities with each other. A network of routes ran through the
> world of Islam and beyond it. Along them moved not only
> caravans of camels or donkeys, carrying silks, spices, glass
> and precious metals, but ideas, news, fashions, patterns of
> thought and behaviour.[24]

The Islamic law of jihad was integral to this process of cyclical
renewal in the lands of the "arid zone", where pastoralists ranged
freely, often beyond the reach of government. After Muhammad
had united the warring tribes of the Arabian peninsula under the
banner of Islam, his successors, the Arab caliphs, sought to establish the rule of Islam over the entire world. Majid Khadduri, author
of a standard academic text on the law of jihad, saw this imperial

aspiration as having been rooted in the traditions of the ancient world. Since the conquests of Alexander the Great, there had been a tendency to move from the parochial to the universal. The theocratic Christian states (Byzantium and the Holy Roman Empire) inherited this aspiration, as did Islam as it expanded outwards from the Arabian peninsula.

> The Islamic state, whose principal function was to put God's law into practice, sought to establish Islam as the dominant reigning ideology over the entire world. It refused to recognise the coexistence of non-Muslim communities, except perhaps as subordinate entities, because by its very nature a universal state tolerates the existence of no other state than itself. Although it was not a consciously formulated policy, Muhammad's early successors, after Islam became supreme in Arabia, were determined to embark on a ceaseless war of conquest in the name of Islam. The jihad was therefore employed as an instrument for both the universalization of religion and the establishment of an imperial world state.[25]

The Islamic state could not expand *ad infinitum*. In the west it was checked at Tours (732), in the east at the Indus valley (*c.*760). Thereafter the world was divided into *dar al-islam* (the Abode of Submission) and *dar al-harb* (the Abode of War). Under the former the inhabitants consisted of Muslims by birth or conversion, or communities of the tolerated or protected scriptural religions (initially Judaism and Christianity, later extended to Zoroastrianism, Buddhism and Hinduism, when Muslims realized that these were scriptural communities) who preferred to hold fast to their own cult at the price of paying the *jizya* (poll tax). Muslims enjoyed fuller rights than non-Muslims; the subjects of tolerated religions enjoyed only partial rights, and submitted to Muslim rule in accordance with special charters regulating their relations with Muslims. *Dar al-harb* consisted of all the states and communities outside the world of Islam. Its inhabitants were often referred to as infidels (*kuffar*).[26]

Formally there existed a constant state of war between Islam and the world outside:

> On the assumption that the ultimate aim of Islam was world-wide, the *dar al-islam* was always, in theory, at war with *dar al-harb*. The Muslims were required to preach Islam by per-suasion, and the caliph or his commanders in the field to offer Islam as an alternative to paying the poll tax or fighting; but the Islamic state was under legal obligation to enforce Islamic law and to recognise no authority other than its own, super-seding other authorities even when non-Muslim communities had willingly accepted the faith of Islam without fighting. Failure by non-Muslims to accept Islam or pay the poll tax made it incumbent on the Muslim state to declare a jihad upon the recalcitrant individuals and communities. Thus the jihad, reflecting the normal war relations existing between Muslims and non-Muslims, was the state's instrument for transforming the *dar al-harb* into *dar al-islam*. It was the product of a warlike people who had embarked on a large-scale movement of expansion.[27]

The Quranic origins of jihad lie in Muhammad's campaigns against the Meccans. Before they submitted to Islam, these were polytheists who "associated" subordinate deities with Allah. Polytheism – *shirk* – is the cardinal religious offence in the Islamic lexicon. Those who "associate" lesser deities with the one divinity are condemned to perdition. The "peoples of the book" are toler-ated, provided they pay the *jizya* in lieu of military service, because their religion in its original form is recognized as consistent with Islamic monotheism. The Jews and Christians are in error not because they worship false gods, but because they have "cor-rupted" the scriptures originally revealed to them by Allah. The doctrine accounts for differences between the Islamic revelation and its Abrahamic predecessors. It may also reflect the gnostic reli-gious milieu of late antiquity in which Islam originated: the Islamic view of Jesus, for example, is similar to that which may be found in many of the gnostic documents discovered at Nag Hammadi in Upper Egypt in 1945.[28] Like the Jesus of the Quran, the Jesus portrayed in many of the gnostic texts found at Nag Hammadi is a "wisdom teacher" rather than a Redeemer. He did not die on the Cross, but a substitute was found to take his place. When applied to Christianity, the Islamic doctrine of the "corruption of the scriptures" is far from being incompatible with the findings of modern scholarship.

Islamic tolerance, in the classical formulations, is not unconditional. Christians and Jews, and members of other faiths once they are deemed to have holy scriptures, are allowed the freedom to practise their religions provided they accept Islamic governance, symbolized by payment of the *jizya*. To use somewhat anachronistic terms, they must remain second-class citizens, subject to certain disabilities. For example a Muslim man may marry a woman from one of the "protected" communities, but the converse does not apply. In a patriarchal society, the message is clear. Christians and Jews – the *ahl al-dhimma* – are social inferiors. Some of these disabilities were elaborated into rules concerning transport (only Muslims ride horses), house construction (a *dhimmi* house may not overlook that of a Muslim) and legal proceedings (a *dhimmi*'s testimony is not worth the same as that of a Muslim).[29] Polytheists enjoy no such protection. The Sword Verse eventually interpreted as superseding other verses referring to warfare was originally directed at Meccan enemies more powerful than the struggling community of Muslims in Medina. Applied to peoples in sub-Saharan Africa, it became a charter for conquest and slavery, even genocide.

The jihad was integral to Islamic expansion. Understood as a political–military struggle, it provided the rationale for the Islamic imperium. For the majority of jurists, jihad was not an individual duty (*fard 'ain*). Hence it was not included as one of the "five pillars" or ritual obligations of Islam – the declaration of faith, prayer, fasting, alms and pilgrimage. The latter are supposed to be observed by individuals regardless of sanction of authority. Theoretically jihad, as *raison d'état*, must be enforced by the state.

It was regarded by all jurists as *fard kifaya*, binding on all Muslims collectively as a group. "So long as the duty was fulfilled by part of the community it ceased to be obligatory on others. The whole community, however, fell into error if the duty was not performed at all."[30]

The law of jihad, based on the Quran and the precedents established by Muhammad in his wars against the unbelievers, insisted on certain limitations. Various categories of persons normally were exempt from fighting, including boys under fifteen, the insane, slaves, women, the ill and handicapped, people too poor to supply themselves with equipment, provisions, a mount or subsistence for their dependants.[31] The Hanafite school of lawyers, in what seems like a egregious example of a self-serving rubric, exempts "the best lawyer in town".[32]

Most of the jurists gave precedence to the *fard 'ain*, the individual obligation, over the *fard kifaya*. Minors cannot take part in jihad unless they obtain their parents' permission. Devotion to parents is an individual duty which prevails over the collective duty. A man who asked the Prophet if his sins would be remitted should he be killed in battle was told: "If you patiently sacrifice yourself, advancing and not retreating, your sins will be remitted but not your debts. That is what Angel Gabriel told me."[33] As an individual duty, repaying a debt has precedence over the collective duty of jihad. If Muslim territory is invaded, however, such limitations cease to apply, since jihad in defence of *dar al-islam* becomes an individual duty incumbent on everyone.

The jihad, as prescribed in the classical legal texts, was subject to certain crucial limitations. Before the Muslims could attack their enemies, they must summon them to Islam, or the payment of the poll tax if they belonged to the Peoples of the Book. According to Rudolph Peters, a leading authority on the law of jihad, "The function of the summons is to inform the enemy that the Muslims do not fight them for worldly reasons, like subjecting them and taking their property, but that their motive is a religious one, the strengthening of Islam."[34] The Malakite school specifies that the summons must be made on three successive days.

If on the fourth day the enemy still refuses to accept Islam or pay the tax, he must be attacked immediately. "All scholars agree," Peters adds, however, "that a summons is not required if this is impossible, for instance when the enemy attacks the Muslims by surprise, or if it would endanger the Muslim position. This last situation arises for instance when it is suspected that the enemy will take advantage of the delay by strengthening his forces, or when the Muslim force is so weak that it can only win by a surprise attack."[35] The fact that the attacks on New York and Washington came without warning does not automatically make them a violation of Islamic law: as with so much in this appalling saga, everything depends on interpretation.

In the classical law of jihad the rules of war were carefully specified. All possible weapons such as arrows, lances, swords and mangonels (subsequently replaced by guns and bombs) were permitted against the enemy. The means explicitly allowed included "drowning them by diverting the course of a river, starving them by cutting off the supply of food and water, by poisoning the water, by throwing boiling oil and by setting them on fire".[36] The use of mangonels – later replaced by canon – was permitted on the ground that the Prophet had used them at the siege of Taif (now the Saudi summer capital) in 631. A hadith was also cited according to which "the Prophet was asked about the children of the polytheists. Could the latter be attacked at night with the possible result that [the Muslims] would hit some of their women and children?" To which Muhammad answered, "They [that is, their children] belong to them . . ."[37]

Some of these methods were subject to certain restrictions: drowning or burning were only allowed if victory could not be obtained by any other method. All the legal schools were agreed that minors and women could not be killed, unless they actually fought against the Muslims: several traditions were cited in support in addition to the "rational" argument that by killing them Muslims damaged their own property, since women and children became slaves on being captured.[38] Most authorities prohibited the killing of noncombatants, such as the aged, the insane, monks, the chronically ill, blind and other handicapped people, farmers and serfs, provided they did not fight or assist the enemy in other ways, such as by giving money or advice. However the Shafi'ite school and the influential scholar Ibn Hazm (of the now defunct Zahirite school) considered it permissible to kill such persons on the ground that the Sword Verse abrogated 2:190 "Fight in the way of God those who fight you, but do not commit aggression". In addition they adduce the following hadith: "Kill the old men of the polytheists and save the lives of their children." As Ibn Hazm and the Shafi'ites only regarded hadiths prohibiting the killing of women and children as authentic, they allowed the killing of all other categories of unbelievers.[39]

Central to the doctrine of jihad are the rewards of martyrdom. The word martyr – *shahid* – has the same root as *shahada* – the declaration or witness of faith. The martyr is the witness to faith *par excellence*. Numerous hadiths attest to the value and privileges of martyrdom. A tradition in the collection of Abu Daud, one of the six collections of hadiths regarded as canonical in Sunni Islam, states that the martyr will be able to save as many as seventy sinful members of his family who would otherwise have been sent to hell.[40] Another hadith, from the collections of al-Bukhari and al-Tirmidhi, states that "no servant [of God] who dies and has goodness with God wants to return to the world, even if he would have the world and all that is in it, except the shahid, for when he sees the bounty of martyrdom (*fadl al-shahada*) he will want to return to the world and be killed again."[41] Muhammad is also quoted as saying: "By the One in whose hand is my soul, I would love to be killed in the path of God and be resurrected, then be killed and then resurrected, then be killed and then resurrected, then be killed."[42] "Count not those killed in the path of Allah as dead . . ." the Prophet tells a woman whose son was killed at the Battle of Badr in 624, the first major engagement between the Muslims and the Meccans. "Your son is in the higher paradise."[43] As Khadduri states, "All these sources give lavish promises of martyrdom and eternal life in paradise immediately and without trial on resurrection and judgement day for those who die in Allah's path."[44] If, as was widely reported, Marwan al-Shehi, one of the leading September 11th hijackers, drank rum and Coca-Cola at a bar in Florida the night before the attack, his infringement of the rule forbidding alcohol would certainly be entitled to forgiveness according to the classical sources.

Suicide, of course, is a sin (see Chapter 3), but suicide that is subsumed in an act of martyrdom may be a different matter. Ibn Ishaq, the first of Muhammad's biographers, records the story of 'Awf bin Harith at the Battle of Badr. "O Apostle of God," 'Awf asked the Prophet, "what makes the Lord laugh with joy at his servant?", to which the Prophet replied, "When he plunges into the midst of the enemy without armour." Upon hearing this, 'Awf drew off his mail-coat and threw it away. Then he seized his sword and fought the enemy until he was killed.[45] Martyrs who died in battle were buried where they fell, not in the unusual type of grave, after washing in a mosque. It is true that a promise of paradise was given to every believer who performed the five basic duties of Islam, but none of them, according to Khadduri, would enable him to gain paradise as surely as participation in the jihad.[46]

Jihad, as is now widely known, means "struggle": it has the same root as *ijtihad*, the interpretative "effort" needed to fathom the law as revealed by God and his Prophet. According to a well-known hadith, jihad is the "monasticism" of faith. "Every nation has its monasticism and the monasticism of this nation is the jihad."[47] Muhammad disapproved of asceticism: there was to be "no monkery" in his community. Jihad held the place occupied by asceticism in early Christianity. On an individual level it meant the struggle against evil. An often-cited hadith equates the "lesser jihad" with war, the "greater jihad" with spiritual and moral endeavour. According to the story, when the Prophet returned from a raiding party, he said: "We have now returned from the smaller jihad to the greater jihad." When asked what he meant by the greater jihad, he replied: "The jihad against oneself." Peters points out, however, that this tradition is not included in any of the authoritative compilations – a fact that has allowed the militant Islamists to reject it as spurious.[48]

Though the remarkable expansion of Islam in the first Arab phase (634–*c*.850) and the conquests of South and Central Asia up to about 1500 owed most to the "lesser jihad" of war, much of the expansion into sub-Saharan Africa and South-east Asia occurred peacefully, along the trade routes. The Sufi *tariqas* (mystical orders) were more effective at securing conversions than armies were, not least because they were more flexible than armies and the "urban scripturalists" who followed in their wake in allowing local cults and customs to flourish within the frame of orthodoxy. Under Sufi auspices Islam developed a vast variety of different colourings, from the legal formalism that established itself in great urban centres such as Baghdad and Cairo to the local cults based on individual saints or holy men, or their descendants, that flourished in rural hinterlands. Aspects of the common or "great" tradition, as it is sometimes called, were usually to be found embedded in local cults. The scripturalist Islam of the urban centres conveyed the cultural prestige attached to what for the vast majority of peoples was *the* civilized world.

After the original Arab empire broke up into states that competed with each other for power and legitimacy, the central orthodox tradition was frequently invoked in justification of war. In a region of the world without fixed boundaries, where the power of the state, radiating from urban centres, progressively weakened in proportion to distance, the religion of the mainstream – urban, scriptural, "Protestant" in its rejection of divine intermediaries – remained the primary source of legitimating authority. (In the minority Shi'ite version, that legitimating authority could only be exercised by a direct descendant of Muhammad, or a leader acting on his behalf.) The Sultan (the word simply means "holder of authority") was obliged, in theory at least, to "enjoin the good and forbid the evil" in accordance with Quranic injunctions. Although *fitna* – strife – was often described as a greater evil than oppression, rebellion could be legitimized as a restoration of the true path of Islam. Tyrants could be removed, for failing to judge (or rule) "in accordance with what God sent down" (that is, the Quran, the "sound" hadiths and the vast edifice of law derived from them). As well as being a doctrine that sanctioned Islamic expansion into non-Muslim areas, jihad became the rubric under which intra-Muslim strife was given legitimacy.

To legitimize such conflicts necessitated the designation of the authority one sought to replace as infidel. In the classical tradition, this was not lightly done. The great theologian al-Ash'ari (d.935), a former Mu'tazilite who became the rationalists' leading opponent, denied the right of popular revolt:

> We uphold the prayer for the welfare of the Imams [that is, caliphs] of the Muslims and the confession of their imamate; and we maintain the error of those who approve of the uprising against them wherever it appeared they have abandoned the right; and we believe in the denial of an armed uprising against them and abstinence from fighting in civil war.[49]

Later jurists tended to justify the caliph's authority on grounds of fear of disorder and anarchy. Some went so far as to justify the authority of any ruler who could effectively maintain order, regardless of his piety or injustice. The justifications were found in Quranic passages against *fitna*, sedition.[50] For example Badr al-Din ibn Jama'a (d.1333) stated:

> If, in the absence of an imam, someone assumes power by force even if he were unqualified and assumes it without *bai'a* [the oath of allegiance to the caliph], his imamate becomes binding and obedience to him is necessary in order to maintain the unity of the Muslims. That he may be unjust, vicious, or lacking in knowledge is of no consequence. If the imamate of force were challenged by another who replaces it by force, the latter becomes the recognized imam in view of the fact that this action is consistent with Muslim interests and maintenance of Islam's unity, in accordance with an utterance of ibn 'Umar who said: "We are on the side of the victor."[51]

Not all authorities, however, took such an authoritarian position. Al-Mawardi, author of a standard work on governance,
al-ahkam al-sultaniyya (The Rules of Authority) which worked
out detailed qualifications and functions of the ideal caliph, argued
that if a caliph did not fulfil, or was incapacitated from fulfilling,
his duties he had no right to remain caliph. But al-Mawardi failed
to explain the legal mechanisms by which a caliph could be
dethroned. The earliest group of sectarians, known as the *khawarij*
or Kharijites, took the extreme puritanical view that the sinner
who failed to repent had *ipso facto* excluded himself from the community, and was hence a *kafir* (infidel). The Kharijites, who survive
in the Ibadi communities of Oman, Zanzibar and the Berber region
of Tahert in western Algeria, were in turn declared infidels by the
Sunni majority. Thus we find hadiths such as: "If a Muslim charges
a fellow Muslim with *kufr* [disbelief] he is himself a *kafir*, should
the accusation prove untrue."[52] "The reproach of *kufr* is equivalent
to murder": the sense of this hadith, whether or not authentic,
carried the prestige of Islam's leading theologian, Abu Hamid al-
Ghazali (d.1111), who held that since a charge of *kufr* levelled
against someone born into Islam carried the implication of apostasy, entailing the death penalty, it should not be lightly made. A
twelfth-century treatise by a judge of Ceuta pronounces *takfir* (the
declaration that someone is a *kafir*) against people who befriend
the Jews and encourage or condone their "rebellion against the
laws", despite the fact that Jews are a People of the Book, and
therefore entitled to protection.[53]

Further from the Islamic heartlands, orthodox Islamic states
were created on the basis of jihads declared against incumbent
regimes deemed to have departed from the "straight path" of
Islamic rectitude. In the 1720s Fulani cattle herders from Mali
founded the West African states of Futa Jallon and Futa Toro on
the basis of jihad movements. During the first decade of the nineteenth century the great Fulani renovator Shehu Usumanu Dan
Fodio (1754–1817) founded an empire in what is now northern
Nigeria by attacking and overthrowing the rulers of Hausaland,
where Islamic practices had been grafted onto court rituals of

pagan origin, using the argument that they ruled in such a way as to give proof that they were unbelievers.[54] The same rationale was deployed in the formation of jihad-based states in the Caucasus (1785–1839), and Kashgar (1820–77) in Xinjiang. A jihad, legitimized by designating Sufi devotional practices as "unbelief", was instrumental in establishing the Al Sa'ud dynasty responsible for the creation of modern Saudi Arabia. In declaring the "Turks" to be infidels who did not rule in accordance with divine commands, the Sudanese Mahdi, quoted at the head of this chapter, had numerous precedents to go by.

The Mahdist movement was only one of the many jihads launched against European or quasi-European rule during the nineteenth century. Almost invariably these movements had a religious underpinning in structures of authority moulded by the Sufi tariqas and buttressed by tribal identities. In times of peace, Sufis are quietist, giving priority to the "greater" over the "lesser" jihad. When *dar al-islam* is perceived as being under attack by infidel forces, or forces that can be construed as infidel, the Sufi organization provides the inspirational and moral basis for the "greater" jihad.

War has a spiritual dimension in the bonds of solidarity forged, of necessity, between fighting men. In tribal societies the bonds between fighters may be primarily genetic: kinship is the basis of solidarity. Muslim leaders fully recognized this fact. In premodern times the sultans recruited their armies in the peripheral regions – among the Turks of Central Asia, Nubians in the Upper Nile regions, Slavs in the Balkans, Daylamis in the mountains south of the Caspian Sea, and Berbers in the Atlas. Eventually such mercenary or slave armies proved unable to resist the superior weaponry and discipline of European armies;[55] but as the example of the original Islamic movement demonstrated, tribal solidarities could be transcended or subsumed within the larger solidarity generated by a charismatic leader who inculcated a common spiritual discipline. The model went back to Muhammad himself, seen by most Sufi orders as the originator of the special spiritual disciplines they inculcated.

Religious practices aimed at self-transcendence (including supererogatory prayers or *dhikrs*, "remembrances" of God, or the whirling dances of the Mevlevi dervishes) can be converted to military use. Before the European drill sergeant had completed his work, the disciplined Sufi adept, given rudimentary military training, could make a better soldier than the "squaddie" pressganged into the army or forced to enlist by reason of debt. In conscious emulation of Muhammad, the *mujahidin* often migrated from a region dominated by "infidelity" to a *dar al-hijra* (territory of migration) beyond the range of infidelity, where the Islamic order could hold sway. In North Africa 'Abd al-Qadir (1808–83), a shaikh of the Qadiriyya order, made the *hijra* to western Algeria where he established a state which the French eventually overran; similar patterns applied to the jihads launched by the Imam Shamil, who resisted the Russian conquest of Chechniya (1834–59) under the spiritual authority of his father-in-law, Sayyid Jamal al-Din al-Ghazi-Ghumuqi, a shaikh of the Naqshbandiyya, and to the Swat Pathans of India's North-West frontier, who created a state, which the British found it politic to recognize, under the Akhund 'Abd al-Ghafur in the 1870s.[56]

As Akbar Ahmed noted in his study *Millennium and Charisma among Pathans*, British encroachments in this area generated a number of millenarian movements which he defines as "a spontaneous, universal and historically short-lived, native reaction to economic or political stimulus, expressed through the presence of foreign troops and administrators". Ahmad stresses the religious--mystical underpinnings of these movements. "The reaction is led by messianic leaders, nationalist heroes and prophets, often claiming mystical talents, promising some form of utopia in the future and reversal to a happier order in the past, and supported by the dispossessed and the rural."[57] However spontaneous they are, such movements tend to fall into the mould of the Muhammadan paradigm, a mould sanctified by history and centuries of cultural programming. "*The historical idiomatic response through which Islamic sentiment expresses itself in times of extreme crisis is jihad.*"[58] (emphasis added)

Such movements, however, were rarely able to challenge the overwhelming power of the Europeans, except in peripheral regions such as Afghanistan where geography and climate created impenetrable obstacles even for modern armies. In India, Sayyid Ahmad Khan (1817–98), the originator of the modernist trend in Islamic thought, argued that since the British did not prevent Muslims from performing their religious duties, jihad against them was unlawful.

The context of Ahmad Khan's writing was significant. In the aftermath of the 1857 rebellion, for which Muslims were largely blamed, educated Muslims such as Sayyid Ahmad, whose forebears had been advisers to the Mughal emperors, experienced discrimination, while educated Hindus benefited from the new imperial administration. Sayyid Ahmad saw that rebellion had been disastrous and argued for an accommodation with the reality of the British Raj that would allow Muslims to prosper. He introduced modern education for Muslims through the Muhammadan Anglo-Oriental College he founded at Aligarh (now a university). The thrust of his teaching led inevitably to a separation of religion and politics and to the secularization of the latter. For this, and for his generally Anglophile views, he was fiercely attacked by his contemporary Jamal al-Din al-Afghani, who could be described as the inspiration behind the modern Islamist movement. Although al-Afghani (he was actually an Iranian Shi'ite, who deliberately concealed his origins to avoid anti-Shi'a prejudice) shared some of Sayyid Ahmad's views about the need for reforming the tradition, he was passionately opposed to any accommodation with imperialism. The Egyptian modernists who were inspired by al-Afghani and his influential disciple Muhammad 'Abduh (1849–1905) defined jihad more broadly than Sayyid Ahmad. Whereas the latter had restricted it to the struggle against religious persecution, "the Egyptian modernists held that jihad was a struggle against all kinds of oppression, religious and political. This implied that the struggle against colonial domination could be classified as jihad – precisely what the Indian modernists had wanted to exclude."[59]

A declaration of jihad is far from being necessarily efficacious. In November 1914 the Muslim world's highest dignitary, the Ottoman Sultan and Caliph Mehmet V, declared a jihad against Russia, France and Britain, announcing that it had become an individual obligation (*fard 'ain*) for all Muslims, whether young or old, on foot or mounted, to support the struggle with their goods and money. As might have been expected, the proclamation, which took the form of a fatwa, or legal ruling, was endorsed by religious leaders throughout the Sultan's dominions. Outside the Ottoman Empire, however, its effect was minimal. In Russian Central Asia, French North Africa and British India the colonial authorities generally had no difficulty in finding *'ulama* (religious scholars) to publicly endorse the Allied cause. Most galling for the Sultan–Caliph, his suzerain the Sharif Hussein of Mecca, Guardian of the Holy Places, refused to endorse the jihad publicly. He had already been approached by the British with a view to launching an Arab revolt against the Turks – the revolt whose success would eventually result in the Sharif's sons Feisal and 'Abdullah being given the British-protected thrones of Iraq and Jordan. The Arabs of Syria, Mesopotamia, Palestine and the Hejaz preferred freedom to "Islamic" rule, even though for many that freedom entailed the risk (soon to be realized) of a new colonialist domination under the "infidel".

In April 1948, one month before Israel's declaration of independence and the declaration of war by the Arab states, a fatwa proclaimed by the mufti of Egypt made it legally obligatory for Muslims to wage the jihad in person, or by means of financial contributions, to come to the rescue of Palestine "since Jewish Zionists attempt by force of arms to establish a Jewish state in Palestine, one of the most noble Arab and Islamic countries, not only in order to take possession of Palestine, but also to dominate all Islamic states and to eliminate their Arab character and their Islamic culture". The real purpose of this fatwa, however, appears in the final sentence: "However, as today the methods of war have become complex, it is obligatory for anyone participating in jihad to submit to the rules that the states of the Arab League lay down for participation in jihad, in order that the expected victory be realized."[60] The caveat was directed at groups of volunteers from the Islamist Muslim Brotherhood who were operating in Palestine without authorization from the Arab governments.

In this and numerous other instances the jihad becomes in effect an instrument of government. Since Ottoman times the muftis, religious authorities licensed to issue fatwas, have come under government control: the fatwa just quoted clearly reflected Egyptian government policy of the day: opposition to the expected declaration of Israel, insistence on a coordinated political response with other Arab League states, opposition to the freelance activities of the Muslim Brotherhood volunteers.

For Habib Bourguiba, the founder of modern Tunisia and an out-and-out proponent of secularism, jihad became the "struggle" for development.

> Tunisia, which is an Islamic country, suffers from a certain degree of decline and backwardness, that bring disgrace upon us in the eyes of the world. The only way of freeing ourselves from this shame is continuous and assiduous work and fruitful and useful labour. Escaping from this backwardness is jihad – an obligation ruled by the same prescriptions as jihad by means of the sword.[61]

In pursuit of this analogy, Bourguiba persuaded the Tunisian *'ulama* to allow workers to be exempted from the Ramadan fast, which he held responsible for slowing production, since *mujahidin* (the warriors taking part in jihad) are exempted from fasting.[62]

The Islamists take a wholly different view of jihad, one that is closer to the classical authorities. The intellectual father of modern Islamism was Sayyid Abu 'Ala Maududi (1903–79) founder of the Jama'at-i-Islami, an organization whose agenda is similar to that of the Muslim Brotherhood in Egypt. Although Maududi claimed that Islam was entirely self-sufficient, being God's final revelation to humankind which superseded all other religions and philosophies, he was strongly influenced by the intellectual climate of the 1930s, particularly the writings of Alexis Carrel, a popular French writer who would later be discredited for his support for the Vichy government. Carrel's animadversions on the "corruptions" of modern living found their way into Maududi's denunciations of the West as a sewer of vice and wickedness. Impressed by the totalitarian movements in Russia, Italy and Germany, he compared Islam favourably with communism and fascism as a movement with the potential to mobilize the masses. The Jama'at-i-Islami with himself as *amir* (commander) had more than a hint of *Führerprinzip* about it. He insisted, however, that the Islamic movement would be free from the destructive features of the totalitarian ideologies because its leadership would be people of proven virtue.

As Olivier Roy stresses, the Islamist political theory developed by Maududi and adapted and brought forward by Sayyid Qutb in Egypt is trapped in what might be called a "vicious circle of virtue". Because the Islamist model is predicated on the belief in government by morally impeccable individuals who can be counted on to resist temptation, it does not generate institutions capable of functioning autonomously. Political institutions function only as a result of the virtue of those who run them, but virtue can become widespread only if society is already Islamic. Maududi believed that the proper observance of Islamic norms, a prerequisite for belonging to the Jama'at-i-Islami, was a guarantee of personal integrity. Unlike the members of secular movements, the Islamists would not be corrupted by power.[63]

Maududi believed that the law had been revealed to Muhammad for all time and for all humanity:

The Quran does not claim that Islam is the true compendium of rites and rituals, and metaphysical beliefs and concepts, or that it is the proper form of religious attitude of thought and action for the individual (as the word religion is nowadays understood in Western terminology). Nor does it say that Islam is the true way of life for the people of Arabia, or for the people of any particular country or for the people preceding any particular age (say the Industrial Revolution). *No! Very explicitly, for the*

*entire human race, there is only one way of life which is Right
in the eyes of God and that is al-Islam.*[64] (emphasis added)

It follows that in the true Islamic state, for which Maududi coined
the term "theodemocracy", the representatives of the people may
be co-opted into the national assembly rather than elected, on
the ground that truly virtuous people will not always put themselves forward. As Yousef Choueiri has observed, Maududi's
theodemocracy is an "ideological state in which legislators do not
legislate, citizens only vote to reaffirm the permanent applicability
of God's laws, women rarely venture outside their homes lest social
discipline be disrupted, and non-Muslims are tolerated as foreign
elements required to express their loyalty by means of paying a
financial levy" (that is, the *jizya*).[65]

A prolific journalist and writer, Maududi was not trained as a
traditional *'alim* (religious scholar) though he retained close links
with the conservative *'ulama* (plural of *'alim*) of India. Initially
opposed to the idea of Pakistan, which he saw as being dominated
by leaders with an unacceptably secular outlook, once Pakistan
became a reality in 1947 he worked ceaselessly to convert the
homeland of India's Muslims into a fully fledged Islamic state.
Maududi has been described as "much the most systematic thinker
of modern Islam".[66] Adapting, without acknowledgement, the
Marxist idea of "permanent revolution" Maududi argued that
jihad was the ultimate political struggle for the whole of
humankind. His tract on jihad merits quoting at length:

> For Islam is not concerned with the interest of one nation to
> the exclusion of others and does not intend to advance one
> people to the exclusion of others. It is not at all interested in
> what state rules and dominates the earth, but only in the hap-
> piness and welfare of humanity. Islam has a concept and a
> practical program, especially chosen for the happiness and
> progress of human society. Therefore Islam resists any gov-
> ernment that is based on a different concept and program, in
> order to liquidate it completely.

... Its aim is to make this concept victorious, to introduce this program universally, to set up governments that are firmly rooted in this concept and this program, irrespective of who carries the banner of truth and justice, or whose flag of aggression and corruption is thereby toppled. *Islam wants the whole earth and does not content itself with only a part thereof. It wants and requires the entire inhabited world.*[67] (emphasis added)

Maududi's writings became available in Arabic translation during the 1950s. They exercised an important influence on Sayyid Qutb, the principal ideologue of the Muslim Brotherhood in Egypt. It is Qutb, the intellectual father of modern Islamist terrorism, whose experience and work must be analysed next. More than any other recent Muslim writer, he is the inspiration behind September 11th.

Chapter Three

The Aesthetics of Martyrdom

Sayyid Qutb was born in 1906 in Musha, a small village near Asyut in Upper Egypt, into a well-educated family. His father, Hajj Qutb bin Ibrahim, was an active member of the Hizb al-Watan, the secular National Party led by Mustafa Kamil, but he was also personally devout. As an adolescent Hajj Qutb had been involved in the anti-British rioting that followed Britain's refusal to consider full independence for Egypt by allowing a delegation (*wafd*) to attend the Paris Peace Conference. In later years the Islamic and nationalist currents would diverge; but during the early part of the twentieth century they ran together. Muslims who were both religiously observant and politically aware shared a common desire to be rid of foreign influence, especially that of the British.

Since 1882 Egypt had been a quasi-protectorate of Britain. Although it became formally independent after the First World War, the country's sovereignty was subject to restrictions which were highly irksome to politically aware Egyptians. British troops retained control over the Suez Canal Zone and the right to station troops throughout the country in the event of war. During the First World War, Cairo became the base from which Britain directed the war against Egypt's former suzerain, the Ottoman Empire. In the Second World War, though technically neutral, Egypt became the base from which the British army fought the Italians and Germans in North Africa, Yugoslavia and Greece. It was also the base from which Britain drew the military support for its contradictory policies in Palestine. Britain's mandate over the former Ottoman territory, which it conquered in 1918, had been conditional on the creation of a Jewish homeland without interfering with the rights of the indigenous people – an impossible condition to satisfy, as practically every commentary on the Balfour Declaration has pointed out. Modern immigration by secular-minded Zionists (as distinct from the small-scale settlement of religious Jews) began in the 1880s but the initial permission granted by the Ottoman sultans was reversed after representations from Arab notables. In the 1920s, Zionist immigration began in earnest. After the Nazi accession to power in Germany in 1933, it increased dramatically. From 1936 to 1939 British troops were involved in suppressing a series Arab revolts sparked off by Jewish immigration; from 1945 as the full extent of German atrocities became apparent, British military efforts were directed mainly against Jewish terrorism. The evils of the British presence in Egypt and Palestine was something about which nationalists and the people we now call Islamists (or, less happily, Islamic fundamentalists) could agree.

The Islamist political movement emerged during the 1930s under the leadership of Hasan al-Banna, a schoolteacher from the new town of Isma'iliyya. Built at the halfway point along the Suez Canal to service the ships that used it, the town epitomized neo-colonialism, with comfortable villas for the canal company's European employees and standardized shacks for the labourers and servants who toiled on the company's behalf. The Muslim Brotherhood, founded by al-Banna in 1928, combined aspects of a political movement with that of a Sufi tariqa, with al-Banna himself (who had a Sufi background) combining the role of shaikh and *Führer*. During the 1930s he expressed considerable admiration for the Nazi Brownshirts; but he may also have been influenced, as were some Hindu nationalists at the same period, by the muscular religiosity of the Boy Scouts and the YMCA. Members, who were recruited from all social classes, from peasants and labourers to merchants and civil servants, were encouraged to take up sports and to avoid the evils of gambling, usury (understood to mean the lending or borrowing of money at fixed interest rates), alcohol consumption and sexual activity outside marriage. They were organized into families, clans, groups and battalions (significantly, the word *kata'ib* is sometimes translated as Phalange, the far-right political organization that supported Francoist Spain). As al-Banna liked to remind his followers, the Brotherhood's primary purpose was religious: "My brothers, you are not a benevolent society, nor a political party, nor a local organisation having a political purpose. Rather you are a new soul in the heart of this nation to give it light by means of the Quran . . . to destroy the darkness of materialism through knowing God."[1]

The spectacular growth of the Muslim Brotherhood, however, made it a political force to be reckoned with: it was wooed alternatively by the monarchy which tried to use the organization to improve its own image in the wider Arab world and as a stick with which to resist its British overlords, and by the left (including on occasions the communists) which sought its support in political strikes and industrial disputes. During the Palestine War of 1948 the Muslim Brotherhood volunteers performed better than the conscripts, earning the admiration of some of the Free Officers who would overthrow the monarchy in an almost bloodless coup in July 1952. In the events leading up to the revolution – particularly the riots of Black Saturday in March 1952, which saw many places associated with British power attacked – it was the Muslim Brotherhood which played the leading part.

Sayyid Qutb's own experience in many ways epitomized that of his generation. He was intelligent, sensitive and highly articulate, and his writings reached beyond his own peers, to the generations that succeeded him. He was brought up as a devout Muslim in a small village. By the age of ten, on his own initiative, he had memorized the Quran. His family, though well-educated, had fallen on hard times, and he went to live with an uncle in Cairo, where he attend the Dar al-'Ulum, a well-known teacher training college where Muhammad 'Abduh, Egypt's leading reformist scholar, had once lectured. His uncle was a supporter of the less militant national party, the Wafd, named after the "delegation" Egypt had been prevented from sending to the peace conference following the Allied victory in the First World War. In Cairo, Qutb fell under the spell of 'Abbas Mahmoud al-'Aqqad (1889–1964), leading light of the so-called Diwan group of Egyptian writers. Their preference was for English rather than French literary models, despite the fact that even in "the Arab countries controlled by Britain it was the French who were more active in the educational field and made the deeper mark on literature".[2] Unlike most other members of the literary elite, al-'Aqqad was self-educated, having completed only primary education. He held the English Romantics, particularly Coleridge and the essayist William Hazlitt, in especially high esteem. Qutb devoured everything he could in translation, becoming generally knowledgeable in the literature and culture of Europe – much more so than his Indo-Pakistani counterpart Maududi. He wrote poetry, short stories, articles and literary criticism, acquiring a considerable reputation. One of his stories, "Ashwak" (Thorns), is a veiled account of his disappointment in love, after which he resolved to remain a bachelor.[3] Coming from a rural background in Upper Egypt he was shocked by the unveiled women he met at work in Cairo. Unwilling to choose a bride from such "dishonourable" women, yet unable for lack of family connections to meet a woman "of sufficient moral purity and discretion",[4] he remained celibate for the rest of his life – a condition he shared with the founder of modern Islamic radicalism, Jamal al-Din al-Afghani.

Having made a name for himself in literary circles, Qutb obtained a job as an inspector in the Ministry of Education. He drafted many projects for the reform of the education system – most of which were trashed by his superiors who included the famous writer Taha Hussein. As a highly regarded writer, Qutb had ready access to space in newspapers and journals. He sharpened his pen with fiery polemics directed against his former boss. During the Second World War, like many educated Egyptians, he became disillusioned with the old-style nationalism of the Wafd party whose leader, Nahas Pasha, chose to collaborate with the British after the High Commissioner, Sir Miles Lampson, forced the king to dismiss his prime minister, 'Ali Maher, who was considered too friendly to the Italians and Germans. Like many Egyptians Qutb also became increasingly angry at the scale of Jewish settlement in Palestine, which he blamed on the British. He became so involved in anti-government and anti-British agitation that the king wanted to imprison him: Qutb was only saved by his old Wafdist connections. In 1948 he obtained a generous government grant to investigate American instructional methods and curricula in primary and secondary education. His superiors appear to have thought that exposure to American culture would moderate his views. Instead it had quite the opposite effect.

Qutb's visit to the United States deserves to rank as the defining moment or watershed from which the "Islamist war against America" would flow. Though Qutb's anti-Western views were already hardening, they had hitherto been directed mainly against Britain, the imperial power in Egypt, Palestine, South Arabia, Transjordan and Iraq. But he was already becoming critical of America. In 1946 he had written an article expressing disappointment at President Harry S. Truman's support for the international committee of inquiry's recommendation that 100,000 Jewish refugees from Europe be immediately admitted to Palestine. While he had not been surprised at the British hands behind the policy, he was disillusioned by America's readiness to support the Zionists, since he had shared with many other Arabs the belief that after the war America would support Arab demands for self-determination. America's refusal to endorse demands for an independent Arab state in Palestine "demonstrated that it was in fact no different in its basic attitude towards Eastern nations than the British, French and Dutch".5 Nevertheless at this stage Qutb's opposition to America was mainly political. During the twenty-one months he spent in the country it matured into cultural and spiritual hostility as well.

John Calvert, who has explored Qutb's American visit more thoroughly than most other scholars, suggests that the Atlantic crossing was itself catalytic. Later, in his multi-volume commentary on the Quran, Qutb recalled how the voyage inspired in him a heightened sense of his personal destiny and moral purpose. Viewing the wintry ocean he recalled the Quranic passage that celebrates the "ships that speed through the sea with that which is useful to men, and in the waters which God sends down from the sky, giving life thereby to the earth".[6] Annoyed by a Christian missionary who proselytized among the ship's passengers, he persuaded the captain to allow him to act as imam, or prayer leader, for a group of Nubian seamen employed by the company. He saw the effect this had on the other passengers, especially a woman refugee from Yugoslavia, as a function of *i'jaz*, the Quran's miraculous ability to move the soul through the power of its language. His sublime feelings were rudely interrupted by the sudden appearance of a "drunken, semi-naked" woman at the door of his cabin. Later he would tell his Arab biographer that she was an American agent planted to seduce him – a suggestion that hardly seems compatible with her inebriated condition. The significance he accorded the incident, however, is itself significant: he must have felt some attraction for the woman since, as his biographer put it, "the encounter successfully tested his resolve to resist experiences damaging to his identity as an Egyptian and as a Muslim". For a virgin (one presumes) of forty-two, this direct encounter with female sexuality "in the raw" was profoundly unsettling.

Qutb landed in New York just before Thanksgiving in November 1949. He was always in delicate health – he suffered from respiratory problems – and the journey had left him exhausted. He regained his land legs by wandering the streets which were already glittering with Christmas decorations. He did not admire the city. It was a "vast workshop, noisy and clamorous". We have no record that he visited the Metropolitan Museum of Art, the Frick collection, Carnegie Hall, or even the Empire State building. He saw only what he wanted to see. He noticed the pigeons which, like the people, he saw as being condemned to live joyless lives amid the traffic and bustle. His vision was "occidentalist". As Calvert suggests, he saw the United States not with fresh eyes, but "through the tinted spectacles of a man long captive to a particular view of the world". Just as many European travellers viewed the Arab–Muslim world through the prism of orientalism, ignoring everything that did not fit their preconceptions, so "Qutb would either purposefully ignore or simply not see anomalies which contradicted a view of America that was congruent with the exigencies of the Egyptian nationalist struggle".[7]

In the New Year, Qutb went to Washington, DC, where he enrolled in Wilson Teachers College to improve his English. "Life in Washington is good," he wrote to his friend Muhammad Jabr, "especially as I live in close proximity to the library and my friends." Thanks to his generous government allowance, he was able to spend up to $280 per month – $100 more than what a "regular" student required. His good humour, however, was not to last. He needed hospital treatment for an undisclosed illness – probably connected with his failing lungs. While in hospital he learned of the assassination of Hasan al-Banna. The killing, by the intelligence services, was in retaliation for the murder of prime minister Nuqrashi Pasha in December by a member of the Muslim Brotherhood's terrorist wing, the so-called "secret organization". Qutb would claim, implausibly, that the hospital staff rejoiced on hearing the news: it seems improbable that many of doctors and nurses at the George Washington University Hospital would have known who al-Banna was. Qutb's sexual frustration, touched with paranoia, shows through. He claimed that a nurse had tried to titillate him by relating the characteristics she sought in her lovers. He paints a lurid picture of her appearance: "thirsty lips, bulging breasts, smooth legs" and her flirtatious demeanour – "the calling eye, the provocative laugh". He castigates his fellow Arabs who succumb to such wiles and date American girls.[8]

After his release Qutb felt lonely and homesick. "How much I need someone to talk to about topics other than money, movie stars and models of cars," he opined to his friend the playwright Tawfiq al-Hakim. At Greeley, near Denver, where he spent six months at the Colorado State College of Education, his isolation deepened. Founded in 1870 and one of several utopian communities established during the nineteenth century, Greeley was a quiet, decorous place. Ironically, in view of the Islamist diatribes against alcohol that would flow from Qutb's disciples, Greeley had remained "dry" in accordance with the wishes of its founders. Qutb took long walks in the quiet, tree-lined streets each of which, he wrote, was "like a garden path". He was struck by how few people ventured out beyond their homes, most preferring to stay on their properties.

Qutb was particularly disconcerted by the attention the denizens of Greeley lavished on their lawns. It was, he thought, symptomatic of the American preoccupation with the external and the material. It exhibited individual selfishness rather than the spirit of community.[9] For a man accustomed to the noise, conviviality and bustle of Cairene life, Greeley must have seemed desolate indeed. Qutb wasn't ignored, however. A college bulletin dated October 1949 shows a picture of him with Dr William Ross, the college president, examining one of his books. The caption identifies him as "a famous Egyptian author . . . of both novels and textbooks" who is "an outstanding authority on Arabic literature and . . . a noted educator in his homeland".[10] As always it was sex that seems to have troubled him most. He was shocked by a conversation with a woman at the college who he reports as saying that sexual intercourse was a "purely biological matter" unaffected by morality.

Given the moral vacuity and amorality he saw in this society, Qutb was surprised by the number of churches in Greeley. "Nobody goes to church as often as Americans do . . . Yet no one is as distant as they are from the spiritual aspects of religion." The churches competed for congregations in much the same way that stores and theatres competed for customers. He cites as an example an advertisement for a church function posted in one of the college dormitories: "Sunday October 1, 6.00 PM Light Dinner; Magic Show; Puzzles; Contests; Entertainment." While clearly disapproving, he was also desperate for company. He joined a church club (he does not specify which denomination) and attended a dance held after the regular evening service in the hall next to the church. The overt sexuality on display disturbed him: "The dancing intensified ... The hall swarmed with legs ... Arms circled arms, lips met lips, chests met chests, and the atmosphere was full of love." Much to his dismay, the evening was hosted by the pastor, who dimmed the lights to create a "romantic dreamy effect" while the gramophone played a popular big-band tune – "Baby, It's Cold Outside".

One senses Qutb's fastidious horror at the social mixing of genders, so different from the world of his home village, where encounters between men and women would have been arranged within the carefully ordered frame of patriarchal, family power. In traditional Muslim societies adolescents do not meet with people of the opposite sex, except with their *mahrams*, to whom they are forbidden in marriage. In cosmopolitan Cairo he avoided contact with "dishonourable" Egyptian females, who painted their faces, wore high heels and midi-length skirts. Though he did not wish to see women revert to their former state of seclusion, he also made it clear that he was unhappy with "their current level of freedom". The health and balance of Egyptian society depended on strictly maintaining separate male and female roles. Charles Dickens, in his account of one of the last public hangings he witnessed in London, described the ghoulish fascination of the crowd as "the attraction of repulsion". Qutb's description of his sexually charged encounters with American women exhibits a similar mixture of fascination and horror. To adapt Dickens's phrase, it might be called "the repulsion of attraction".

In traditional Islamic societies, women are veiled for the "protection of men". Their sexuality is considered so potent, their charms so compelling and so tempting to men, that strict segregation is considered necessary for the maintenance of social harmony. The same word, *fitna* – strife or disorder – is used for sexual misdemeanours, social–political conflicts and the civil wars that split the infant Muslim community after the death of the Prophet Muhammad. The word *harim*, meaning the area reserved for women in the traditional household, shares the same root as *haram* – forbidden, taboo or sacred. Sexuality belongs to the realm of the sacred: to see it flaunted in a church setting must have been for Qutb profoundly disturbing.

Qutb's whole attitude towards the "pagan" (*jahiliyya*) culture he discerned in his native Egypt was coloured by his American experience. Though his English improved greatly it seems significant that he withdrew from the courses he was auditing on American Education, Secondary Education and Oral Interpretation just prior to the final examinations. As an audit student he was not required to undergo exams, but there seems to have been reticence, if not arrogance, in his refusal to subject himself to appraisal. As Calvert remarks, "One searches Qutb's writings in vain for references to strenuous academic challenge of the kind that features prominently, for instance, in Taha Hussen's account of his studies in France." Determined in his dislike of everything American, the last thing Qutb wanted was to have his proficiency judged on American terms.

Qutb spent the final months of his American sojourn in California, staying in San Francisco, Palo Alto and finally San Diego. Of American culture, and Americans generally, he remained determinedly disdainful. "Jazz," he told his fellow Egyptians, "is [their] favourite music. It is a type of music invented by Blacks to please their primitive tendencies and desire for noise." High culture had to be imported from Europe; in any case it was not much appreciated, because of American ignorance and shallowness. In one of his accounts Qutb explains how during his "tenth visit" to the San Francisco Museum of Modern Art he was transfixed by a certain French painting (he does not specify which) and contemplated it for four hours during which time dozens of people passed by, casting at the painting only cursory glances. "How many people," he asked, "understood what they were looking at?" The passage is revealing for its combination of naïvety and aesthetic sensitivity. Never having visited Europe, Qutb was evidently unaware that the ability to read and absorb paintings is as rare in Paris or London as in New York or San Francisco. But the passage also shows that he was no philistine. His disdain for American popular culture was aesthetic as much as moral.

The same may be said of his understanding and appreciation of
Islam. Unlike the Islamists who would fall under the spell of his
writings, his passion for the Quran was primarily literary and aesthetic. Highly sensitive to the qualities of its language, it remained
for him the source of inspiration, as distinct from a programme of
action he advocated for his followers. His belief in *i'jaz*, the miraculous quality of its language, far from being the product of
unthinking dogmatism or village traditionalism, was rooted in a
Romantic ideal of the aesthetic sublime – an idea that owes as
much to Kant and Coleridge (whose ideas he absorbed through
al-Aqqad) as to traditional Quranic scholarship. Leonard Binder,
in a searching analysis of Qutb's work, dwells on this often-
neglected dimension of his religious thought. Qutb, he says, "seems
to have adopted the post-Kantian aesthetic of liberal individualism
that was the legacy of European romanticism to the cultural elite of
the colonial world".[11] Like so many modern thinkers in the West
he professed to despise, Qutb believed that art did not merely
reproduce life, it reproduced the immediate experience of life. As
Wordsworth famously described it, poetry was "emotion recollected
in tranquillity". In thus rather riskily applying the category of art
to the Quran – a posture that leaves it open to literary–critical
analysis of the kind applied by Nasr Abu Zaid – Qutb joined
"many thinkers who argue that in the field of religion as in the
communicative sciences generally it is consciousness and not
knowledge upon which truth, or reality, or Being, is to be
grounded. In particular, Qutb is to be associated with those who
have argued or intimated that the aesthetic is the appropriate form
of discourse on religious, social and historical matters."[12]

In taking up an aesthetic view of his religion, however, Qutb was
not referring to the role of the artist as an interpreter, or conveyer,
of the cultural consciousness of a particular era (which is how a
nonbeliever knowledgeable in Arabic literature might understand
the "revelation" of the Quran). His concern was with "the role of
revelation which conveys, by means of a divine art, a transcendent
religious consciousness".[13] As Binder explains in an extended and
nuanced discussion that can only be crudely summarized here,

Qutb's aesthetic approach towards Islam and the Quran in particular would find much common ground with the liberals and
modernists who accepted the reality of the modern secular state. As
is the case with modernist theologies in Christianity and Judaism,
the aesthetic approach to the Quran as an artistic rather than factual or historical truth "diminishes the force of rationalist or
objectivist doubts and places greatest burden of belief upon individual consciousness".[14] But as Binder points out, this strategy is
also risky since "individual consciousness is a matter about which
it is difficult to be absolutely certain for any continuous and lengthy
period. The argument for the aesthetic ordering of the world as a
way of rendering it meaningful was Nietzsche's last resort in the
struggle to escape from nihilism."[15]

After proclaiming the Death of God (or rather, as Michel
Foucault noted, the "death of his murderer") Nietzsche succumbed
to insanity. For a man as sensitive and intelligent as Qutb the idea
that consciousness was the "ground of being" was as precarious as
it was for Nietzsche. The solution was to be found in political
activism – the solution adopted by some of Nietzsche's spiritual
progeny who found an escape from meaninglessness in Hitler's
Reich. For Qutb, the teaching of the Quran was not merely
intended to affect the emotional attitudes of Muslims: it was "also
meant to convince them that the external social experience is to
be brought into conformity with the aesthetically defined inner experience of truth".[16]

Qutb joined the Muslim Brotherhood late in 1951, the year after
he returned to Egypt and resumed his job in the Ministry of
Education. "I was born in 1951," he would later say, renouncing
his early publications.[17] These were dramatic times. In 1951 Nahas
Pasha, the Egyptian prime minister, under pressure from a public
still fuming from Egypt's defeat in the war against the new state of
Israel, which many people blamed on corruption at the highest
levels, tore up the Anglo-Egyptian treaty. The Muslim Brotherhood
came out in support of the government, calling for a jihad against
the British. Qutb applauded the freelance, but tolerated, harass-
ment of British forces in the Canal Zone by Muslim Brotherhood

volunteers. The massacre of twelve auxiliary police by British forces caused massive riots in Cairo; clubs and hotels frequented by foreigners were attacked, along with bars, cinemas and restaurants. Entire districts of the city were destroyed. The Muslim Brotherhood took the leading part in these events, and when in July 1952 the Free Officers led by Colonel Gamal 'Abd al-Nasser placed General Naguib, a devout officer acceptable to the Muslim Brotherhood, at the head of their junta, the political future of Egypt as an Islamic state seemed assured. The honeymoon, however, was not to last. Naguib was forced into retirement, to be replaced by Nasser as head of the junta and eventually president. The Muslim Brotherhood collaborated with the communists in opposing Nasser's renegotiation of the Anglo-Egyptian treaty: Qutb was in charge of the liaison. The government accused Hasan al-Hudaibi, al-Banna's successor, of planning "to overthrow the present form of government under cover of religion". The "secret apparatus" was revived.

In October 1954 in Alexandria, a botched attempt was made on Nasser's life. Qutb was one of dozens of Muslim Brothers arrested. Tortured, tried and convicted for his part in the alleged conspiracy to overthrow the regime he was sentenced to twenty-five years' hard labour. The six months he spent in the notorious Tura prison camp on the southern outskirts of Cairo were traumatic. He was abused by his jailers, before his deteriorating health (and the intervention of influential friends) secured his transfer to the prison infirmary. His continuing ill-health secured his early release in 1964, thanks to the intervention of the Iraqi president, 'Abd al-Salam 'Arif, but the respite was short. Enmeshed in another alleged plot against the state he was arrested in August 1965, condemned to death and hanged a year later, on 29 August 1966 – despite representations from influential Arab leaders, including the Iraqi president.

During his sojourn in prison and out of it Qutb produced his two most influential works: his multi-volumed Quranic commentary *Fi zalal al-Quran* (In the Shade of the Quran) and the tract *Ma'alim fi'l-tariq* ("Signposts on the Road"). The latter has been usefully compared to Lenin's *What Is To Be Done?*, the tract which, in combination with the *Communist Manifesto* (1848) of Marx and Engels, stoked the fires of the Bolshevik Revolution in Russia.

Qutb's tract deserves to be treated at length, for more than any other text it articulates both the rage and the revolutionary energy underpinning the Islamist movement. It also reveals the extent to which the values and aspirations of the movement are rooted in classical Islam, while also significantly departing from it.

The tract begins by addressing the crisis facing not just the Islamic world, but the whole of modern civilization. "Mankind today is on the brink of a precipice, not because of the danger of complete annihilation which is hanging over its head – this being just a symptom and not the real disease – but because humanity is devoid of those vital values for its healthy development and real progress."[18] Even Western civilization is aware of these unhealthy values. In the East (that is, the Soviet bloc) the situation is similar. The initial attractions of Marxism have declined as it has been reduced to a state ideology far removed from its doctrinal foundations. Such an ideology can only prosper in a society that has become degenerate, or cowed into submission by prolonged dictatorship. For the same reasons, Qutb avers, Western hegemony is coming to an end, not because of the loss of economic and military power, but because the West has been deprived of those "life-giving values which once enabled it to become the leader of humanity". There is a vital need for new leadership which will preserve and develop the material fruits of the creative genius of Europe, whilst providing humanity with a way of life that is positive, constructive and practicable, yet fully in tune with human nature. Islam alone possesses these qualities.

Islam, however, cannot fulfil its role except by taking concrete form in a society, or, rather, in a nation. No one will listen to an abstract theory that is not given concrete expression in a living society. Viewed from this perspective the true Muslim community has been extinct for centuries. It is now "buried under the debris of the man-made traditions of several generations, and is crushed under the weight of those false laws and customs which are not even remotely related to the Islamic teachings. In spite of all this the modern Muslim world calls itself the 'world of Islam'." Despite the apparent "beauty" of European technology the growing bankruptcy of Western civilization makes it necessary to revive Islam.

> The Muslim community today is neither capable of nor required to present before mankind great genius in material inventions, such as would make the world bow its head before its supremacy and thus re-establish once more its world leadership. Europe's creative mind is far ahead in this area and for a few centuries to come we cannot expect to compete with Europe and attain supremacy over it in these fields. Hence we must have some other quality, a quality that modern civilization does not possess ... in these fields ... To attain to the leadership of mankind we must have something to offer besides material progress, and this other quality can only be a faith and a way of life that both promotes the benefits of modern science and technology and fulfils basic human needs.[19]

Qutb then proceeds to the core of his argument: the parallel between modern society and the "paganism" (*jahiliyya*) against which the Prophet Muhammad successfully waged war "in the path of God".

> If we look at the sources and foundations of modern modes of living, it becomes clear that the whole world is steeped in *jahiliyya*, and all the marvellous material comforts and high-level inventions do not diminish [this] ignorance. This *jahiliyya* is based on rebellion against the sovereignty of Allah on earth. It attempts to transfer to man one of the greatest attributes of Allah, namely sovereignty, by making some men lords over others. It does so not in the simple and primitive ways of the ancient *jahiliyya*, but in the more subtle form of claiming that the right to create values, to legislate rules of collective behaviour, and to choose a way of life rests with men,

without regard to what Allah has prescribed. The result of this rebellion against the authority of Allah is the oppression of his creatures.[20]

Today we too are surrounded by *jahiliyya*. Its nature is the same as during the first period of Islam, and it is perhaps a little more deeply entrenched. Our whole environment, people's beliefs and ideas, habits and art, rules and laws, is *jahiliyya*, even to the extent that what we consider to be Islamic culture, Islamic sources, Islamic philosophy and Islamic thought are also constructs of *jahiliyya*! This is why the true Islamic values never enter our hearts.[21]

The beauty of the new Islamic system cannot be appreciated until it takes concrete form. To bring it about, there must first be a revival in one Muslim country, enabling it to attain the status of world leadership. To achieve this aim there must be a vanguard which holds to a steady course, marching through the vast ocean of *jahiliyya* which has encompassed the entire world. It must remain aloof from this all-encompassing *jahiliyya* while also keeping some ties with it. The role of the vanguard is to read the landmarks and signposts on the road, so that it will recognize the starting place, the nature and the responsibilities of this journey as well as its ultimate purpose.

The Muslims in this vanguard must know the landmarks and the milestones on the road to this goal . . . [They] ought to be aware of their position *vis-à-vis* this *jahiliyya*, which has struck its stakes throughout the earth. They must know when to cooperate with others and when to separate from them; what characteristics and qualities they should cultivate . . . How to address the people of *jahiliyya* in the language of Islam; what topics and problems to discuss with them; and where and how to obtain guidance in all these matters. I have written Signposts for this vanguard which I consider to be a waiting reality about to be materialized.[22]

Qutb outlines the emergence of this vanguard in terms that recall the Sufi movements which played such a vital part in the development and articulation of Islam throughout the world. It would be wrong to see these movements as wholly mystical or quietist, as avoiding social action. During the nineteenth century Sufi movements such as the Naqshbandiyya and Qadiriyya were at the forefront of resistance to colonial domination in the Caucasus and Algeria. This resistance drew on spiritual resources similar to those described by Qutb:

A man has faith in this belief, which emanates from a hidden source and is enlivened by the power of God alone; the existence of the Islamic society virtually begins with the faith of this one man . . . This individual, however, receives the revelation not in order merely to turn it in on himself, but to carry its spirit too: such is the nature of this belief . . . The immense power that has carried it into this soul knows with certainty that it will carry it further still . . . When three believers have been touched by the faith, this credo means to them: "you are now a society, an independent Islamic society, separate from the jahiliyya society which does not have faith in this. From that point onwards the Islamic society will grow apace: the three become ten, the ten become a hundred, the hundred a thousand, the thousand twelve thousand." The society has become a movement that will permit no one to stand apart . . . The battle is constant, the jihad lasts until the Day of Judgement.[23]

In a remarkable passage Qutb instructs his "vanguard" how to read the Quran. The passage is highly significant because of the way it explicitly links the custom of the "pious ancestors" as the first generation of Muslims are often called in modernist writings, to what scholars of fundamentalism call "proof-texting" – the practice of taking passages from scripture out of context, to be used as talismans rather than as sources of spiritual feeling or ethical guidance. The first generation, says Qutb,

... did not approach the Quran for the purpose of acquiring culture and information, nor for the purpose of taste or enjoyment. None of them came to the Quran to increase his sum total of knowledge for the sake of knowledge itself or to solve some scientific or legal problem or to remove some defect in his understanding. He rather turned to the Quran to find out what the Almighty Creator had prescribed for him and for the community in which he lived, for his life and for the life of the group. *He approached it to act on what he heard immediately, as a soldier on the battlefield reads "Today's Bulletin" so that he knows what is to be done ... At most he would read ten verses, memorise them and then act upon them.*[24] (emphasis added)

Here the fabric of traditional exegesis, according to which any one statement in the Quran must be balanced by all the others, is completely cut away. The Quran whose claims to literary and aesthetic perfection are regarded by pious Muslims as self-validating, has often been treated as a kind of fetish. This is how it came to be regarded in many premodern societies where the book itself was invested with magical potency, becoming a kind of votive object. But it is strange indeed to find someone as sophisticated as Qutb positively endorsing such a seemingly unscholarly approach to the divine text. One suspects that this passage may be informed by his own perception of the Quran's literary and aesthetic qualities: for Qutb himself ten memorized verses may well have yielded the aesthetic and spiritual satisfaction mere infidels would find in works of music or art. As we have seen he was no philistine: his contempt for Americans lay in his perception of *their* philistinism. In the hands of his less sophisticated disciples, however, his "soldiers on the battlefield", the text would become an operational manual, a seventh-century time bomb loaded with menace.

Not that Qutb can be exonerated for the "misuse" to which the divine text would be put by his disciples. The sections on jihad in *Signposts on the Road* are explicit in rejecting any idea of the struggle as being spiritual or defensive. Qutb accuses writers who argue that jihad is purely defensive as being apologetic and defeatist, of succumbing to the "wily attacks of the orientalists" who distort the concept of Islamic jihad. These people confuse two issues: the statement that "there is no compulsion in religion" (Quran: 2.256) with the historical fact that Islam expanded by eliminating all the obstacles that stood between the people and Islam, preventing them from accepting the sovereignty of God. These two principles, Qutb says, are not related. The causes of Islamic jihad should be sought in the very nature of Islam and its role in the world, its high principles, which have been given by God. It was for the implementation of these principles that God appointed Muhammad, declaring him to be the last of all prophets and messengers. Anyone who understands Islam will know that jihad is not a "defensive movement" in the narrow sense of what is technically called a "defensive war".

> *It is a movement to wipe out tyranny, and to introduce true freedom to mankind, using whatever resources are practically available in a given human situation.* (emphasis added) If we insist on calling Islamic Jihad a defensive movement, then we must change the meaning of the word "defense" to mean "the defense of man" against all those forces that limit his freedom. These forces may take the form of beliefs and concepts, as well as political systems, based on economic, racial and class distinctions. At the advent of Islam the world was full of such systems just as the present-day jahiliyya abounds in various systems.[25]

Qutb continues:

> When we take this broad meaning of the word "defense", we understand the true character of Islam in that it proclaims the universal freedom of every person and community from servitude to every other individual or society, the end of man's arrogance and selfishness, the establishment of the sovereignty of Allah and his lordship throughout the world and the rule of

the divine Shari'a [Islamic law] in human affairs ... When Islam calls for peace, its object is not a superficial peace which requires only that the part of the earth where the followers of Islam are residing remain secure. *The peace of Islam means that* din *[that is, the law of the society] be purified for Allah, that all people should obey Allah alone, and every system that permits some people to rule over others be abolished.*[26] (emphasis added)

In his detailed exegesis of the jihad verses in the Quran, Qutb follows the classical commentators mentioned in Chapter 2 who interpreted the passages as a progressive licence for war. In particular he relies on the Syrian theologian Ibn Qayyim (d.1350), a member of the Hanbalite school, who stated that the Muslims were first restrained from fighting, then they were permitted to fight, then they were commanded to fight against the aggressors, and finally they were commanded to fight against all the polytheists. Qutb does not explicitly identify the *jahiliyya* society with polytheism, but the implication is there. Nor does he explicitly advocate violence; but that implication is also there.[27]

It is most important to note that there are currents of thought whose origins are not acknowledged in his text. The message of revolutionary anarchism implicit in the phrase that "every system that permits some people to rule over others be abolished" owes more to radical European ideas going back to the Jacobins than to classical or traditional ideas about Islamic governance. Similarly the revolutionary vanguard Qutb advocates does not have an Islamic pedigree, though historically there have always been tribal forces that sought to "purify" Islam from religiously improper accretions. The vanguard is a concept imported from Europe, through a lineage that also stretches back to the Jacobins, through the Bolsheviks and latter-day Marxist guerrillas such as the Baader–Meinhof gang (see Chapter 4).

The idea of a vanguard or revolutionary elite that acts in the name of future generations, rebuilding society in line with higher, transcendent Truth (whether that truth be conceptualized in terms of the general will, the historical destiny of the proletariat, or the nation) is common to most modern radical political movements. Qutb legitimizes his call to arms by reference to the classical Islamic tradition. As we have seen, this appeal to the example of the Prophet Muhammad and the early caliphs cannot be dismissed as spurious. The classical tradition was formed during the period of expansion that accompanied the Arab conquests. As I have suggested elsewhere, Islam – in the mainstream Sunni tradition, if not always for the Shi'ite minority – is "programmed for victory". Its religious institutions were predicated upon the attainment of imperial power. "Can anyone say," Qutb asks rhetorically, referring to Islam's first great territorial expansion under Muhammad's "rightly guided" successors,

> that if Abu Bakr, 'Umar or 'Uthman had been satisfied that the Roman [that is, Byzantine] and Persian powers were not going to attack the Arabian peninsula, they would not have striven to spread the message of Islam throughout the world? How could the message of Islam have spread in the face of such material obstacles, the political tyranny of an absolutist state, the socio-economic system based on races and classes, and supported by the military might of tyrannical governments? It would be naïve to assume that a call to free the whole of humankind throughout the world may be effected by preaching and exposition of the message alone. Indeed because "there is no compulsion in religion" it strives through preaching and exposition when there is freedom of communication and when people are free from all extraneous pressures. But when the above-mentioned obstacles and practical difficulties are put in its way, it has no recourse but to remove them by force so when it is addressed to the people's hearts and minds, they are free to accept or reject it with open minds.[28]

The totalitarian menace is clear: anything that stands in the way of Qutbist preaching constitutes an "obstacle" to religious "freedom".

The argument is not dissimilar to that deployed by communists during the 1930s. Qutbism (or Islamism as we should now call it) is distinctly modern, both in its adoption of the revolutionary vanguard and in the way it addresses a contemporary phenomenon, the modern crisis of faith.

Leonard Binder, in his penetrating critique of Qutb, argues that

> . . . the possibilities of a benign dialogue between Islam and the West are limited even for the believers among us, because the gap in understanding is really constituted by the fact that ours is an unbelieving society, as Muslims clearly perceive, while theirs is a believing society . . . The very forms of the discourse of belief in our society [that is, theology] are already embedded in the critique of finitude as a suppressed premise.[29]

The conception of God in modern Western thought begins with individual subjectivity. Critical philosophy since Descartes has gradually undermined and exposed the metaphysical presuppositions of the medieval deity, ultimately derived from Plato, underpinning premodern Western culture. As Don Cupitt, a leading liberal theologian argues, Kant tried to show that these "absolute presuppositions" could be proved, but only in a way that involved abandoning the old metaphysical idea of God. "Instead of being objective truths propping up an objective God, Kant made them into just structural presuppositions and postulates of our knowledge and our moral action."[30] Kierkegaard, drawing on the subjectivism inherent in Luther's "justification by faith", argued that the "what" that is believed can be subsumed into the "how" of believing it. As Cupitt explains: ". . . if one were to get *being* a Christian right, as a matter of the kind of self one is and the way one's life is oriented, it would be unnecessary to mention the objective content (of what one) believed." It could "fall away, no longer needed",[31] a piece of discarded cultural scaffolding. The influential Protestant theologian Rudolph Bultmann took Kierkegaardian subjectivity much further by "demythologizing"

Christianity altogether; C.G. Jung drove the final nail into the coffin of the pre-Kantian metaphysical deity by locating the Ground of Being in the unconscious. Traces of the social and public claims of religion survive in the Anglo-Saxon world, in the rituals of monarchy or the "civil religion" that permeates American institutions, despite the formal constitutional separation of Church and State, as symbolized on the dollar legend "In God We Trust". But in the main Binder's remark is valid: in the pluralistic world of modernity ours is not a believing *society*. Where individuals are free to choose their beliefs, the public domain has to be religiously neutral, a-theistic. Religious liberty requires that belief be confined to the realm of private consciousness.

Such ideas are far from being foreign to Islam. In some of its esoteric traditions, divine judgement is wholly spiritualized and internalized, the external creator God giving ground, as it were, to the "god within". Heaven and hell become principles or "persons", individualized states of mind or being.[32] But Qutb and his disciples deliberately eschewed a spiritual interpretation of Islam. For them it was much more than "religion": it was the blueprint for the correct social order, the model for the ideal society ordained by God. In the struggle against imperialism or neocolonialism, the "spiritual" jihad must give way to the "jihad of the sword". To internalize the message, to spiritualize it as the Sufis had always done and as the Isma'ilis did after the collapse of the legitimist (Fatimid) caliphate, was to accept defeat. The pre-Kantian metaphysical deity demanded action as well as prayer. In Qutb's fiery rhetoric the Enlightenment and the political and economic power flowing from it are simply "a mask for the crusading spirit", a new attempt by the old enemy, Christendom, to crush the believers.[33]

Qutb was fully aware of the challenge posed to the pre-Enlightenment metaphysical deity by modern philosophical thought. As we have noted, he adopted a post-Kantian aesthetic in viewing the Quran as "art". He was no backwoods mullah. Intellectually he could hold his own with the best of the minds produced by Egypt's Westernized elite. Nor can his rebellion be explained simply in terms of the reification or essentializing discourse of cultural nationalism: in order to "defend" a culture from "outside" encroachments, one must first define it as being fundamentally different from that which is supposed to be attacking it.

Egypt is not India. Maududi's definition of modern society as *"jahiliyya"* was in some ways a natural outcome of two conditions: the long experience of Indian Islam as a precarious Muslim island surrounded by an ocean of "pagan" Hindus, to which was added the humiliation of the replacement of the Muslim Mughals by the British as the country's rulers. Egypt, by contrast, has always been part of the Mediterranean world. European merchants had been trading there since before the Renaissance. Modernization was initiated not by external forces (though Bonaparte's 1798 occupation was a catalyst) but from within the frame of Islamic rule, under the Mehmet 'Ali dynasty. True, that dynasty's financial problems resulted in the British military occupation in 1882, but the last vestiges of British rule had ended with the Suez Crisis in 1957. Nasser was no imperialist stooge. Indeed, though he turned to the Soviet Union in order to finance the high dam on the Nile at Aswan which he regarded as an economic and political necessity, he became (with Tito, Nkrumah, Nehru and Sukarno) a leading advocate of the Nonaligned Movement: the very outlook that Qutb himself had advocated. There was undoubtedly political disappointment among the Muslim Brothers that Nasser's policies were insufficiently "Islamic", but this of itself seems insufficient to account for Qutb's absolutist and uncompromising hostility.

Violence breeds violence, aggression is interactive. It seems reasonable to hazard that the militancy of *Signposts on the Road* may have been engendered partly by the appalling treatment Qutb, a cultivated, educated man, received at the hands of the Egyptian police. There is some empirical evidence to support this view. In a recent study one of Egypt's leading sociologists, Sa'd al-din Ibrahim, found a close correlation between extremist attitudes among Islamist groups and their responses to police brutality. Some had their spirits broken by torture, deciding thereafter to opt for a more moderate stance. Others were hardened by the experience, which produced the response: "How could Muslims treat their Brothers in such a way?" In the latter case the conclusion was: "This is not how Muslims behave; *ergo*, such people are not true Muslims."[34]

For the Islamist hard-liners who would follow him, Qutb's general diagnosis of the *jahiliyya* state crystallized into the act of *takfir*: declaring such a state, its officials or its leaders, *kuffar* or *kafirun*, unbelievers. In due course the status of society and government *vis-à-vis* belief or unbelief became a major subject for debate among the radicals and the point of bifurcation between the different Islamist groups. Positions ranged from the moderate Muslim Brotherhood attitude, consistent with Hanafi law, that no one who makes the Shahada – the declaration of faith – can be considered an infidel, to the extremist position of the group called the Society of Muslims (dubbed by the press al-Takfir wa-l-Hijra), who redefined the whole of society as *jahiliyya*, and emulated the Prophet's example by withdrawing from "Mecca" completely, worshipping in separate mosques, performing their own marriage ceremonies and seeking to construct new utopian Madinas in the desert.

Qutb was small and delicate, perhaps unusually susceptible to pain. One doubts, however, if his rage against the "*jahiliyya*" state would in itself have been sufficient to propel him to martyrdom. He spent most of his time in prison in the infirmary, which allowed him to write *Signposts on the Road* and his commentary on the Quran – something that would have been denied healthier, and perhaps less well-connected prisoners. When *Signposts on the Road* appeared in November 1964, Nasser at first personally intervened with the censorship authority to allow it to be published. It was then reprinted five times before being finally banned.[35] The success of the book doubtless sealed its author's fate. "If you want to know why Sayyid Qutb was sentenced to death," wrote the Muslim Sister Zaynab al-Ghazali, "read *Signposts*."[36] Qutb was too dangerous for Nasser, in or out of prison. Few believe the charges against him; but by the same logic, he could probably have saved his life if he had chosen to moderate his stance as so many other Muslim Brothers would do in the course of time. Qutb's martyrdom, partly if not totally, was voluntarily espoused. Martyrdom in his case was a considered political act, a time bomb planted at the epistemological heart of Egyptian culture – a culture riven not so much by divisions between "Islam" and "secularity" as between competing understandings of the received faith tradition.

Behind the political purpose of his martyrdom there lay Qutb's personal conviction and his personal philosophical commitment. This is not easily deciphered. Binder explores the contradictions in Qutb's thought, between a human-centred idea of Islam (*al-tasawwur al-islami* – the Islamic Conception) associated with movement, dynamism, activity and change on the one hand, and his argument that by simply "practising Islam, by doing what Islam commands, eschewing any intellectual debate or justification, and by affirmatively accepting the consequences of that practice, one becomes a true Muslim and one gains paradise." In a manner of speaking, says Binder, Islam "replaces the aesthetic in a rather uncertain adaptation of Heidegger's ontological phenomenology".[37]

Qutb's ontological Islam is thus linked to the "ownmost being" of the believing Muslim, in a manner that urges him to act out, to realise, to practice that faith as an expression of his being, and not with regard to practical political or social consequences of that act. When we consider once again that the absolute foundation of Islam, and of the freedom of the individual Muslim to act, is the *hakimiyya* [sovereignty] of God, then the characteristic Islamic act becomes the defiance of jahili activity. *Thus is the groundwork laid for acts of martyrdom which appear to be suicidal and/or hopeless acts of political terrorism.*[38] (emphasis added)

This view of Islam, Binder concludes, is "quite modern and quite distinctive (and) beset by many contradictory themes, suggesting the ambivalence of Sayyid Qutb and the intensity of his personal struggle to give his own martyred life Islamic meaning."[39] The same can be said, *a fortiori*, of those much less intellectually gifted, but much more technically proficient, "martyrs" who followed in his wake.

Chapter Four

A Fury for God

Media discussion about suicide bombings and the novel phenomenon of suicide hijackings after the attacks on New York and Washington inevitably raised the spectre of martyrdom and its rewards. In a witty and angry article attacking "the devaluing effect that religion has on human life", Britain's best-known atheist advocate, the biologist Richard Dawkins, suggested that the sexual misery experienced by "testosterone-sodden young men too unattractive to get a woman in this world" could make them desperate enough to go for the "72 virgin brides, guaranteed eager and exclusive" promised for martyrs in the next life.

> If death is final, a rational agent can be expected to value his life highly and be reluctant to risk it. This makes the world a safer place, just as a plane is safer if its hijacker wants to survive. At the other extreme, if a significant number of people convince themselves, or are convinced by their priests, that a martyr's death is equivalent to pressing the hyperspace button and zooming through a wormhole to another universe, it can make the world a very dangerous place. Especially if they also believe that that other universe is a paradisical escape

from the tribulations of the real world. Top it off with sincerely
believed, if ludicrous and degrading to women, sexual promises, and is it any wonder that naïve and frustrated young men
are clamouring to be selected for suicide missions?[1]

The answer to this question must be speculative, since none of the
"successful" suicide bombers or hijackers is available to fill in
questionnaires about their sexual desires or preferences. The flaw
in Dawkins's article is not his assumption that young men at their
sexual peak may suffer from frustration, especially if they are religiously observant, since Islam like other religions forbids sexual
activity outside the legal marriage contract. It is his assumption
that suicide bombers or hijackers are necessarily naïve or primarily
inspired by Islamic teachings about personal immortality.

   The Quran contains no unambiguous condemnation of suicide. In a passage that is often cited, "And do not kill yourselves
(*anfasakum*)",[2] the term *anfasakum* was interpreted in classical
commentaries to mean "one another". A number of hadiths,
however, left no doubt that Muhammad disapproved of suicide.
The person who committed suicide forfeited paradise. In Hell he
would be condemned to repeat the very act by which he killed
himself. The Prophet refused to say the customary prayers for the
dead in a case of suicide. In later times, under pressure of circumstances or family grief, the legists would differ as to whether
or not suicides should be accorded funeral prayers: in many cases
they erred on the side of compassion. After a cautious and
nuanced discussion of the subject in the *Encyclopedia of Islam*,
Franz Rosenthal concludes:

   Yet, even if we take into account the likelihood that suicides
   were hushed up wherever possible because of religious scruples,
   and the fact that the bulk of available biographical information
   concerns scholars who were most sensitive to the religious
   injunction against suicide and pays hardly any attention to
   other, numerically much stronger classes of the population, the
   impression prevails that, everything considered, suicide was of

comparatively rare occurrence. The assumption that the teachings of Islam were an effective deterrent may well be true.[3] (emphasis added)

Unlike the kamikaze pilots who operated within a culture that sanctioned suicide, the Arab suicide bombers and pilots are bucking tradition by killing themselves. The religious legitimacy of these acts is, to say the least, highly questionable. The suicide bombings are referred to not as "suicides" but as acts of "self-martyrdom", *istishhad*. The fatwas that provide them with legitimacy have been issued by jurists in the Gulf and in Pakistan. There is argument not only about the validity of such legal opinions, but about the authority of the individuals who issue them.[4] They need to be balanced by the rulings of clerics such as Shaikh Fadlallah, spiritual leader of the Lebanese Hizbollah, who explicitly condemned suicide bombings.[5] Given the ambiguity of Islamic teachings about suicide – with the weight of tradition firmly against it – one needs to probe further in seeking an explanation. The wave of suicide bombings in the Middle East began with the Shi'a in Lebanon before being adopted by the Islamist group Hamas in Israel–Palestine. Although religious arguments are used to legitimize the suicide bombings in the Palestinian case, it would be wrong to see the motivation as exclusively or even primarily religious. It is driven rather by a combination of realpolitik and despair. From a realpolitik perspective the technique, however horrendous, has been effective in achieving its purpose, which is to provoke the Israelis into massive reprisals designed to alienate, and radicalize, the whole Arab population against the continuing occupation and the illegal Jewish settlements. As this book went to press, the suicide bombings were no longer confined to the Islamists. Increasingly the martyr–bombers were being recruited from nonreligious individuals and parties, including young women and members of the semi-Marxist Popular Front for the Liberation of Palestine and the secular al-Aqsa Martyrs Brigades. The scale of the carnage, and Israel's response to it, forced the internationalization of the issue, with moderate Arab states threatening to undermine America's "war against terrorism" by their refusal to cooperate. The Iraqi leader, Saddam Hussein, was the chief beneficiary of this escalation, since it diverted the Bush administration from its stated aim of removing him from power. But the suicide bombing is also a gesture of rage and despair at the failure of the Oslo peace process and the continuing and systemic humiliation of the Palestinian people by the Israeli army.

The argument used by Dawkins that suicide bombers are essentially naïve, religious youngsters lured by promises of sex in paradise belongs to a long tradition of Christian polemics about Islam. Classical Muslim exegesis – which the Islamists tend to bypass – takes a more sophisticated, less literal view of the heavenly rewards promised to the believer: the Imam Ghazali (d.1111), the greatest of the medieval theologians, saw the sexual imagery in the Quranic descriptions of paradise as inducements to righteousness: "It is a foretaste of the delights secured for men in paradise, because to make a promise to men of delights they have not tasted would be ineffective . . ."[6] Ghazali, in his book of marriage, dwelt on the delights of conjugal sex, emphasizing the importance of pleasure for the female partner in a way that anticipates the Western sexual manual by almost a millennium. His argument, like that of numerous other exegetes, is not that sex in paradise is a reward for abstinence in this world, but rather that a state of spiritual fulfilment can only be described in terms of experiences that are familiar.[7]

That is not to say, however, that Muslims who volunteer for suicide missions understand Quranic passages promising sexual satisfaction in paradise metaphorically. We have seen from Qutb's writings that he advocated and justified "proof-texting" the Quran, bypassing the traditional scholarly hermeneutic. The Prophet Muhammad's contemporaries, he wrote in *Signposts on the Road*, did not approach the Quran for taste or enjoyment but to act on what they heard immediately as a soldier on the battlefield receives his orders. As we saw earlier there are plenty of verses in the Quran which, taken singly and out of context, can be used as "operational briefings" in the Islamist "war against paganism". Understood literally the lure of sex in paradise could come into this category.

There is evidence that the suicide bombers and hijackers have adopted this approach. Research has shown that the overwhelming majority of the leaders of Islamist movements have scientific educational backgrounds and qualifications. Their intellectual training, I would suggest, makes them more susceptible to monodimensional or literalist readings of scripture than their counterparts in the arts and humanities whose training requires them to approach texts multidimensionally, exploring contradictions and ambiguities. Mohammed Atta's disapproval of Nasr Abu Zaid's literary–critical approach to the Quran is an obvious case in point. He cannot, alas, be interviewed. But it seems reasonable to suppose that he shared the intellectual outlook of other Islamist leaders. A clue may be found by spooling back a quarter of a century to the beginnings of modern Islamist terrorism in Egypt.

Two groups of Islamist militants would emerge after Qutb's death in 1966. The first was the jihadist group led by Salih Sirriyya (1933–74), a Palestinian, which tried to seize control of the Technical Military Academy in the Cairene suburb of Heliopolis on 18 April 1974. The aim of the conspirators, some of whom were students at the academy, was to arm themselves with weapons and to assassinate the President, Anwar al-Sadat, who was scheduled to pass by in his motorcade. Sirriyya had been a member of the Islamic Liberation Party (Hizb al-Tahrir) founded by his fellow Palestinian Taqi al-Din al-Nabhani (1909–77) in 1952. In contrast to Qutb, al-Nabhani did not regard the whole of Muslim society as having lapsed to the condition of *jahiliyya*. That condition was rather confined in countries with Muslim majorities to the regimes and the ruling elites who had imported Western legal systems. The long-term aim of Hizb al-Tahrir was the ambitious project of restoring the universal caliphate.

This office had gradually fallen into abeyance from the eleventh century when the 'Abbasid rulers had yielded power to their pretorian guards, recruited mainly from Central Asian Turkish tribes who then ruled in their name. The office had been revived by the Ottoman sultans in the second half of the nineteenth century to assert their rights over Muslims in the Russian and British empires. The abolition of the caliphate by the Turkish National Assembly in 1924, which sparked off rioting in India, was resented by al-Nabhani and his supporters as an example of colonial interference, the rise of Turkish nationalism having coincided with the dismemberment of the Ottoman Empire by the victorious Western powers in 1917–18. In a sense Hizb al-Tahrir continued the tradition of Ottoman loyalists who had looked to the sultan–caliph as the last hope for a universal, independent Islamic state. Al-Nabhani, however, criticized the Ottoman state for being purely military, and for having tried unsuccessfully to stave off defeat by adopting the Western-inspired secular reforms known as the Tanzimat. Rejecting Western democracy as disbelief (*kufr*), al-Nabhani only allowed limited forms of expert consultation (*shura* and *mashura*) in his version of the restored caliphate. His idea of the caliphate was an Islamic dictatorship directly elected by secret ballot according to universal adult Muslim suffrage. The Hizb al-Tahrir was established to bring this about. It adopted a vanguardist position significantly different from Qutb's. Rather than being the spearhead of the new order which would know when to engage with and when to withdraw from the wider society, al-Nabhani aimed to impose the Islamic order by the exercise of state power acquired through the missionary endeavours of his party.[8] Al-Nabhani's agenda was described in somewhat crude terms by 'Umar Bakri Muhammad, former head of its British branch: "The nation of Islam is like a woman . . . Inject her with thought until she becomes pregnant and then she will deliver the baby of the Islamic state."[9] Although al-Nabhani rejected the idea of seizing state power directly by force, the implication was evident to some of his followers, including Sirriyya.

Sirriyya's plan went disastrously wrong. The guards fired on the mutineers before they left the grounds of the Academy. A trial was held at which Sirriyya and his top aide were sentenced to death and executed. Twenty-nine others received prison terms. Sixty were released. To avoid political embarrassment the government went to great lengths to implicate foreigners in the conspiracy, blaming the plot on Libya, with whom relations had become strained.[10]

After the fall of the Taliban, a manuscript was found in a house in Qandahar, Afghanistan, which gave new details about Sirriyya's "martyrdom", confirming his importance as the first of Qutb's disciples to emulate the man described in the document as "the cornerstone of our movement". It was written by Ayman al-Zawahiri, a former paediatric surgeon and the leader of the Egyptian Jihad group who became Osama bin Laden's deputy after joining the al-Qa'ida organization. It was published in *al-Sharq al-Awsat*, the Arabic newspaper based in London.[11] According to al-Zawahiri, after the death sentences had been passed on Sirriyya and two of his associates, the government tried to negotiate with them over a request to President Mubarak for clemency. One of the three Talal al-Ansari made the request, and his sentence was duly commuted to life imprisonment. Sirriyya and his colleague al-Andalusi heroically refused.

> One day the political prisoners gathered around Sirriyya, in one of the small open spaces which the prison authorities allowed him during his otherwise solitary confinement, and urged him to submit a mercy plea. But he said to them with the certainty of the believer: "What authority does Anwar al-Sadat have that he can order to prolong my life even a moment? Look at this miserable prison, this repulsive food that we're given, these blocked-up toilets where we empty ourselves of that food. If this is the world (*al-dunya*) in its reality, why should we hold on to it?"[12]

Despite formal differences in their theoretical outlook, the spirit of Sayyid Qutb clearly lived on in Salih Sirriyya.

The second group of Islamist militants to emerge after Qutb's death was led by Shukri Mustafa (1942–77) and called itself the

Society of Muslims (Jama'at al-Muslimin) but was generally known as Takfir wa-l-Hijra (TwH – Excommunication and Hijra). Technically *takfir* means the pronouncement or declaration that someone is an infidel. TwH acquired the name on account of its Qutbist view that the whole of Egyptian society, not just the leadership, was in a state of *jahiliyya*, from which they concluded that the appropriate response must be *hijra* (emigration or withdrawal).

Mustafa was born in June 1942 in Abu Khurus near Asyut, not far from Qutb's birthplace of Musha, but he moved to Asyut when his father repudiated his mother under the Islamic system of unilateral divorce for men. In 1965 he was arrested for distributing Muslim Brotherhood pamphlets while attending the University of Asyut's school of agriculture. He spent the next six years in prison, imbibing the works of Maududi, Qutb and Ibn Taymiyya, the celebrated Hanbali legist who had been particularly adamant in his condemnation of religious and legal practices derived from Christianity or observed by the Mongol rulers of his day.

Many of the brethren who read Qutb's *Signposts on the Road* during this time interpreted its message with circumspection. Since one could not pronounce the *takfir* openly on Egyptian society while continuing to live in it without incurring the charge of *ilhad* – heresy – the *takfir* must be done secretly, in the heart, while the true believer continued to observe the outward conduct of an ordinary Muslim. These moderate Islamists actually prayed on Fridays before an imam whom they privately regarded as being apostate.[13] (The approach was similar to that of the Shi'a who, when faced with persecution, are permitted to adopt *taqiyya* [dissimulation], conforming outwardly to Sunni legal practices or making their allegiance [*bai'a*] to Sunni rulers, while secretly maintaining loyalty to the True Imams of the House of 'Ali.) These moderate Islamists, like the Isma'ili Shi'ite movement which held power in Egypt from 969 to 1171, believed in acquiring power gradually through a system of progressive initiation. Power would be gained as the movement grew within the *jahiliyya* society; inside the movement the initiate would learn more about its aims as he moved up the ranks of its organization.

Mustafa's group took the much more radical approach of complete religious and social separation. They prayed at home, refusing to attend Friday prayers or to visit mosques other than family (private) mosques where the prayers were led by imams of their persuasion. The men trimmed their beards and wore their gowns in imitation of the way the earliest sources described the *sunna* (practice or custom) of the Prophet. In this they resembled the Ikhwan (brethren) of Central Arabia, the Wahhabi fanatics who had assisted Ibn Sa'ud's conquests during the 1920s. Like the Wahhabis, TwH saw themselves as the only true Muslims in an ocean of infidelity. They rejected the vast intellectual apparatus of "cumulative tradition", including the edifice of law represented by the four legal schools of Sunnism, preferring to exercise *ijtihad* (individual interpretation) which in practice meant following the rulings of Shukri Mustafa himself. After Mustafa's release from prison in 1971, when Sadat began easing up on the Muslim Brotherhood and its affiliates to counter his repression of the Left, his movement grew rapidly, achieving a membership of around 2,000 by 1976. Members abandoned jobs as employees of the *jahiliyya* state. Though mostly well-educated, they kept themselves by manual labour, hawking and growing vegetables. Rents were paid by money sent by members living in Kuwait and Saudi Arabia.[14]

The group attracted widespread media attention by recruiting young women who were married to the society's men under a simplified *nikah* (exchange of contract) ceremony unsupervised by the state. In a society where the bride's virginity is a precious token of exchange for the housing and furniture provided by the groom or his family, the scandal of unregulated marriage was compounded by the marginal status of the group, who lived – like poor foreigners and prostitutes – in cheap furnished lodgings where key money was not required. As Gilles Kepel relates:

This "leading of women astray" outraged public opinion, and provided the headline material and unnumerable photographs for the Egyptian press. In the newspaper stories, the scenario never varied: seduced by the captivating words of Shukri or one of his disciples, a young girl deserts the paternal home and hearth, abandons her studies, and goes to live among the group.[15]

Yet, as Kepel makes clear, TwH's "alternative" lifestyle not only claimed Islamic legitimacy. It acted as a living reproach to a rapidly urbanizing society in which young people were denied sexual fulfilment because of the prohibitive cost of housing. Unlike Christianity, Islam places a very positive value on sexual activity while strictly prohibiting sexual relations outside the marriage contract. In many traditional Muslim societies the young are encouraged to marry at puberty, or soon afterwards. The contract is usually negotiated between families and requires that furniture and housing be provided by the groom. Although rents in Egyptian cities such as Cairo were supposed to be fixed by law, the excess of demand over supply enabled landlords to charge "key money" for unfurnished property, equivalent in many cases to the cost of the freehold, a sum well beyond the reach of most couples, even among the educated. In consequence, a great many young people have had to delay marriage. TwH's *hijra* from mainstream society gave young people something that Islamic teachings insisted upon as a right – the right to sexual fulfilment denied by the *jahiliyya* society.

> In their furnished rooms, the Society's members created a tiny, genuinely Islamic society of their own, based on their understanding of Islam. Here their lives changed radically: they married young, housing was immediately available without payment of key-money, and the values of Egyptian society no longer applied. Diplomas were considered mere scraps of paper, the mosques [administered by] the Ministry of Waqfs [regarded as] temples for the worship of medieval annotators, and Israel as an enemy [considered] on the same footing as the iniquitous prince and his administration.[16]

Mustafa insisted that if one of the partners of a couple joined TwH but not the other, their marriage ties were annulled: this of course underlined the claim of TwH to represent the only true Muslims in a sea of *jahiliyya*. Under Islamic law, as the Abu Zaid case demonstrates, divorce is automatic if one of the partners is a polytheist. Stories appeared alleging that Mustafa exercised *droit de seigneur* over his female acolytes and arranged all the marriages himself; the stories are consistent with his status as a charismatic "cult" leader comparable to Joseph Smith, Sun Yang Moon or David Koresh.

Personal tensions and rivalry with the Hizb al-Tahrir, which tried to poach his members, led to the Mustafa group's downfall, though a group of the same name, based in Algeria, is now reported as being part of the al-Qa'ida organization, and is on the list of proscribed terrorist organizations issued by the US State Department. Raids on the homes of dissident members to "chastise the apostates" in imitation of the first caliph, Abu Bakr, eventually led to the arrest of fourteen members of the group. In July 1977, members of the group disguised as policemen kidnapped Shaikh Muhammad al-Dhahabi, a former minister of Waqfs (religious trusts) who had incurred the group's ire by declaring them Kharijites – "seceders" after the rebels who "went out" of the early Muslim community in 661. The group's demands included the release of their prisoners, apologies by the media, publication of one of their tracts and 200,000 Egyptian pounds in cash. When the government refused to give in, Mustafa had al-Dhahabi executed (though some Islamists claim, inevitably, that the former minister was shot by the police).[17]

At his trial in November 1977 Mustafa made a comprehensive theological statement that indicates the Qutbist influence on his thought. The Quran was delivered in Arabic. The only tool that might be needed for its interpretation was a good dictionary. Taking as his text 2:216 "God knows and you know not", Mustafa argued that everything that came after the Quran and the authentic tradition that established the Prophet's *sunna* (custom) was invalid. Following the four legal schools of Sunnism amounted to idolatry.

According to Mustafa, Islam had been in decline ever since men ceased to draw their lessons directly from the Quran and the

Sunna, and instead followed the tradition of the imams who founded the law schools. These had "closed the gates of *ijtihad*" (individual interpretation) so their texts would become objects of veneration. They had become idols (*asnam*) worshipped like the pagan deities of the *jahiliyya*. The gates of *ijtihad*, however, had not been closed to everyone. Though ordinary people were expected to abide by the rulings of the legal scholars belonging to the schools, innovative rulings remained open to the leaders, so that fatwas could be issued to suit their interests, making illegality legal. Examples were fatwas by Mahmud Shaltut, the rector of al-Azhar university during the Nasser period, who declared banking interest lawful; or Shaikh Su'ad Jalal, who declared that beer did not fall under the prohibition of alcohol (he became known as Shaikh Stella, after a popular brand of Egyptian beer).[18] Like Qutb, Mustafa was especially critical of the mixing of the sexes and illicit sexual activity, punishable according to the Shari'a, but not according to Egypt's imported civil code. The *'ulama* had been accomplices in this abrogation of the Shari'a.

Although Mustafa's claims were annoying to the religious establishment, his most damaging statement came in reply to the question "What would the Society of Muslims [TwH] attitude be if Jewish [i.e. Israeli] forces invaded Egypt?" Mustafa replied: "If the Jews or anyone else came, our movement ought not to fight in the ranks of the Egyptian army, but on the contrary ought to flee to a secure position."[19] Mustafa's position was a direct challenge to the legitimacy of the Egyptian state in its struggle against Israel, which at the time of the trial was still occupying most of the Sinai peninsula. In subsequent questioning Mustafa drew attention to the absurdity of the government's policy which guaranteed jobs for graduates on civil service salaries fixed at very low rates – a virtual invitation to corruption since state employees could only hope to live by moonlighting or extorting bribes for their services. Writing of Cairo at this time, Kepel states that "an illiterate peasant woman who arrives in the city and manages to land a job as a foreigner's maid will be paid more or less double the salary of a university assistant lecturer".[20] Mustafa's critique of the system was far from being that "of a fanatic from a bygone century" which was how he was presented in the Egyptian press and media. Rather, in his own way and in language accessible to the mass of the population, he was challenging the social and economic realities of life in Egypt, exposing the underlying politics.[21]

One significant theme to emerge from the trial of Shukri Mustafa was the educational background of the accused. At the trial, and in interviews with the authoritative newspaper *Al-Ahram*, the military prosecutor General Muhammad 'Abd al-Halim Makhluf pointed out that neither Mustafa nor other leaders of the group had been trained in Quranic studies. He had "claimed to interpret the Quran and the hadiths, but he knew no more about either than he did about Arabic grammar, of which he was wholly ignorant".[22] During Mustafa's original detention from 1965 he had read "deviant" books, which secret police officers who testified at the trial identified as being works by Qutb and Maududi. This had enabled Mustafa and Mahir Bakri, the "group's philosopher", who had only received secondary education, to mislead young people, many of whom were well educated. The influence of Qutb and Maududi, as well as modernists such as Afghani, Abduh, and the leading Hanbali scholars, including Muhammad ibn 'Abd al-Wahhab and Ibn Taymiyya, was confirmed in subsequent interviews.[23]

When asked how such an ignorant pair could have persuaded better-educated people to join their group, the general made a statement which may retrospectively have acquired considerably more significance than it conveyed at the time. If the members of the group had any culture, the general said, "it was limited to that conferred by university disciplines such as medicine or engineering", both of which were powerless to remedy the "religious vacuity" (*al-faragh al-dini*) regarded by the general as the bane of young Egyptians. The youth, he stated in his opening statement at the trial, "are no longer educated in religion".[24] Kepel cites this remark as indicative of the arrogance of the military, an instance of the crude and high-handed way the government tried to exclude the al-Azhar religious establishment from participating in the trial, although the victim, Shaikh al-Dhahabi, had been one of their own. Kepel goes on to detail the subsequent acrimony existing between the two pillars of the Egyptian state.

The state's reliance on the army rather than on the much more problematic ground of religious tradition is a recurring motif in the political life of modern Muslim countries. In Turkey, Syria, Iraq, Jordan, Egypt, Tunisia and Algeria, the army exercises political control, directly or indirectly, and in all these cases it strives to contain or counter political opposition expressed in religious terms. In Sudan and Pakistan the military has sometimes sought to appease or adapt the Islamist current for its own purposes. General Zia ul-Haqq, Pakistan's former military ruler, courted popularity and tried to outflank the Islamists in devotion to Islam by introducing the "Hudood Ordinances", a version of Shari'a law administered by the army. In Sudan, General 'Umar al-Bashir allowed the Muslim Brotherhood to exercise real power under Hasan al-Turabi, the Islamist leader of the National Front, until a coup by the General in December 1999 which led to Turabi's house arrest. The current Pakistani ruler, General Pervez Musharraf, precariously holds the banner of secularism aloft in an army that has been heavily infiltrated by Islamists, hoping that a Taliban defeat in neighbouring Afghanistan will not lead to a rout of Pakistan's traditional Pushtun allies by the predominantly Tajik and Uzbek Northern Alliance. But to see General Makhluf's statement in purely political terms is to miss an important sociological point. The Egyptian Islamists may indeed be victims (or exploiters) of "religious vacuity". Apart from a few al-Azhar-trained scholars – the dissenting rebels in a predominantly politically quiescent religious establishment – the vast majority of Islamists in leadership roles have been drawn from the ranks of applied scientists, notably physicians and engineers.

In the aftermath of the 1974 and 1977 trials of the Sirriyya and Mustafa groups the sociologist Sa'ad al-din Ibrahim obtained permission to interview the "second echelon" cadres who had been sentenced to lengthy prison terms (the leaders of both groups had been executed, adding to the list of Islamist martyrs). Ibrahim's research team took care to build up relationships with the prisoners, who at first refused to see them. When the researchers eventually overcame the prisoners' reluctance to be interviewed, they were given "honesty tests" by their subjects, with the same questions repeated at different intervals. The researchers were also "shadowed" by members of the groups who were not in jail, to see if they were contacting members of the Mukhabarat, the secret police. When confidence had been established, Ibrahim's team spent approximately four hundred hours interviewing 34 Islamist militants – 21 from the Military Academy group and 13 from TwH.

Their social backgrounds were broadly similar: 21 had been born in villages or small towns and were recent comers to big cities. Most had come to universities in Cairo, Alexandria or Assyut after completing secondary school. Half were living with room-mates or alone, away from their families. Two-thirds of their fathers had been government employees, mostly in the middle grades of the civil service. It was safe to conclude, wrote Ibrahim, "that the class affiliations of most members of Islamist groups are middle to lower-middle class".[25]

Their educational and occupational attainments were higher than those of their parents. Twenty-nine of the 34 were either university graduates or were enrolled in college at the time of arrest. The remaining 5 had completed secondary school. Of the 16 who could be classified by occupation, 12 were professionals employed by the government, 3 were self-employed professionals and one was a bus conductor. Almost all recruits had majored in the natural sciences and maths, demonstrating both high motivation and competence. Ibrahim concluded:

> The typical social profile of members of militant Islamic groups could be summarised as being young (early twenties), of rural or small-town background, from middle and lower-middle class, with high achievement motivation, upwardly mobile, with science or engineering education, and from a normally cohesive family. It is sometimes assumed in social science that recruits of "radical movements" must be somehow

alienated, marginal, anomic, or otherwise abnormal. Most of those we investigated would be considered model young Egyptians.[26]

Elbaki Hermassi's study of members of the Islamist movement in Tunisia (Movement de la Tendence Islamique, or MTI) comes to strikingly similar conclusions. A large percentage of the membership, which included a substantial number of women, were of rural origin. Although Hermassi does not explicitly refer to the academic disciplines of his sample, 80 per cent were university students, with three-quarters of the leadership consisting of either secondary school teachers or university students. According to Valerie Hoffman, numerous other studies corroborate Ibrahim's observation that the majority of students in the movement are in the prestigious and competitive faculties of medicine, science and engineering.[27] The bias is confirmed by the fact that since the mid-1970s the professional associations of medicine and engineering in Egypt have been under Islamist control. Hoffman notes that a similar intellectual bias is evident in Pakistan, where all of Maududi's successors as leaders of the Jama'at-i-Islami attended modern schools and obtained graduate degrees in science, with the broader leadership of the movement also drawn from the modern professional or business sectors. Only 8 per cent have been recruited from the more traditional classes ('ulama, landlords, traditional medical practitioners).[28] The same pattern is discernible in Iran where, in contrast with Sunni-majority societies, the Shi'ite clergy have absorbed much contemporary rational thought into their theology. The coalition of militant leftist and Islamists which helped to bring down the Pahlevi regime in 1978–79 was sharply divided along disciplinary lines, with the Islamic guerrilla movement, the Mujahedin-e-Khalq, drawing its members mainly from students in the natural sciences, whereas Marxist Feda'i guerrillas were drawn largely from students in the humanities and social sciences. The former were mostly recruited from the traditionally religious middle classes, whereas the latter came mainly from the new middle class of secular-minded teachers, civil servants and professionals. There were three times as many women among the Feda'is as among the Mujahidin. Hoffman concludes:

> A consistent pattern emerges, across all these different coun-
> tries, of fundamentalists drawing heavily from students and
> university graduates in the physical sciences, usually students
> with rural or traditionally religious backgrounds. These
> movements seem to attract the recent beneficiaries of the
> expanded university systems in all of these countries, people
> who have, therefore, likely made recent adjustments to a
> modern urban intellectual and cultural environment after
> being raised in a fairly traditional milieu.[29]

Given that the Islamists are mostly drawn from among students with technical educations based on knowledge in subjects such as medicine and engineering which has been "imported" from the West, their use of language in politics is remarkable. One of the most interesting sections in Ibrahim's report concerns the way the political outlook the militants share with many other political movements, including Western social democracy, is cast in a vocabulary that refuses to acknowledge its origins:

> The militants' socio-economic programme appears very close
> to the moderate socialism of, say, the British Labour Party or
> even President Nasser. *But any suggestion to that effect invari-*
> *ably produces an outraged response. Islam is not to be likened*
> *to any man-made doctrine or philosophy.* It would be more
> acceptable to say that British socialism resembled Islam. Some
> of them attributed Mao Zedong's success in China to his emu-
> lation of Islam, rather than his Marxism. The militants often
> use words such as the poor – *al-fuqara'*, the wretched *al-*
> *masakin* and the weak on the earth (*al-mustad'afin fi-l'ard*) –
> to designate those whom leftists term "working class", the
> "exploited" or the "proletariat". The militants use terms such
> as the "corrupt on earth" (*al-mufsidun fi-l'ard*) and the unjust

(*al-zalama'*) to mean those whom secularists refer to as "exploiters" or "oppressors".[30] (emphasis added)

The determination to present ordinary political ideas as "Islamic" is the one of the hallmarks of the Sunni Islamist movement. It is much less prominent among the Shi'a. For example 'Ali Shari'ati, a prominent Shi'ite intellectual who helped to inspire the Islamic revolution in Iran, acknowledged his debt to Marx, Fanon and Sartre in his writings, as well as the influence of the great French orientalist Louis Massignon, whose lectures he attended in Paris. Maududi, as we have noted, makes positive references to Alexis Carrel, a French writer with close links to fascism, but in general there is a refusal to acknowledge "imported" foreign influences, to entertain the possibility of cultural exchange.

This attitude of cultural intransigence is consistent with the traditional Sunni insistence on the primacy of revelation over reason. Although historically the Arabs took over, and advanced, the learning of the Greeks and other peoples of late antiquity, making the advances in mathematics, optics, medicine and other disciplines that are often seen as laying the foundations for the humanism of Renaissance Europe, the dogma that revealed knowledge supersedes or encompasses knowledge acquired by the exercise of reason has remained part of the Arab–Muslim cultural outlook into the twenty-first century. Its origins lie in the defeat of the Mu'tazila during the 'Abbasid period, a populist revolt against the intellectual elitism represented by the court of al-Ma'mun (see pages 39–40).

The prodigious intellectual achievements of subsequent generations of Muslims always occurred in the face of populist pressure. The courts fostered talents that were placed at the disposal of ordinary Muslims in the magnificent public buildings we associate with the civilizations of Islam at their height. But despite the achievements of individual Muslim scientists, cultural attitudes as a whole remained hostile to borrowing, experimentation and innovation which are fundamental to scientific method. Education remained a limited preserve, because of the systematic hostility to the introduction of printing on the part of the *'ulama*.[31] The high rates of illiteracy in countries such as Afghanistan and Pakistan have been major obstacles to development and to the introduction of reformist or modernist trends in the way Islam is interpreted. The supremacy of revelation over reason made philosophy the marginal pursuit of an intellectual elite which preached one truth to itself (founded on speculative inquiry) and another (based exclusively on revelation) to the people. The philosopher Ibn Rushd is better known by his Latin name, Averroës, because it was through Latin that his works became most widely available. Despite his speculative outlook, he doubled as an Islamic judge empowered to enact the judgements laid down by God.

The disciples of Sayyid Qutb were caught in the same cultural trap as Averroës. For them Islam was self-sufficient. Nothing needed to be adopted, adapted, borrowed from the hated Other, the West, except for its technological products which, for self-serving, psychological reasons, they regarded as neutral, non-contaminating.

The scientific background of the Islamists has an important bearing on their readings, not only of the foundational texts of Quran and Hadith, but also of Qutb's own writings. As Martha Mundy has observed, in adopting literalist readings of the legal tradition the Islamists have tried to reconstruct Islamic legality not by a return to the *spirit* of the original reforms suggested by writers such as Hasan al-Banna and Sayyid Qutb, but by the *word*.

Unlike the legal modernists who sought to harmonize Islamic tradition with contemporary realities, the literalists refused to entertain any suggestion of historical relativity. Hence, for example, Mustafa's rejection of the whole corpus of Islamic legal tradition. The traditions of textual analysis enshrined in the great law compendia represent a developed sense of history, of the history of a tradition of commentators and interpreters. But while legal reformism retained the medieval tradition of historical textual analysis and the glosses of the scholars as sources for variant readings, the Islamist movement had no patience with such decadent elaboration.

Indeed, literalism is the essence of the "proof-texting" advocated by Qutb. As Martha Mundy puts it, "The text of
instruction takes the form of a manual of procedure; the law that
of a list of injunctions; the defence that of an outraged homily."[32]
People with legal training, either in the tradition of Islamic *fiqh*
(jurisprudence) or in the tradition of modern civil law, are conspicuous by their absence from the leadership of the Islamist or
religious reform movements of most Arab lands today. The situation is different in Shi'ite Iran where clergy are trained in the
traditions of medieval legal scholarship, and where the Mu'tazilite
belief (not dissimilar to that of St Thomas Aquinas) that God
will not act contrary to reason still holds sway. In the Sunni
world, alongside the populist preachers "stand men of technical,
military and scientific education".

The explanation Mundy offers is primarily sociological:

> With some reason does normative, juridical idealism attract
> men trained in science. To the local university come men
> licensed by a professional certification obtained from
> abroad – from a university of the core – and tied for life to the
> distant sources of the scientific truths in which they deal. Yet
> so long as such scientists remain at home they become virtu-
> ally barred from any serious role in the certification of
> scientific truth. Irremediably the discourse of "hard" science
> is produced elsewhere. What answer for self-respect? . . . A
> tradition of legal idealism is pressed to provide another model
> for the production of truth. The search opens for an unchang-
> ing indigenous criterion begging no certification from outside,
> for a criterion that can overrule by moral force the shifting
> truths of the committees of specialists.[33]

In a similar vein James Rupert dwells on the theme of marginal-
ization, describing Islamist students in Tunisia as "would-be
professionals – engineers, lawyers, doctors" alarmed at the bleak
prospects they face where "economic development has stagnated
and prospects for climbing into the country's elite classes seem

slight".[34] Bearing in mind the scientific background of most Islamists Nazih Ayubi suggests:

> ... these movements have emerged not really as an expression of moral outrage against a modernisation that was going "too fast", but rather as a reaction to a developmental process that was not going fast enough ... The Islamists are not angry because the aeroplane has replaced the camel; they are angry because they could not get on to the aeroplane. There is little doubt in my mind that had Nasserism (and other similar developmental projects) "delivered" in the sixties, we would not be witnessing the same political revival of Islam that we see today.[35]

Ayubi's argument would be more persuasive, however, if Islamism in particular and religious fundamentalism in general were limited to regions where "developmental projects" similar to Nasserism have failed, or if the Islamists were drawn exclusively from the ranks of aspiring professionals who failed to get decent jobs. This is conspicuously not the case in Malaysia or Indonesia, Muslim-majority countries in which Islamists are well represented, where before the recent economic crisis industrialization had been proceeding apace. India, also industrializing rapidly, has seen a surge in Hindu fundamentalism comparable both to the rise of Islamism in the Middle East and South Asia and to the appearance of new religious movements (NRMs) in Korea and Japan. In the 1980s and 1990s, Protestant fundamentalism raised its profile in the United States, one of the world's most developed economies.

It is not just an infrastructural epiphenomenon, the ghostly by-product of socio-economic forces, though socio-economic forces doubtless play an important part in generating the psychic and social discontents that fundamentalists try to address.

What was particularly chilling about the attacks on New York and Washington was that they were planned and executed by people whom Ibrahim sees as being "model Egyptians". The chief planners – if we are to believe newspaper reports, were Ayman al-Zawahiri, the paediatric surgeon who appears to have brought his faction of Islamic Jihad into al-Qa'ida in 1999 after splitting with the majority over their cease-fire with the government, and Mohammed Atta, the architect and town planning expert. Both were men whose education, training and proficiency could have guaranteed them a position among the elite of technocrats and professionals whose social eminence tends to be greater in less developed societies than it is in the West. Both these men could doubtless have made successful careers in Europe or America had they chosen to do so. To fathom the significance of the Islamist attacks on America one must look beyond the reductionism that would see it as an act of destructive rage by a gang of "religious fanatics" or "frustrated professional wannabes".

Valerie Hoffman sees "psychosocial alienation", not the blocking of careers, as the basis of the Islamist appeal. "Islamic fundamentalism is primarily a revolt of young people who are caught between a traditional past and a higher secular education with all its implications of Western intellectual impact and contact with the materialistically oriented culture of the modern urban environment."[36] Here, she argues, the issue of identity is crucial, reflecting as it does "the conflicting anxieties created by the necessity of finding one's own identity in a world of confusing choices". The issue, she suggests, is most acute in areas where the Western cultural impact has been strongest: "in the cities, in the universities, and particularly in the faculties of science, where the embrace of Western learning is most complete".[37]

Susan Waltz makes a similar point. "Liberal arts students studying Western ideas are exposed to the evolution of those ideas and to the weaknesses of Western culture, whereas students in science and technology are more apt to see Western culture as monolithic and properly hegemonic."[38] In the view of these students the belief that the "West" is wholly materialistic, devoid of spiritual values, which is Sayyid Qutb's case derived from his aesthete's disdain for the philistinism and vulgarity he chose to find in America, acquires a different colouring. "They come to see their lives bifurcated between an Islamic culture that provides moral values, community and spiritual satisfaction, and a Western culture that provides access to the material improvement of their lives." Islamism is the mirror image of orientalism, a dualistic perspective, in which the West "continues to serve as the standard by which Muslims evaluate their own culture".[39]

Sexuality, Hoffman suggests, is at the heart of this crisis because this is the area where young Muslim males may feel most exposed to the transgressive allure of Western lifestyles and to the restrictions of their own. Modernity is seductive: Satan is a tempter, not a tyrant. Since Muslim cultures tend to draw boundaries around social behaviour, emphasizing external rather than internal moral constraints, governments – or more pervasively "the West" – are blamed for the availability of temptations. Imported American dramas such as *Dallas*, *Knott's Landing* and *Falcon Crest*, showing human behaviour in situations dominated by lust, greed and selfishness, are seen as undermining the Muslim family by introducing aspirations towards materialism and sexual immorality.[40]

Outside the Shi'ite tradition of passion plays commemorating the death of the Imam Hussein or the shadow puppet plays of South-East Asia, there are few indigenous traditions of drama. US television shows are taken, not as entertainments which actually affirm moral values by dramatizing moral failings, since if the "bad guys" are not actually caught, the sufferings they cause to others are invariably revealed, but as accurate representations of American or "Western" life. For example:

> ... in *Islam and the Orientation of the Contemporary Muslim Woman*, the Egyptian writer Muhammad al-Bahi depicts the West as a society that has fallen prey to a "sexual revolution" of brothels, pornography, and casual intercourse, where normal marital relations are nonexistent and people sell their children in order to buy cars. He warns Muslim women that if they pursue Western-style liberation, Muslim society will likewise soon be plagued with nude nightclubs, nude beaches, pornographic films and massage parlours.[41]

A tract distributed by the Islamic Associations (*al-jama'at al-islamiya*) warns that it is the strategy of international Zionism to effect the collapse of Muslim society by exposing the youth to sexual relations on film "so that they will no longer remain sacred . . . Their greatest concern will be to quench their sexual desires. Then morals will collapse."[42]

The discomforting effects of Western seduction are compounded by an obsession with sexual purity. According to the Moroccan feminist writer Fatima Mernissi, this may be due to the fact that the typical unmarried male's contact with his own sexuality is in a context deemed impure according to Islamic norms – sodomy and masturbation. "It is no wonder," she comments, "that women who have such tremendous power to maintain or destroy a man's position in society, are going to be the focus of his frustration and aggression."[43] Mernissi's observation is consistent with the theories of Wilhelm Reich who noted that most sexually frustrated males internalize their feelings at the level of moral or religious defence rather than channelling them into a rebellion against social or economic repression.

Here, however, it is the exceptions that may prove the rule: in a minority, sexual anomie may generate feelings of rage directed at the "West" as the source of both of temptation and the corruption of morals. In his comparative study of fundamentalist movements in America and Iran, Martin Riesebrodt argued that religious fundamentalism is above all a protest movement against the assault on "patriarchal structural principles in the family, economy and politics", with sex – or more specifically, the control of female sexuality – looming large in both discourses. As Riesebrodt observes, American fundamentalists like John R. Straton, pastor of Calvary Baptist Church in New York, writing in the 1920s, described the corrupting role of women in images that are strikingly similar to the jeremiads of today's imams and ayatollahs:

The most sinister and menacing figure of our modern life is the cigarette smoking, cocktail drinking, pug dog nursing, half-dressed, painted woman, who frequents the theaters, giggles at the cabarets, gambles in our drawing rooms or sits around our hotels, with her dress cut "C" in front and "V" behind! She is a living invitation to lust . . .[44]

Revolutionary Islamist groups like the Fedayan-i Islam denounce unveiled women in similar, if more dramatic, language, claiming, "Flames of passion rise from the naked bodies of immoral women and burn humanity to ashes," causing young men to neglect their work. More than half the provisions of a 1981 Iranian law codifying Quranic prescriptions – 107 out of 195 articles – are concerned with sexual activities, ranging from adultery and homosexuality to unrelated persons of the same sex lying naked under a blanket.[45]

Riesebrodt sees the obsessive concern with sexuality common to American and Iranian fundamentalisms as a reaction to broader anxieties resulting from rural displacement and economic change. The symptoms of patriarchal decline manifest themselves in the spheres of the family and sexual morality; but the true causes may lie in those very processes Max Weber regarded as integral to modernity: the expansion of large-scale "rationalized" operations, entailing formalized and codified relationships, at the expense of small businesses based on paternalistic relations between an employer and employees.[46] In resisting such aspects of Weber's "disenchantment" of the world, Riesebrodt argues, fundamentalism can indeed be termed "antimodern". Reality, however, forces it to absorb many of modernity's salient features. What it cannot sustain in the face of structural transformation it attempts to impose symbolically. Male–female segregation can no longer sustained by traditional domestic arrangements, since women are required in the workforce. Instead it is achieved by sartorial coding – long hair and skirts for American women, "Christian" haircuts (short back and sides) for their menfolk; the chador for Iranian women, the beard – a mark of sex and piety – for men. The forms of public religiosity may mask, but do not necessarily reverse or even delay, the processes of secularization.[47] Sexuality is an important part of the story for the way in which the sense of personal selfhood is constructed around it. Our sense of self is affirmed at its most intimate and vulnerable in sexual activity. It is a sacred area where, as al-Ghazali noted, the virtuous Muslim couple experiences a foretaste of the divine. It is an area in which "Western values" are perceived as especially menacing. Muslim women seeking to gain admittance to public spaces previously reserved for men have responded to these concerns by adopting "Islamic dress", a style of clothing which symbolically defuses the threat posed by women in a male-dominated social order by desexualizing the woman's body.

Fear and hatred of the "West" have many causes above and beyond the issue of sexuality, as I hope to show. The jihad tradition, as I have also tried to show, is programmed into the historical memory, or "social imaginary" of contemporary Islam: there is an abundance of material from the Quran, the hadith literature and the Prophet's biographies which, if taken out of context, could be used to justify an attack on an enemy designated as being the "infidel". None of this means, of course, that "Islam is to blame": merely that intellectual resources exist in this tradition, as in most others, for taking up arms in the face of a perceived threat. In this case, I would suggest, the threat is really to an identity created in the typically modern, "third world" context where the child of the village, or rural suburb, encounters the adult beneficiary of a modern, technical, scientific education. Qutb, the man of letters, courted martyrdom in order to resolve the contradiction between a personal identity forged in the traditional faith of an Egyptian village and the reality of the *jahiliyya* world he encountered in America and Cairo.

For students trained in the sciences, that contradiction may be even more problematic than it was for Qutb. The two sources of knowledge or awareness underpinning the dual identity of the village Muslim and applied scientist are imperfectly integrated. The religious mind inherited from the village or suburb is conditioned to believe that knowledge is "Islamic", that all truth is known to, and comes from, Allah. The scientist operates in a field of epistemological doubt: and modernity itself, as Anthony

Giddens reminds us, consists in the "institutionalisation of doubt". Uncertainty is as fundamental to modern science as belief in the pre-Kantian metaphysical divinity is to the main-stream of Sunni Islam whose divines since the nineteenth century set themselves against incorporating post-Enlightenment think-ing into their theological outlook. As Daniel Easterman (the Islamic scholar Denis McEoin) has made clear, the real scandal the post-Enlightenment West holds for many Muslims is that knowledge acquired through doubt has proved far more power-ful in creating material prosperity than revealed knowledge. This need not matter for spiritually minded Muslims who eschew material prosperity or place it in the context of the mystical humanism taught by Ibn 'Arabi and other masters, in which the "complete human being" (*al-insan al-kamil*) is perceived as the microcosm of the divine, the ultimate reality. Modern Sufis and many Shi'ites in the Ithna'ashari (Twelver) and Isma'ili (Sevener) traditions have found ways of accommodating their modern and Islamic identities without undue stress by drawing on these ideas. But for those Muslims beholden to what I have called the "Argument from Manifest Success", in which the early conquests of Islam are seen as demonstrations of God's approval, even proofs of His existence, the scandal of Western post-Enlightenment success may be unbearable. As Easterman puts it:

> Much modern Muslim writing tries to play down the tri-umph of the West by emphasizing the dark side of the European and North American experience, the inner angst of a bankrupt civilization on the verge of collapse. The problem is that Islam itself is peculiarly vulnerable on this score. There is very little point in sneering at the material success of others if at the same time one measures one's own achievements by precisely the same criteria: the unprecedented triumph of Muslim arms, the glories of the Abbasid, Andalusian or Mughal empires, the scientific advances of the Islamic Middle Ages.[48]

One way out of the dilemma in which the dual identity of the villager-turned-scientist is reinforced by the epistemological dualism of religion (certainty) and science (uncertainty) is to pretend that religion already contains the truths of science. A popular book by the French surgeon Maurice Bucaille argues on the basis of highly eclectic readings of the Quran that a great quantity of modern scientific knowledge, from biology to cosmology, is already in the divine text, waiting to be exposed by the modern scientifically aware exegete in the light of contemporary knowledge. The problem with Bucaillism, as Parvez Hoodbhoy, a theoretical physicist working in America and Pakistan, has noted, is that the Quran contains "not a single *prediction* of any physical fact which is unknown up to now, but which could be tested against observation and experiment in the future".[49] However appealing rhetorically, Bucaillism simply does not stand up to analysis by people trained in the sciences. Apart from its failure to supply testable predictions, it cannot deal with the shifting patterns in the paradigms and hypotheses through which human knowledge advances.

Since for the vast majority of Muslims Islam is a religion of orthopraxy rather than orthodoxy, in which it is proper conduct, rather than correct belief, that offers the path to salvation, the contradiction between the intellectual grounds of received tradition and the intellectual basis underpinning contemporary reality may not be experienced acutely. But the people who join Islamist movements are not so easily satisfied. Like all radical political and philosophical projects, the movements attract people who are not content to make pragmatic accommodations, who seek to make the world conform to their ideas of what is just, harmonious and right. The intransigence of the world, its refusal to conform to the "straight path" laid down by "God and His Messenger" is experienced for them in our time as acutely as it was experienced by Nietzsche and his contemporaries a century ago, when the demise of the metaphysical divinity was afflicting the sentient minds of Europe.

In the neo-Kharijite tradition exemplified by TwH, the response to the world's intransigence was to rebuild the world from scratch, to withdraw from the *jahiliyya* by "migrating from Mecca to Medina" in order to build an alternative society. That, in a modified way, is what many of the more moderate Islamist groups have also sought to do in the universities and in the poorer parts of the cities. Before *jahiliyya* power can be overcome, society must be rebuilt "from below". To borrow Christian terminology, the solution is "postmillennial" and world-constructing: before the Messiah comes, we must make a world fit to receive him. The jihadist groups, by contrast, have opted for the much more extreme approach, predicated on seizing state power from "above". The eschatology is implicit: the jihadist group responsible for the murder of Sadat in October 1981 believed that the removal of "Pharaoh" would spontaneously induce an Islamic revolution comparable to that which had occurred in Iran two years earlier. In the event, the only disturbances that did occur were in Asyut, far from the capital.

The Military Academy group which intended to murder Sadat in 1974 evidently had the same idea. The influences operating on the jihadist groups, however, are not so obvious as might appear at first sight. As Ibrahim pointed out, the group refused to use "imported" leftist terminologies, preferring instead to employ terms taken from the "authentic" Islamic lexicon. In the discussions preceding the attack on the Military Academy the survivors interviewed by Ibrahim could only remember one occasion when the leader, Salih Sirriyya, was unable to sway the *shura* (consultative) council to his point of view: the timing of the attack. At that time Sirriyya estimate their chances of success at only 30 per cent. All but one other member argued that even if success was not assured, they should go ahead with their plan anyway. The action would be an outrage or "fury for God" (*ghadba lil-allah* – a term Ibrahim astutely translates into English using a well-known phrase from the lexicon of European anarchism: "propaganda by deed").

Ibrahim's terminology reveals the hidden, unacknowledged influence of what one suspects may have been the Baader–Meinhof gang. An extreme leftist group with close connections to the Palestinian revolutionary movement, their exploits were making headline news throughout the world, and especially in the Middle East. Known to themselves as the Red Army Faction (RAF) the group was led by Andreas Baader, a high-school dropout, his lover Gudrun Ensslin, a trainee teacher, and Ulrike Meinhof, a journalist and former editor of *Konkret*, a left-wing magazine. Most of the members of the group were well-educated and came from middle- or upper-middle-class families. Like the Islamist scientists and technocrats, they could have expected fulfilling, financially secure professional or business careers. Soon after their inception in 1970 they received some training in a refugee camp controlled by the Marxist Popular Front for the Liberation of Palestine (PFLP) in Jordan. The Palestinians gave them weapons and instructed them on how to create a cell structure which the authorities would find it hard to penetrate. On returning to Germany they began by robbing banks. During one of these raids they killed a policeman. Meinhof commented: "We say the person in uniform is a pig – that is, not a human being – and thus we have to settle the matter with him. It is wrong to talk to those people at all. Shooting is a matter of course." One of their slogans became "*Don't argue, destroy.*"[50] In the spring of 1972 the RAF struck at high-profile targets to publicize their aims, which were to oppose the US military presence in Germany and to draw attention to the continuities existing between the modern West German government and the former Nazi regime. They attacked US army bases at Frankfurt and Heidelberg, killing four US servicemen, and the Axel Springer press building in Hamburg, injuring thirty-eight people. (The Springer newspapers had been particularly hostile to the 1968 student movement of which all the RAF leaders had originally been part.) The three leaders were arrested in June 1972 along with nineteen other people. In December 1975, members of the RAF joined with Carlos Ilych Sanchez – known as "The Jackal" – in holding hostage eleven oil ministers from the OPEC oil-cartel at their meeting in Vienna. After a few hours Chancellor Bruno Kreisky gave in to their demand to be flown with their hostages to Algeria. There they were set free along with terrorists, although three people had been shot in Vienna. The hostages, who were mostly Arabs, included Shaikh Ahmad Zaki Yamani, the Saudi oil minister. He believed that "Carlos" had intended to kill him and an Iranian minister in order to warn pro-Western states against taking a "soft line" with Israel. They had the Algerian government to thank for their survival. The Libyan leader, Colonel Qadhafi was generally blamed in the press as being the instigator of the raid, earning him the title of "paymaster of terrorism".

In May 1976 Ulrike Meinhof was found hanging dead in her cell at the specially built high-security complex at Stammheim near Frankfurt where the terrorists were held and tried. The authorities claimed she had committed suicide. RAF members and their sympathizers believed she had been murdered by state employees, just as Rosa Luxemburg, their heroine, had been in 1920, along with Carl Liebknecht, leader of the German Social Democrats. In July RAF members took part with Palestinians in the hijacking of an Air France jet to Entebbe, Uganda. Two RAF members were killed when Israeli commandos rescued the passengers. The crisis of terrorism in Germany reached its peak in April 1977, when the RAF shot and killed Siegfried Buback, the general state prosecutor, who had been one of the foremost advocates of stricter anti-terrorist measures. In July the trial of Baader, Ensslin and their colleague Jan-Carl Raspe finally ended. All three were sentenced to life imprisonment. In retaliation the RAF killed Jurgen Pronto, head of one of Germany's large commercial banks (one of his assassins was his own goddaughter) and kidnapped Hanns-Martin Schleyer, a former SS man who had become president of the employers' association, killing all four of his bodyguards. When the government refused the RAF's demand that they release Baader, Ensslin and several other prisoners from Stammheim, in October 1977 the RAF joined with Palestinians in hijacking a Lufthansa jet. The jet finally landed in Mogadishu, the Somali capital, where members of the West German anti-terrorist unit, assisted by Britain's SAS, managed to free all the passengers, killing or capturing the hijackers. On hearing the news of the successful storming of the airliner, Baader and Ensslin shot themselves with smuggled pistols. Raspe hanged himself with wire. A day later, Schleyer's body was found in the boot of a car across the French border in Alsace. Thereafter the movement declined, although they still engaged in some high-profile actions with their French counterparts, Action Directe.

Ideologically, the Baader–Meinhof gang and the Islamist group led by Sirriyya appear poles apart. The RAF were ultra-leftist utopian communists, committed to spreading world revolution. Their Arab collaborators were on the far left of the Palestinian revolutionary spectrum. Nevertheless they shared with the Islamists a common internationalist outlook. Both groups were violently anti-American and opposed to the "Zionist occupation" of Palestine supported by America. Both groups were romantic idealists in their moral–political outlook, both held utopian ideas. True, the Islamist utopia of a revived caliphate may be past-oriented, while the communist utopia was located in the future, but that would make little difference in organizational and practical terms. Formally communists are atheists – an aspect of revolutionary doctrine that has made it difficult for communism to win converts in the Muslim world outside the ranks of the Westernized intelligentsia, except in the Central Asian republics formerly controlled by Russia. But in a broader sense revolutionary idealism is religious by definition, based as it almost invariably is on a transcendental eschatological imperative. Revolutionary utopias are heavenly kingdoms created on earth by "saints".

Ulrike Meinhof, the RAF's leading intellectual, had been deeply religious in her youth. According to Jillian Becker, "She was an ambitious, love-hungry child." Her education had made her into both a puritan and a rebel, the one never reconciled to the other. She was "sentimentally drawn" into utopian communism, insistent on her moral superiority. "The sort of insight into self which makes moral absolutism impossible was not within her capability." Speaking of Meinhof's suicide, for which she provides detailed and convincing evidence, Becker concludes:

There is good reason to believe that [Ulrike] had long dreamed of personal glory, of having a heroic role to play, since the days of her girlhood in Oldenburg; also that she had not matured emotionally, so that adolescent extremism, "absoluteness" and dogmatic moral idealism continued with her into middle age. Martyrdom was all that was left to her in Stammheim prison, and martyrdom was, after all, the highest form of heroism which her country in her formative years, as well as the religion by which she was deeply affected, had provided for her admiration and ambition.

Apologists for her said she "thirsted for justice" and that it was a burning sense of injustice suffered by others that drove her to terrible punitive acts against an unjust society. But unless she is seen as some avatar of vengeance set above humanity to scourge it, it must be charged against her that she was neither just nor humane.[51]

There seem to be several similarities between the personalities of Ulrike Meinhof and Mohammed Atta, though the details of Atta's life, and those of his fellow conspirators, are still sketchy. More will doubtless become available after the historians of September 11th have picked over his career more thoroughly. Journalistic accounts revealed a deeply troubled personality: an overbearing father, a mother who held him on her lap long after most small boys have turned into little macho men. Even in his twenties the short and slight Atta would sometimes sit on his mother's lap. "I used to tell her that she was raising him as a girl," Atta's father told *Newsweek*, "but she never stopped pampering him." Atta seems to have been obsessive, meticulous and anally retentive. Working part-time as a draughtsman for Plankontor, an urban planning firm in Hamburg, while he studied for his master's degree, he produced extremely detailed, colour-coded diagrams in fine ink. He would occasionally smile, but was hardly ever seen to laugh. Like Qutb he was obsessive about women. In the will dating from 1996 found in the suitcase that did not make it onto the doomed American Airlines flight 11, and later published by *Der Spiegel*, he wrote:

Those who will sit beside my body must remember Allah and
pray for me to be with the angels. I don't want pregnant
women or a person who is not clean to come and say goodbye
to me because I don't approve of it. I don't want women to go
to my funeral or later to my grave. I only want to be buried
next to good Muslims. My face should be directed east
toward Mecca.[52]

Like Qutb, Atta seems to have been tortured by the attraction he
felt for the sleazy sides of Western life in Hamburg (which has more
brothels than most other German cities), and by taboos about
bodily purity. According to Adam Robinson, a writer with close
connections to the British intelligence community, he remained a
"heavy drinking, sexually deviant individual who, to satisfy himself,
beat the prostitute he regularly hired".[53] I do not know if this is
actually true, or simply part of a programme of character vilification orchestrated by the intelligence services. But of his confusion
and anxiety about sexuality there seems little doubt. By all accounts
he was a man who was very far from being mentally unstable, but
filled with unresolved anger and rage. His problematic sexuality
seems to have been deeply bound up with his religiosity.

The skills he and his team deployed in executing the September
11th attacks owed everything to their disciplined technical backgrounds. The suicidal martyrdom they embraced in their final,
horrendous act of destruction was not so much the result of some
naïve faith in a paradisical future, but the final solution they found
to a profoundly tragic personal predicament. The pre-Kantian,
metaphysical deity taught in the mainstream academies of Islam in
Egypt and Saudi Arabia had failed them catastrophically. In a
world dominated by the post-Enlightenment West, the Argument
from Manifest Success was collapsing everywhere. These highly
educated products of Western technical education had begun to
experience what Paul Tillich called the "shaking of the foundations". In adopting the Islamist ideology, they were "protesting
too much". Their faith in the benign and compassionate deity of
Islam had begun to wobble. Their final act was not a gesture of

Islamic heroism, but of Nietzschean despair. Their Islamist lineage is not in doubt. Like the Military Academy group they conceived the deed they committed on September 11th as an Outrage, a Fury for God. The Baader–Meinhof slogan – *Don't argue, destroy!* – could well have been their own.

Chapter Five

Cultural Schizophrenia

Since its foundation in the 1920s, the modern Saudi kingdom has been considered a byword for Islamic orthodoxy. The rulers of the kingdom style themselves officially "Custodians of the Two Sanctuaries" – a reference to the holy shrines of Mecca and Medina. The former, an ancient shrine known to Pliny as Macorba, was the Prophet Muhammad's birthplace, where he received the first of the divine revelations that make up approximately half the material contained in the Quran. The latter was the oasis settlement to which he and the first Muslims emigrated in the *hijra* in 622 CE, where he created the original Islamic polity which expanded, by persuasion and force of arms, to cover most of the Arabian peninsula before his death in 632. The Grand Mosque at Medina, where Muhammad is buried, is the second holiest shrine after Mecca. The Saudis acquired the Hijaz, the Islamic holy land where both shrines are located, by conquest in 1926. The original Saudi state was created in the eighteenth century out of an alliance between a reformer of the Hanbali school, Muhammad ibn 'Abd al-Wahhab, and Muhammad al-Sa'ud, tribal chief of Najd, of which the modern capital, Riyadh, is the centre.

Ibn 'Abd al-Wahhab, like many previous Islamic reformers, had preached a return to the purity of the early Islam of the Prophet

Muhammad and the "rightly guided" caliphs, an Islam free from the accretions and practices, such as the custom of worshipping at the tombs of Muslim saints and asking for intercessions, adopted during more than a millennium of "cumulative tradition". Ibn 'Abd al-Wahhab's first targets were local forms of *shirk*, meaning polytheism or the "association" of lesser beings with God, such as the image of Dha'l Khilsa – against which apparently infertile women rubbed their buttocks in the hope of fertility, or the cult of the male palm tree where women prayed for husbands.[1] The celebration of feasts connected with the birth of sacred persons including the Prophet Muhammad were also attacked. Religious scholars of the Hanbali school, to which Ibn 'Abd al-Wahhab laid claim, had attacked such practices many centuries previously. For example Ibn Taymiyya (d.1328), the Hanbali scholar widely admired and emulated by modern Islamists, inveighed against un-Islamic borrowings from Christianity in his "On the Necessity of the Straight Path" (*kitab iqtida al-sirat al-mustaqim*) a text that may be found today in Islamic bookshops in London and Birmingham, as well as Cairo and Lahore. For Ibn Taymiyya – who lived in Syria and Egypt, both of which had substantial Christian minorities – the beginning of Muslim life was the point at which "a perfect dissimilarity with the non-Muslims has been achieved".[2] Ibn Taymiyya argued that celebrations of the Prophet's birthday or the construction of mosques around the tombs of Sufi shaikhs were unacceptable borrowings from Christians: "Many of them [the Muslims] do not even know of the Christian origin of these practices. Accursed be Christianity and its adherents!"[3] Ibn 'Abd al-Wahhab's followers went even further than Ibn Taymiyya by designating Muslims who took part in religiously reprehensible practices as "infidels". Mere affiliation with Islam – for example, by pronouncing the *shahada* in front of witnesses – was insufficient to prevent a Muslim from being a polytheist. The definition of *kufr* applied not only to idolatrous religious practices, nor was it confined to non-Islamic monotheism. It described non-Wahhabi co-religionists as well. Ibn Abd al-Wahhab justified this exclusiveness by reference to Muhammad himself (who, for example, fought the Jewish monotheists at Khaybar and the Byzantine Christian monotheists at Tabuk). As 'Aziz el-Azmeh explains, in Wahhabism "the hallowed principle of Sunni Islam, according to which all those who profess the *shahada* are Muslims, is rejected in favour of the assertion often made by Wahhabite divines that even reserve towards the necessity of pronouncing non-Wahhabites generically dubbed *mushrikun* (polytheists) to be *kuffar* (unbelievers) and of fighting them in itself constitutes *kufr*." Sulayman bin 'Abdullah, a prominent descendant of the movement's founder, banned not only alliance with *kuffar*, but virtually any contact with them whatsoever.[4] Anyone still practising polytheism, as defined by the Wahhabis, he said, should be declared an infidel and killed.[5] Wahhabi doctrine encouraged the Saudi warriors to be utterly ruthless in battle: every campaign was a jihad, with the most extreme implications of that doctrine. "All who are taken with arms," wrote the Swiss traveller Jacob Burckhardt of the early Saudi armies, "are unmercifully put to death. This savage custom has inspired the Wahhabies with a ferocious fanaticism that makes them dreadful to their adversaries."[6]

By the middle of the eighteenth century CE the alliance between the Al Sa'ud dynasty and Ibn 'Abd al-Wahhab enabled the movement to become the dominant force in the Arabian peninsula. The combination of military force and religious enthusiasm proved devastating. One after another the shaikhdoms of Central Arabia fell before the Saudi forces. The Saudi ambition to take over the Muslim holy land after attacks on Mecca in 1803 and Medina in 1805 was only thwarted when the ruler of Egypt, Mehmet 'Ali, sent his son Ibrahim Pasha with a modern army to protect the holy land.

Saudi fortunes were revived in the early twentieth century when 'Abd al-'Aziz ibn 'Abd al-Rahman al-Sa'ud (better known as Ibn Saud), a tall, charismatic scion of the Al Sa'ud, reclaimed his ancestral lands in Najd from the pro-Ottoman Rashids in 1906. In 1932, after conquering al-Hasa in the east, the Hijaz in the West and the province 'Asir on the borders of Yemen, Ibn

Saud established the modern "Arab Saudi kingdom" for which he won international recognition. In emulation of his ancestors, Ibn Saud used the power of religion to advance his political aims. The shock troops, known simply as the Ikhwan (Brethren), who spearheaded the twentieth-century Saudi revival, originated in a movement among the Harb and Mutair tribes in al-Artawiyya, a locality in the steppelands about 200 miles north of Riyadh. Inspired by Muhammad's example and the teachings of Ibn 'Abd al-Wahhab, the Ikhwan abandoned their nomadic ways to create agricultural settlements, called *hijras*, modelled on the community founded by the Prophet at the oasis settlement of Medina. In accordance with hadiths describing the Prophet's appearance, or attributed to him, and in order to distance themselves from their nomadic pasts, the Ikhwan wore the headdress without the head-rope or *agal*, originally a method of hobbling camels. They cut their *thawbs*, or gowns, short above the ankles, trimmed their moustaches and grew their beards long, as they imagined, in imitation of the Prophet.

Ibn Saud supported the settlements with money, and paid for preachers. Following the classical paradigm of Medina, the *hijras* became militarized, and in due course the Ikhwan became Ibn Saud's most valuable fighting asset. Their religious enthusiasm made them formidable fighters. "I have seen them hurl themselves on their enemies," wrote Hafiz Wahba, an adviser to Ibn Saud in later years, "utterly fearless of death, not caring how many fall, advancing rank upon rank with only one desire – the defeat and annihilation of the enemy. They normally give no quarter, sparing neither boys nor old men, veritable messengers of death from whose grasp no one escapes."[7] With their hijra colonies located at strategic points all over the Najd plateau, the Ikhwan could be mobilized at great speed, a rapid deployment force *avant la lettre*. In supporting the movement, Ibn Saud was spared the cost of a standing army. "He had to bear the expense of paying modest subsidies and giving presents to the tribal leaders, of providing land and seeds, of paying for the preachers and to some extent of providing arms and ammunition but he avoided the enormous overheads of accommodation, supply, administration, training and personnel problems."[8]

In reuniting most of the Arabian peninsular, Ibn Saud, like his forebears, consciously modelled himself on the Prophet Muhammad, who fourteen centuries earlier had welded the feuding tribes of the Arabian peninsula into an Islamic "super-tribe", the *umma*, under divine authority. There was, however, a crucial difference. The Arab conquest, like that of Ibn Saud, was the outcome of a movement, part religious, part secular, that could only sustain its inner cohesion by maintaining its outward momentum. The early Islamic state, as suggested earlier, had to expand continuously in order to maintain this momentum, which was only exhausted after a century, when the Arab advance was checked in central France and the Indus valley. The tribes had been inspired by the desire for booty as well as the belief that they were enacting the divine will. As the early conquests proceeded, the distribution of booty was institutionalized through a system of stipends or direct salary payments.[9] In the greatly altered conditions of the early twentieth century, when airplanes and armoured cars overtook the camel as military vehicles, the momentum of the Ikhwan movement promoted by Ibn Saud could not be sustained.

The British, who effectively replaced the Ottomans as Arabia's imperial suzerains, acquiesced in Ibn Saud's conquest of the Muslim holy land. Their client, the Sharif Hussein of Mecca who had launched the Arab revolt against the Ottomans with British help, proved no match for the wily and skilful ruler of Najd. Beyond central and western Arabia, however, the expansion of his movement was blocked to the north by British client states of Transjordan and Iraq, granted, under British auspices, to the Sharif Hussein's sons, the Amirs (later Kings) 'Abdullah and Faisal, and to the south and east by the Yemeni mountains and the British protectorates of South Arabia (later South Yemen, now Yemen), Oman and the Gulf. When the camel-mounted Wahhabi warriors reached British-protected boundaries, they were met with withering fire from the planes and armoured cars of the Royal Air Force and the Transjordanian Frontier Force.

In its initial expansion the Arab conquest had washed over many of the high cultural systems of late antiquity, and in the course of its development it absorbed their learning to which it gave a distinctive Islamic colouring. The process of Islamization was a gradual one: at first the Arab armies kept themselves distinct from the subject populations, whose religions (Judaism and Christianity) they respected. In the course of centuries a majority of the "protected" or subject populations (*ahl al-dhimma*) adopted Islam, by marriage, or conversion. What came to be described as "Islamic civilization" was really a creative synthesis of Graeco-Roman, Hebraic and Iranian cultural traditions made possible by the opening up of a common market in goods, services and ideas extending from the Indus Valley to Spain. The Arabs, under Muhammad's Quraishite tribe, initially provided the military leadership (though they would rapidly be replaced by military leaders from the steppelands of Central Asia), while the "final revelation" of the Quran, understood as the veritable Word of God transmitted in Arabic, guaranteed the hegemony of Arabic in the religious sciences. But in many other cultural areas, the non-Arab peoples were able to assert themselves within the new Arabian imperium: the universalism of Islam, its claim to be the final revelation crowning and superseding, but not replacing, revelations previously vouchsafed to earlier prophets in the monotheistic tradition, allowed for a degree of cultural tolerance unprecedented in pre-Enlightenment times.

The neo-Wahhabi movement launched by Ibn Saud is in many ways similar to the original Islamic movement. As Fred Donner has suggested, the first Islamic state initially founded by Muhammad represented the control by a sedentary commercial elite of townsmen, the Meccan Quraish, over the rest of Arabia's warring tribesmen in order to "recapture" trade that had shifted to new routes. After Muhammad's death, when most of the nomads rebelled against the new Islamic polity, his successors Abu Bakr and 'Umar subdued the tribes by force of arms and redirected their energies outwards into the lands made available by the defeats of the Persian Empire and the Byzantine provinces. The

Arab migrations followed hard on the conquests "because the political and perhaps economic interests of the Islamic ruling elite were best served by a large-scale emigration of tribesmen into the conquered domains. The migrations were the result of state policy, planned in its general outlines by the state and implemented by the state's offer of various incentives to the emigrants" including the institutionalization of plunder through the system of stipends. Just as the Prophet's *hijra* to Medina demonstrated the superiority of settled over nomadic life, so the policy of the early caliphs was designed to encourage the settlement of the previously warring tribes in the newly conquered territories. According to a hadith attributed to the second caliph, ʿUmar (r.634–44), "The sooner one settles, the sooner one receives a stipend."[10]

Unlike the early Islamic polity, the Saudi state was blocked in its outward expansion. Faced by the mechanized and air power of the British, Wahhabism turned in on itself. Religious zealotry was converted into the ideology of a unique political phenomenon: a quasi-totalitarian dynastic state based on the absolute supremacy of a single clan, the Al Saʾud. ʿAziz el-Azmeh has given us a cogent analysis of this transformation. The early Saudi polity consisted of a trade state at the core, a tribute state at the periphery. Like other clans the Al Saʾud made their living out of property (including animal husbandry and agriculture) as well as trade. Their political and geographical expansion was serviced by the extraction of taxes or dues from subject populations through a complicated system of clientage backed by superior military power. An important source of these taxes was the trade of Qasim, in particular the twin cities of Buraida and ʿUnaiza which sat astride the caravan routes between Madina, Basra and Kuwait. ʿUnaiza has been described as the "Paris of Najd", a gorgeous city of mud-brick buildings grown rich on the pearl trade. The British explorer St John Philby particularly admired the city for its religious tolerance. The city merchants paid taxes to the local dynasty, the Rashids, who in turn guaranteed its protection. Under Saudi hegemony, however, ʿUnaiza lost its former political autonomy. Its once fine buildings are now mostly abandoned or in ruins.[11]

As the dominant power in Najd, the Al Sa'ud initially resembled their predecessors the Rashids. Other tribes such as the 'Utaiba, Al Murra, the Mutair, and the 'Aniza (of which Al Sa'ud was a sept) had similar arrangements by which they took an active part in trade and also taxed the artisans and merchants of the towns. The Wahhabi version of Islam, however, provided the Al Sa'ud with the ideological fuel by which the less militant tribes could be subordinated and eliminated politically. To be considered other than *kuffar*, idolators worthy of death, they had to be incorporated into the system dominated by the Saudi clan. Thus the tribes became tributaries to the centre of power. This entailed not only their subjugation to taxation (in kind such as camels) but also their political exclusion. The centralization of taxation under the Saudi state implied the political eradication of the subordinate tribes. "This new political right exclusively exercised by the centre," says al-Azmeh, "derived from the tribal concept of protection – *himaya* – exercised by central authority, in the same way that nomadic tribes had hitherto offered protection in return for taxation."[12] Under the Saudi system nomads, agriculturalists and townspeople became equally subject to Saudi power.

In Arabian history, war has been the primary means by which tribal groups maintained their cohesion and identity, with prowess in war the inevitable theme of tribal epics. It was clearly impossible for the Saudi state simultaneously to detribalize society while maintaining the tribes as units with a tributary status. The agricultural settlement fostered by Ibn Saudi was one way out of this dilemma: the nomads were converted into agriculturalists. The other was outright military supremacy. During the conquest of the *hijaz*, the Muslim holy land, Ibn Saud had great difficulty in restraining his holy warriors. He had to intervene personally to prevent the Ikhwan from slaughtering the official delegation of Egyptian pilgrims bearing the *kiswa*, the black silk covering of the Ka'ba, the cube-shaped temple at the centre of the sanctuary in Mecca. The Ikhwan regarded these, and all other pilgrims, as "idolators". Despite Ibn Saud's efforts, some forty pilgrims were killed. After the conquest of the Hijaz, and embarrassed by Ikhwan raids into

British-defended territory in Iraq, Ibn Saud decided to disband them altogether, incorporating the loyalists among them into the National Guard, after defeating the rebels at the Battle of Sabillah (1929).[13] In suppressing the rebellious Ikhwan, Ibn Saud made sure that he kept the Najdi *'ulama* on his side: on the crucial issue of the right of the Ikhwan to continue the jihad against their enemies, the *'ulama* ruled in 1927 that this was a question left to the Imam (a position Ibn Saud inherited from his father, 'Abd al-Rahman).[14] He legitimized the subjugation of the non-Saudi tribes by imposing the canonical alms tax, the *zakat*, one of the five "pillars" or religious obligations of Islam. According to al-Azmeh, zakat was just one of the many ways in which Wahhabism used the Shari'a law to homogenize society and subject it to the control of the House of Saud, by removing local customary usages and local privileges.[15]

Given the role of Wahhabism as a force for centralization, the terms "feudal" and "medieval" often applied to the Saudi monarchy are somewhat misleading. Saudi absolutism undoubtedly has its feudal aspects. But in its political dimension it seems closer to the absolutism of eighteenth-century France than to the medieval monarchy of, say, pre-Tudor England, where a complex variety of political and religious forces were permitted to flourish within the overarching duopoly of church and monarchy. Ultimately, however, any European analogy must seem inappropriate, because European societies have long ceased to be tribal. Land and property have either been privatized, or are held as public trusts by state or local public authorities.

In modern Arabia the old concept of usufruct, by which property (such as water or grazing rights) tended to be shared out in accordance with complex interlocking arrangements between different pastoral users organized in clans, has been replaced by the tribal absolutism of the Al Sa'ud who effectively own the state. After the suppression of the Ikhwan by Ibn Saud, the formerly Wahhabite polity became the Saudi polity. Two features of Hanbali law, in particular, were used on uphold the family's prerogatives: *ijtihad* and *maslaha* – the right of independent reasoning and public interest. Both have become instruments of modernization in the hands of the ruling clan. Thus the Wahhabi–Saudi alliance clears the ground for economic development, by methods such as "constant social invigilation" by the ubiquitous religious police, the *mutawwi'un*, who enforce observance of prayer times and fasting during Ramadan as well as the exclusion of women from public spaces. Wahhabism cuts two ways: on the one hand it can be used to facilitate modernization, as for example when the late King Faisal used the pretext of *maslaha* to allow insurance on commercial goods. Traditional Islamic teaching forbids insurance. On the other hand the concept of *ijma'*, the consensus of the religious scholars, can be deployed to uphold what are really tribal customs: as in the well-known case of the ban on women drivers. The eminent Shaikh 'Abdullah bin Baz issued a fatwa upholding the ban when, inspired by the sight of female GIs driving US army trucks, a group of educated Saudi women who had foreign driver's licences staged a highly publicized "drive-in" in Riyadh. "Driving by women contradicts the Islamic traditions followed by Saudi citizens," an edict issued by the interior ministry stated. "The *'ulama* have determined that driving degrades and harms the sanctity of women."[16]

The ban on driving is probably the least of the human rights deprivations suffered by Saudi women, who risk death by stoning if convicted of adultery – a punishment more applied in upholding the honour of men than in preserving the "sanctity of women". A ghost-written narrative based on the testimony of a Saudi princess gives a detailed description of the death by flogging and stoning of a women taken in adultery.

> A large crowd had gathered since early morning . . . [J]ust as they were becoming angry with impatience in the hot sun a young woman of about twenty-five years of age was roughly pulled out of a police car . . . [Her] hands were bound. Her head hung low . . . A dirty rag was used to gag her mouth and a black hood was fastened around her head. She was forced to

kneel. A large man, the executioner, flogged the woman upon her back fifty blows. A truck appeared, and rocks and stones were emptied in a large pile . . . [A] group of people, mostly men, rushed towards the stones and began to hurl the rocks at the woman. The guilty one quickly slumped to the ground and her body jerked in all directions . . . [T]he rocks continued to thud against her body for what seemed to be an interminable time. Every so often, the stones would quieten while a doctor would check the woman's pulse. After a period of nearly two hours, the doctor finally pronounced the woman dead and the stoning ceased.[17]

The account cannot be authenticated, for obvious reasons, but it is consistent with other accounts, including both the 1980 docudrama *Death of a Princess*, which caused a major diplomatic row between Britain and the Saudi kingdom, and the secretly filmed execution of a woman shown on BBC *Panorama* in 1996, leading to the collapse of the Saudi-funded BBC Arabic television service. In its 1997 report on Saudi Arabia, Amnesty International produced a substantial dossier of "arrest and detention abuses, secret trials, torture, flogging and amputation, and the abuse of women".[18]

Suspects are invariably arrested without a judicial warrant, held incommunicado beyond any judicial supervision, and detained for lengthy periods without trial . . . Those charged are tried behind closed doors . . . Disregard for the right to fair trial has been a key factor in Saudi Arabia's catalogue of gross human rights violations over the years. Thousands of political and religious activists, including prisoners of conscience, have been arbitrarily deprived of their liberty because of lack of independent and impartial judicial supervision over the arresting and interrogating authorities. The lack of such supervision has allowed the security forces to make torture an institutionalised practice with full impunity.[19]

Foreign workers on whom the kingdom depends for jobs that the former bedouin are too lazy, or insufficiently educated, to do themselves are particularly vulnerable to abuse, since employers can use the judicial system against them. According to a 1996 US Department of State report on Saudi Arabia:

> [T]here have been many reports of workers whose employers have refused to pay several months, or even years, of accumulated salary or other promised benefits ... The labour system abets the exploitation of foreign workers because enforcement of work contracts is difficult and generally favours Saudi employers. Labour cases can take many months to reach a final appellate ruling, during which time the employer can prevent the foreign labourer from leaving the country; alternatively, an employer can delay a case until a worker's funds are exhausted and the worker is forced to return to his home country.[20]

In August 1997 more than one hundred Filipino citizens staged a sit-in at the Philippine Labour Compound in Riyadh to protest at their government's failure to aid their repatriation. According to the Asia-Pacific Mission for Migrant Filipinos (APMMF) there were approximately five hundred stranded Filipinos in Riyadh alone.

> Most of them had grievances lodged at the Saudi Court against the employers or sponsors for contract violations such as non-payment of wages, long hours of work, poor working and living conditions, sexual and physical abuses. Others became stranded after they were forsaken by their sponsors and "run away" [sic] from their employers.[21]

Amnesty International states that the Saudi criminal justice system "is designed to cater primarily for the might of the state with total disregard for the individuals' right to fair trial".[22] But the state, as al-Azmeh argues, is really the "family":

Wahhabite fundamentalism puts forward a model whose task
is to subject local societies with their customs, authorities,
devotions and other particularities to a general process of
acculturation which prepares them for membership in the
commonwealth whose linchpin and exclusive raison d'être is
the absolute dominance of the House of Saud.[23]

There are no pure models of development. To state that the evolution of Saudi Arabia has been "distorted" by the presence of oil
would imply that there is some ideal–typical normative model of
development against which all others must be measured.
Nevertheless the discovery of the world's largest petroleum
deposits, one quarter of its proven reserves, within about a decade
of the Saudi conquests had incalculable consequences, not only
for the country, but for the rest of the Muslim world. In most
countries the process of modernization has had to be accompanied
by the intellectual adjustments necessary to sustain a modern economy. The most significant of these adjustments has been the
privatization of religion, its removal from the sphere of social
action into the realm of private, spiritual thoughts and experience.
Private beliefs, however eclectic or out of line with public assumptions, need not affect the workings of modern societies so long as
they remain private. Modern technology depends on an open-ended
epistemology based on the "institutionalization of doubt" – the
pragmatism of trial-by-error in which nothing is taken for granted,
least of all the existence of supernatural forces capable of influencing
or intervening in natural processes.

A partial exception to this picture is the United States where,
uniquely amongst industrialized societies, an artificial system of
Church–State separation has encouraged anti-modern ideas such
as "scientific creationism" and homophobia to survive and even
to flourish in protected enclaves insulated from the operations of
the "real" world. But the only reason ideas such as "six-day creationism" are able to persist in America is that they have a limited
effect on public action. Fundamentalist establishments such as
the Institute of Creation Research near San Diego are expensive

luxuries paid for by deluded philanthropists: they may have a negative impact on the teaching of science in schools, but by and large they do not obstruct research into space technology, computer software or superconductors. Where religious ideas do impact on public policy, as in the opposition to abortion and the equal rights amendment for women (ERA), gay marriages, or alcohol consumption or, from the liberal end of the spectrum, in favour of full civil rights for ethnic minorities, religion has to muster its forces democratically, to participate in public debate. The very idea of having to argue a religious case democratically is a mark of secularization, a recognition that post-Enlightenment pluralism has come to stay. The unacknowledged truth behind the "wall of separation" between church and state constructed by the Founding Fathers is that American society is insulated from religion, with its potential for ideological absolutism and destructive intolerance.

Thanks to the geological accident of oil (which the Al Sa'ud regard as a divine gift) Saudi Arabia has been able to create the outer shell of modernity – four-lane highways, motor vehicles, air-conditioned supermarkets, high-rise buildings, state-of-the-art banks and the latest design in airports – without undergoing the spiritual changes – the epistemological revolution, the institutionalization of doubt – that made modernity possible. To some degree this applies to other countries outside the European matrix that gave birth to the Enlightenment and the scientific revolution: Korea, Japan, and now China, for example, have seen remarkable spiritual movements, from the Unification Church (the Moonies) and the Japanese New Religious Movements with their female prophets, to the Falun Gong sect in China, now suffering persecution as part of the "war against terrorism". All these movements, however, are syncretic, reflecting the diversity of the influences that have come to bear on their societies. Their very existence is proof of religious pluralism, one of the hallmarks of modernity. They do not enjoy official sanction. By and large they do not affect the business of government although, as in China, they may challenge the governing party's ideological monopoly. In Saudi Arabia,

Wahhabism not only enjoys official sanction: it functions as both the state religion and the ideology used to legitimize the tribal absolutism of the Al Sa'ud. "Wahhabism remains pervasive not only in the educational system, the media, and public discourse in general, not to speak of its spectacular performances in the shape of the public punishment of errants and criminals, much reminiscent of the Roman circus. Indeed the Saudi–Wahhabite alliance reminds one of one principle of Roman statecraft, *panis et circenses.*"[24]

Public worship by non-Muslims is forbidden, in accordance with an alleged hadith of the Prophet Muhammad to the effect that there can be no two religions in Arabia. The *'ulama* enjoy a privileged position in Saudi society. Some of their leaders, the Al al-Shaikh, who claim descent from Muhammad ibn 'Abd al-Wahhab, are connected to the Al Sa'ud by marriage. Though generally loyal, the *'ulama* have often challenged (*sotto voce*) both the absolutism of the Al Sa'ud and their modernizing agenda. They are also primarily responsible for the kingdom's intellectual backwardness, for the cultural schizophrenia it suffers in its relationship with modernity.

The former chief mufti, Shaikh 'Abdullah bin Baz (who died in 1999) was a hugely influential figure in the kingdom. In 1982 he won recognition as the recipient of the King Faisal Award for international services to Islam. The same year he published a book entitled *Jarayan al-shams wa'l qamar wa-sukun al-ard* (The Motion of the Sun and Moon, and the Stationarity of the Earth) which held to the pre-Copernican, geocentric cosmology according to which the earth is the centre of the universe and the sun moves around it. The cosmology is consistent with Quranic references to the "seven heavens" which modern scholars would see as referring to the Ptolemaic cosmology that held sway before the discoveries of Kepler, Copernicus and Galileo. Bin Baz's position has incorrectly been described as stating that the "earth is flat". He was, however, on record as stating that the 1969 moon landing was a television fake (a view he shared with some Americans). In an earlier article the venerable shaikh had threatened all who challenged his pre-Copernican views with a fatwa of *takfir*, pronouncing them infidels. He did not repeat this fatwa in his 1982 book, which was just as well, as it would have anathematized Prince Sultan bin Salman bin 'Abd al-'Aziz, the son of the mayor of Riyadh and grandson of the kingdom's founder. Prince Sultan is the Muslim world's only officially certified astronaut. "Carried aloft in NASA's space shuttle, [he] could certainly have commented on the Shaikh's thesis if he had not been preoccupied with the urgent task of determining the direction of Qibla [Mecca] for his prayers."[25]

The cultural schizophrenia from which Saudi Arabia suffers is masked to some degree by censorship at home and the privileges enjoyed by the ruling clan who, like eighteenth-century European aristocrats, are permitted freedoms denied to the kingdom's other subjects. At home, "academic freedom is non-existent, with permanent blanket-bans imposed on such topics as biological evolution, Freudian psychology, Marxist economics, Western music and Western philosophy. Some professors have testified that government and religious informers monitor their performance in the classroom."[26] Members of the ruling clan and some of the wealthier families, however, may compensate for these deficiencies by studying abroad. Strict censorship applies to the government-owned media. The "censors work hard to remove any unwelcome references to politics, criticisms of Islam, references to religions other than Islam, mention of pork or pigs, references to any alcoholic beverages, and all sexual material in songs and other foreign broadcasts".[27] Attempts by the *'ulama* to ban satellite dishes, however, have not been successful. Although the government has banned the import, sale and installation of such equipment since 1994, dishes are still used and people subscribe to satellite decoding services. Even the powerful *mutawwi'in* (religious police) cannot prevent the wealthier and more privileged members of Saudi society from having satellite dishes, importing forbidden videos, or enjoying bootlegged liquor. Modern technology allows cultural schizophrenia to penetrate not just the home, but the individual psyche as well.

The regime not only controls the domestic media: through its ownership of Arabic-language media based abroad it operates a strategic defence against outside scrutiny. Two major Arabic-language newspapers based in London, *al-Hayat* and *al-Sharq al-Awsat*, are Saudi-owned, as are Orbit Television, the Arab Media Corporation and the Saudi Research and Marketing Company which publishes more than fifteen dailies, weeklies and monthlies. According to Simons, the kingdom may "dominate as much as 95 per cent of the Arabic language newspapers, magazines and radio and television stations throughout the Arab countries and beyond". Domination can be direct, as when the family maintains total ownership, or indirect, "when Saudi money or intimidation guarantees support for the Saudi regime".[28] Influence and censorship, however, have their limits in a global culture dominated by television. Al-Jazeera television, the station based in Qatar, is freely available throughout Saudi Arabia and able to broadcast Osama bin Laden's videotapes attacking the Saudi regime and its American supporters. The attack on the World Trade Center was headline news in every publication. Publicly applauded by some Palestinians, the images of the planes hitting the Twin Towers had a special kind of impact in Saudi homes. For many Saudis of the younger generation, Osama bin Laden was already a hero. Exceptionally tall, like Ibn Saud (an important asset in a tribal society when physical prowess still lingers in the social memory), he had conveyed all the vigour and dignity that the ageing monarch, the obese and semi-invalid Fahd, lacked. In his videotapes, bin Laden conveyed the calm serenity of the Prophet, the Chosen One of God whom even the pagans of Mecca used to refer to as "al-Amin" (the Trusted One). Like the Prophet he had given up the comforts of a worldly, prosperous life in order to fight for social justice against the enemies of God. No Saudi who watched the attack on America could doubt that the "human cruise missiles" were also aimed at its protégé, the House of Saud.

Oil is not just Saudi Arabia's primary national resource: it is first and foremost private, family property. The bulk of the revenue is paid to the king before it is registered as national income. The royal family decides on its needs, and government officials are obliged to act accordingly. The 6,000-odd princes and princesses linked to the Al Sa'ud are entitled to approximately $20,000 a month each in addition to the "working" salaries they may receive as government officials or their commissions from business deals. With every royal child or princess considered a "prince", an "ordinary" Saudi prince with two wives and ten children could receive around $260,000 per month in addition to any official or commercial salary. In 1996 a Saudi economist estimated that the royal family was costing the state at least $4 billion a year.[29] The Saudi system is widely described as "corrupt", but the word is hardly appropriate seeing that tribal ownership of the country's oil wealth is consistent with the early Islamic tradition of stipends maintained out of booty and of inheritance laws that explicitly favour the transmission of wealth to one's kin. "Corruption" implies the transgression of social or legal norms. Such corruption undoubtedly exists as it does in most other governmental systems. But the use of the word "corruption" to describe the Saudi system more comprehensively would imply that the system as a whole is susceptible to "reform", that it could endure or even flourish if only the Saudis would "clean up their act". This is not just offensive to the Al Sa'ud, who see themselves as legitimate owners (as well as divinely instituted guardians) of the country's wealth; it is, structurally speaking, naïve. The Saudi system of plunder and patronage is so embedded into the country's political, social and economic cultures that to reform it would be to destroy the kingdom altogether.

A clear example is the system of *kafala*, sponsorship, which al-Azmeh sees as tantamount to the extraction of money (*khuwwa*) under the old nomadic system of plunder. Under Saudi law a non-Saudi cannot initiate or fully own a business in Saudi Arabia without a *kafil*, or sponsor. Sa'd al-din Ibrahim met one such sponsor, Abu Hamad, an illiterate bedu, who amused himself by acting as the driver for the head of a UN mission concerned with education. Abu Hamad shrugged off suggestions that he should

attend literacy classes – pointing out with satisfaction that he
earned more than his client, a man with a PhD and at least twenty
years of continuous formal education. Abu Hamad's salary as a
driver was a minute proportion of the money he earned as a *kafil*.
He drove mainly for pleasure: it was the only skill he possessed.
The bulk of his earnings were derived from two groceries, a toy
shop, a garage, a barbershop and a tailor's. He was neither able nor
willing to learn any of the skills involved in these enterprises. He
hired others to do the work – or, more probably, others approached
him to be their *kafil*. As a *kafil* he was the partner to, or full-time
employer of "Egyptians, Palestinians, Syrians, Yemenis and
Pakistanis. These and other nationals put up the capital, skills and
labour. He gives them the only legal coverage by lending his finger-
print (later his signature) and contractual arrangements to obtain
licensing." In return Abu Hamad, "a very pious and fair man",
obtains 50 per cent of the profit. Other, more greedy *kafils* may
appropriate as much as 80 per cent of the profit in exchange for the
same legal cover.[30]

The Abu Hamads, of course, are near the bottom of the system
of institutionalized plunder that governs in Saudi Arabia. Between
the Abu Hamads and the Al Sa'ud come what Ibrahim calls the
"lumpen capitalists", a class of entrepreneurs who are "neither
fruitfully productive, nor completely parasitic, but something in
between". Unlike his Western counterpart, the Saudi entrepreneur
does not take any risk with his capital: indeed he may start without
any capital at all. Ibrahim synthesizes his research into "lumpen
capitalists" with a detailed description of an ideal–typical figure he
calls 'Abdullah.

A member of one of the tribes of central Najd, 'Abdullah receives
his college education in Egypt before obtaining a degree in social
sciences at one of the West Coast universities in the US. Returning
to Saudi Arabia with an MA in planning and public administration, he presides over a segment of the kingdom's Five Year Plan
before resigning, at thirty-four, to start his own company. This
undertaking, a "conglomerate" from the start, deals with a multiplicity of activities: import–export, feasibility studies for private

and public institutions, consulting in engineering, management and social services delivery systems, road construction, public buildings and housing, power and water stations; hotels, hospitals and supermarkets. In less than five years "'Abdullah" and his partners are all multi-millionaires. The "miracle" of this phenomenal "success", says Ibrahim, is all the more startling since the "conglomerate" began with the equivalent of $50,000 as capital, a four-room villa as a temporary headquarters, a telephone, a telex hook-up, and two typists with 'Abdullah as the only full-time member out of five partners. Ibrahim's conclusion is a classic description of cultural schizophrenia:

> The story of 'Abdullah is that of several thousand Saudis who are seen at home in flying white robes, quite vigilant about the Kingdom's traditions and Islamic rituals. They are the same jet-setters in Pierre Cardin business suits making multi-million-dollar deals in Paris, London and New York or spending hundreds of thousands in gambling casinos in Monaco and Las Vegas. The 'secret' of success for the new Saudi entrepreneurs is the accident of geology (oil), education, government service and the economic boom of the 1970s. Since there is no risk, the only thing that differentiates one entrepreneur from another is his ability to assemble a "group" as partners in a private company. The ideal group consists of individuals who are blood relatives or close friends but who are strategically located in Saudi social and governmental structures. Because the state is the number one spender, it follows that the most profitable business must be transacted with the government. It helps if one or more of the partners is in the government, and in on the planning of the next five years' projects. They would have valuable and advance information as well as access to former technocratic colleagues or even former subordinates who by that time would be making the decisions. It is also imperative for the group to have at least one high-ranking connection for political coverage in times of crisis. Most

successful groups have a link with a member of the royal
family.[31]

Of the royal family's origins enough has been said. Their
future is much less certain. For more than six decades the Al
Sa'ud have shown an impressive instinct for survival. Despite the
tensions that will always exist between the siblings of multiple
marriages – Ibn Saud is recorded as having sired 45 sons by at
least 22 different women, with an unrecorded number of daugh-
ters – the family has refrained from public in-fighting. Disputes
between the brothers are for the most part settled behind closed
doors. In line with tribal custom, the succession (following the
death of Ibn Saud in 1953) passed down the line of his sons in
approximate order of seniority. Ibn Saud's eldest living son Saud
inherited the throne in accordance with his father's wishes. An
ineffectual personality and profligate spender, he was deposed
after eleven years by an *ad hoc* council of princes in favour of his
brother Faisal, a much more impressive leader. Faisal, who had
distinguished himself in his father's time as the conqueror of the
Asir province bordering Yemen, helped to widen the appeal of
Wahhabism within the emerging Islamist movement by giving
refuge – and university jobs – to leading members of the Muslim
Brotherhood driven into exile by the Nasserist crackdown in
Egypt. A staunch opponent of Arab nationalism, Faisal supported the royalist forces in Yemen against the Egyptian-backed
republican government that overthrew the monarchy in 1962.
Nasser's disastrous engagement in Yemen depleted and demoral-
ized his army, contributing to Egypt's catastrophic defeat by
Israel in the 1967 Six Day War. Though generally regarded as a
man of intelligence and personal integrity, with relatively progressive views on such delicate topics as the education of women
(he had formally abolished slavery in 1962, when acting as
Crown Prince and prime minister), Faisal understood that the
kingdom's stability depended on maintaining family solidarity.
He was obsessively anti-communist, and his opposition to Israel,
though never translated into policy, transgressed the line separating

anti-Zionism (opposition to Jewish settlement in Palestine) from anti-Semitism (hostility to Jews as people and to everything Jewish). Under Faisal's rule the volume of annual oil revenues increased by a factor of more than 50, from about half a billion dollars in 1964 to nearly $28 billion in 1974. Faisal was extremely generous to members of the family and selected favourites. According to the Palestinian writer Said Aburish, far from taking control of the royal purse as is sometimes claimed, Faisal merely compensated friends and family in "more subtle ways" than his predecessors, by scheduling land as *aradi amariyya* (princely land) and parcelling it out among friends. The well-known former oil minister Shaikh Ahmad Zaki Yamani told his biographer that he owned more than $300 millions' worth of land given him by the King.[32] In March 1975 Faisal was assassinated by his nephew, Faisal ibn Musaid ibn 'Abd al-'Aziz, a former student at Berkeley and the University of Colorado at Boulder who in 1970 had been arrested for conspiring to sell the drug LSD and prevented from leaving the kingdom. Ten years earlier Faisal's elder brother Khalid had been shot dead by the police after leading a pro-Wahhabi demonstration against the introduction of television. The mother of both princes had been a member of the Rashid clan overthrown by Ibn Saud in his early campaigns: perhaps some inherited rage at the patriarchal custom of marrying the women of defeated rivals may have played its part in the rebellions of both princes.

Within three hours of Faisal's assassination the senior princes obtained *'ulama* approval for the succession of Khalid, who had been nominated Crown Prince in 1965, passing over his elder brother Muhammad. The latter, though the third surviving son of Ibn Saud, had been passed over by the consensus of senior princes because of his fierce temper, which was periodically exacerbated by bouts of heavy drinking. The real power under the gentle, sickly Khalid, however, was exercised by the Crown Prince, now King, Fahd (b.1921). Though renowned for massive losses sustained at the gaming tables in London and on the French Riviera, Fahd was considered effective and decisive. His elevation to the key role of

Crown Prince and successor to the monarch coincided with the rise of his uterine brothers – Sultan (b.1927), 'Abd al-Rahman (b.1931), Turki (b.1933), Naif (b.1934), Salman (b.1936) and Ahmad (b.1940). This group of brothers (known as the Sudairi Seven or Al Fahd) are the sons of Hassa al-Sudairi, Ibn Saud's favourite wife to whom he was twice married. According to one reckoning, the Sudairis and their sons occupy some 63 government posts, notably the ministries of defence (Sultan), interior (Naif) and the governorship of Riyadh (Salman). The sons of Faisal, though popular, were left out of the loop. The Foreign Minister, Prince Saud ibn Faisal, reportedly told the late King Hussein of Jordan that he was "no more than an office boy".[33] The family balance, however, required that the next in line of succession, 'Abdullah (b.1923), be nominated Crown Prince as next in seniority. 'Abdullah commands the National Guard into which many of the former Ikhwan fighters were integrated. If and when he succeeds to his ailing brother's throne, a crucial test for the dynasty's stability will be the choice of his successor as Crown Prince. Next in seniority would be the relatively unknown Bandar (b.1923), but it seems unlikely that the Sudairi clan would give up its power to a nonentity when its younger members are still in their relatively vigorous sixties. The youngest of the sons of Ibn Saud, Hamoud (b.1947) is still comparatively youthful. Theoretically the shift of power to the third generation, namely the grandsons of Ibn Saud, could be deferred until the mid-2020s.

Though very little about the politics within the ruling family reaches the Western press, the jostling for power may already be under way. The ailing King Fahd is well known for his indulgence towards his children. His sixth son, Muhammad, is reported to have received $1.3 billion in commissions from contracts with the Philips electrical company worth $6.7 billion – a figure inflated to five times the consultants' estimates in order to accommodate commissions from both Philips and its subcontractors. Fahd is known to be exceptionally fond of his 23-year-old son 'Abd al-'Aziz, who has been granted ministerial status along with other privileges. A soothsayer reportedly predicted that 'Abd al-'Aziz will die in his son's absence: the young man is kept in constant attendance at his father's side.[34]

The future of the dynasty is problematic, to put it mildly. The only real certainty remains, for the foreseeable future, the constant and increasing demand for cheap Saudi oil. If oil is the lifeblood of the industrial economies of Japan and the West, Saudi Arabia is the heart (or, more precisely, the valve of the Middle Eastern heart) that keeps it pumping. Saudi Arabia contains 263.5 billion barrels of proven oil reserves and up to ten thousand million barrels of ultimately recoverable oil. This is more than a quarter of the world total.[35] Four of Saudi Arabia's neighbours – Iran, Iraq, Kuwait and the United Arab Emirates – each boast a total of about 10 per cent so, added together, the Middle East oil reserves amount to between 60 and 65 per cent of the world total. In addition the kingdom's proven gas reserves are estimated at 204.5 trillion cubic feet, ranking it fifth in the world (after Russia, Iran, Qatar and the United Arab Emirates).[36] The cost of extracting Middle East oil is low: because the crude is of high quality and reasonably near the surface, it costs barely a dollar per barrel to lift out of the ground.[37] Recent efforts to diversify the economy have barely reduced the kingdom's dependency on oil. Massive investment in irrigation and agriculture has enabled the kingdom to become the world's sixth largest exporter of grain, but the costs are formidable. In 1989, Saudi farmers were being paid $533 per ton to produce wheat available on the world market for $120. The expansion of Saudi Arabia's agriculture is limited by the scarcity of suitable land (about 2 per cent of the total area) and water. Already the nonrenewable aquifers containing fossil waters laid down millions of years ago are becoming depleted at an alarming rate.

Oil and oil-related products still account for about 90 per cent of the kingdom's foreign currency earnings. Although the industry has been "indigenized" since 1975 when the American ownership in Aramco (once the largest single US investment in any foreign country) passed to Saudi Arabia, the industry is highly mechanized and automated, employing a relatively small number of

people. Before the Saudi takeover of Aramco fewer than 16,000
Saudis were employed in the industry, the vast majority of them in
the lower, unskilled and semi-skilled jobs, rather than at the man-
agerial and technical levels. Writing in 1982, Ibrahim remarked
that most of the high-level jobs were performed by "expats",
who made up as much as 43 per cent of the workforce. "In other
words, the social organisation of the oil industry in Saudi Arabia
has kept the natives, by and large, outside its intricate operating
'secrets' or 'know-how'. If this was logically understandable in
the 1930s when oil was first drilled, it is quite odd and socially
alienating that this remains the case fifty years later."[38] Since the
1970s the situation has changed to some degree, with the
"Saudiization" of the extraction industry and increasing investment by the government in oil-related "downstream" industries
such as refineries and petrochemical plants. Through Saudi-
Aramco the country has acquired substantial refining interests in
petroleum-importing countries: for example under a joint venture
with Texaco signed in 1988, the national oil company gained
access to a refining and distribution network spanning twenty-six
states in the southern and eastern United States; in 1991 it
acquired a 35 per cent stake in South Korea's largest oil refining
company, Ssangyong Oil.[39]

Controlling the kingdom's oil wealth is both the prerogative and
the *raison d'être* of the House of Saud. As a tribal elite, its members
have educated themselves in the intricacies of the world market and
developed a shrewd understanding of their position in the world.
Though lacking the sophistication to be found in the historically
more advanced cultures of the region such as Iran and Egypt, they
have shown themselves to be considerably more adaptable and
resilient than, say, the Pahlavi family that ruled in Iran from 1923
to 1979. Though sometimes accused of arrogance, they are less elit-
ist and more in touch with different strands of popular opinion
than the Pahlavi regime was during the latter years of its power.
The principle of *shura* (consultation) does not approach the relatively open democracy which now exists in Iran, where the Shi'ite
clergy, for all their conservatism, have had to accept the reality of

a parliament elected by universal adult suffrage (from an approved list of candidates) which will challenge and contest the rulings of the Guardianship Council dominated by senior members of the clergy. But consultation does exist in Saudi Arabia, between the princes and the *'ulama*; and the *diwans* held on a regular basis by senior princes and ministers do, in theory at least, provide citizens with the opportunity to meet their rulers and put forward their complaints.

The Saudi "oiligarchy" (sic) legitimizes itself by reference to the formula that "God's Book and the Sunna of his Prophet" are the Constitution. The formula is somewhat ambiguous. On the one hand it permits the government to rule without the formal agreement of organized political opinion, provided Islamic legitimacy is found for its actions. This is not particularly restricting, since the Quran and the Sunna are both open to a wide variety of interpretations. Generally speaking, it means that the princes must carry the *'ulama*, the qualified religious scholars, with them, or at least take note of their opinions. The religious establishment, though weak in relation to the monarchy, cannot be wholly ignored or brushed aside. For important decisions the government must obtain *fatawa* (legal rulings) to show that they are governing in accordance with Islamic law. The downside of this formula, from the Saudi point of view, is that in the absence of open and institutionalized democracy, opposition is most effective when it takes on a religious colouring. Although, as in most Sunni countries, a majority of the *'ulama* tend to go with the flow of power, since the dangers of anarchy are considered to be worse than those of tyranny, a governmental system that claims Islamic legitimacy without specifying the formal terms of that legitimacy (such as one finds, for example, in the 1979 Islamic Constitution of Iran) will always be more vulnerable to religious than to secular opposition.

As the world's largest oil producer, Saudi Arabia is thoroughly integrated into the world's industrial economies. Outside special interest groups such as Arab or Palestinian nationalists who would like to see its immense wealth more equitably distributed, or used as a "weapon" against Israel, the technocrats who control the oil industry under the aegis of the Al Sa'ud have generally been respected for their shrewdness and sagacity in controlling such a strategically sensitive commodity. Because of the industrialized world's dependence on oil the price has a direct impact on the prosperity, not just of exporters and importers, but of the whole of the global economy. A low price helps to promote economic growth by providing cheap energy for importers. Exporters, however, are slow to benefit, since the profits they have for investment in their own economies will also be low. A high price may benefit producers in the short term, but not in the longer term, because a higher price invariably leads to a reduction in demand. High prices contribute to inflation, slow economic growth and a large trade deficit for oil importers. Low prices, however, create lower rates of "energy intensity" – measured in terms of energy use per dollar of gross domestic product (GNP) – because the financial incentives for investment in energy conservation are reduced.[40] The United States is "by far the most energy-profligate nation on the planet".[41] With less than 5 per cent of the world's population, it consumes 65 per cent of its energy. It currently imports about 11 million barrels of oil per day, around one seventh of the world's total production,[42] most of which comes from the Middle Eastern oilfields. Although this figure could be reduced to 5 or 6 million barrels per day by serious conservation measures, there is, in contrast to Europe, a remarkable absence of political will to curb this profligacy. Within days of taking office, President George W. Bush – whose campaign received more than a million dollars from Esso, an oil company that refuses to invest in renewables and actively campaigns against international measures to curb global warming – withdrew from the Kyoto protocols, the flawed, but so far the only, international mechanism for the reduction of greenhouse gases. Large sections of the American public are in denial about the human causes of climate change. They want cheap oil for their poorly insulated homes and offices which rely on inefficient central-heating systems in winter and air-conditioning in summer, not to mention cheap air travel and the gas-guzzling sports utility vehicles (SUVs) that crowd their freeways. British cars now average 35 miles per gallon of petrol consumed; US cars average 20 miles per gallon while four-wheel-drive SUV monsters average a scandalous 9 miles per gallon. While some Washington officials may be aware that the nation's oil dependency makes it vulnerable to political and economic forces outside its control, there are not many votes in energy conservation measures. A recent proposal by the National Academy of Sciences for increases in petrol tax along European lines was dismissed by a senator from Virginia as "just flat ignorant" – a phrase that accurately reflects the views of the current administration.

While neither Saudi Arabia nor its leading customer, the United States, want oil prices to be "too low" or "too high",[43] establishing the boundaries between these parameters has been a complex process of trial and error, not least because of the vagaries of international politics.

For most of the century after the commercialization of oil (1860–1960), prices remained steady at between $1 and $2 per barrel. These very low prices, which were restored after the disruption of the Second World War, contributed substantially to the post-war recovery of Europe and Japan both of which, unlike the United States, had to depend almost wholly on imported supplies from the Middle East. Oil replaced coal as the major energy source for industry, transport, commerce and households. Between 1960 and 1972, world consumption increased by 150 per cent, or 7 per cent per year. The Arab–Israeli war of 1973, when Saudi Arabia and its partners in the petroleum exporters' organization OPEC drastically cut production in order to put pressure on Israel and the United States, led to a dramatic increase in prices, plunging the Western world into a major economic recession. In response to the OPEC cartel's stranglehold on supplies, the US Secretary of State Henry Kissinger spearheaded efforts to create an International Energy Agency to coordinate efforts by consumer countries to store substantial amounts of oil as a precaution against future shortages. The US strategic petroleum reserve was established by President Gerald Ford in 1975.

Further disruption of supplies resulted from the Iranian revolution of 1978–9 and the war that followed between Iran and Iraq
(1980–88), during which prices temporarily reached more than
$40 per barrel, causing a fall in demand as new, more expensive,
sources of oil were developed. Aware of the danger that the Iranian
revolution might spread to the oil-rich Eastern Province, which
has a substantial Shi'ite population, the Saudis sought to improve
their relations with the West, and particularly the United States.
With US support they backed Saddam Hussein against the ayatollahs, while using their dominance in OPEC to increase output. The
strategy not only stabilized prices, it rewarded the Saudis by giving
them a larger share of the world market. They pursued the same
strategy when, enraged by the Emirate's refusal to raise the price of
oil and to help fund Iraq's postwar recovery, Saddam Hussein
invaded Kuwait in 1990. The Saudis made up for the loss of Iraqi
and Kuwaiti outputs – which pushed the price of oil up to $30 a
barrel – by raising production, helping to keep prices within the
range of $15–$20 per barrel.

The price stability, however, was not to last: a combination of
factors – the economic crisis in Asia, unusually warm weather in
America and Europe, United Nations authorization for the resump-
tion of Iraqi oil exports frozen since the Gulf War, as well as
OPEC's unwise decision, initiated by Saudi Arabia, to increase production – came together late in 1997 to create a glut on the market,
driving prices down to an average of $13 per barrel, levels not seen
since the first oil shock of 1973. The drop was rapidly followed by
a surge in prices, prompting further increases in output. Aware that
high prices over a long period of time would be harmful, the Saudis
and other OPEC members have engineered a mechanism for sta-
bilising prices within a band or "basket" ranging between $28 and
$22 per barrel: if the price goes above $28 for twenty consecutive
trading days, OPEC production is automatically increased by half
a million barrels per day; if it falls below $22 for ten consecutive
days, production will decrease by the same amount. If the new
system works, forcing oil prices to reduce their oscillations by
means of a "snake-in-the-tunnel" mechanism similar to the means

by which the European Monetary System (EMS) controlled fluctuations in the old pre-Euro currency exchange rates, the Saudis will be seen as significant contributors to world economic stability. The "natural" or rhythmic oscillations of business cycles with the vast implications these have for jobs, markets and welfare in the industrialized and developing world are difficult enough to manage without violent oil price fluctuations. As the leading custodians of this most volatile natural resource, the Saudis have a vital interest in the economic stability of the West.[44]

The interdependence of the Saudi Arabian economy with those of the West, and particularly with that of the United States, is underpinned strategically and financially by military power. According to one, highly critical estimate by the Cato Institute, America "wastes" between $30 billion and $60 billion a year on safeguarding Middle Eastern oil supplies even though its oil imports during the 1990s averaged only $10 billion a year.[45] The lion's share of this spending goes on defending the oilfields of the Gulf, most of which lie in Saudi Arabia. Whether the American government or its British counterpart really "wastes" all this money, however, is a moot point. The costs of defending Saudi Arabia from its enemies have largely been borne by the Saudis themselves. They have poured their vast petrodollar surpluses into the pockets of American and British arms manufacturers, enabling the latter to fund the research and development necessary to create new generations of weapons for future sales to the region. Thus the mutual dependency generated by oil is reinforced by arms dependency: put very crudely, the Western governments need Saudi and other Gulf money to develop weapons they sell to the Saudis and other Gulf states in order to support their own arms industries. The issue is complicated, however, both by American military support for Israel, which amounts to some $3 billion per year, and by opposition on the part of Israel's friends in the United States to the supplying of arms to Arab countries that could be used against the Jewish state.

Two examples should suffice to demonstrate the complexity of this issue. In 1976, when America had already replaced Britain as

Saudi Arabia's main arms supplier, an order for 2,000 Sidewinder air-to-air missiles was reduced to 850 under Jewish pressure on Congress, while an order of 1,500 Maverick air-to-surface missiles was reduced to 1,000. An editorial in *Near East Report*, the newsletter of AIPAC, the powerful American–Israel Public Affairs Committee lobbying organization, commented that "the Arabs" already had a three-to-one advantage over Israel.[46] The second, even more complicated, example involved what might be called the "electronic castration" of the 1982 airborne warning and control system (AWACS) deal, worth $8.5 billion, the largest single armaments sale in US history. The deal, signed by the Reagan administration, went through after much opposition. It has subsequently been suggested that the AWACS software "was configured to reduce the effectiveness of the Saudi system against the type of US-manufactured jet fighters used by the Israeli air force." Additionally, the system was designed to be heavily dependent on the US. It contained a "digital look down link" allowing the US military to collect electronic intelligence gathered by the AWACS planes nominally under Saudi control. This enabled US F-15 fighters stationed offshore to act as instant reinforcements to the sixty F-15s sold to Saudi Arabia with the approval of President Jimmy Carter in 1978. The AWACS deal, in effect, made Saudi Arabia the US's biggest aircraft carrier fleet in the region. According to Anthony Cordesman, a specialist in air strategy:

[E]ach main Saudi air base had the basic support equipment for 70 US F-15 fighters in addition to supplies for its own F-15s. The package meant that Saudi Arabia would have all the necessary basing, service facilities, refuelling capability, parts and key munitions in place to accept over-the-horizon reinforcement from USAF F-15 fighters. No conceivable improvement in US airlift or USAF rapid deployment and "bare basing" capability could come close to giving the US this rapid and effective reinforcement capability . . . The facilities that would become part of the Saudi system would also help to strengthen US ability to deploy forces from the eastern Mediterranean and project them as far east as Pakistan . . . No conceivable build-up of US strategic mobility, or of US staging bases in Egypt, Turkey, Oman, Somalia, or Kenya, could act as a substitute for such facilities in Saudi Arabia.[47]

Strategic considerations may have determined these massive arms sales, but so did commercial interests, since Western arms suppliers, notably Britain and the United States, sold the Saudis weapons systems they knew to be inappropriate or too sophisticated for a wealthy, but culturally undeveloped country. Steve Tipping, an arms dealer and former associate of Mark Thatcher, son of the British prime minister, put it with offensive bluntness: "You can make the silly rag-headed buggers buy anything."[48] In a society where personal relationships count for more than formal office-holding, in the mid-1980s the junior Thatcher was able to exploit his mother's status to act as middleman in the al-Yamamah deal, a series of defence contracts worth some £10 billion and made possible by the blocking of US arms sales to Saudi Arabia by Congress. The ethics were hotly debated in Britain – as was the appropriateness of Mark Thatcher's reported £12 million commission. In terms of the British national interest, however, the logic was inescapable: one of the al-Yamamah contracts, worth £5 billion, for the sale of forty-eight Tornado aircraft reportedly saved 19,000 jobs at the British Aerospace plant in Warton, Lancashire. Given the size of the contracts, the largest arms deal in British history, the benefits extended far beyond British Aerospace.

American military collaboration with Saudi Arabia extended beyond mutual security interests in the region. Under the Reagan administration the Saudis acted as a conduit for the US-backed insurgencies in Nicaragua and Angola. The Saudi interest in the arms trade was served in other ways. Apart from the commissions received by the numerous intermediaries, such as Adnan Khashoggi, son of Ibn Saud's doctor and an intimate of the royal

family, military patronage offered a strategy for the integration of
the nomads, always a potentially disruptive element in Saudi society. As Ibrahim notes, few of the original nomads have opted for
the sedentary life; but under modern conditions, the nomadic life
has changed fundamentally. The camel is now an object of leisure
"converted from a means of survival to a luxury sport". "The tent,
the camel, the sheep, the horse and the sword are still there. But
cascading over them are the truck, the radio and the machine gun."
Now blessed with trucks, the bedouin can move much more rapidly from place to place than they did in the past. The herd still
remains their major economic base: but the milk, the meat and the
camel-hair they obtain for their tents is supplemented with cash
obtained from working in the oilfields or the armed services. Most
of the tribesmen, according to Ibrahim, would like their sons to
enter the armed forces, preferably as airforce pilots.

> Commanding this and people appeals to them . . . If courage,
> chivalry and constant moving are part of the Bedouins' nor-
> mative system, then commanding an airforce supersonic
> fighter seems to come very close. Commanding a tank, an
> armoured vehicle or a truck still reflects the same normative
> system. Little wonder, therefore, that most of the Bedouins
> who opted for modern occupations ended up in the Saudi
> Army, the National Guard or as Truck Drivers. In this sense
> [they] may have avoided the sharp dichotomous choices
> which may otherwise negate one another.[49]

The advantages to the Al Sa'ud of militarization should not be
dismissed too lightly. Military analysts who dwell on the inability
of the "rag-headed buggers" to use their expensive weaponry
mistake its primary purpose, which is to keep potentially disruptive former nomads happy and loyal. The Saudi armed forces are
a form of massive subsidy aimed at buying bedouin loyalty: by
1990 the kingdom's annual spending per soldier had reached a
figure of $223,592, compared with $66,000 for the US and
$6,960 for Iraq.[50] In the biggest test it faced prior to the terrorist

attacks inside the kingdom during the 1990s, that strategy was successful. In November 1979, inspired by the Iranian revolution and expectations associated with the new Islamic (hijri) century, a group of Islamist radicals led by Juhaiman al-'Utaibi seized control of the Sanctuary in Mecca, which they held for nearly three weeks against the national guardsmen and Saudi special forces advised by French special military units. Juhaiman's pamphlets against the House of Saud, issued in the name of the Mahdi Muhammad 'Abdullah al-Qahtani, declared the Saudi rulers infidels in almost identical terms to those used by bin Laden a generation later.

A former student at the Islamic University of Medina founded by Muslim Brotherhood exiles during the 1960s, Juhaiman combined some of the radical Qutbist ideas with the more traditional Wahhabi doctrines propagated by bin Baz who taught law at the university. Juhaiman, however, rejected the chief mufti's acquiescence in Saudi rule. In a pamphlet in 1978 he accused the Najdi *'ulama* of having been bought by the Saudis, directing his scorn particularly at bin Baz, who had originally encouraged Juhaiman and his group: "Ibn Baz may know his Sunna well enough, but he uses it to bolster corrupt rulers."[51] The test of Juhaiman's rebellion – which coincided with rioting among the Shi'a of the Eastern Province – was a crucial one for the national guard, as he himself had once belonged to its 'Utaibi section, having been brought up in the Ikhwan settlement of Saghir in the Qasim area. Part of the 'Utaiba tribe was involved in the rebellion against Ibn Saud in 1929. The Ikhwan descendants in the national guard, however, including the 'Utaiba elements, stood firm against Juhaiman's attempts to rouse them by appealing to their recent past. After a battle lasting more than two weeks, the rebels finally surrendered. The official government casualties were 127 dead and 461 injured. Some 117 rebels were killed, including al-Qahtani. Most of those who eventually surrendered, including Juhaiman, were decapitated.

According to Brisard and Dasquié a significant member of Juhaiman's network was spared: Mahrus bin Laden, a son of

Muhammad bin Laden, the Yemeni-born contractor whose company had undertaken the restoration and enlargement of the
Sanctuary during the reign of King Saud.[52] According to numerous
accounts of the siege of Mecca, the Saudi forces and their French
advisers were only able to flush out the rebels from the warren of
cellars under the sanctuary after consulting the plans belonging to
the bin Laden company. If the claim of Mahrus's involvement is
true, it seems probable that Mahrus, who now looks after family
business in Medina, was spared as a quid pro quo.

Chapter Six

The Seeds of Terror

The roots of al-Qaʻida were put down in the ten-year war fought by the *mujahidin* – the "holy warriors" – against the Russians in Afghanistan after the Soviet invasion of 1979. According to the "blowback" thesis advanced by John Cooley in his excellent book, *Unholy Wars*, the CIA financed and backed the Afghan *mujahidin* through its Pakistani counterpart, the Interservices Intelligence directorate (ISI). The US and its allies, including Britain, France and Portugal, helped during the 1960s and 1970s by the Shah of Iran, found ways of "waging proxy wars in Africa and Asia against adversaries they feared: often real or token allies of Moscow".[1] After the Soviet leader Leonid Brezhnev sent the Red Army into Kabul to prop up an ailing pro-communist government, the Carter administration, persuaded by the viscerally anti-communist Polish-born National Security Adviser Zbigniew Brzezinski, saw in the "foolhardy Soviet invasion" not only a major international threat, but an opportunity to undermine the "already tottering" Soviet empire in Central Asia. America's love affair with Islamism became a marriage of convenience, consummated through an alliance with General Zia ul-Haqq, Pakistan's Islamist military dictator who had his own reasons for wanting to rid Afghanistan of the generally pro-Indian Soviets. In cooperation with the ISI (which provided logistical support) and the Saudis who contributed nearly $4 billion to the Afghan jihad between 1979 and 1990, the CIA "managed the raising, training, equipping, paying and sending into battle against the Red Army in Afghanistan of a mercenary army of Islamist volunteers" many of them "religious fugitives from their own governments or soldiers of fortune from all over the world".[2] The US contribution in arms and money during the 1980s reached approximately $6 billion.[3] Throughout the campaign, the CIA adopted a hands-off approach. It did not want to give the Russians a propaganda weapon by having any of its agents caught on the ground.[4]

Even in the training of more than 50,000 Muslim mercenaries to fight the Russians, the CIA chose the proxy method. Pakistani ISI officers and a few key Afghan guerrilla leaders were first secretly schooled in the service training centres of the CIA and the US Army and Navy Special Forces in the United States. Main training took place under the watchful eyes of the Pakistanis and sometimes a very few CIA officers – in Pakistan, and, eventually, in areas of Afghanistan free of Soviet troops and the Communist Afghan government. Various open and hidden channels and stratagems were used to send arms supplies. Early in the war, the Americans gave Pakistan full control of training and allocation of the cash resources, weapons and logistical support for the holy warriors. A variety of sources financed the war, and the post-war conversion of the fighters into international terrorists. First came the US taxpayers' funds during President Ronald Reagan's two administrations (1981–89). Saudi Arabia's private and public contributors, like bin Laden, matched American funds dollar for dollar. The fraudulent BCCI bank and the drugs trade provided more billions.[5]

The jihad against the Russians was a triumph: an important, if not the decisive factor in the collapse of the Soviet Union and its Central Asian empire. In 1989, under the presidency of George H.

Bush, a former director of the CIA, that organization celebrated its "victory" with champagne. But Afghanistan itself lay in ruins, wasted by the jihad and the civil war between rival tribal factions that followed once America had turned its back. By 1994 the two Islamic powers, Saudi Arabia and Pakistan, allied with the United States, the world's only remaining superpower, had hatched the Taliban, widely seen as a "monster of Islamist extremism". At first the Pakistani-armed Taliban who were mostly students from religious *madrasas* or seminaries in the tradition of Deoband, a nineteenth-century reformist movement based in India, brought some order and stability to the areas under their control which had been ravaged by warlords and bandits. But the price paid by Afghan society was horrendous.

> It included the virtual enslavement and sequestration of women and crushing of all opposition to the Talibans' super-rigorous pretended Sunni Muslim, laws and protocols of conduct. Transgressors suffered the harshest punishment systematically inflicted since the Europe of the Middle Ages and the Inquisition. There were: beatings or floggings for violations of dress codes for men or women or of prescribed beard lengths or shapes for men; amputations of hands and feet for theft; stoning to death for adultery; burial alive for sodomy – punishments carried out in public.[6]

The longer-term consequences were even more dire, if such were possible: the conversion of the *mujahidin* "freedom fighters" into "terrorists". My purpose in this chapter is not to detail the jihad in Afghanistan and its aftermath, which has been done in admirable accounts by John Cooley, Michael Griffin and Ahmad Rashid, but rather to highlight some of its dynamics, to show how the seeds of terrorism (as distinct from its roots) were spread by the Islamist movements sustained and funded by conservative Muslim states, particularly Saudi Arabia, with the active participation of Pakistan and the United States. The attacks on September 11th which cost nearly 3,000 American lives were a direct consequence of the CIA's policies during the Reagan years and afterwards.

After September 11th and ever more so after October 5th, when the American bombing of Taliban positions in Afghanistan began, the Western media, taking its cue from President George W. Bush and prime minister Tony Blair, spared no efforts in drawing attention to the appalling record of human rights under the Taliban, the public executions, the corporal punishments, the treatment of women. Almost no one drew attention to the fact that identical charges of human rights abuses can be made against Saudi Arabia, America's closest Arab ally. In the Saudi context the bigotry and fanaticism of which the Taliban were universally accused were quietly overlooked. The Saudis are much wealthier than the Taliban. They control a fair portion of the world's most vital commodity. They own newspapers and property in London and New York. No one would consider bombing their cities, or stopping the flow of funds emanating from their oil wells from reaching "religious fanatics". As harbourers of the al-Qa'ida organization the Taliban had to be dealt with. But in the wider context of the religious and intellectual forces represented by al-Qa'ida, the Taliban were simply scapegoats or fall guys. Al-Qa'ida put down roots in Afghanistan, a "failed" or pariah state under the control of an unholy coalition of drug lords and religious zealots. But the soils in which it grew were tended and nurtured by the oil states under the noses of their Western customers.

Saudi Arabia is the world's leading exporter not only of petroleum but of "hard" or fundamentalist Islam, that version of the faith that insists on the strict observance of outward rules of behaviour (orthopraxy) whilst systematically attacking, or undermining, the more esoteric or mystical variants of the faith that tend towards widening the religion's appeal whilst facilitating accommodations with modernity. Although the extreme Wahhabism that regards all non-Wahhabis as "infidels" has been softened since the Saudis became custodians of Mecca and Medina, the ruling family's dependence on the *'ulama* for their legitimacy allows the latter a free rein propagating religious extremism abroad. Saudi religious imperialism finds expression in three related but critical areas, all of which flow from the state's official Wahhabi ideology: hostility to non-Islamic religions, including Judaism and Christianity; anti-Sufism and anti-Shi'ism.

The caliph 'Umar enforced the hadith attributed to Muhammad (but contradicted by the exemplary treatment he accorded to the Jews of al-Khaybar) that there "should be no two religions in Arabia" because of the presence of the Two Sanctuaries of Medina and Mecca. Consonant with that policy the Saudis do not permit the public observance of religions other than Islam, although "fellowship meetings" of Christians are tolerated, provided their numbers are small. Filipinos have been deported for holding "fellowship meetings" that the *mutawwa'in* regard as being too well-attended.[7] During Operation Desert Shield when American troops were stationed in Saudi Arabia, military personnel wearing crosses or stars of David were required to keep them hidden under their clothes; the red crescent replaced the red cross on US ambulances and hospital tents, and soldiers were advised not to take bibles outside US military compounds.[8] Abroad the Wahhabi influence is expressed less directly, in the patronage extended to Muslim polemicists, such as the late Ahmad Deedat, a South African preacher of South Asian origin who received the 1986 King Faisal Award for International Services to Islam. In pamphlets, videos and public performances Deedat "uses humour and scurrilous innuendo to make sure his audience sees Christianity, the Pope, the Catholic church and the Bible as unworthy of respect ... [and] invites his audience to join him in an infantile and sneering assault on central tenets of the Christian faith".[9] Whilst in a truly secular society Deedat's polemical style should be tolerated, if not encouraged, as healthy religious knockabout, his popularity among Muslims living in Western countries must be contrasted with the universal outrage that greeted the publication of Salman Rushdie's novel *The Satanic Verses* in 1988 when British Muslims, including organizations funded by Saudi Arabia, were all but unanimous in demanding that the book be withdrawn. Muslims living in the

West rightly see themselves as victims of Islamophobia – manifestations of which have increased markedly since the September 11th attacks. The racial disharmony between Asian Muslims and whites that erupted into major riots in Bradford and several other British cities during the summer of 2001 cannot, of course, be attributed to a single cause, but the religious climate fostered by Wahhabism and Saudi sponsorship of anti-Christian and anti-Jewish religious polemics undoubtedly contributes to negative perceptions of Islam in the West.

A more pernicious trend, which tends to reinforce anti-Christian polemic, is Wahhabi hostility to Sufism, the esoteric or mystical tradition in Islam. Like Ibn Taymiyya before him, Muhammad Ibn 'Abd al-Wahhab regarded any manifestation of devotion apart from the formal religious observances enjoined on Muslims – the five times daily prayer, fasting during Ramadan, the payment of _zakat_, and attendance at the Hajj at least once during the believer's lifetime – as religiously suspect. In particular he condemned the practice of seeking intercession from saints by praying at their tombs. Like the seventeenth-century puritans who condemned the forms of Catholic worship, including the "miracle" of Christ's bodily presence at the mass and the prayers offered to the Virgin Mary or the saints, the Wahhabis are violently opposed to the idea that holy persons, living or dead, can make intercessions with God. For them "the excessive veneration of the deceased who enjoyed a holy reputation was a first step that had led people to idol worship in the past".[10] The Wahhabis gave expression to their hatred of "idolatry" by smashing the tombs of saints and the domes that often covered them.

Implicit in the Wahhabis' anti-Sufi iconoclasm was an attack on popular and non-Arab versions of Islam. In countries such as Egypt and Morocco, peasants, nomads and even townspeople have long relied on the intercessionary powers of saints to ask for favours, or to bring them closer to God. Since celibacy is positively discouraged, individual holy men often founded saintly lineages which became the sources of religious authority and non-coercive social power: for example in the Atlas region, in Southern

Arabia and in the North-West Frontier region of India (now Pakistan) saintly families occupied strategic positions as mediators between competing tribal groups or the guardians of vital resources such as wells. The role of the Sufi orders in the definition and dissemination of Islamic values in premodern societies cannot be overestimated. Nonliterates, whether they are Arabs or non-Arabs, do not have direct access to the Quran. The Sufi religious orders that grew up over the centuries fulfilled the role of the medieval Church in Europe. By means of the personality cults associated with "saints", both living and dead, people outside the limited range of a manuscript-based culture became part of the Islamic universe. Beyond the Arabic-speaking world, in sub-Saharan Africa or South Asia, Sufism was the primary agency for the dissemination of Islam. But Wahhabism, however, by emphasizing the absolute primacy of the Quran, an Arabic text, and the Prophet's "Arabian" *sunna*, while ignoring the cumulative traditions that had grown up over the centuries under the umbrella of Sufism with its multiplicity of regional variations, was in effect attacking regional identities, subjecting non-Arabs to Arab linguistic and religious authority.

The Saudis are able to disseminate and impose their narrow and literalistic version of Islam not only because of their wealth, but also because of the quasi-caliphal role they enjoy as Custodians of the Two Sanctuaries. As rulers of Mecca they control access to the Hajj, setting annual quotas for the numbers of pilgrims allowed to attend from each country. According to their Sufi-oriented critics, the Saudis use their prodigious wealth to systematically drown the voices of mainstream Islam. Thus according to 'Abd al-Hakim Murad (Dr Tim Winter), a lecturer in Islamic studies at Cambridge, many, even most Islamic publishing houses in Cairo and Beirut are now being subsidized by Wahhabi organizations which prevent them from publishing traditional works on Sufism, while in other works requiring them to remove passages that Wahhabis consider unacceptable.[11]

A leading agency for the dissemination of Wahhabism has been the World Islamic League, established in Mecca in 1962 under the chairmanship of Shaikh 'Abdullah bin Baz, the pre-Copernican cosmologist. With access to Saudi money, the agency has disposed of considerable funds for training missionaries through such organizations as the European Council of Mosques and the Islamic Coordinating Council of North America. In its work among Muslim minorities in Europe, the World Islamic League has lent its support to Islamic organizations that share its fundamentalist or nonaccommodationist approach, including (in Britain) the spiritual mentors of the Taliban, the Deobandi sect, the Tablighi Jama'at, the Ahl-i Hadith and the Jama'at al-Islami (the Pakistani version of the Muslim Brotherhood founded by Maududi in 1941).[12] The Saudi-sponsored *da'wa* (missionary) organizations preach against the Sufi-oriented Islam of groups such as the Barelwis who control about half the mosques in Britain. The Barelwis, who take their name from Ahmad Riza Khan Barelwi (1856–1929), a *pir* (Sufi leader) of the Qadiri order which had roots in the Muslim rural communities of North India, adhere like other Sufi and Shi'i groups to the gnostic concept of the Divine Light which filters down from Muhammad to the *pirs*, living and dead. The Barelwis attach particular importance to the *Mawlid al-Nabi*, the Prophet's birthday, which is celebrated in many Muslim countries including Egypt, but never in Arabia. The Barelwis honour the Prophet by a period of ritual standing, during which his presence is supposed to be among them, as Christ's is during the Mass. Like Ibn Taymiyya, who regarded the celebration of the Prophet's birthday as an unacceptable borrowing from Christianity, Wahhabis and their fellow travellers vigorously oppose this and other Barelwi practices, which they regard as idolatrous. Thus bin Baz in his capacity as chairman of the Muslim World League issued a fatwa in 1982 declaring the event and the devotions surrounding the Prophet's birthday celebrated all over the Muslim world with lights and festivities, an "evil innovation".[13] At a conference I attended in London in May 1985 organized by the World Islamic Mission (which was founded by the Bradford-based Barelwi leader Pir Maroof Hussein Shah), 3,000 British Barelwis passed a series of resolutions

... condemning Saudi officials for confiscating and allegedly destroying translations of the Quran by Ahmad Riza Khan [Barelwi] and devotional books; complaining about the draconian measures to which Muslims in Medina and Mecca were exposed when they sought to celebrate the Prophet's birthday; seeking assurances that remaining sites associated with the Prophet, his family and companions would be respected and maintained; objecting to the fact that the World Islamic League, ostensibly intended to foster Muslim co-operation, was staffed almost entirely by Wahhabis, who accounted for only 2 per cent of the Muslim community worldwide.[14]

The Saudis use their financial power to export Wahhabism not only to Europe but to the United States. According to the Bengali Sufi writer Zeeshan 'Ali, now living in the US:

Muslims from Bangladesh in the US, just like any other place in the world, uphold the traditional beliefs of Islam but, due to lack of instruction, keep quiet when their beliefs are attacked by Wahhabis in the US who all of a sudden become "better" Muslims than others. These Wahhabis go even further and accuse their own fathers of heresy, sin and unbelief. And the young children of the immigrants, when they grow up in this country, get exposed only to this one-sided version of Islam. Naturally a big gap is being created. Every day that silence is only widening.[15]

Hisham al-Kabbani, a Lebanese-born Sufi living in America, estimates that 80 per cent of mosques in the United States are "under the control of Wahhabi imams who preach extremism".[16] While this figure may be exaggerated, few would deny that the Islamist trend, fostered by petrodollar funding, is becoming dominant amongst observant Sunni Muslims in the United States.[17] The anti-Sufi trend in American mosques is in marked contrast to the reception of Sufism in the wider North American culture: a collection of poems by the great Sufi poet Jalal al-Din Rumi (1207–73), translated by Coleman Barks, has been high on the US best-seller lists for a decade.

Saudi religious imperialism is not directed only against Sufi devotional practices. Operating independent Islamic religious establishments outside Wahhabi control is illegal in Saudi Arabia, and members of the Shi'a minority, which comprises about 10 per cent of the world's Muslims, are particular targets. In 1802 the Wahhabis invaded Iraq and wreaked devastation on the holy cities of Najaf and Kerbala, where the first two Imams of the Shi'a, 'Ali and Hussein, are buried. Since the Saudi conquest in 1902, al-Hasa (now the Eastern Province of Saudi Arabia) where the population are mainly Shi'a has been subject to the draconian rule of the Wahhabi bin Jaluwi family, to whom the Al Sa'ud are related by marriage. According to Human Rights Watch, the Twelver Shi'a, who constitute about 8 per cent of the population, suffer discrimination in employment as well as limitations on their religious practices. Books on Shi'a jurisprudence have been banned, while the traditional annual mourning procession of 'Ashura, commemorating the martyrdom of the Prophet's grandson, the Imam Hussein, is strongly discouraged. At least seven Shi'a religious leaders remain in prison for violating these restrictions. The situation facing members of the Isma'ili (Bohra) branch of the Shi'a, who live in the south-eastern province of Najran, is even worse. In April 2001 an Isma'ili religious leader was arrested on charges of practising sorcery, which carry the death penalty.

The charge of sorcery as applied in modern Saudi Arabia is not just a hangover from a brutal and ignorant past. It has been used by the Al Sa'ud as an instrument of persecution against both individuals and groups. In a notorious case that came to the attention of Human Rights Watch, a charge of sorcery was brought against a Syrian national, 'Abd al-Karim Mara'i al-Naqshbandi, who was executed in 1996 for undertaking "the practice of works of magic and spells and possession of a collection of polytheistic and superstitious books". Al-Naqshbandi's conviction resulted from a dispute with his employer Prince Salman bin Sa'ud bin 'Abd al-'Aziz, a nephew of King Fahd. According to submissions made by al-Naqshbandi prior to his execution, Prince Salman, "a particularly demanding employer, with a history of abusing his employees" as well as "a long history of improper religious, financial and sexual behaviour", had threatened to kill him if a group of debtors defaulted on a loan. Terrified, the Syrian sold his wife's jewellery in order to make a payment of approximately $16,000 on behalf of one of the debtors. "In a moment of weakness and fear" he obtained from a Sudanese shaikh an amulet containing verses from the Quran. Though such amulets are widely used as protective devices in Saudi Arabia, this particular amulet, which he had left in an office drawer, became the basis of the sorcery charge in a subsequent dispute when al-Naqshbandi refused to give false testimony against a fellow employee. After his execution, al-Naqshbandi's family told Human Rights Watch that the Governor of Riyadh, Prince Salman bin 'Abd al-'Aziz, uncle of Prince Salman bin Sa'ud, had admitted to the Syrian ambassador that their kinsman had been wrongfully executed, and had offered to pay compensation in the form of blood money (*diya*). When the family demanded an apology, however, the offer was withdrawn.[18]

The charge of sorcery levelled against the Isma'ilis appears to be part of a wider pattern of vilification used by the Al Sa'ud and their religious police against religious or political dissenters, or people who fail to cooperate in the schemes of greedy princes. By some accounts, members of the Saudi religious police raided an Isma'ili mosque, closed it down, and confiscated its books. Protesters then assembled in front of the home of Najran's provincial governor, Prince Mash'al bin Sa'ud bin 'Abd al-'Aziz. The details are unclear: according to Agence France-Presse, the Interior Ministry deployed forces overnight amidst warnings that the protesters were liable to be "arrested, questioned, and tried in keeping with Islamic law". According to the Saudi Press Agency, citing the Interior Ministry, security forces raided not a mosque but the home of an "illegal resident" who was "practising sorcery". During the search and after the "sorcerer" was arrested, the Saudi Press Agency said, one member of the security forces was shot and injured. At a demonstration at the governor's headquarters calling for the release of the alleged sorcerer, protesters fired guns and burned vehicles, killing one member of the security forces and injuring others. There was no independent confirmation of the numbers killed, injured and arrested in the days that followed. Official government statements tried to downplay the incident. There is no record that the United States or other governments friendly to Saudi Arabia have protested against the religious persecution of Shi'a Muslims in Saudi Arabia, or that they have expressed any public reservations about the judicial system of a country that sentences "sorcerers" to death.

Fortunately the ruling family of Saudi Arabia is in no position to pursue alleged sorcerers outside its own jurisdiction. The *'ulama*, however, have been permitted to do the next best thing, which is to swing Saudi foreign policy in an anti-Shi'i direction, with the help of their American allies. The fall of Shah Mohammad Reza Pahlavi in 1979 and the Islamic revolution that followed were major defeats for US policy in the Middle East. The Shah had been a trusted ally: a major purchaser of American armaments, and a vital member of the "Northern Tier" of pro-Western states on the southern borders of the former Soviet Union stretching from Turkey to Pakistan. The seizure of Americans working in the US embassy in Tehran by students following the "Imam's line" under the direction of the Ayatollah Khomeini inflamed American public opinion. Night after night, television viewers were told how many days the hostages had been held. The explicit anti-Americanism of the Iranian revolution, with demonstrators chanting "Death to America", "Down with the Great Satan" and burning US flags, created the overwhelming impression that "Islamic fundamentalism" as represented by "the Ayatollahs" ruling in Iran was at the forefront of an anti-Western revolution directed primarily against American interests.

This was true to a certain degree. In their rhetoric the ayatollahs appeared more hostile to their distant enemy, America, than they were to their communist neighbour, the Soviet Union, with whom they shared a common interest in petroleum development and common opposition to Israel. The impression was reinforced in October 1983 when, in the aftermath of Israel's invasion of Lebanon the previous year, 241 US and 58 French marines from the 5,800-strong multinational force that replaced Israeli troops in Beirut were massacred in suicide bombings by Iranian-backed Shi'ite militias, leading to America's ignominious withdrawal.

During the Iran–Iraq war, American policy moved away from the traditional aim of maintaining the balance of power between the two dominant states of the region towards outright support for Iraq. Full diplomatic relations were restored in 1984. In 1987 the US navy effectively intervened against Iran, which had been attacking Western shipping, by re-registering Kuwaiti oil tankers under the US flag. America's Saudi ally backed Saddam Hussein with money enabling him to prolong the war at a prohibitive cost to Iran. The policy, aimed at containing the Iranian revolution, proved successful when, in 1988, the ailing Ayatollah Khomeini was forced to "swallow poison" and to accept unequivocally UN resolution 598 which called for an immediate ceasefire and the withdrawal of all forces to the internationally recognized frontiers, without naming Iraq as the aggressor, as Iran had previously demanded.

In the longer term, however, US support for Saddam proved disastrous. Emboldened by his success against Iran, he turned on the Kurdish separatists in the north, destroying a thousand villages with bombs and poison gas. On 2 August 1990, enraged by Kuwait's repudiation of an OPEC production target aimed at raising the price of oil to $18 a barrel – a measure Iraq needed to pay its war debts – Saddam invaded Kuwait with an army of 100,000. It may have been a bargaining ploy, but efforts by the Arab League, led by Egypt and Jordan, to sort out the "Arab domestic" crisis were scuppered by Egypt, acting under US pressure.[19] Within a week President George H. Bush had ordered the deployment of US troops in Saudi Arabia, forming the major part of the coalition forces sent to the kingdom to deter an invasion by the Iraqi forces based in Kuwait.

The decision by King Fahd to "invite" American troops into Saudi Arabia remains highly controversial. It has been claimed that

the king and the Saudi ambassador in Washington, Prince Bandar,
son of the defence minister Prince Sultan bin 'Abd al-'Aziz, were
misled by satellite photographs produced by US Defense Secretary
(now Vice-President) Richard Cheney and Chief of Staff (now
Secretary of State) Colin Powell, showing 100,000 Iraqi soldiers
massing near the border, with one of three Iraqi divisions advancing through Kuwait to the Saudi frontier.[20] However an
enterprising Florida newspaper, the *St Petersburg Times*, published
photographs bought from Soyuz-Karta, the Soviet satellite, which
showed that the Iraqi build-up in Kuwait was only about one-fifth
of the 250,000 troops and 1,500 tanks claimed by the administration.[21] Although there was no unambiguous evidence of Saddam
Hussein's intention to move beyond Kuwait, there was panic in
Washington that the Iraqi dictator would seize the Saudi oilfields,
pushing up the price of gasoline in Middle America – something
that no administration hoping for re-election would dare to risk.
After a stand-off lasting nearly six months, Operation Desert Shield
gave way to Desert Storm; and following intensive bombardment
of Iraq, the coalition forces led by the US liberated Kuwait.
Hundreds of ill-armed and ill-trained Iraqi soldiers were killed in
what correspondents described as a "turkey shoot". Thousands
more surrendered. Saddam Hussein's elite Republican Guard, however, escaped.

Sticking to the book of his UN remit, President Bush demurred
at invading Iraq. When a revolt among Shi'a deserters from Suq al-
Shuyukh, a town under American control, spread to several other
Shi'a-dominated towns including the holy cities of Najaf and
Kerbala, the rebels received no support from coalition forces. The
Americans and their Saudi allies feared that the Iranians were using
the revolt to install an Iranian-style Islamic republic in Iraq,
although a conference of Iraqi opposition groups in Beirut claimed
that, despite the prominent role of the Tehran-based Supreme
Council of the Islamic Revolution in Iraq, the uprising was secular.
"The prospect of a fragmented Iraq, with the Shi'a south lining up
with Iran, worried the rulers of Saudi Arabia and Kuwait, not to
mention the US administration."[22] The collapse of the rebellion

was followed by brutal Iraqi repression of the Shi'a, including the inhabitants of the southern marshlands which the Iraqis drained, forcing the exodus of some 70,000 people, mainly Shi'a, to Iran. In contrast, the coalition allies, led by the US and Britain, actively assisted the Sunni Kurds, by providing a "safe haven" under UN auspices in northern Iraq. Viewed from a sectarian perspective, Western policy in the Gulf has had a decisively "pro-Sunni" bias, consistent with the virulent anti-Shi'ism of the Wahhabi movement. Although Iraq's population is between 50 per cent and 60 per cent Shi'a, the effect of Western policies in the two Gulf wars was to shore up the Saddam dictatorship which is dominated by the Arab Sunni minority.

I am not suggesting that Washington's policy was consciously influenced by anti-Shi'a sectarian bias: merely that where Saudi and US interests converged geopolitically, the effect was to encourage "good" Saudi or Wahhabite "fundamentalism" at the expense of the "bad" variety promoted by Tehran with its more explicitly anti-Western thrust. The perception is reinforced when one considers the Afghan jihad in which al-Qa'ida originated. According to Cooley, covert American funding for the Islamist movement long predated the Soviet intervention in Afghanistan. In 1971 the CIA through Kamal Adham, the wealthy Saudi intelligence chief and brother-in-law of King Faisal, gave its blessing to a Saudi offer made by King Faisal to the rector of al-Azhar, Shaikh 'Abd al-Halim Mahmoud. It was an offer the latter, leader of Sunni Islam's most prestigious academy, could hardly refuse: $100 million for a campaign throughout the Muslim world to fight "communism and atheism", twin evils which King Faisal regarded as virtually indistinguishable from Zionism. Saudi funding assisted Sadat in the secret preparations he made for the 1973 October War against Israel, compensating for the absence of the Soviet military advisers he had expelled the previous year. Sadat balanced his shift to the right, opening up the Egyptian economy to Western investment and Western markets, by easing up on the Muslim Brotherhood and their fellow travellers, a relaxation that backfired when he himself was shot down in October 1981 by the jihadist Lieutenant Khalid al-Islambouli at a parade to mark the eighth anniversary of the Egyptian "victory".

By then the Afghan jihad was well under way. Alarmed at the "loss" of Iran in February 1979, President Jimmy Carter had sent Brzezinski to Cairo to woo Sadat for the anti-communist cause, to "get him on the team". Experts in Washington knew that "enlisting Sadat's Islamist critics and opponents as ideological leaders or recruiters was a key to raising a volunteer army of Egyptian mercenaries".[23] Several of the Afghan *mujahidin* who would be needed to fight the Russians had been educated in Egypt where they imbibed the Islamist militancy encouraged by Muslim Brothers newly released from jail and by sections of the al-Azhar establishment. Sadat's support for the Afghan jihad with Soviet weaponry or copies of Soviet weapons manufactured in Egypt went some way towards appeasing his Arab and Islamist critics who accused him of "selling out" the Palestinians in the Camp David treaty he signed with Israel in 1979, in which the Sinai peninsula was returned to Egypt without a guaranteed Israeli withdrawal from the Occupied Territories on the West Bank and Gaza.[24]

An important beneficiary of the relaxed climate towards the Islamists in Egypt was Shaikh 'Umar 'Abd al-Rahman, the blind cleric who had been imprisoned in the 1960s and 1970s for his diatribes comparing President Nasser to the unjust tyrannical figure of Pharaoh in the Quran. Rehabilitated by Sadat after Nasser's death, Shaikh 'Umar was sent back by the government to the al-Fayyum oasis, where he had built his reputation as a fiery Islamist, and then on to al-Minya and Asyut University in Upper Egypt, always a centre of Islamist activity, where he preached, interpreted and disseminated the message of Maududi and Qutb. In 1977 he evaded a new crackdown affecting the Islamists in Egypt after the Takfir wa-l-Hijra episode (see Chapter 4) by moving to Saudi Arabia, where he taught in the Imam Muhammad ibn Sa'ud University in Riyadh. Hundreds of students heard his uncompromisingly anti-Western message. An influential contact he made in Saudi Arabia was Hasan al-Turabi, the Sudanese Muslim Brotherhood leader who would form a profitable political and business partnership with

Osama bin Laden during the mid-1990s. A document circulating among the *'anquds*, the self-contained cells or "bunches of grapes" which made up the Islamist groups, so that if one were "plucked" it would not affect the others, conveyed the Shaikh's affirmative answer to theoretical question: "Is it lawful to shed the blood of a ruler who does not rule according to what God sent down?" Later, when asked for a specific ruling about Sadat, without being informed of the plot to kill him, the Shaikh was cautious: "I cannot say he has definitely crossed the line into infidelity."[25] The Shaikh was twice acquitted of conspiracies to overthrow the Egyptian government: at the trial of Sadat's killers in the spring of 1982, and shortly afterwards at the trial of 300 members of the al-Jihad movement to which Islambouli and his mentor, 'Abd al-Salam al-Farag, had belonged. However Shaikh 'Umar served six further years in prison for his subversive preaching, before travelling to Peshawar, Pakistan, in 1988 to aid the Afghan jihad.[26]

For the Islamists the Afghan jihad was a famous victory. The *mujahidin*, fired by religion, defeated the might of the Soviet Union, the world's second superpower. Adopting the slogan of the Islamic revolution – "Neither East, nor West, Islam is best" – the *mujahidin* rejected the offer, put forward by the Russians at UN-sponsored talks in Geneva, of a limited phased withdrawal to end the fighting. Professor 'Abd al-Rasul Sayyaf, leader of Ittihad-i Islami, a Saudi-funded jihad organization, stated their position in forthright terms:

> Infidels, whether they be communists, crusaders or Zionists, are one in their enmity towards Islam. In an attempt to block the path of the mujahidin they import solutions from America, Russia or Paris. But they know well that if the jihad continues, it will culminate in the establishment of Islamic rule in Afghanistan . . . Therefore, they have breast-fed and brought up some people who are prepared for negotiations . . . These people have not shared in our jihad . . . they only speak for themselves. The solutions of the Afghan issue

will stem from the trenches of war and not from Washington, London, Paris or Moscow.[27]

The realities were somewhat different. As already noted, the *mujahidin* were armed and trained by the CIA through its Pakistani counterpart the ISI. Training the Pakistani trainers were members of the US special forces: the Army's Green Berets and the Navy SEALS (sea/air/land commando teams), both of which were veterans of major paramilitary operations that the CIA had managed in Indo-China. The Green Berets in particular had trained "native" guerrillas to fight communist forces in Vietnam and Laos.[28] Selected Green Beret officers, many of them seasoned Vietnam veterans, took "draconian secrecy oaths" before beginning their assignments at places such as the John F. Kennedy Special Warfare Center at Fort Bragg, North Carolina, and Camp Peary, Virginia.[29] The subjects taught "included use and detection of explosives; surveillance and counter-surveillance; how to write reports according to CIA 'company' standards; how to shoot various weapons, and the running of counter-terrorism, counter-narcotics and paramilitary operations. There were also classroom courses in the all-important subject of recruiting new agents, couriers and assorted helpers."[30] Other special military units would, in time, join forces with the Green Berets. "They would train a huge foreign mercenary army; one of the largest ever seen in American military history. Virtually all would be Muslims. They would fervently believe that God had commanded them to fight His enemies, the Godless Communist and foreign Russian invaders. Their earthly rewards would be glory and generous pay. For those who died as martyrs, the rewards would be in heaven."[31]

Unlike communist guerrilla training operations, or even the programmes aimed at winning "hearts and minds" in Vietnam, the political indoctrination was minimal: the proxies in America's jihad against Russia knew all about the evils of "atheist communism". They were not required to learn about the virtues of American democracy or the canons of the Constitution. Where Vietnamese peasants were taught, however crudely, to value the teachings of

Marx, Engels, Lenin and Mao Zedong, few if any of the *mujahidin*, including their commanders, would even have heard of Benjamin Franklin, George Washington, Thomas Jefferson or the guru of Reaganomics, Professor Milton Friedman.

In Pakistan and in the tribal areas of Afghanistan the money and arms that brought in recruits were administered by the ISI. Zia ul-Haqq, Pakistan's military dictator, readily consented to participation in what was ultimately America's jihad against the Soviet Union. Victory by the *mujahidin* in Afghanistan would be to his country's advantage, especially if they were under Pakistani control. It would boost his regime's Islamist credentials. These had cooled considerably since the Muslim League and Jama'at-i-Islami had withdrawn their support for him when he postponed elections indefinitely. Fronting the jihad for Washington would also thaw the frost that had entered US–Pakistani relations since Zia, responding to India's first nuclear weapons test in 1974, had boosted Pakistan's nuclear programme: under the Symington Amendment, the US Congress had suspended military supplies.[32] Grander ambitions loomed for Zia ul-Haqq: the dream of carving a new Mughal empire between infidel "Hindustan", "heretic" Shi'ite Iran and "Christian" Russia, embracing a revitalized Islamic Central Asia.[33] This was an ambition that harmonized both with the Saudi religious outlook and America's desire to isolate and neutralize Iran.

During the jihad against the Soviets, Pakistan and its American backers operated a deliberate policy of fragmentation in Afghanistan. General Zia had been a military adviser in Jordan during the Black September of 1970 when King Hussein, as he saw it, was forced to use the army against the Palestinian guerrillas, who had become "overmighty subjects" in his realm. Zia had been determined to avoid Hussein's problem which he saw as a consequence of the way the main Palestinian guerrilla organization, al-Fatah, had been able to wrest control from the Palestine Liberation Organization, the latter having been recognized by the UN and most member states as the "sole representative" of the Palestinian people, with its own treasury and tax system. To promote fragmentation in Afghanistan, the Zia government officially recognized six mutually hostile Islamic parties as representatives both of the refugees and of the *mujahidin*; a seventh, 'Abd al-Rasul Sayyaf's Ittihad-i Islami, was added later – although it had no social base in Afghanistan – because of the Saudi support it received for its Wahhabi religious outlook. As Brigadier Yousef, director of the ISI's operations from 1983–87, would write: "It was then a firm principle that every commander must belong to one of these seven parties, otherwise he got nothing from ISI."[34] Pakistan insisted that only religiously oriented parties could operate from its soil: it refused to recognize the Pashtun nationalist party, the Afghan Millat, or to permit members of the former ruling clan, the Durrani Pashtuns, whose exiled leader King Zahir resided in Rome, to receive funds or to contact the resistance directly in Pakistan.[35] At the same time Pashtun religious nationalism was encouraged. Of the seven parties funded through the ISI, only Ahmad Shah Mas'ud's Jama'at-i Islami was led by a non-Pushtun Tajik.[36]

By the summer of 1983, between 80,000 and 150,000 full-time guerrillas were operating in Afghanistan, in addition to hundreds of thousands of part-time Afghani and Pakistani fighters. Paid out of Arab and American funds, the full-time fighters were handsomely rewarded. In one of the world's poorest countries, they were earning between $100 and $300 a month.[37] Although the CIA and ISI were supposed to manage the logistics through the seven approved political groupings, in practice pay and supplies for the fighters in the field came directly from the outside donors.[38] The Islamist parties obtained more than the traditionalists; they received more than two-thirds of the weapons, with the lion's share going to the anti-American Islamist extremist Gulbuddin Hikmetyar and the Saudi-sponsored Sayyaf. The allocations were decided not by the CIA on the basis of strategic criteria, but by the Arab donors:

> The ISI claimed that its decisions reflected objective analysis of military effectiveness, not political favoritism toward Hikmetyar and Sayyaf. As dubious as this claim is, there is no

doubt whatever that the Arab donors decided on the basis of political preference. Old-regime parties, which received no Arab cash to pay for the transport of weapons or the operation of offices, often sold weapons to pay these expenses. This desperate strategy corroborated the ISI's opinion that the old-regime parties were corrupt.[39]

In a guerrilla war fought a generation earlier on different terrain, political fragmentation of the resistance might have proved fatal: in fighting the Americans in Vietnam, the communist leader Ho Chi Minh and his commander General Vo Nguyen Giap both saw a centrally directed "people's war", created out of the union of the military and political will, as the key to strategic success. For the communists, political education and party propaganda preceded military activity. According to Giap the guiding principle for the people's war was "armed propaganda: political activities were more important than military activities, and fighting less important than propaganda; armed activity was used to safeguard, consolidate and develop the political bases".[40] For the Afghan guerrillas it could be argued that propaganda and "political education" were not required to precede military activity because the population, unlike Giap's peasants, was already imbued with the Islamic faith after ten centuries of "indoctrination". After all, the different political groups all shared the same objective, which was to rid Afghanistan of the "atheist Soviets", and restore it to the rule of *dar al-islam*. This, however, would be a naïve view, both assuming a far greater degree of political consensus among the Islamists than existed, and ignoring differences between them and Afghan traditionalists.

Unlike the Americans in Vietnam, the Soviets were defeated in Afghanistan without a far-reaching revolutionary transformation being made in the resisting society. The key factor was a change in the military technology made available to the guerrillas. It was the heat-seeking Stinger missiles, supplied to the *mujahidin* by the United States from 1986, that turned the tide of the war. With electronic guidance systems, who needs political education or even basic literacy? The revolutionary discipline necessary for the development of martial skills that Mao and Giap and their political commissars had instilled into the communist cadres and through them into the peasant guerrillas was downloaded into the weapon itself. All that was needed was a couple of days' training. "The Stinger is the most effective hand-held anti-aircraft missile in use, a 'fire and forget' weapon that locks onto the heat radiated by helicopter and airplane engines."[41] Once the Stingers were deployed, the Soviets lost the total air superiority they had formerly enjoyed. Around 900 Stingers were supplied to the Afghans. By 1989, when the Soviets began their withdrawal, 269 Soviet planes and helicopter gunships had been shot down. As Ahmad Shah Mas'ud, the charismatic commander of what would later become the Northern Alliance (murdered in a suicide bomb attack on 9 September 2001) observed, "There are only two things the Afghan must have: the Quran and Stingers."[42]

In the Pakistani refugee camps or tribal areas where most of the *mujahidin* were recruited, not only was there no "political education" in democracy or such "Western values" as internationally agreed standards of human rights or education for women. Such values were positively discouraged, since they were to be associated with the communist "enemy". The communist "evil empire" the *mujahidin* were so heroically resisting on behalf of Western "civilization" had brought to the Central Asian Republics almost universal literacy, gender equality, clean water, basic medical care, paved roads, mechanized agriculture and electricity – along with alcohol, corrupt family coteries, inefficient collective farms, and a corrupt, inefficient bureaucracy. The communists in Kabul had made female emancipation and employment one of their priorities. When the Taliban took control of Kabul in 1996, an estimated 150,000 women held jobs in healthcare, teaching and the bureaucracy; the Taliban strictures on female participation in education affected 106,256 girls, 148,223 boys (taught by female teachers) and 7,793 women teachers.[43] In short, many of the features of life that would be taken for granted in Billings, Montana, or in Jefferson City, Iowa, would be found (albeit at a less affluent level) in the Central

Asian Republics and the extension of the civilized urban culture of Tashkent, the Soviet Union's third city, into Afghanistan as a result of the Soviet invasion. Compared to villages of Soviet Central Asia, rural Afghanistan was still in the dark ages. During the jihad and afterwards, Afghan women died because their husbands would not allow them to be treated by male doctors. Wounded Afghan fighters died because they refused amputations out of concern over the condition of their bodies on the Day of Resurrection, or would not allow intravenous drips between sunrise and sunset during Ramadan.[44] Geopolitics apart, the American mid-West had far more in common with the Soviet mid-East than either had culturally or socially with Afghanistan's secluded valleys. Rural Afghanistan had barely experienced the beginning of modernity. Social and cultural values, however, did not enter American calculations. As one of the jihad's leading champions, Representative Charles Wilson (Democrat, Texas) put it: "There were 58,000 [American] dead in Vietnam and we owe the Russians one."[45] The mujahidin never did even the score for America: the Red Army losses, officially put at about 14,000 dead and missing between 1979 and August 1988, only reached about a quarter of the American figure.[46] But the Afghan people paid dearly: at least one million people lost their lives during the Soviet occupation and the resistance it encountered.

The war in Afghanistan was not just a source of misery for its people: because of its character as a "global jihad" against "atheism" it spread far beyond the country's borders. The bacillus was the Sunni version of Islamism, encouraged by Saudi Arabia and its US ally. The most militant version of Islamism has now, for reasons of expediency and political correctness, been renamed "terrorism", a semantic shift which is supposed to distinguish the method from the doctrine.

The carrier was the army of volunteers who flocked to fight the jihad from all over the Muslim world, and from places where Muslims resided, including Europe and the United States. Just as the apportionment of US funds and weaponry was left to the

Pakistanis, so the raising of volunteers for the struggle was left to
the Islamists, through the network of Islamic charitable organizations that acted as conduits for funds from Saudi Arabia and the
Gulf as well as private contributions from Muslims in the Gulf and
in the West. To a man, the volunteers were radicals or hard-line
Islamists whose religious outlook was congenial to the Saudis.
They were known as the Afghan Arabs. Although they came from
all parts of the Islamic world, the majority were Arabs from the
non-oil world – Sudan, Chad, Mauritania, Somalia and Yemen –
while as many as 5,000 Saudis, 2,000 Egyptians and 2,800
Algerians were reported to have joined.[47] By 1990–1, the peak
time for foreign volunteers despite the Soviet withdrawal, there
were already 4,000–5,000 non-Afghan fighters in the Peshawar
area. Since the start of jihad in 1980, according to Cooley at least
10 times that number had either trained or fought in
Afghanistan.[48] Among the Pashtuns the Afghan Arabs "gained a
reputation for enforced marriages, excessive brutality and an intolerance of the local Hanafi ritual, though they fought with
conspicuous courage in the border areas adjacent to the North-
West Frontier Province".[49] After the Americans began bombing
Taliban positions in the autumn of 2001, most of the Taliban fighters rapidly melted away: but the Afghan Arabs, like the Hitler
Youth in Germany in 1945, fought to the last, true to their
Wahhabi heritage.

    Two international Islamic organizations, the World Islamic
League chaired by bin Baz and the Tablighi Jama'at, played a
major role in organizing and funding the recruits. The League's
participation is hardly surprising, since as already stated, it acts as
the foreign arm of Wahhabi religious policy. The involvement of
the Tablighi Jama'at is more problematic. Cooley sees it as deserv-
ing much more investigation and attention than it has received to
date.[50] Explicitly nonpolitical and widely seen as such, the Tablighi
Jama'at (Preaching Association) was founded in India in 1926 and
is one of the fastest-growing Islamic missionary movements in the
world. Its annual conference at Raiwind, near Lahore in Pakistan,
is attended by about a million members, making it the "second

largest religious congregation of the Muslim world after the *hajj*".[51] Its annual conference in North America normally attracts about ten thousand. Its annual European gathering at Dewsbury, West Yorkshire, regularly attracts eight thousand.[52] Founded by Muhammad Ilyas (1885–1944), an alumnus of the reformist college of Deoband, the Tablighis sought to inject the spirit of inner piety into Islamic observance by preaching: in Protestant terms the movement resembles Wesleyan Methodism. Like Methodism it appeals especially to recently displaced rural migrants, which accounts for its success among Muslim immigrants in Europe and North America. In Islamic terms it has been described "both as a reinvigorated form of Islamic orthodoxy and as a reformed Sufism"[53] whose success "owes much to the dedicated missionary work of its members and followers, its simple, noncontroversial and nonsectarian message, and its direct, personal appeal to and contacts with individual Muslims".[54] Like the Mormons, the Tablighis rely on door-to-door "invitations" to join their ranks and spread the word for God. "Their program of asking Muslims to leave their families, jobs and home towns for a time and join in a system of communal learning, worship, preaching and other devotional activities has proved enormously effective in building up a community-type structure with close personal relationships and mutual moral–psychological support."[55] In view of its explicitly nonpolitical outlook (Tablighis are forbidden to engage in sectarian controversy, or to discuss politics when proselytizing), its success in recruiting jihadis may seem surprising. An explanation may be found in its "concentric" Sufi-style organization – whereby "an inner group of full-time Tabligh personnel is surrounded by an outer ring of more experienced members and an outmost circle of more loosely attached collaborators"[56] – which facilitates secrecy, while its nonpolitical orientation made it "easy to spread its message in the armed forces of Pakistan", especially among non-commissioned officers (NCOs). According to Mumtaz Ahmad, the Tablighi Jama'at "received a great boost during the government of President Zia ul-Haqq, who was concerned to develop Islamic spirit among the Pakistani military". He adds that "an active member of the Jama'at" ran the ISI between 1991 and 1993, directing Pakistan's Afghan operation both through conventional intelligence techniques and through holding Sufi *dhikrs* or rituals with selected acolytes.[57] On the basis of interviews with a senior member of the secularist and authoritarian regime of President Zine al-Abidine ben 'Ali of Tunisia and an unnamed "senior but independently minded journalist", Cooley reports that Tablighi emissaries "began discreetly to approach and proselytise" young Tunisians, especially in the suburbs of Tunis and other cities, in the 1980s during a period when President Habib Bourguiba was actively repressing the Islamists, imprisoning real or suspected militants. Tablighis would appear as volunteer imams in the prisons, which enabled them to gain access to prisoners during Friday prayers. Released prisoners considered reliable were offered free trips to Pakistan to study in *madrasas* (seminaries) in the Lahore area. After six weeks of pious activity during which little or nothing was said about the jihad in Afghanistan, ISI officers, "usually in mufti, would then appear and offer opportunities for training in weapons, self-defence and 'more advanced' subjects".[58]

In North America, by contrast, recruitment was conducted much more openly. A place that would gain in significance as a focus of terrorist activity after the 1993 bombing of the World Trade Center was Al-khifa Afghan Refugee Center on Atlantic Avenue in Brooklyn, which was registered as a charitable organization "to provide for the needs and welfare of the Afghan people particularly the refugees due to the Soviet invasion".[59] In fact it had very little to do with refugees, but acted as the recruitment hub and fundraising centre for Muslims living in the United States who wanted to fight the Soviet invasion. It was known to Arab and Muslim travellers from abroad, and to Arab-Americans who met and worked there, as the "al-Jihad" centre. More than two hundred volunteers for the jihad in Afghanistan passed through its doors.[60] Officially the funding came from charitable donations for Afghan refugee relief in the United States. Unofficially, as Cooley suggests, there may have been "hard-to-trace suitcases full of cash and anonymous bearer cheques, of bank drafts, from the World Islamic

League, the Tablighi Jama'at and other missionary and charitable organizations located in Pakistan. Often they were bankrolled by Saudi Arabian public and (later on, as the jihad wound down) private funds, such as those supplied by the multi-millionaire renegade Saudi construction tycoon, Osama bin Laden."[61]

Bin Laden's career is now well-known to the world through the numerous articles and profiles that appeared in the Western press after September 11th. They differ, however, on points of detail. Certain facts are well-established. Others are much less certain. What follows is partly conjectural, since I have not had the opportunity to verify the published sources on which this account is based. Psychologically the narrative that describes Osama bin Laden as a "born-again" Muslim who turned to religion after a misspent, self-indulgent youth seems plausible. There are pictures of him as an adolescent in Europe, wearing loud Western clothes and flared jeans, which are consistent with this narrative. Disinterred from obscurity by the international press, there seems no reason to doubt their authenticity. However, there is disagreement about the extent to which Osama's behaviour in adolescence and early manhood deviated from Islamic norms. Some accounts deny that he was ever a "playboy" with strong attachments to alcohol and prostitutes.

Like several other leading merchant families in Saudi Arabia, including that of Khalid bin Mahfouz, the bin Ladens came from the Wadi Hadhramaut in the former Aden Protectorate (now the Republic of Yemen), the seventy-mile canyon with its fabled cities that runs inland and almost parallel to the southern coast of Arabia. The tall mud-brick dwellings, fortified singly or grouped together to form defensive walls, attest to the centuries of tribal feuding that interrupted business or agriculture, while the mazes of corridors and interior dead-ends that would defeat any uninvited outsider indicate the importance attached to strict female segregation. Hadhramis were renowned for their conservatism and strict Islamic observance, as well as their business and engineering skills, which date back hundreds of years to the Himyaritic kingdoms of antiquity. Though few Europeans ever visited the valley before the

1930s, the Hadhramis maintained extensive trading and familial contacts with the island of Java (now part of Indonesia): within the premodern world of Islam, before colonial interventions, the Hadhramis had an internationalist outlook. Osama's father, Muhammad bin Laden, emigrated to Jeddah with his brother 'Abdullah around 1930, beginning work as a porter or perhaps a small builder, before founding his own construction company. Thereafter his fortunes shadowed those of the ruling dynasty. He built palaces for princes and was the main contractor for the extensive rebuilding of the Sanctuary in Mecca in the 1950s, becoming close both to King Saud and his brother Faisal in the process. During the crisis over Saud's abdication, he acted as Faisal's fixer, playing a key role in persuading the king to step down in favour of his younger brother, a favour that can only have improved his business. By the time Shaikh Muhammad, as he was known, was killed in a flying accident in 1967, the chain of companies he headed was the biggest private contractor of its kind in the world.[62]

Osama, who was born in 1957, was the seventeenth son of Muhammad, who, like many of the Saudi princes he emulated, had four wives, one of which he was in the habit of changing regularly.[63] Osama's mother was Syrian. Divorced by her husband soon after Osama's birth, she was apparently disliked by other members of the family for her foreign ways and independence of mind. She was nicknamed, disparagingly, *al-'abda*, the slave woman. Osama was one of fifty-two children sired by Muhammad, but his mother's only son. Even before her husband's death she "was forced into a background role in his life, unlike the mothers of his siblings". Osama is said to have bitterly resented the epithet *ibn al-'abda* his siblings attached to him. Brought up in luxury in his father's palace in Jeddah, he was tutored privately at home before attending the exclusive private school of al-Thaghr. An English teacher, Brian Fyfield-Shayler, recalls him as being unusually courteous, but also as being "quiet, retiring and rather shy".

Accounts differ over the extent to which Osama sowed his "wild oates" in Lebanon before returning to university in Saudi Arabia.

"Adam Robinson", the pseudonymous author of a book that appeared within three weeks of the September 2001 atrocity, states that while enrolled in Broumanna High School in Lebanon, Osama led the life of a typical Saudi "playboy", frequenting three well-known nightclubs, Eve's, the Casbah and the Crazy Horse, where "his table, one of the finest in the house, [was] centrally placed near the stage, and when he arrived it was already well-stocked with Dom Perignon and Black Label in anticipation".[64] The seventeen-year-old Osama, "debonair in his sports jacket and neat black trousers, or alternatively a handmade suit, was the perfect host. No one was allowed to want for anything; no expense was spared."[65] Robinson relates that when Osama returned to Jeddah on the outbreak of the Lebanese civil war in 1975, his family refused to allow him to study abroad again because of his bad behaviour. Robinson states that he was sent to study economics and Islamic economic theory at the King Abdul Aziz University in Jeddah. Bored by both topics, he was only an average student and spent his leisure hours binge-drinking in private villas with wealthy friends. According to other versions he studied public administration and civil engineering and would later use his professional knowledge in Sudan and Afghanistan.[66] Robinson says the only luxury he was permitted – apart from alcohol, the privilege of the upper echelons of Saudi society, whose family connections allow them to avoid the attentions of the religious police – was a conspicuous canary-yellow Mercedes SL450, with burnt-orange interior, air conditioning, cruise control and electric windows, regularly to be seen cruising up and down al-Malek Road.[67] Redemption, according to this account, came through Salim, who persuaded his younger brother to accompany him on the Hajj in 1977. Eschewing the red-carpet treatment reserved for royals and other VIPs, the brothers joined the throng of ordinary pilgrims to perform the Hajj – an arduous and demanding series of rituals spread over several days. After the Hajj it appears they may have visited the cave at Mount Hira, near Mecca, where Muhammad is said to have received the first revelations from God, transmitted by the Archangel Gabriel.

Osama, who had read the Quran as a child and had visited the site before, is related to have been profoundly moved on this occasion. He returned to Jeddah a changed man. He gave up drinking, dropped his former companions, sold the Mercedes, grew his beard, and threw himself into the Islamic studies he had previously neglected. This account, if true, fits the paradigm of the modern "born-again" Muslim like Sayyid Qutb, who flirts with the seductions of "Western" culture or hedonism before "reverting" to Islam. An unnamed Saudi business colleague of the bin Laden family who was quoted by the British journalist Simon Reeve sees the behaviour as typical: the wealthy young Saudis "have all this money and they think they are the kings of the world, and they start spending money like water. As soon as they leave Saudi [Arabia] they forget their religion. They would go to Beirut and buy whores and get drunk, and then eventually they have this religious crisis – and some of the young [bin Laden] brothers became very religious. I remember one of the brothers went off and spent weeks praying in the desert."[68]

It seems probable that Osama first came under the influence of the Muslim Brotherhood at King Abdul Aziz university in Jeddah. Leading Muslim Brotherhood members who taught there included Muhammad Qutb, the brother of the Islamist martyr, who carried forward his brother's radical, pan-Islamist mantle, while stopping short of endorsing the view that contemporary society was all *jahiliyya*. Muhammad Qutb shared with the more moderate Muslim Brotherhood leadership, including the Supreme Guide 'Umar al-Tilmisani, the view that while the term *jahiliyya* characterized the *Zeitgeist* of contemporary Muslim society, which must be resisted by preaching, to pronounce the *takfir* would be to risk falling into the heresy of the Kharijis, the charge made by the religious establishment against the Takfir wa-l-Hijra group in Egypt. Without formally renouncing his brother's views, Muhammad Qutb subtly reinterpreted them to fit the more moderate line advocated by the Muslim Brotherhood's leadership. For the newly "reverted" or born-again Osama (chastened, perhaps, by memories of excess in Beirut), the message was warmly appealing. The following is an edited paraphrase of Muhammad Qutb's message:

The Islamic community [*umma*] has been left in ruins. It has become weakened and divided into small nations. The seeds of internal conflict have been planted and nurtured by the West. Every effort has been made to draw society away from its religious foundations, keeping people in ignorance and luring them with worldly desires. Attempts at reform within an Islamic framework are still being suppressed. Religious practising Muslims have become outcasts in their own societies. And yet it is the will of Allah, the Almighty, that this religion will survive – and not only survive, but make a comeback. For while Islam is no longer "fashionable" in Muslim countries, people in the West itself are beginning to discover the truths that Muslims themselves have neglected.

Even those who have not yet "discovered" Islam have noticed the great spiritual famine that has taken hold of Western culture. They are now seeing for themselves how the new "freedoms" they acquired fail to bring satisfaction to the human soul. Humankind in general is in a state of chronic anxiety and despair. The present political, social and economic systems have failed to realize justice or to bring peace of mind to humanity. Man longs to believe in a purpose behind his existence. He is finally beginning to understand the real need for a belief in God, for nothing else can take its place – not a faith consisting of mere words and rituals, or of spiritual disciplines that neglect human needs, but a religion that includes every aspect of humanity: the mind, the body and the soul. Islam is the only religion on earth that includes and satisfies all these requirements.

In spite of the obvious difficulties which appear to us now, Muhammad Qutb concludes, the obstacles will lessen as more and more people seek an improvement and turn back to reason and to God. "When men awaken and seek out the truth, they will find

Islam. How long will this take? That is not important. The reward
for those who work towards that end is guaranteed by Him who
created the heavens and the earth, and the result is in His hands. By
the will of God, Islam has survived its darkest hour. And by His
will, it can again spread its light to every corner of the earth."[69]

After graduating, Osama joined the family firm. So pleased were
the family at the return of their prodigal son that they brought him
straight into senior management, overseeing projects and negotiat-
ing high-level contracts. His leisure hours were now spent in the
mosque. Influenced perhaps by Muhammad Qutb, he was pious,
but not yet radical. He was horrified when Juhaiman and his
acolytes took over the Grand Mosque in November 1979. Still
accepting the legitimacy of Saudi rule, Osama roundly condemned
their act as a violation of the Sanctuary and treason against a
lawful Islamic government.

The following month, the Soviet Union invaded Afghanistan.
Thereafter the Afghan jihad became Osama's cause. The crisis rad-
icalized him. He had never been to Afghanistan, but the invasion
affected him profoundly. Non-Muslim forces were occupying a
Muslim country. "When the invasion of Afghanistan started, I was
enraged, and went there at once," he would later tell an inter-
viewer. "I arrived within days, before the end of 1979."[70]

Chapter Seven

Jihad in America

Prince Turki al-Faisal, the youngest son of King Faisal, is regarded as the cleverest of the late king's sons. With an "undisciplined wispy beard and thick round glasses",[1] he enjoys a reputation for personal integrity, which is doubtless why the family put him in charge of foreign intelligence, a position he held until August 2001, when he was replaced by Prince Nayef. Though considered honest and serious, Prince Turki's approach to life is not without style. When visiting Harvard University in 1990, it is reported that 40 hotel rooms were booked for him and his entourage, encompassing two whole floors, with sand and palm trees brought into the building to create an oasis effect.[2] In talking to the British author Robert Lacey, he expressed his conviction that the oil of Arabia was no geological accident. "Arabia is rich today as it has never been before, and many simple people in this country believe that it is for one reason and one reason only – because we have been good Muslims ... Many simple people believe this, and I believe it also. Everything comes from God and oil is no exception."[3] The sense of divine purpose doubtless underwrote Prince Turki's conviction that victory in the Afghan jihad was foreordained. At the same time it was the kingdom's duty to support the jihad by every means possible, which was why he gave his encouragement and support to his friend Osama bin Laden's mission in Afghanistan. During the jihad in Afghanistan, with Turki's backing, Osama effectively acted as an "arm of Saudi intelligence". In Peshawar he set up the Maktab al-Khidamat (MAK), the Office of Services, a support organization for Arab volunteers that would evolve in the course of time to become the core of al-Qa'ida.[4]

The inspiration for this organization, as for the jihad generally, was a charismatic Palestinian *'alim* (singular of *'ulama*), 'Abdullah 'Azzam (1941–89), a graduate of al-Azhar and, after Sayyid Qutb, the most influential of all the exponents of the modern jihadist movement. 'Azzam was born in a village near Jenin in British-occupied Palestine. In 1966 he graduated with a degree in Islamic studies from Damascus University. The following year, when his home town of Jenin, along with the rest of the West Bank and Gaza, was captured by Israel, he escaped to Jordan where he joined the Palestinian jihad against Israel. His talents were seen, however, to be in preaching and propaganda rather than fighting, and he was sent to the University of al-Azhar, where he received a master's degree in Shari'a law, before returning to Jordan to teach at Amman University. The following year he returned to al-Azhar to study for a Ph.D in Islamic jurisprudence, which he obtained two years later, in 1973. In Cairo he was drawn into Islamist circles, and he became friendly with the family of Sayyid Qutb, as well as with Shaikh 'Umar 'Abd al-Rahman, who would become the Egyptian jihadist spiritual leader. In the late 1970s 'Azzam returned to Amman to teach Islamic law at the University of Jordan, but he was dismissed for his opposition to what he regarded as the faculty's secular outlook, and he moved to the more congenial milieu of the King Abdul Aziz University in Jeddah, where bin Laden may have attended his lectures. After the Soviet invasion of Afghanistan he decided to devote all his energies to the impending jihad, and he moved to Pakistan.[5] Like Shaikh 'Umar 'Abd al-Rahman he appears to have worked with the CIA in their campaign to recruit foreign volunteers to fight the Soviets. A documentary shown on ABC network television in July 1993 revealed that during 'Azzam's time in the US in the 1980s he visited no fewer than 26 states in search of funds and volunteers.[6] Though ostensibly recruiting for the Afghan jihad, it seems likely that he also signed up Palestinian volunteers for Hamas, the Palestinian resistance organization. His writings make it perfectly clear that the Afghan war was part of a wider programme of Islamic irredentism. The struggle to expel the Soviets was simply the prelude to the liberation of Palestine and other "lost" territories, including al-Andalus (Spain).

> The Jihad in Afghanistan is the right of every able Muslim in order to turn Communism away, and the Afghan jihad has been judged to be a *fard 'ain* [individual obligation] like prayer and fasting, which a Muslim is not permitted to neg-lect . . . Jihad is now . . . incumbent on all Muslims and will remains so until the Muslims recapture every spot that was Islamic but later fell into the hands of the *kuffar* [infidels]. Jihad has been a *fard 'ain* since the fall of al-Andalus, and will remain so until all other lands that were Muslim are returned to us . . . Palestine, Bukhara, Lebanon, Chad, Eritrea, Somalia, the Philippines, Burma, Southern Yemen, Tashkent and al-Andalus . . . The duty of jihad is one of the most important imposed on us by God . . . He has made it incum-bent on us, just like prayer, fasting and alms [*zakat*]. Such duties are divine obligations. The forbidding of jihad is *kufr*, which strays from faith . . .[7]

Central to 'Azzam's preaching were the themes of martyrdom and sacrifice. Expatiating upon the well-known hadith that the "the ink of the scholar is worth more than the blood of the martyr", he insists that the two fluids are of equal value:

> The life of the Muslim Umma is solely dependent on the ink of its scholars and the blood of its martyrs . . . so that the map

of Islamic history becomes coloured with two lines: one of them black, with the ink of the scholar's pen; the other one red with the martyr's blood. It is even more beautiful when the two become one, so that the hand of the scholar which expends the ink and moves the pen is the same as the hand which expends its blood and moves the Umma to action. The extent to which the number of martyred scholars increases is the extent to which nations are delivered from their slumber, rescued from their decline and awakened from their sleep. History does not write its lines except with blood. *Glory does not build its lofty edifice except with skulls. Honour and respect cannot be established except on a foundation of cripples and corpses.* Empires, distinguished peoples, states and societies cannot be established except with examples of such as these martyrs. By the likes of these martyrs, nations are established, convictions are brought to life and ideologies are made victorious ... Indeed those who think that they can change reality, or change societies, without blood sacrifices and wounds, without pure, innocent souls, do not understand the essence of our religion. They do not understand the method of the best of Messengers (may Allah bless him and grant him peace). (emphasis added)

In the same tract 'Azzam celebrates the heroic examples of Abu Bakr (r.732–4, the first caliph, who fought the apostate tribes in Arabia and brought them back into the fold of Islam) and Ahmad ibn Hanbal (780–855, founder of the law school to which Wahhabism is heir, who resisted torture in opposition to the doctrine that the Quran was "created" in time [see page 39–40]). The implication is clear. When the Umma goes astray and espouses false doctrines, God sends an individual or small group of people who will rescue it from perdition and restore it to the path of truth. This small elite, says 'Azzam,

are the ones who carry convictions and ambitions. And an even smaller group from this band are those who flee from the worldly life in order to spread and act upon these ambitions. And an even smaller group from this elite, the cream of the cream of the cream, are those who sacrifice their souls and their blood in order to bring victory to these ambitions and principles. It is not possible to reach glory except by traversing this Path.

The elite, par excellence, were the Afghan Arabs who would come to form the inner core of al-Qa'ida, along with other international volunteers. The success of the enterprise was entirely God's: no reference is made to the possibility that the *mujahidin*'s helpers – the Saudis, the CIA, the ISI and the American technicians who created the Stinger missiles, with their electronic guidance systems – had any influence on the war, even as God's chosen instruments.

The Jihad initially began as a few drops, until Allah decided to ignite the sparks within this blessed people and explode the Jihad, blessing with it the land of Afghanistan and the rest of the Muslims until its good encompassed the whole World. Some thought that the Earth had become devastated and that this Umma had been drained of the thirst for martyrdom. Therefore, Allah exploded the Jihad on the land of Afghanistan and groups of youths from the Islamic World marched forth to Afghanistan in search of Jihad and martyrdom. Indeed this small band of Arabs, whose number did not exceed a few hundred individuals, changed the tide of the battle, from an Islamic battle of one country, to an Islamic World Jihad movement, in which all races participated and all colours, languages and cultures met; yet they were one, their direction was one, their ranks were one and the goal was one: that the Word of Allah is raised the highest and that this religion is made victorious on the Earth.

'Azzam's tract includes a famous hadith from the collection of al-Tirmirdhi detailing the rewards the martyrs can expect in paradise:

Indeed the martyr has seven special favours from Allah: all his sins are forgiven at the first spurt of his blood, he sees his place in Paradise as his blood is shed (before his soul leaves the body), he tastes the sweetness of *iman* (faith), he is married to 72 of the Beautiful Maidens of Paradise, he is protected from the Punishment of the Grave, he is saved from the Great Terror (on The Day of Judgement), there is placed upon his head a crown of honour a jewel of which is better than the whole world and everything in it and he is granted permission to intercede for 70 members of his household to bring them into Paradise and save them from the Hell Fire.[8]

The rhetoric appears medieval and traditional: 'Azzam presents himself as an orthodox *'alim* in the Hanbali tradition. Since Islam, under divine guidance, contains the answers to all human problems, to acknowledge outside influence would be to undermine his purpose. The political ideology revealed in its entirety to Muhammad fourteen centuries ago is complete, self-sufficient. It does not need to adapt itself to modern circumstances. Stinger missiles are irrelevant. All that is needed is faith.

Smuggled into the discourse, however, wearing, as it were, an Afghan burqa, is an idea that is rarely found in the Saudi–Hanbali tradition to which 'Azzam formally lays claim. It is the notion, adopted from Sayyid Qutb, of a dedicated vanguard or elite, the "cream of the cream of the cream" of Islamic youth, spearheaded by the Arabs, that will bring about the restoration of Umma at its fullest extent, recovering the lost domains of Palestine, Bukhara (the former Islamic Amirate now part of Uzbekistan) and Spain.

Qutb's ideas, as suggested earlier, were "invisible" adaptations of the revolutionary or political vanguardism to be found in both Bolshevism and fascism. The quest for social justice that 'Azzam and other members of the movement, including Ayman al-Zawahiri, shared with Qutb and with Shi'ite ideologues, such as 'Ali Shari'ati, owe much to Marxist and socialist ideas, though it is only Shari'ati who openly acknowledges and critiques them.[9]

But the fascist parallels go deeper than the Marxist ones. In his explicit hostility to reason (alluded to in the reference to Ahmad ibn Hanbal's struggle against the Mu'tazilite doctrine of the "created" Quran) it is not Marx, grandchild of the Enlightenment, but Nietzsche, an anti-rationalist like the anti-Mu'tazilite al-Ash'ari, whom 'Azzam echoes. The attachment to the lost lands of Palestine, Bukhara and Spain (unlike a rational and humane concern for Palestinian rights) is, like Mussolini's evocations of ancient Rome, nostalgic in its irredentism, its "obliteration of history from politics".[10] The invocation of religion is consistent with the way fascism and Nazism used mythical modes of thought to mobilize unconscious or psychic forces in the pursuit of power, a task made easier in a population sanctified by a millennium of Islamic religious programming. Georges Sorel, sometimes seen as the intellectual father of fascism, declared that "use must be made of a body of images which, by intuition alone, and before any considered analyses are made, is capable of evoking as an undivided whole the mass of sentiments which corresponds to the different manifestations of the war undertaken by Socialism". Mussolini, to whom Sorel in his later years lent his support, saw fascism as "a religious conception in which man is seen in his immanent relationship with a superior law and with an objective Will that transcends the particular individual and raises him to conscious membership of a spiritual society".[11] In the same line of thinking Alfred Rosenberg, the Nazi ideologue, stressed the other-worldly, spiritual aspect of Hitler's racial theories: "The life of a race does not represent a logically-developed philosophy nor even the unfolding of a pattern according to natural law, but rather the development of a mystical synthesis, an activity of soul, which cannot be explained rationally."[12]

It would be much too reductive to redefine Islamism as "Islamofascism", but the resemblances are compelling. The social, political and cultural contexts in which these two ideologies have flourished are different. Fascism took root during the 1920s and 1930s in European societies that had already experienced a long exposure to modern thought and industrialization. None of the countries that adopted fascism had suffered from foreign occupation or direct colonial rule. The ideological bases of the two movements, however, do share common features. Fascism reacted both to the uncertainties of liberalism and to the chiliastic post-Enlightenment modernism of communism by seeking refuge in nostalgia and by refusing to acknowledge the contingent nature of the contemporary realities brought about by historical and social change. In the words of a recent analyst:

> Abandoning the concept of class and class struggle, fascism masquerades as the representative of all classes, conceived as a single national unit; fascism obliterates history from politics and fills the space with nature; fascism appropriates the concept of revolution, applies it to its own activism, and declares revolution to be nothing other than one manifestation of the universal war.[13]

The formulation can be adapted for significant parts of the modern Islamic world, including Afghanistan, where it is tribalism rather than "class" that is abandoned in order to facilitate, by concealing, the extension of tribal power under the guise of a national–religious purpose; while for "the concept of revolution" may be substituted the "reversion" or "return" to Islam under the leadership of the vanguard of the pure. In the Islamist discourse the space filled under fascism by "nature" is taken by the religion itself, conceived of as "*din al-fitra*", the "religion of nature" or *al-tariqa al-mutawasita*, the "middle way" between the "extremes" of Left and Right, communism and capitalism.

'Abdullah 'Azzam was a powerful influence on Osama bin Laden. Robinson sees the relationship between the two men as "part mentor/disciple, part father/son" but, as he himself explains, the respect was mutual. When 'Azzam arrived in Peshawar, he established the Bait al-Ansar (House of the Helpers, named after the Ansar who helped the Prophet Muhammad and his fellow Meccans after the migration to Medina), where he received and trained the first volunteers to arrive for the Afghan jihad. With help from Osama he went on to establish the Maktab al-Khidamat (see page 202) which bin Laden transformed into an international network for recruiting experts with specialist skills, from medical doctors to engineers and bomb-makers.[14] Backed by Osama's money and organization, 'Azzam became the leading intellectual light of the jihad, acknowledged as such by *Time* magazine. Osama boosted his mentor's reputation by including him in stories of heroic battles against the Red Army, though according to Robinson, 'Azzam rarely left the safety of Peshawar.

Osama's own military exploits became legendary, though how much is fact and how much "spin" is uncertain. There seems little doubt that were he alive today 'Azzam would be the leader of the movement. Bin Laden quotes him frequently in the polished propaganda videos released on the al-Jazeera channel. For example in the video bin Laden released in November 2001, after the US bombing had begun, he quoted directly 'Azzam's endorsement of terrorism (*irhab*) against the Soviets.

> We are terrorists, and terrorism is our friend and companion. Let the West and East know that we are terrorists and that we are terrifying as well. We shall do our best in preparation to terrorize Allah's enemy and our own. Thus terrorism is an obligation in Allah's religion.[15]

There is little doubt that 'Azzam always intended in principle to carry the jihad beyond Afghanistan to the liberation of other "occupied" Islamic lands and that bin Laden shared his views. It is not yet clear, however, at what point bin Laden and his mentor developed the specific hostility towards the United States that became their hallmark. Even though they failed to acknowledge it they cannot have been wholly unaware of the help the *mujahidin* received from the US in their struggle against the Soviets. An important turning point appears to have been the battle of Jalalabad in March 1989, a month after the Soviet withdrawal. The previous year, on 17 August, General Zia had been killed

(along with the US ambassador, the ISI chief and other digni-
taries) in an air crash that has never been fully explained, though
it is widely thought to have been arranged by the Soviet KGB. The
ensuing elections arranged after more than a decade of military
rule were won by Banazir Bhutto, the Oxford-educated daughter
of the former leader of the Pakistan People's Party (PPP) and
prime minister Zulfikar 'Ali Bhutto, who had been executed for
treason and corruption after the military coup which brought Zia
to power in 1977. Although she blamed Zia for the judicial
murder of her father, Bhutto knew she was vulnerable to the
Islamists in the military. Like Lyndon B. Johnson she considered it
safer to have her enemies "inside the tent pissing out" than the
other way round, and to this end she appointed General Hamid
Gul, "the most fervent Islamic ideologue in the army",[16] as head
of the ISI.

Despite the Soviet withdrawal, foreign recruitment for the jihad
was accelerated under Bhutto, with special "tourist" visas, often
accompanied by free airline tickets, issued to Muslims wishing to
join the Afghan jihad. Up to 20,000 militants arrived in Pakistan
during the late 1980s, most of them Arabs, though they also
included Muslim Filipinos, Bosnian Muslims and Kosovan
Albanians.[17] The first test of the new policy was to be a major
offensive on Jalalabad, still held by Afghan government forces, but
without their Soviet allies. Convinced by Gul and his colleagues
that a major *mujahidin* push on Jalalabad would rapidly lead to
the fall of Kabul and the pro-communist government of President
Najibullah, Saudi Arabia and the United States provided a massive
amount of help. The result was a massacre of catastrophic proportions. The lightly armed, ill-disciplined and uncoordinated
mujahidin were slaughtered *en masse* by the artillery left behind by
the Soviets as they tried to storm the city's defences. Bin Laden and
'Azzam saw the result, which all but destroyed the *mujahidin* forces,
as a deliberate conspiracy on the part of the US, working through
its Pakistani allies. Yossef Bodansky, a US anti-terrorism expert,
while not exonerating the US policy, sees the hand of Pakistani
realpolitik.

Islamabad knew that such a frontal assault could only result in massive carnage of the attackers, who were not tightly controlled by Pakistan. As a result the Afghan resistance that had endured almost a decade of fighting the Soviet-DRA [Afghan government] forces was so decimated it could not longer constitute a viable fighting force. The road was open for Islamabad to organize and field its own "mujahidin" force, now known as the Taliban.[18]

'Azzam made no secret of his view that Pakistan, Saudi Arabia and the US were responsible for the betrayal of the *mujahidin* at Jalalabad. His pamphlets, speeches and sermons made him powerful enemies. He was murdered, along with two of his sons, by a car bomb in Peshawar after Friday prayers on 24 November 1989. No one claimed responsibility for the bomb which was activated by a sophisticated, remote-controlled device.[19] The suspects include: Mossad, the Israeli intelligence agency, whose involvement is not implausible, since 'Azzam was a supporter of Hamas, some of whose leaders have recently been victims of "targeted killings" by Mossad; the Soviet KGB or its Afghan adjunct, KHAD; the ISI or even the CIA, for whom 'Azzam was becoming an obvious embarrassment.[20] The most likely candidate is an Afghani terror group controlled by the ISI.[21]

The widespread accusation that bin Laden was behind the killing seems highly improbable. Islamist websites that support bin Laden and al-Qa'ida still carry 'Azzam's name. Profoundly distressed by the loss of his friend and spiritual guide, the battle-hardened Saudi *mujahid*, now aged thirty-two, lost little time in taking on 'Azzam's mantle. His organization al-Qa'ida ("the base") continued the work of MAK in providing support for the Afghan Arab volunteers. According to Cooley, the Saudi intelligence chief Prince Turki insisted that bin Laden maintain his programme of training volunteers despite the Soviet withdrawal. General Gul certainly concurred. When asked by Ahmed Rashid if he was not "playing with fire" by inviting Muslim radicals from Pakistan's ostensible Islamic allies, endangering Pakistan's own foreign policy, the intelligence chief replied, "We are fighting a jihad and this is the first Islamic international brigade in the modern era. The communists have their international brigades, the West has NATO, why can't the Muslims unite and form a common front?"[22] The idea was to ensure the survival of a mobile strike force that could be deployed to fight Islamic causes anywhere.

For the US and the West the Islamist "victory" in Afghanistan was, to put it mildly, problematic. As Samuel Huntington, the Harvard political scientist, would write:

> The war left behind an uneasy coalition of Islamist organisa-
> tions intent on promoting Islam against all non-Muslim
> forces. It also left a legacy of expert and experienced fighters,
> training camps and logistical facilities, elaborate trans-Islam
> networks of personal and organisational relationships, a sub-
> stantial amount of military equipment including 300 to 500
> unaccounted for Stinger missiles and, most important, a
> heady sense of power and self-confidence over what had been
> achieved and a driving desire to move on to other victories.[23]

Despite the Jalalabad disaster, the *mujahidin* eventually over-
came resistance by the Afghan government forces. Bin Laden returned to a hero's welcome in Saudi Arabia. His brother Salim having died in a flying accident in Texas, Osama was able to use the bin Laden companies as a resource for training fighters for the next phase of the jihad. When he visited Jedda's coffee shops, he found himself mobbed like a football star; his picture, cut out of newspapers, hung next to that of the King.[24] He began to frequent Islamist shaikhs, holding discussion groups and giving speeches and sermons in dissenting mosques. Tapes of his ser-
mons and speeches were circulated throughout the kingdom: a quarter of a million authorized tapes are reported to have been sold. By the time of Saddam Hussein's invasion of Kuwait in August 1990, he was already a threat to the royal family, an overmighty subject, an Arabian Earl of Essex with a dangerously large popular following. Still professing loyalty, he presented a

ten-page plan for the defence of the kingdom, offering his family's construction equipment for the building of defences and proposing to raise a corps of battle-hardened "Afghan Arabs" to stiffen the Saudi forces' resistance to the Iraqis, should they invade. He also warned Riyadh against inviting "infidel" US troops to defend the holy soil of the Hijaz, a misgiving shared by many conservative *'ulama*, despite the fact that Saddam Hussein's presumed target, the oilfields of Dhahran, lay more than a thousand miles to the east.

All the senior *'ulama* were categorically opposed to the allowing of non-Muslim troops into the kingdom. It was only after prolonged discussion with the King that bin Baz, as grand mufti, "reluctantly gave his endorsement to the idea on condition that solid proof be presented as to the [Iraqi] threat".[25] Finally, after Defense Secretary Dick Cheney promised that US troops would not remain in the kingdom "a minute longer than they were needed", the King persuaded a meeting of 350 *'ulama* in Mecca to agree to the presence of US forces on a strictly temporary basis.[26]

The presence of American troops in the Arabian Peninsula, despite the "figleaf" accompaniment of Muslim coalition allies, including Egypt, Syria and Pakistan, fanned the growing Islamist temper. Like the Palestinians who rallied to Saddam, the Islamists in Arabia gave priority to the jihad against America over concerns about Saddam Hussein. Bin Laden responded to the mood. While carefully refraining from attacking the royal family, he urged a boycott of US goods. "When we buy American goods, we are accomplices in the murder of Palestinians. Americans make millions in the Arab world out of which they pay taxes to their government. The United States uses that money to send $3 billion a year to Israel, which uses it to kill Palestinians."[27] The Al Sa'ud responded by demanding that bin Laden cease his attacks on the Americans; when that failed, the royal house put pressure on his family, threatening to sever their lucrative ties with the monarchy, which could push them to bankruptcy. Concerned for his family's interests, on which he still depended, bin Laden accepted an invitation from Hasan al-Turabi to make his base in Sudan.

Preoccupied with the crisis in the Gulf, and confused about the potential Islamist threat, American officials seem to have been caught off guard by the reorientation of the jihadist movement against America's allies. Shaikh 'Umar 'Abd al-Rahman, spiritual leader of the Egyptian jihadist group responsible for the assassination of Anwar al-Sadat, visited New York in 1987 and again in 1990, when he decided to stay. Following its catastrophic failure to anticipate the fall of the Shah, the CIA appears to have thought that it might be worth grooming him as a potential future leader of Egypt. Although he was on a list of known terrorist advocates, having been indicted in Egypt for his part in the plot to assassinate Sadat in 1981, and had been on the State Department's "terrorist watch" list since 1987, he was given a tourist visa in 1987 and a multi-entry visa in 1990. Later, government officials would claim that the visas were issued because of "computer errors" from differences in the way his name was transliterated from Arabic; but the multiple entry visa, issued in Khartoum, was approved either by a CIA officer working undercover, or by a local employee who may have been working for Sudanese intelligence.[28]

The militant Islamist shaikh's stay in New York from 1990 was arranged by 'Azzam's right-hand man in America, Mustafa Shalabi, a chemist with an electrical contracting business in Brooklyn and the founder of the al-Khifa Refugee Center. After the Soviet withdrawal from Afghanistan in 1989, Shalabi and 'Abd al-Rahman had had a falling-out which was much publicized in New York Muslim circles. Apparently neither the CIA nor the FBI had any of their agents in the congregations. Shalabi, who had a reputation for honesty and piety, wanted to consult the donors about what to do with a considerable quantity of cash in hand. The shaikh wanted to divert it to the jihad against America's ally, the "infidel" Egyptian government. In his sermons he began attacking Shalabi for being a "bad Muslim". Posters appeared in mosques all over the New York area accusing his former ally of financial mismanagement. On 1 March 1991 Shalabi was found stabbed to death in his Coney Island apartment, two days before he was due to join his family in Pakistan. No one has been charged with the murder. Thereafter the al-Khifa Center was taken over by the Shaikh's loyalists. In a country where homicides are commonplace, Shalabi's murder evidently attracted little official attention, even though the suspicion pointed to acolytes of a man well known for his extreme views and the known associate of the assassins of a friendly foreign head of state.

The sequel is very well known. Staffed by 'Abd al-Rahman's loyalists, the al-Khifa Center became one of the points of contact for the terrorist attack on the World Trade Center on 26 February 1993.

The other was a small mosque above a toyshop in Jersey City where Shaikh 'Umar had been urging his congregation to "hit hard and kill the enemies of God in every sport, to rid [the world] of the descendants of apes and pigs fed at the table of Zionism, communism and imperialism".[29] The Shaikh's rhetoric, an "open incitement to violence"[30], had been monitored by the FBI since 1990 when one of his followers, el-Sayyid Nusair, had been charged with the murder of the racist extremist Rabbi Meir Kahane at the Marriott Hotel in midtown Manhattan in November 1990. A former CIA "asset" who had been recruited to undermine Jewish-American opposition to the Vietnam war, Kahane regarded Arabs as "jackals" and African-Americans as "savages" and "animals". He openly advocated the expulsion or ethnic cleansing of Palestinian Arabs from the Israeli-occupied West Bank. At Nusair's trial the jury – selected after twenty peremptory challenges by the defence aimed, apparently, at excluding whites – acquitted Nusair of murder, a verdict Justice Schlesinger described as "devoid of common sense and logic" which went "against the overwhelming weight of evidence". Nusair was sentenced to 15–17 years' imprisonment, the maximum penalty, on firearms charges, which meant he would be eligible for parole after six years.[31] The intended getaway driver for the attack, Mahmud Abu Halima, was Shaikh 'Umar's chauffeur. He would later be extradited from Egypt for his part in the 1993 plot to blow up the World Trade Center.

The 1993 World Trade Center bombing, which caused six fatalities and injured more than a thousand people, raises a question of vital importance to any consideration of al-Qa'ida and the American response to the string of terrorist acts it is assumed to have committed, including the September 11th attack. Two writers who have thoroughly investigated the 1993 attack, Simon Reeve and Laurie Mylroie, believe that Iraqi intelligence may have been involved in the attempt, which occurred on the second anniversary of the liberation of Kuwait. Reeve concurs with James Fox, the former director of the FBI's New York office, whom he quotes as saying, "Although we are unable to say with certainty the Iraqis were behind the bombing, that is the theory accepted by most of the veteran investigators."

According to the scenario put together by Reeve, who bases his account on a large number of unnamed "American investigators" and "intelligence sources", the master bomber known by his alias "Ramzi Yousef" was born 'Abd al-Basit in 1968, the son of a Baluchi father with Pakistani nationality and a Palestinian mother. His parents met in Kuwait and brought up their family in the suburb of Fuhayil, an area "vibrant with immigrant life", where Palestinians comprised about 40 per cent of the population along with Iraqis, Egyptians, Pakistanis and Indians.[32] The Baluchi tribesmen, who live in a remote, desert area divided by the border between Pakistan and Iran, are radically hostile towards the Shi'a, who comprise the majority of the Iranian population. During 'Abd al-Basit's teenage years his father openly espoused Baluchi nationalism, which takes an anti-Shi'i form, especially in the areas under Iranian control. This made him sympathetic to Wahhabism, the established version of Islam in Saudi Arabia.

In 1984, when 'Abd al-Basit was sixteen, his family obtained a passport for him from the Pakistani consulate in Kuwait. His father, an engineer with the Kuwaiti national airline, was fed up with the bad treatment meted out to guest workers in Kuwait, and intended to return with his family to Pakistani Baluchistan. 'Abd al-Basit, now eighteen and intent on improving himself, persuaded the family to send him to study in Britain. In November 1986, after obtaining a visa from the British consulate, he flew to London where there may have been a relative to keep an eye on him. After improving his English at a college of further education in Oxford, he moved to the West Glamorgan Institute of Higher Education in Swansea, now the Swansea Institute. Here he studied for a Higher National Diploma in computer-aided electrical engineering. His major project was the application of computer design to geometric Islamic patterns.

However, according to Reeve he also took a course in micro-electronics which the FBI believed could have helped him build the nitroglycerine-activated bombs he made for the World Trade Center and subsequent terrorist enterprises.[33] Reeve interviewed 'Abd al-Basit's tutors at Swansea who described him as "hard-working" and conscientious. Staff at the institute were "anxious to dispel any suggestion they might have trained the master terrorist. 'His project was quite innocuous' said one of his former tutors. 'Nothing that might be useful for a bomb-maker.'"[34] Unnamed student contemporaries report that he frequented the student bar and the Uplands Tavern, a local pub with a corner dedicated to its most famous customer, the poet Dylan Thomas.

Despite his penchant for alcohol and other "infidel" pleasures, 'Abd al-Basit was targeted by Islamists, who were active among students in the Swansea area.

> Until Yousef [that is, 'Abd al-Basit] arrived in Swansea he was an empty vessel, a politically naïve young man with limited experience of life and the world. His father had instilled a sense of passion and pride in young Ramzi, but it was events in Asia and the influence of friends in the Muslim Brotherhood that would turn Yousef into a committed terrorist.[35]

According to Reeve's scenario, 'Abd al-Basit visited Afghanistan during his summer vacation in 1988 where he trained in one of the jihadist camps funded by Osama bin Laden, learned bomb-making skills, and taught electronics to other fighters. Here, crucially, he met and befriended Mahmud Abu Halima, his Egyptian co-conspirator in the World Trade Center bombing. A stamp in the passport issued in 1984 shows that he returned to Swansea via London Heathrow on 6 September 1988.[36]

After completing his studies in 1989, 'Abd al-Basit returned to Kuwait, where he still had connections, and may have obtained a job in the Ministry of Planning. He was there when the Iraqi forces invaded the emirate in August 1990. Half-Palestinian by birth, he strongly sympathized with the Palestinian cause. Taking his cue from the PLO leader Yasser Arafat, who supported the Iraqi action, he joined other Palestinians in Kuwait in collaborating with the Iraqi invaders. Thereafter, the trail goes cold – until his arrival at New York's John F. Kennedy airport in September 1992 to plan the World Trade Center bombing. According to Reeve, "the consensus of opinion among Pakistani and American investigators is that he travelled in the Gulf, Pakistan and possibly even to Britain using a false passport". Reeve devotes a considerable amount of space to detailing possible links Yousef/'Abd al-Basit may have had with Ihsan Barbouti, an Iraqi businessman with a company in Texas and "a notorious international fixer who helped Libya and Iraq establish their chemical weapons programmes, and is believed to have been the architect of the Libyan Rabta chemical weapons plant".[37] The implication – though this is not clearly spelt out – is that the link with Iraqi intelligence would have come via these connections. Mylroie sees the Barbouti connection as the likely source of the cyanide traces found in the aftermath of the World Trade Center bomb.[38] Reeve concludes that "while the evidence of Iraqi involvement in the rest of Yousef's crimes is virtually nonexistent, the evidence of Iraqi involvement in the twin towers bombing is strong".[39]

The other terrorist crime for which Yousef would eventually be convicted in the United States was the murder of a Japanese passenger on board a Philippines airline flight from Cebu to Tokyo in December 1994. This was evidently a test run for the nonmetallic plastic and nitroglycerine device he intended to use in the "Bojinka" plot to simultaneously bomb eleven American airliners, killing thousands of people and spreading mayhem throughout international aviation. The details of the "Bojinka" plot were found on an abandoned computer in a Manila hotel, which he fled after causing a fire by mixing chemicals in his bedroom. Picked up in Pakistan in a swoop by Pakistani and FBI agents, where he was betrayed by a South African Muslim colleague, Ishtiaq Parker, who received more than $2 million for his trouble, 'Abd al-Basit was brought to the United States for trial in 1995. In 1996 he was sentenced to 250 years in prison and fined $5 million to prevent him from benefiting from newspaper articles, and he is now serving out his time in the high-security federal penitentiary at Florence, Colorado – thought to be the safest prison in the world.[40] Reeve claims there are many other terrorist crimes for which he has not been indicted. They include a "botched attempt to assassinate the Pakistani Prime Minister, Benazir Bhutto; the bombing of a major Shi'i shrine in Mashhad, Iran; and a failed attempt to bomb an embassy in Thailand in March 1994". Reeve believes that Yousef also met with Oklahoma City bomber Terry Nichols in the Philippines; and that there is a "wealth of circumstantial evidence" to suggest that Yousef was linked to the Oklahoma City bombing.[41] Mylroie points out, however that "the only plots in which Yousef was demonstrably involved were the Trade Center bombing and the conspiracy to bomb US aircraft. Reeve's claim that Yousef was connected with other terrorist plots rests, in each case, on uncorroborated assertions and flimsy evidence".[42]

Mylroie's treatment of 'Abd al-Basit/Yousef is more thoroughly documented than Reeve's. Described on the jacket of her book as an expert on Iraqi affairs, Mylroie acted as an adviser to Bill Clinton's 1992 presidential campaign, and she examined transcripts of court proceedings, telephone records and the forensic evidence produced at the New York trials in considerably more detail than Reeve. Her views have received public endorsement from James Woolsey, former director of the CIA, from Vincent Cannistrano, former CIA counter-terrorist chief, from Richard Perle, former Assistant Secretary of Defense, well-known for his hawkish views, and, most significantly, from Paul Wolfowitz, the current Deputy Secretary of Defense, widely regarded as the leading "hawk" in the administration of George W. Bush.

The essence of Mylroie's case is that Ramzi Yousef/'Abd al-Basit was an Iraqi agent. He may have worked with al-Qa'ida, and certainly collaborated with the Arabs in the Islamist circles surrounding Shaikh 'Umar, including Abu Halima, but he was himself no Islamist. His interest in women and the glitzy world of the Western *jahiliyya* is also noted by Reeve, who states that while Yousef "clearly enjoyed the 'sinful' pleasures of 'the West' in Wales, America and the Philippines, he also loved blowing them up". Reeves comments that he shares this apparently contradictory behaviour with bin Laden, who also "embraced decadent Western values during his late teens and early twenties" along with many other Islamic militants who "profess admiration and even love of Western culture".[43] This is surely overstated: drawing on our earlier analysis of Sayyid Qutb, it would be much more accurate to say that the prevailing attitude towards Western culture among Islamists ranges from ambivalence to outright hostility. Those who have admired or even loved "Western culture" have invariably ended by rejecting it, like Qutb, who renounced all the literary works he produced before embracing the Muslim Brotherhood. Unlike bin Laden and Qutb, however, there is no suggestion that Yousef/'Abd al-Basit experienced a Damascene conversion, after which he became a "born-again" Muslim. Until his incarceration he exhibited a flirtatious attitude towards Western women incompatible with the "modest" demeanour (including the avoidance of eye contact) towards the opposite sex adopted by the vast majority of genuine Islamists. When, instead of death, he was sentenced to life imprisonment he visibly breathed a sigh of relief in court – an unlikely response for a "Muslim fanatic" eager to embrace the rewards of martyrdom. After examining the evidence, Mylroie concludes that "Yousef" was not 'Abd al-Basit at all, but someone who stole his identity.

The crucial details from the evidence advanced by Mylroie concerns three passports, or copies thereof, produced by Yousef/'Abd al-Basit, two of them Pakistani and one from Iraq. When "Yousef" arrived at New York's John F. Kennedy airport on 1 September 1992 he produced an Iraqi passport and claimed political asylum.

After being briefly held as an illegal entrant, during which time his fingerprints were taken, his request for asylum was granted. On 11 November Yousef, representing himself as 'Abd al-Basit, a Pakistani national, went to a Jersey City police station and reported his passport as stolen. On 31 December he went to the Pakistani consulate in New York to obtain a new passport, presenting photocopies of 'Abd al-Basit's original 1984 passport (issued when he was sixteen) and part of the "stolen" Pakistani passport originally issued to 'Abd al-Basit by the Pakistani consulate in Kuwait in December 1988 when he was twenty. The photocopies of the 1988 passport did not include pages that would have contained a Kuwait entry stamp showing he was in the emirate when the Iraqis invaded.[44] The passport photographs on the Iraqi and 1988 Pakistani passports match each other: both show a young man with a neatly trimmed but quite bushy beard. The 1984 and 1988 pictures look similar at first glance, given the overall similarity of features shared by the beardless boy of sixteen and the young man of twenty. Closer inspection, however, even of the copies of copies reproduced in Mylroie's book, suggests a clear possibility that the 1988 image has been manipulated to suit the features of the bearer of the Iraqi passport, a relatively easy task using computers with scanners. The discrepancy between the two images is most evident in the size and positioning of the ears. The sixteen-year-old has a Mickey Mouse left ear that seems disproportionally large in relation to the size of his head. The tip of the lobe aligns with the left nostril. The face in the 1988 image has much smaller, neater ears, the lobes of which are aligned with the mouth. Even granted the poor quality of the pictures and the slightly different angles from which they were taken, a careful look suggests that they are not the same person. Since ears do not grow smaller, the head (which grows at a much slower rate than other parts of the body, even in adolescence) would have had to enlarge at an impossible rate to "catch up" with the ears as shown in the 1988 picture.

Interestingly, Mylroie fails to mention the giveaway differences between the two sets of ears. Instead she focuses on the difference between the subject's height as registered in the 1984 passport (140 cm − 4 feet 7 inches) and the 1988 passport (170 cm − 5 feet 8 inches) and the US immigration department's statement that 'Abd al-Basit, aged twenty-four in 1992, was 6 feet tall. Even if boys often put on a spurt in adolescence, it is improbable, if not impossible, that 'Abd al-Basit could have grown 30 cm or 13 inches between the ages of sixteen and twenty, especially since the twenty-year-old had already achieved an impressive growth of beard. Sex hormones stop growth, causing the bones to fuse. "Even if we set aside the Iraqi passport as unreliable and concentrate only on the Pakistani passports, how likely is it that 'Abd al-Basit, who was 4 feet 7 inches when he was sixteen and 5 feet 8 inches when he was twenty, could have been 6 feet tall when he was twenty-four"?[45] Compared to Mylroie's meticulous examination of 'Abd al-Basit's height, Reeve's comment is vague and unconvincing: "It is not unheard of for late developers to sprout a few inches in their late teens."[46]

These differences and discrepancies are explained by the hypothesis that "Ramzi Yousef" assumed 'Abd al-Basit's identity after the Iraqi invasion of Kuwait, when the latter was in the emirate and in all probability was killed along with other members of his family. As Mylroie suggests, 'Abd al-Basit's passports could easily have fallen into the hands of Iraqi intelligence, along with the thousands of passports and other documents they obtained in Kuwait. The Iraqis intended, she says, that the US authorities should think that Yousef and 'Abd al-Basit were the same person. For this purpose they laid a false trail, including not only the substitution or manipulation of passport photographs, but also the substitution of fingerprints. After the bombing, Yousef's name came to the attention of the US authorities as one of the prime suspects as a result of a "harsh interrogation" (a euphemism for torture) of Abu Halima by the Egyptian security police.[47] US officials then looked into their immigration records. They suspected that Yousef was the same man as 'Abd al-Basit, who left New York for Pakistan using the latter's 1988 Pakistani passport on 27 September, the day after the bombing. To confirm that Yousef and 'Abd al-Basit were one and the same person, the Americans sent the Kuwaiti authorities copies of Yousef's fingerprints. These matched those held in 'Abd al-Basit's file in the Kuwaiti interior ministry. Mylroie believes that during the occupation of Kuwait by Iraq in 1990–91, Iraqi intelligence substituted for the real 'Abd al-Basit's fingerprints those of their agent "Yousef" to create a false identity.[48] Mylroie adduces several other facts in addition to the evidence of the passports to support her thesis that Yousef/'Abd al-Basit was an Iraqi agent. Muhammad Salameh, a Palestinian who had frequented jihadist circles in Peshawar, was arrested a few days after the bombing when he tried to retrieve his $400 deposit for the van used to transport the bomb: hardly the action of a street-smart terrorist. Mylroie concludes that he had been deliberately left in the lurch by Yousef, who had plenty of money, in order to take the rap for the bombing along with the other Islamist amateurs, including Shaikh 'Umar 'Abd al-Rahman. An examination of Salameh's telephone record revealed that he ran up huge charges for calls to his uncle in Iraq, Abu Bakr, a former member of a Palestinian guerrilla unit under Iraqi control.[49] Mylroie surmises that the plot originated with Salameh who confided plans for a low-level terrorist operation in New York to avenge the imprisonment or to try to secure the release of el-Sayyid Nusair, his fellow Palestinian serving a sentence on firearms charges connected with the shooting of Rabbi Meir Kahane. Abu Bakr's phone would have been tapped by Iraqi intelligence which, appraised of the amateurish plot being concocted by Salameh and his friends, sent one of their top professionals, Ramzi Yousef, to take over the operation.

There was nothing amateurish about the World Trade Center bomb, which was brewed in an apartment rented by Salameh and Yousef in Jersey City. It consisted of more than half a ton of urea nitrate, wrapped in plastic bags inside cardboard boxes, with added "boosters" composed of lead azide, magnesium, ferric oxide and liquid hydrogen gas. The highly unstable nitroglycerine detonator had to be suspended in cool water to insulate it from shock or changes in temperature on the journey to Manhattan.[50] Yousef would later disclose that the aim had been to topple one of the twin towers onto the other, causing a phenomenal number of deaths. In the event the tubular structure of Yamasaki's towers proved equal to the challenge. The force of the explosion blasted through six levels of the North Tower's underground car parks where the bomb had been planted, scattering material at a rate of almost 20,000 feet per second. A seven-ton steel girder from the North Tower was ripped off and thrown forty feet, slamming into a brick wall which collapsed onto five maintenance workers who were eating their lunch.[51] Since the basement floors used for the car parks formed the huge building's horizontal supports, the engineers were worried that their greatly weakened state could lead to a "progressive collapse" and worked through the night to insert emergency girders.[52] There were traces of sulphuric acid and sodium cyanide in the lockers used by the bombers and in the debris after the blast. If the sodium cyanide had combined with the sulphuric acid and vaporized, instead of burning, the people trapped in the North Tower would have been asphyxiated in a cloud of cyanide gas.

On the basis of these chemical facts alone, Mylroie questions if "it is reasonable to suppose that this most ambitious terrorist bombing ever was solely the work of *émigré* Muslim extremists in New York? Could they have conceived of such a plot – toppling one tower onto another, amid a cloud of cyanide gas – let alone executed it?"[53] Although Israeli intelligence suspected the hand of Iran in the bombing, Mylroie concludes that Iraq was the much more likely candidate because of its known record in the production and use of chemical weapons.[54] There is further evidence of Iraqi involvement in the case of another conspirator, 'Abd al-Rahman Yasin. A US citizen, he was born in Bloomington, Indiana in 1960, when his Iraqi father was a graduate student at the University of Indiana. Yasin, who was charged with helping to mix the chemicals for the bomb, had been picked up after Salameh's arrest and questioned by the FBI. He cooperated with the Feds, giving them details about the van used in the bombing and the safe house in Jersey City where the bomb was put together. Unaccountably the FBI released him without holding his passport. The day after his questioning he flew to Jordan and from there went on to Baghdad, where he resides to this day.[55]

The final plank in Mylroie's case against Iraq involves a second Arab government, the Sudan, at that time a close ally of Iraq, in the second Islamist bombing conspiracy supposedly intercepted by the FBI, for which Shaikh 'Umar and ten others were convicted. The plot involved simultaneous attacks on the United Nations head-quarters, the Jacob K. Javitz Federal Office building, headquarters of the FBI, and the Holland and Lincoln tunnels under the Hudson river linking Manhattan island with New Jersey. The so-called "second bombing conspiracy", in Mylroie's words, "was actually a sting operation that the FBI initiated to teach the Muslim extrem-ists a lesson". The FBI employed a double agent, Emad Salem, a former lieutenant in the Egyptian army whose services they had used prior to the World Trade Center attack, but had dispensed with shortly beforehand, apparently on the ground that he was too unreliable to be worth the miserly $500 a week they were paying him, although he would claim, inevitably, that had they held on to him he would have exposed the World Trade Center conspiracy before it matured. The FBI now paid Salem $1.5 million to expose the Islamists surrounding Shaikh 'Umar by setting up a new bomb factory. Ibrahim Siddig 'Ali, a Sudanese friend of Abu Halima with US residency, who helped him to escape to Egypt after the bomb-ing, fell in with Salem's scheme, choosing the targets and enlisting other conspirators, who included several Egyptians and Sudanese, a Palestinian, two African-American converts and a Puerto Rican convert. Salem rented a warehouse in the Jamaica district of Queens which the FBI bugged with concealed microphones and video cameras. In June 1993, after recording nearly a month's worth of evidence, the FBI made their swoop, catching twelve of the conspirators red-handed as they were mixing fuel and fertiliz-ers.[56]

After some hesitation the Clinton administration indicted Shaikh 'Umar along with the actual participants in the plot on a charge of "seditious conspiracy", a catch-all law dating back to the period following the Civil War and originally used against supporters of the Confederacy who continued to resist the federal government.[57] The charges also included the plot to bomb the World Trade

Center, the murder of Meir Kahane and the attempted bombing of
the United Nations, the Federal Building and the two tunnels.[58]
None of those convicted in the second bombing conspiracy, however, was charged with actually taking part in the World Trade
Center bombing.[59] The government's case was merely that "some
of those who participated in the Trade Center bombing, like
Muhammad Salameh, were inspired to do so by Shaikh 'Umar's
fiery rhetoric".[60]

The seditious conspiracy law makes it possible to charge people
for participating in a conspiracy without having to prove that they
had been involved in any of the "overt acts" resulting from it. As
the *New York Times* explained:

> Because the law does not require the government to prove
> that the defendants committed any overt acts to further their
> conspiracy – or even that they knew all the acts the others
> committed – some criminal defence experts say the law comes
> perilously close to punishing people for their beliefs or
> speech."[61]

The use of the conspiracy act was necessary to catch Shaikh 'Umar
in its net, since his connection to any overt acts was somewhat
tenuous.

Though his rhetoric may have been fiery, when it came to
actions Shaikh 'Umar was quite cautious, as we have seen in the
case of the assassination of Sadat. When Salem asked him if it was
permissible to attack the United Nations building, he was told, "It
would not be forbidden, but it would muddy the waters for
Muslims." When Salem, still hoping to incriminate the Shaikh,
then asked, "Do we do it?" the Shaikh replied, "No, find a plan to
inflict damage on the army, the American army, because the United
Nations would harm Muslims, harm them tremendously."[62] As
Mylroie comments, "Shaikh 'Umar's view of Siddig 'Ali's schemes
constituted less than a ringing endorsement."[63] The FBI did not
want to indict Shaikh 'Umar, as James Fox, the New York director,
made clear. They considered that there was insufficient evidence

against him to press criminal charges. Instead they wanted him deported. They were overruled by the Attorney General, Janet Reno.[64] The Shaikh is now serving a life sentence for his part in the "seditious conspiracy". The Islamists see him, not without cause, as having been incarcerated not for his actions, but for his beliefs.

In contrast to the Shaikh, two much more active participants in the second bombing conspiracy were never indicted because they enjoyed diplomatic immunity. Siddig 'Ali had two "friends" at the Sudanese mission to the United Nations, Siraj Yousef and Ahmad Yousef Muhammad, both of them members of the Sudanese intelligence service. They had offered to provide him with diplomatic numberplates so he could get a bomb-laden vehicle into the parking garage under the UN building. Soon after the plotters were arrested on 24 June 1993, the CIA intercepted a call from Sudan's UN ambassador to Hasan al-Turabi, leader of the Sudanese Muslim Brotherhood (known locally as the National Islamic Front), now under house arrest but at that time the real power behind the military government of General 'Umar al-Bashir. The ambassador protested to al-Turabi that two people on his own UN mission staff had been involved, without his knowledge, in the attempted bombing of the UN – the body to which he was accredited. According to Vincent Cannistrano, former counterterrorism chief at the CIA, al-Turabi responded curtly, telling his ambassador to "Mind your own business."[65] At the time the Clinton administration told a *New York Times* columnist that they had "no conclusive evidence that Sudanese or Iranian intelligence services were involved with the Muslims ... accused of plotting to bomb the United Nations and other sites".[66] The mention of Iran was a red herring: as Mylroie points out, at that time Iran had no reason at all to bomb the United Nations, given that UN Security Resolution 598 ending the Gulf War favoured Iran by stating that Iraq had been the aggressor and demanding that Iraq pay Iran tens of millions of dollars in reparations. Iraq, by contrast, had close ties with Sudan, which had supported it in the Gulf War and may have helped to provide it with chemical weapons. According to Mylroie, "Sudanese intelligence had been involved in choosing the targets for the conspirators, and the distinct possibility exists that Sudan was fronting for Iraq".[67]

Though closely argued, Mylroie's thesis is far from being conclusive. The whole purpose of using surrogates for acts of terrorism – as the US showed in its jihad against the Soviet Union in Afghanistan – is to enjoy "deniability". In attacking the United States under the "false flag" of Islamism, Iraq (and in the case of the second bombing plot, its Sudanese ally) would have been adopting the same strategy used by America in Afghanistan. Within the greatly restricted sphere of military operations imposed on Saddam Hussein after Desert Storm, Ramzi Yousef's clever bombs would have been the equivalent of the Stinger missiles sent by the Reagan administration to the *mujahidin*. Ramzi Yousef himself, one presumes, would avoid "coming clean" about his membership of or involvement with Iraqi intelligence, out of loyalty to Iraq or out of concern for the safety of family members, whoever they happen to be. The Islamists themselves would be reluctant to admit that they were being manipulated by the agents of a dictatorial regime they regarded as unacceptably secular, even if they had their suspicions. Like the *mujahidin* in Afghanistan who tended to deny, or underplay, the importance of American electronics in securing their divinely inspired victory over the Russian infidels, the motley collection of Islamists in New York and New Jersey liked to think of their struggle against the "satanic" United States as proceeding from their own, divinely inspired, mission.

Inadvertently or otherwise, the US justice system may have contributed to this false, or inflated, Islamist self-image. "We prosecute individuals. We don't do state sponsorship," Andrew McCarthy and Gil Childers, the two chief prosecutors in the Rahman and World Trade Center trials, told Mylroie.[68] The law enforcement model of counter-terrorism has been adopted with reasonable success in mainland Britain and Northern Ireland. However none of the terrorist organizations operating in these countries have had significant state sponsorship in recent years, though at one time the IRA received support from Libya and the Soviet Union. Indeed the increasing successes British governments achieved over the IRA were contingent on the ending of the semi-official sponsorship that came from the Irish Republic during the 1970s when the Catholic community was perceived in the Republic as suffering unfair treatment, and the pressure exercised by British diplomacy on the unofficial sponsorship of republican terrorism, through Noraid and similar charities, from the Irish expatriate community in the United States. Criminalizing terrorism, however, tends to evade the question of sponsorship by focusing on the evidential requirements for individual prosecutions to the exclusion of wider issues. As James Woolsey argues, "Trials are not general searches for truth and insight. They are legally circumscribed fights, a kind of jurisprudential trial by combat."[69] Specifically Woolsey notes that the US judicial system serves to keep the intelligence community and the National Security Council in the dark once proceedings have started.

> Grand jury secrecy, as codified under rule 6(e) of the Federal Rules of Criminal Procedure, severely restricts the flow of information to the rest of government from investigations such as this one, where the facts should compel the government as a whole to look at national security issues as well as the needs of law enforcement. The rule permits grand jury material to be shared with other law enforcement authorities in certain cases – for example, to help solve or help prosecute other cases – but there is no exception to permit intelligence officers to see such material in order to make an assessment about possible foreign government support for a terrorist act.[70]

Mylroie believes that the enormous publicity surrounding the New York bombing conspiracy trials had a deleterious effect on national security policy during the Clinton years.

> [I]t was the separation of the criminal question from the national security question in the first two major bombing conspiracies to occur on Clinton's watch that gave rise to the

notion that a new terrorist threat to America had emerged, and
that major acts of terrorism were no longer state-sponsored,
but rather the work of individuals and loose networks.[71]

In his foreword to the 2001 edition of Mylroie's book, produced
after September 11th, Woolsey endorses her thesis about the 1993
World Trade Center attack, which he describes as "brilliant and
brave", and asks whether September 11th might not have had state
sponsorship from Iraq. Writing on 27 September he says:

> Few hard facts are available publicly . . . as of today. Osama
> bin Laden appears to have been involved, but a key question
> remains: Did he and his network act alone? Investigating a
> major terrorist attack is necessarily a long and painful
> process, and this investigation is particularly difficult, given
> the magnitude of the assault and the steps taken by the attack-
> ers to hide their tracks and give false leads. But precisely
> because a trail has been left that points so obviously to bin
> Laden, the nagging question for those of suspicious mind is
> whether there may have been a senior partner hiding in the
> shadows, carefully concealing its role from investigators and
> now encouraging us to look elsewhere . . .

The Clinton White House, he adds, had a propensity to start with
the impression it wanted to create and then to work backwards
from it. It wanted to avoid the bad news that would result from a
clear confrontation with a state, the casualties that would be likely
to follow hostilities. Given these priorities, "blinkers that would
leave state actions outside your field of view will help serve your
purpose".[72]

Mylroie herself in her post-September 11th conclusion is in no
doubt about the identity of this "senior partner":

> If we could recover the understanding of terrorism that we
> had a decade ago, we would recognize that a state is behind
> the September 11 assault and the biological attacks that have

followed. And we would ask, Which state could it be? The only reasonable answer is Iraq, with which we are still at war. After all we bomb Iraq on a regular basis and maintain an economic siege that is itself an outgrowth of the Gulf War. It is only to be expected that Saddam would take action against us . . . What is the probability that bin Laden carried out the September 11 assault without assistance from a state? *Next to zero* . . . (emphasis added)

Mylroie insists that if the United States fails to assert that Iraq was involved and to take the appropriate measures, Saddam will have little reason to desist.

We already have the clues to show us that Iraq is probably involved. Bin Laden has known ties to Iraqi intelligence. Bin Laden's aims, moreover, coincide with Iraq's agenda: to overthrow the Saudi government, to end the US presence in the Gulf, and to have the sanctions on Iraq lifted. In Baghdad, where any mass protest must be officially sanctioned, Iraqis have marched in support of bin Laden . . . Saddam is the only world leader to have publicly praised the September 11 attacks and who suggested that they were justified.

She concludes with a quote from the speech the Iraqi leader made the day after the attack:

Regardless of the conflicting human feelings about what happened in the United States yesterday, the United States reaps the thorns that its rulers have planted in the world . . . Those who consider the lives of their people as precious and dear must remember that the lives of people in the world are also precious and dear to their families.[73]

The presumption of innocence appropriate to criminal processes is difficult to apply when it comes to states since the whole point of operating under "false flags" is to maintain deniability. State complicity will usually only emerge in retrospect when evidence from widely differing sources is gathered and coordinated. As Fred Halliday observes:

> The record of terrorism in the Middle East in recent years suggests ... that in many cases the degree of state involvement in acts of violence by apparently independent or underground groups is greater than at first sight appears: not all, but many terrorist groups have received support from states, even if these groups originated in an autonomous manner.[74]

Although direct proof is hard to come by, suspicion of state involvement with operations blamed on al-Qa'ida is strong. It is now thought likely that bin Laden's organization was involved in training the Somali tribesmen, followers of General Mohamed Aidid, who killed eighteen US servicemen in Somalia in October 1993, ten months after landing on a highly publicized humanitarian mission prompted by public responses to televised images of starving children. Before the US intervention, Turabi's Sudan, backed by Iran, was spreading Islamist influence among the fractious Somali tribes whose internecine struggles were largely responsible for the famine conditions. For the Islamists, the humanitarian intervention was merely a pretext for the extension of the American military presence in the area: the arrival of the marines heralded a new phase of US imperialism aimed not just at Somalia, but also Sudan itself.

Bodansky maintains that despite the mutual animosity between Iran and Iraq, the former enemies collaborated with Sudan to strengthen its resistance against the United States. The Iraqi embassy in Khartoum was beefed up with Iraqi intelligence agents; Saddam Hussein's son Qusayy was placed in personal charge of Iraqi policy in the Horn of Africa region. Detachments of trained experts, including Iranian Pasdaran, Lebanese Hizbollah, Arab – mainly Egyptian – "Afghans" and local Islamist elements from Sudan, Somalia and Eritrea, helped by weapons and money supplied by bin Laden, were secretly deployed in Somalia prior to the

"Black Hawk Down" incident – the shooting down of a helicopter – which led to the withdrawal (or the "expulsion", as the Islamists preferred to call it) of US troops from the Horn of Africa.[75] Sudan was behind the assassination attempt on the Egyptian president, Husni Mubarak, during his visit to Addis Ababa, the Ethiopian capital, in June 1995; according to Bodansky, bin Laden, as part of Turabi's inner circle, "played an integral part in formulating the plot", which failed thanks to the split-second thinking of Mubarak's driver.[76]

Bodansky sees the hand of Iran behind the al-Qaʻida suicide bomb attacks on the US embassies in Nairobi, Kenya, and Dar es-Salaam, Tanzania, in August 1998, the atrocities in which 224 people, most of them Kenyans and Tanzanians, were killed. No state employee, however, was indicted in the East Africa bombings, for which two of bin Laden's associates were prosecuted. Bodansky suggests that internal power politics, in addition to state-sponsored terrorism fostered by Iran and Sudan, played its part in the attacks on American service personnel in the Arabian peninsula attributed to bin Laden and his al-Qaʻida network. Inside Saudi Arabia some fifteen to twenty-five thousand Islamist sympathizers of bin Laden and dissident religious shaikhs such as Salman bin Fahd al-Udah from Buraida found support among more than five thousand trained "Arab Afghan" veterans, many of whom were more than capable of sophisticated acts of terror against US personnel. In November 1995 a car bomb exploded in front of the Military Cooperation Building in Riyadh, where dozens of American service personnel were eating their lunch. Of the six people killed in the blast, five were Americans: Saudi sources admitted that the operation was meticulously planned and highly sophisticated. The following summer nineteen American servicemen were killed in the massive bomb that exploded at the Khobar Towers residential complex near Dhahran.

Nevertheless, at the time of writing no conclusive evidence has been produced that Iraq was behind the September 11th attack. There are reports that between April 8 and 11 Mohammed Atta flew from Virginia Beach to Prague for a meeting with Ahmad

Khalil al-Ani, the Iraqi consul, said to be Saddam Hussein's intelligence officer in the Czech capital. The columnist William Safire, writing in the *New York Times*, reports that the meeting was confirmed by Czech intelligence, which kept al-Ani under "constant visual and wiretap surveillance", and senior US intelligence officials.[77] The reports, however, have been denied by Russian intelligence sources and unnamed European officials. Czech intelligence sources quoted by *Newsweek* in May 2002 acknowledged they may have been mistaken and that no such meeting took place. Based on Kurdish sources in northern Iraq, Jeffrey Goldberg's investigation, published in the *New Yorker*, concluded that Iraqi intelligence had collaborated with al-Qaʻida for years and that the two organizations had been involved in running a terrorist group, Ansar al-Islam, operating in the Kurdish-held areas of northern Iraq. According to Goldberg, senior al-Qaʻida operatives had been received in Baghdad as early as 1992.[78] Rather than remaining a purely intelligence matter, the whole issue of possible Iraqi involvement has been snared in the arguments within the Bush administration over extending the "war against terrorism" to Iraq. Whereas "doves" in the State Department, concerned with the international ramifications of extending the war, have given more emphasis to Saddam Hussein's alleged manufacture and stockpiling of weapons of mass destruction, the "hawks" in the Pentagon are more inclined to expose the evidence of "smoking guns". A senior US counter-terrorism official interviewed by Bergen refused to draw any conclusions whatsoever from the reported meeting between Mohammed Atta and Ahmad al-Ani. As Bergen puts it, "one meeting does not an al-Qaʻida–Iraqi conspiracy make".[79]

After the Taliban had been eliminated by American bombing in Afghanistan, White House rhetoric pointed increasingly towards an extension of the "war against terror" to Iraq, suggesting that the administration might have intelligence about Iraqi involvement too sensitive to be made public. President Bush's State of the Union address in January 2002, in which he bracketed the highly improbable trinity of Iraq, Iran and North Korea as an "axis of evil", produced a chorus of protest from European leaders, including the foreign ministers of Germany and France and the European Commissioner for Foreign Affairs, Chris Patten. Informed observers (including Patten) saw inclusion of Iran in the speech as highly injudicious, since it would solidify feelings against the United States instead of allowing the differences between the pro-Western reformists under Khatami and the hard-liners led by the supreme religious leader Ayatollah Khamenei to develop. The inclusion of Iran in the "axis of evil" seemed particularly ungrateful and inept, in view of the positive role, widely acknowledged by the Americans, that the Islamic Republic had played in establishing the interim Afghan government under Hamid Karzai, a kinsman of ex-king Zahir chosen by Washington. Other commentators, however, believed paradoxically that the inclusion of Iran in the "axis of evil" could improve the prospects for Khatami and his supporters: realizing that their government was being tarred with the terrorist reputation for which hard-liners in the judiciary and intelligence services were responsible, the pro-democracy reformers would be pushed into adopting more aggressive positions.[80]

Few people doubted, however, that the primary target of Bush's speech was Iraq, and newspapers began to predict a war as early as the summer of 2002, though sources in the Pentagon and the State Department were reported as saying that preparations for a war could take at least a year.[81] Particular significance was attached to a shift in the language of Secretary of State Colin Powell, previously considered a "dove" on the issue, who stated that "regime change would be in the best interests of the Iraqi people".[82] It was far from clear, however, how the outcome of a successful war against Iraq would be different in 2002 from that predicted by the president's father in 1991, when the US held back from destroying the Republican Guard and pursuing Saddam Hussein to Baghdad for fear of dismembering the country into mutually antagonistic Kurdish, Sunni and Shi'i states. A Shi'i state on the borders of Kuwait and Saudi Arabia was hardly compatible with US interests in the region. Either the new policy had not been thought through (which seemed unlikely), or Saddam's renewed capability for producing weapons of mass destruction was considered to be so menacing that Iraqi dismemberment was considered the lesser risk. The "axis of evil" speech and the prospects of war with Iraq, seen as a manifestation of American unilateralism, also threatened to sour relations between the US and the European Union, especially Germany and France.

Given the administration's previous demonization of bin Laden and the angry rhetoric of the "war against terrorism", the shift of focus from al-Qa'ida to Iraq was significant. In the view of Sir Michael Howard, one of Britain's most distinguished military historians, the "war" on terrorism had been a "terrible and irrevocable error" from the start. The British in their time had fought many "wars" against terrorists, in Palestine, Ireland, Cyprus and Malaysia – but they labelled them "emergencies", never "wars". "This meant that the police and intelligence services were provided with exceptional powers, and were reinforced where necessary by the armed forces, but all continued to operate within a peacetime framework of civil authority." The rhetoric of war tended to create a "war psychosis" that was wholly counter-productive for the strategic objective of winning "hearts and minds" in order to deprive the terrorist networks of local support. Above all, talk of war raised unrealistic and inappropriate expectations:

> Figures on the Right, seeing themselves cheated of what the Germans used to call a *frisch, fröhliche Krieg*, a short, jolly war in Afghanistan, demand one against a more satisfying adversary, Iraq; which is rather like the drunk who lost his watch in a dark alley but looked for it under a lamp post because there was more light there. As for their counterparts on the Left, the very word "war" brings them out on the streets to protest as a matter of principle. The qualities needed in a serious campaign against terrorists – secrecy, intelligence, political sagacity, quiet ruthlessness, covert actions that remain covert, above all infinite patience – all these are forgotten or overridden in a media-stoked frenzy for immediate results, and nagging complaints if they do not get them.[83]

After the US bombing of Afghanistan, Howard's prognostications appeared to have been borne out. Hundreds, if not thousands, of civilians had been killed – in several notorious cases as a result of false intelligence deliberately fed to American commanders by Afghan factions looking to settle old scores. Despite the triumphalist claims of Washington, the Afghan campaign, in terms of its original objective of capturing bin Laden "dead or alive", had been a failure. At the time of writing the Saudi renegade was still thought to be alive and safe somewhere in the North-West Frontier, in the mountainous borderlands between Afghanistan and Pakistan where local tribes formerly backed by the ISI were sympathetic to his cause.

As we have seen, bin Laden's organization was never more than semi-autonomous, even at its inception, when it may have operated as an arm of Saudi intelligence controlled or supported by the Pakistani ISI, with CIA backing. It only came to public attention in the West (as opposed to Afghanistan) after the attacks on American forces in Saudi Arabia in 1995 and 1996 and on the US embassies in East Africa in 1998. In each and every case there has been speculation of state involvement. The soundness of such speculation, however, is problematic, as is the question, Which state? Like Mylroie, Yossef Bodansky takes the *prima facie* view that states are behind terrorism, but he seeks to show how bin Laden has manipulated state sponsorship to his advantage:

Bin Laden ... is not an evil "Lone Ranger" but rather a principal player in a tangled and sinister web of terrorism-sponsoring states, intelligence chieftains, and master terrorists. Together they wield tremendous power throughout the Muslim world and wreak havoc and devastation upon their foes. In order to understand Osama bin Laden, one must comprehend the world in which he operates. Bin Laden has always been – and still is – part of a bigger system, a team player and a loyal comrade at arms. The terrorist operations in several parts of the world now attributed to bin Laden were actually state-sponsored operations perpetrated by dedicated groups of

Islamists. Bin Laden's own role in this network has increased, and his stature has risen tremendously. Thus, the Osama bin Laden of the late 1990s has evolved in response to key events and associations that shaped his life and molded his world-view. Ultimately, however, bin Laden, his colleagues, and the states sponsoring them are all key components of the dominant megatrend in the Muslim world – the rise and spread of radical militant Islamism.[84]

The evidence for state sponsorship of terrorism is difficult to establish conclusively since in order to achieve deniability, governments and their agents will take care to cover their tracks. In the murky, looking-glass world of intelligence and counter-terrorism, the evidence is rarely conclusive. The intelligence files of the sponsoring countries are closed, the briefings given to writers by counter-terrorism experts may be contaminated by political prejudice or partisanship. Since their sources cannot be checked, the evidence produced by journalists or counter-terrorism experts such as Bodansky has to be taken on trust, and it is difficult to have complete confidence in writers who show themselves to be sloppy, inaccurate, partisan or tendentious on significant points of detail.[85] A more fruitful approach, in my view, would be to explore the broader political contexts in which the culture of terrorism takes root.

There can be little doubt that terrorism (or, to use a more neutral term, freelance military activity that may be encouraged, but not necessarily controlled, by governments) flourishes in circumstances where the state is perceived as corrupt or alien, ethnically or religiously unrepresentative or otherwise partisan and unrepresentative of the cultural and political aspirations of the population over which it governs, or a significant part thereof. State sponsorship is part of the story, but so also is the sense of injustice that occurs when the state is seen as being alien or the tool of foreign interests. The state may be experienced as oppressive in many societies, especially in the developing world where modernization and industrialization raise expectations for all, while

granting their benefits to the few. In much of the Islamic world,
however, the perception of injustice is especially acute. As I hope to
show in Chapter 8, the modern Islamic state's legitimacy is fragile,
Although it is simplistic to see the Islamist movement, with all the
violence it generates, as being part of a wider "clash of civilizations", there are historical factors which provide both the models
and the contexts for the kind of revolutionary action that are hallowed and sanctified in the Islamic tradition.

Chapter Eight

A Clash of Civilizations?

In a widely read article in *Foreign Affairs* in the summer of 1993 later expanded into a book, Samuel Huntington, professor of government and strategic studies at Harvard University, argued that after the end of the Cold War, future conflicts would occur between the "tectonic plates" of civilizations formed by centuries of cultural programming. The attacks of September 11th enormously boosted Huntington's argument. The Italian prime minister, Silvio Berlusconi, used Huntington's ideas to argue the case for Western cultural superiority. ("'We' have Mozart and Michelangelo, and 'they' don't," as Edward Said caustically summed him up.)[1]

According to Huntington:

> . . . the fundamental source of conflict in this new world will not be primarily ideological or primarily economic. The great divisions among humankind and the dominating source of conflict will be cultural. Nation states will remain the most powerful actors in world affairs, but the principal conflicts of global politics will occur between nations and groups of different civilizations. The clash of civilizations will dominate global politics. The fault lines of civilizations will be the battle lines of the future.[2]

Civilizations are differentiated from each other by "history, language, culture, tradition, and most important, religion". Foremost among the future clashes predicted by Huntington was a conflict between a revitalized Islam and China, on the one hand, and the West on the other. "The dangerous clashes of the future are likely to arise from the interaction of Western arrogance, Islamic intolerance and Sinic assertiveness."[3] The Huntington thesis has come in for a good deal of criticism. Said attacks the cultural essentialism underlying his concept of a "civilization" as something discretely marked off from its neighbours. Huntington, he says, is really an ideologist looking for another cold war between the "West" and "the rest", who makes his "civilizations" and "identities" into "sealed-off entities" purged of the "myriad currents and countercurrents that animate human history". Such interactions have over centuries made it possible for "that history not only to contain wars of religion and imperial conquest but also to be one of exchange, cross-fertilization and sharing".[4]

Huntington's definition of a "civilization" is certainly unusual. Despite Berlusconi's comments, it is not the sum of the high cultural products in art and architecture, literature or manners that are often associated with the term but something rather less penetrable. "A civilization is a cultural entity" with "villages, regions, ethnic groups, nationalities, religious groups" all having "distinct cultures at different levels of cultural heterogeneity". The culture of a village in southern Italy may be different from that of a village in northern Italy, but both will share in a common Italian culture that distinguishes them from German villages. European communities, in turn, will share cultural features that distinguish them from Arab or Chinese communities. Arabs, Chinese and Westerners, however, are not part of any broader cultural entity. They constitute civilizations.

The definition of a civilization as something composed of villages seems plausible enough, until one remembers that northern Italian villages (for example in the Alpine Alto Adige) are much more like Austrian (that is, German) villages in neighbouring Tyrol in appearance than they are like villages in Tuscany; while Sicilian villages, for example around Trapani in the western, flatter part of the island, are more like Tunisian villages than their "civilizational" counterparts further north. This is hardly surprising since the climates of Sicily and Tunisia are similar, as are those of the Alto Adige and the Austrian Tyrol. Huntington's definition, however, does not depend on the external, environmental influences that might mould a civilization's domestic architecture (and the lifestyles that go with it), but rather on a combination of historical–cultural factors, including religion, and the elusive, subjective factor of identity.

"A civilization," he writes, "is . . . the highest cultural grouping of people and the broadest level of cultural identity people have short of that which distinguishes humans from other species. It is defined both by common objective elements, such as language, history, religion, customs, institutions, and by the subjective self-identification of people." While acknowledging that people have different "levels of identity" and that the composition and boundaries of civilizations are subject to change, he nevertheless seems to imply that membership of one's "civilization" is non-transferable, since the civilization to which a person belongs "is the broadest level of identification with which he intensely identifies". The implication that Westerners, Arabs and Asians share no broader cultural relationships and constitute mutually exclusive civilizations ignores the ways in which all three can participate in modernity, when they have access to it, and are equally adept at using its products: the fact that people of 115 nationalities were present in the World Trade Center when it was attacked is a case in point. The argument also fails to address the vital issue of education, both in terms of its content and its relationship with development – not to mention the wider, problematic relationship that all cultures have in reconciling "tradition" and "modernity". An educated Muslim or Chinese person, especially if they share common professional or cultural interests, will often have more in common with, say, their southern English counterpart than the latter may have with his or her supposed civilizational comrade from a Newcastle housing estate. The element of subjectivity or choice Huntington allows in his definition of identity contradicts the cultural determinism of his argument.[5]

According to Huntington the clash between Islamic and Western civilizations flows "from the nature of the two religions".[6] Both faiths are "universalistic and missionary".[7] Conflicts between them are less likely to be centred on territory than on "broad intercivilizational issues such as weapons proliferation, human rights and Western intervention".[8] Huntington is clearer on "the distinctive character of the West" than on the distinctive character of Islam. "Christianity, pluralism, individualism and the rule of law ... political democracy, human rights, cultural freedom are Western ideas, except by adoption."[9] Restricting himself as he does to rather broad abstractions, he does not enumerate equivalent contrasting values for his "Islamic civilization" beyond stressing the centrality of "clan, family and tribe" to Muslim identity.[10] He stresses the "non-negotiable character of religious demands"[11] without addressing the content of such demands. His is a stimulating, but also a frustrating book: it stimulates a very generalized kind of discussion without focusing on specific details. The reason, one suspects, may partly be ignorance: his discussions of Islam display a very superficial knowledge of the tradition.

Nevertheless one does not have to go all the way with Huntington – or his critics – to recognize that there is a good deal of force in his argument. Setting aside the interactions that may exist between members of different "civilizations" at the local level, where there are mixed communities of people from different religions and ethnicities living in very similar ways, the concept of "civilization" as the largest unit of collective self-identification short of humanity has a certain plausibility, especially when general cultural factors and ways of living are given primacy. "Islam" and the "West" share common religious roots in the religious traditions of Western Asia, but their central institutions are configured in significantly different ways. Islam shares with Judaism and Christianity, its Abrahamic siblings, a common millenarian dynamic. The early, Meccan passages of the Quran are full of warnings about the Day of Judgement when men and women will be held accountable for their deeds: it is far from clear from such passages that what is being referred to is a judgement in the afterlife. The warnings delivered to people who fail to heed God's messages sound both imminent and terrestrial. The apocalyptic strand in Islam seems less prevalent in the majority tradition of Sunnism, because Muhammad's victory over the Meccans was in its own way an apocalyptic event that happened in "real" historical time: the Muslim conquest or "opening" of Mecca towards the end of Muhammad's life was the judgement of God. The millennial spirit, however, is not exhausted by its partial fulfilment. It is a constant in human affairs, especially in the Abrahamic traditions. Like the aftershocks of a great earthquake, millennial movements continued to shake the Islamic world as different tribal groups espoused the cause of the Mahdi (often but not always a descendant of 'Ali) in movements aimed at bringing about the restoration of peace and justice to a world torn asunder by strife. In Shi'ism the millennial idea is institutionalized in the belief in the Hidden Imam, who will return one day to restore peace and justice on earth.

Religions, however, cannot be defined exclusively in terms of formal doctrines or religious practices. They are better conceived of as symbolic languages or communication systems through which a vast range of human impulses, private and social, are given expression. Western encroachments, conceived as alien and hostile, have frequently stimulated millenarian responses among Sunni Muslims: the Swat Pathans and the Baqqara tribes that supported the claims of the Sudanese Mahdi in the 1880s are obvious examples. Another is the millennial movement led by Juhaiman al-'Utaibi who occupied the Grand Mosque in Mecca in November 1979 in the name of the Mahdi 'Abdullah al-Qahtani, shaking the Saudi monarchy to its foundations.

The deeper basis for all such movements, whether or not they occur within the frame of Islam, lies in the human psyche. The eschatological hope for messianic deliverance, howsoever conceived in its details, has a universal appeal. The basis for this appeal, one suspects, lies in the promise of escape from the burden of individual selfhood framed by the inevitability of death, the ultimate condition of chaos and dissolution. As Harold Bloom reminds us, "religion, whether it be shamanism or Protestantism, rises from our apprehension of death. To give a meaning to meaningless is the endless quest of religion . . . When death becomes the center, then religion begins."[12]

Citing with approval what Ernest Becker calls religion's "denial of death", Mark Juergensmeyer links this denial directly to the symbols of violence to be found in most of the great religions, including Hinduism, Judaism, Buddhism, Christianity, and Islam, all of which "offer ways of avoiding what humans know to be a fact: eventually they will die". "[W]hat strikes me is the way religion has employed symbols of violence not only to deny death but to control all that is intimately related to death: disorder, destruction and decay. By evoking and then bridling images of warfare, religion has symbolically controlled not only violence but all the messiness of life."[13] When religious texts or the cultures they engender portray warfare, whether it is the battles of the Israelites in the Old Testament, the epic struggle of the Nephites in the Book of Mormon, the references to the Battle of Badr in the Quran or the famous discourse between Lord Krsna and Arjuna in the Bhagavad Gita, the effect in each case is similar: in Juergensmeyer's words "they are presenting an almost cosmological reenactment of the primacy of order over chaos". In Christianity, Jesus's horrifically painful death by crucifixion acquires meaning as "a monumental act of redemption for humankind, tipping the balance of power and allowing a struggle for order to succeed".[14] Islam re-enacts the bloody sacrifice performed by Abraham when animals are slaughtered in their thousands at the 'Id al-Adha (Feast of Sacrifice) at the conclusion of the Hajj ceremonies. We have seen in the first chapter of this book how the hijackers' letter made use of the language employed in this ritual. But images of violence pervade the Islamic tradition in many other places, especially in the *sira* (biographical) literature depicting the Prophet as a battle-hardened warrior. Muhammad, like all great exponents of the art of prophecy, offered two ways out of the predicament of death: personal

immortality for people who kept his law, and collective immortality for "the best community" created by God for "enjoining what
is good and forbidding what is evil". The jihad (in its "greater" and
"lesser" versions) encompasses both.

Jihad or "struggle" is as essential to Islamic identity and self-
definition as the Mass is to Catholicism. Although the conditions
of its application vary greatly, its value and centrality to the tradition cannot be denied. Militancy of a kind is built into the Islamic
faith tradition. In Shi'ism, as in Christianity, the violence is ritualized, taking a symbolic form in the self-inflicted flagellations that
form part of the 'Ashura ceremonies commemorating the death of
the Imam Hussein, the Prophet's grandson. In the majority Sunni
tradition, violence in the form of warfare is linked historically to
the Islamic imperium. As I have suggested elsewhere, Islam is "programmed for victory".[15] Its formative period occurred during a
period of physical expansion unprecedented in the history of religion. The contrast with Christianity and the "civilization" it
engendered is instructive.

For the first three centuries, Christianity evolved as an underground cult or mystery religion, one of several in the cultural
landscape of late antiquity. The "long and perilous" rise of
Christianity was organic and self-directing. As Rodney Stark has
argued, its central doctrines of loving one's neighbour, given practical expression in caring for the sick in the plague-ridden cities of
the Roman empire, dramatically improving their chances of survival, "prompted and sustained attractive, liberating and effective
social relations and organizations".[16] Christianity succeeded as a
revitalization movement within the Roman empire because it
offered a "coherent culture entirely stripped of ethnicity".[17]

Universalism was built into Christianity. The Church as the
"body of Christ" became the model for the corporate institution
which transcends the mere sum of its membership, substituting for
old identities a new identity and allegiance devoted to Christ,
whose return to establish the Kingdom of God on earth was
expected imminently. The martyrdom of those early Christians who
refused on a point of principle to make even a token submission

to the religious authority of the Roman emperors made a huge impression in a culture conditioned by cruelty. Both Peter Brown and Rodney Stark have emphasized the impact that the highly publicized heroism of Christians must have had as they calmly faced dangerous animals or refused to fight for their lives.[18] Christianity not only encouraged the celibacy that created an elite class of religious specialists whose primary allegiance was to the institution rather than to their families (though in due course patrician families would come to dominate the Church, as in Renaissance Italy). It encouraged exogamy among the laity, facilitating the ethnic mixing that came to characterize most Western societies.[19] The central rite of Christianity, a feast that was open to all believers, was aimed at breaking down social and ethnic barriers through the ritual sharing of food. Eventually the social cohesion fostered by the cult commended it to the Emperor. After the conversion of Constantine in 334, Christianity became the ideological underpinning for Roman power. In the capable hands of Augustine of Hippo, the dangerous belief that the Kingdom of God would be fulfilled on earth, with all the problems this held for worldly authority, was spiritualized and ritualized. Henceforth the Kingdom was not to be of *this* world. The City of God was a spiritual idea, a kingdom of mind and spirit. The eschatological hope of a better "world to come" was kept alive through liturgies. Attempts to enact it literally, to actualize the programme charted, for example, in the Book of Revelation, were suppressed by a Church whose mission was seen by its critics as being the systematic frustration of its founder's intentions.

Muhammad, unlike most of the prophets whose heritage he claimed for his message, lived to preside over the Kingdom, though he died before its massive, sudden expansion brought it from the Arabian margins into the centre of the civilized world. In contrast to Christianity, whose universalism was built into its central rituals, Islamic universalism was contingent rather than insitutional. The Quran is ambiguous: there are passages of universal import which suggest a message directed to the whole of humankind. There are also passages that refer to an "Arabic Quran" and to the existence of prophets or divine messengers among non-Arab peoples: the implication of these passages is that Islam is a religion for the Arabs, a people with a rich oral tradition who lacked a scripture. Possessing a written scripture was a prerequisite of cultural respectability: having the Quran allowed the Arabs to think of themselves as a people comparable to the other Peoples of the Book. Initially no attempt was made to convert the latter: after the first conquests the Arab warriors were housed in separate cantonments to keep them away from the cities. Converts – who had a material interest in conversion, since by becoming Muslims they avoided paying the *jizya* (poll tax) – were absorbed gradually into the Arab system, by marriage, by conviction or through the desire for social advancement, becoming initially "clients" (*mawali*) of the various Arab tribes.

The supra-tribal project initiated by Muhammad was never completed during his lifetime. After his death in 632, its leadership was commandeered by his own tribe, the Quraish who, like Constantine, seized the historical advantage offered by a new monotheist legitimacy. Muhammad may have intentionally signalled this appropriation. After one of his last Arabian battles he gave a disproportionately large share of the booty to his former Meccan adversary Abu Sufyan and his sons Mu'awiya and Yazid, thereby laying the foundations for the Umayyad dynasty. As Jean Lambert writes:

> All of the subsequent history of Islam can be understood as the gradual reconquest of the state by its original enemies, the Meccan families. The same founding model of the *hijra* will serve to legitimate new forms of power, inserting into Islam an explosive contradiction as every believer can refer to the original model to overturn the state in its historical form, denounced as imposture.[20]

That original model was constructed around the jihad against polytheism, in defence of divine unity, or, to use the stronger term, unicity – *tawhid*. Tawhid found its political expression in the idea of the Umma, the transcendental community. If the rituals of prayer (arranged non-hierarchically, with carefully coordinated bodily movements, as in the gymnastic displays beloved of totalitarian regimes) and the rites of the Hajj and 'Umra, are the religious expressions of this idea, jihad is the means of attaining it.

For the majority of believers the "greater" jihad, or, to use a more neutral term, the "soft" jihad, remains the struggle against evil, against temptation, against the passions and impulses of the ego. Among those who adhere to the "lesser" jihad – which we may perhaps call the "hard" jihad – positions vary considerably. Given that most of the world is divided into discrete territorial units, Ibn Khaldun's idea of jihad as part of the process of "cyclical renewal" in Islam is problematic, to put it mildly. The extension of European power into the Islamic world created a twofold process of change: the fixing of frontiers and the fixing of dynasties. Arrangements between European powers, the suppression of slavery and piracy and, later, the acquisition of mineral rights and the franchises and monopolies granted to oil companies demanded that frontiers be fixed territorially. In order that such arrangements could be made permanent (for example in the cases of the treaties that bound the Gulf shaikhdoms to Britain) formal provision had to be made for the succession.

This was a radically new arrangement in what Marshall Hodgson calls the "Afro Eurasian Arid Zone"[21] where pastoralists had ranged for centuries over broad belts of territory at different seasons in search of grazing. In pastoral regions, property and territory are not coextensive, as they came to be in Europe, a region of higher rainfall where the enclosure of land made commercial sense for the landowner. Peasants can be taxed, their surpluses squeezed out of them, if necessary, by physical force (as happened to the ryots, in India, under the Mughal zemindars).[22] Nomads are harder to tax, because of their greater mobility and military skills. The Islamic state as it developed after the collapse of the Arab caliphate was communal rather than territorial. Islamic law, as it developed, was also communal in orientation: as Lawrence Rosen has shown in his study of Shari'a courts in Morocco, its primary purpose was conflict resolution (as distinct from enforcing the writ of the state).[23] The authority of government diminished in proportion to distance from the city. The model of jihad suggested by the philosopher of history Ibn Khaldun applied in a region of the world where the cities and fertile valleys had always been vulnerable to attack by the tribal peoples of the margins – what Moroccans expressively called the *bled al-siba* (lands of insolence).[24] Dynastic rule had been subject to change in accordance with what might be described as a Darwinian system of political ecology. For much of the Muslim world, modernity arrived on the wings of colonial conquest: the new territorial arrangements were supported by colonial armies, or armies under colonial tutelage using imported weaponry.

In Transjordan, Iraq and the South Arabian Protectorate, treaty arrangements and frontier defences were enforced and maintained by the Royal Air Force. In much of the Arab world, new weaponry consolidated the hold of the dynastic states. Whereas in premodern times the power of the rulers was notionally conditional on "enjoining the good and forbidding the evil"[25] (in accordance with a Quranic phrase understood to mean, retrospectively, the upholding of the Shari'a law), the power of enforcement made possible by enhanced bureaucracy, better policing, expanded intelligence services and armies that ate up an ever-growing portion of GDP enabled dynastic or quasi-dynastic governments to impose themselves far more effectively on civil society than they had been able to in the past. In the West the growing power of the state over civil society, intrinsic to the modernizing process, was balanced by democratic institutions which rendered state officers accountable to their electorates. The supersession of democracy, or its perversion, in Russia, Italy, Spain and Germany and the states of Eastern Europe proved that the accountable side of the bargain could be suspended without adversely affecting the process of modernization, at least in the short term. The forms of democracy, rooted in the traditions of Northern Europe, were predicated on the formal distinction, inherited from Roman law, between public and private realms. Representative assemblies are "bodies" disposing of portions of that sovereignty originally vested in monarchy, and subsequently acquired by "the people".

On the international scale, the grids superimposed by the Western states that formatted Muslim countries onto two-dimensional spatial maps, conferring sovereignty on whoever happened to control the frontiers, were further buttressed by the international system, with all its powers of patronage. However, the boundaries thus established often conflicted with the affective realities of loyalty, faith and allegiance. The Kurdish people of upper Mesopotamia had their homeland carved up between Iran, Iraq and Turkey. Palestinians were driven from a substantial part of their homeland by European settlers and later by Jews of Middle Eastern origin in order to make room for the Jewish national state. Iraqi Shiʿites were made to fight against their Iranian co-religionists in an army commanded by their traditional Sunni enemies. Somali pastoralists who had wandered freely into the Ogaden uplands were arrested as intruders by Ethiopia because of a boundary drawn by the colonial powers. The Durand line separating the British Indian Raj from the frontierless zone of the Hindu Kush created a boundary separating different segments of the Pushtun (Pathan) tribes where none had existed before. For a substantial part of the world's population the modern national states, heirs to the European empires they displaced, were experienced as new and alien phenomena, transplanted onto a culture that had organized itself politically along very different lines.

The economic arrangements that accompanied this process were also experienced as coming from an alien source. The capitalist revolution that transformed the globe, and is continuing to transform it as that revolution spreads to South Asia and the Pacific Rim, is integral to modernity. It has become universal through the emergence of the global market. Few of even the most strident critics of globalization believe that this situation can be reversed, that the world can be deglobalized into discreetly separated trading units. For its critics, however, who include most of the Islamists as well as adherents of other political movements such as the VHP in India which emphasize "cultural authenticity", the forms of economic power that dominate the globe are not neutral, either culturally or in terms of values. In my view, their critique is correct. The forms of modernity, including its most important vehicles – the business corporation and its handmaid, the modern national state – are distinctively Christian (and not just Protestant) in their origins. When bin Laden and his associates refer to the "Jews and Crusaders" in their 1998 fatwa they may be using archaic language, but expressing a view of the contemporary world situation that has some basis in historical realities.

The corporate institutions that accompanied the rise of capitalism in the West – including parliamentary assemblies and other institutions of representative government – are imprinted by a distinct type of cultural patterning directly traceable to Western Christianity. Attempts to export them to or impose them upon the Islamic world have not been very successful. Given the importance of the Christian–capitalist revolution for the whole world – and not just the western part of it – it seems legitimate to ask why this revolution did not appear in the Islamic world, since until the thirteenth or fourteenth centuries CE the Islamic world was in many respects more "advanced" than Western Europe in terms of urbanization, wealth, trade and the quality of civil life.

Various economic and technical factors have been advanced to explain the takeoff of the West that led to its global dominance in the eighteenth century. Deeper ploughs increased the agricultural yield. Improved tools enabled forests to be cleared more rapidly, improvements in ship design and navigational skills made possible the discovery – and subsequent plunder – of the Americas. Above all, the introduction of moveable type – the Gutenberg revolution – generated a massive extension of literacy and significantly contributed to the Protestant Reformation and the Enlightenment. None of these technological factors taken in isolation provides a sufficient explanation by itself. Most of these transforming technologies existed in other parts of the globe, for example in China, where the Sung dynasties (960–1279) presided over an industrial revolution in the manufacture of tools and weapons unparalleled before the nineteenth century.

It was not so much the technologies themselves as the institutional forms and legal mechanisms invented by Western Christianity that created the furnace in which the accumulated changes were forged into something new and qualitatively different. I would suggest that Max Weber's famous "Protestant ethic", based on the "this-worldly asceticism" of monks-turned-merchants, was the outcome of this process rather than its cause. The mechanisms, or the legal mechanics to be more precise, that fostered the development of capitalism in Western Europe are the result of many complex interactions. The structures of feudal society allowed ambiguous areas of overlapping jurisdiction to emerge in Western societies – peasant commons, manorial courts, larger territorial entities under the nominal jurisdiction of a great seigneur, and of course towns, with their own freedoms. The monarch at the apex of this structure was theoretically rather weak, given that he was only the grantor-in-chief of the various liberties and franchises that made up Western society, and that he depended on his vassals for military support. Western Christianity, however, in its Catholic, pre-Protestant version makes its own distinctive contribution in the authority it furnishes for the legal structures that underpinned the bourgeois–capitalist revolution.

Two recent scholars, Maxime Rodinson in *Islam and Capitalism* (Harmondsworth, 1977) and Peter Gran in *The Islamic Roots of Capitalism* (Austin, 1979) have argued that Islam was no obstacle to capitalist development because there was little in Muhammad's teaching that contradicted the kind of rationality that Weber regarded as a prerequisite for capitalist development. Generally speaking there is almost nothing in the Quran, apart from the prohibition on alcohol, that would not have been thoroughly congenial to Thomas Jefferson or other eighteenth-century deists. It is mistaken, however, to assume that capitalist institutions as such were an outcome of the Reformation, as Weber's theory implies. The corporate structures that make capitalism possible developed out of three distinctively Christian doctrines – none of them "rational" in the Weberian sense, all of them fundamental to Catholicism. All are conspicuously absent from Islamic teaching, which is one reason why Islam was much admired as a more rational faith than Christianity by a significant number of eighteenth-century deists and *philosophes*. They are the doctrine of the incarnation of Christ through which the divine takes human form; the bodily resurrection of Christ; and the doctrine of vicarious atonement according to which there is "no salvation or remission of sins" outside the Church.

All three doctrines were institutionalized and took secular forms without losing their distinctiveness. They interacted with each other and certain vestigial remnants of Roman law to form the basis of the unique legal corporative institutions that characterized late medieval and early modern North-West European societies – especially in France, Germany, Britain and the Low Countries, the nurseries of modern capitalism.

In his celebrated essay *The King's Two Bodies* Ernst Kantorowics described how the mystical body of Christ, which is central to the Christian liturgy, acquired a sociological meaning in the later Middle Ages. The *corpus mysticum*, previously understood to mean the sacrament or "host", became the organized body of Christian society united in the sacrament of the Altar.[26] In due course, the mystical body of Christ, understood as the community of Christians, became secularized. "*Corpus mysticum* proper came to be less and less mystical as time passed on, and came to mean simply the Church as a body politic or, by transference, *any body politic of the secular world*." (emphasis added)[27] The emerging group structures of secular life in northern Europe – towns, cities, guilds and so forth – acquired public legal recognition as "bodies" parallel with and comparable to the Church. Under charters from the king (or sometimes the bishop), the Western city acquired its own *corpus mysticum*, its fictional identity which allowed the group personality of the organism to transcend the sum of its individual component parts. In due course "the greatest of artificial persons" became, in the words of Pollock's *First Book of Jurisprudence*, "the State".[28] When royal sovereignty was contested by the people, the mystic body came to be vested typically in an assembly, whose members represented parts of the body politic.

Thus in a republic the mystic body of the crown was transferred to "the people" – not as an aggregate of individuals, but as a *fictionalized abstraction*. The mystical–mythical person of Christ, a half-man, half-human chimera, became the modular structure or building block out of which Western capitalism emerged.

The mystic qualities of fictional personhood were devolved not just to parliaments, but also to joint stock companies and public corporations with tradable shares. Within the boundaries of what F.W. Maitland, a famous commentator on the laws of England, suggests might be called "English fellowship law" lie virtually all the institutions that make up the public sphere in the West:

> . . . the churches . . . religious houses, mendicant orders, nonconforming bodies, a presbyterian system, universities old and new, the village community . . ., the manor . . ., the township, the New England town, the counties and hundreds, the chartered boroughs, the guild in all its manifold varieties, the inns of court, the merchant adventurers, the militant "companies" of English *condottieri*, . . . the trading companies, the companies that become colonies, the companies that make war, the friendly societies, the trades unions, the clubs, the group that meets at Lloyds Coffee House, the group that becomes the Stock Exchange and so on even to the one-man company, the Standard Oil Trust and the South Australian statutes for communistic villages.[29]

In short, the Western corporation, the cultural and legal descendant of the mystic body of Christ, is at the origin of the peculiar society we have come to know as the "West", whose cellular structures are multiplying (some people would say, like a series of carcinogenous growths) across the globe.

The outcome of this somewhat complex argument is clear: the legal fiction of group personality was the prerequisite for a capitalist revolution. To some degree, my argument reinforces the Huntington thesis by stressing the peculiarity of Western institutions and their specific cultural bases. Group personality – the legal fiction invented by the Church on the basis of the fictive personality inherited from Roman law – generates group identities: witness the company liveries worn by the wealthier merchants and traders in London and other cities in early modern times, to distinguish themselves from the humbler journeymen and artisans. The corporation commands a special kind of group loyalty that, crucially, transcends the interests and ties of kinship. The burgers not only become a class (which they may arguably constitute in other, non-Western societies) but they become conscious of themselves as separate, distinct and powerful. Rembrandt's magnificent group portraits such as *The Staalmeesters* exemplify this corporate authority, as does one of his most theatrical paintings, the *Nightwatch*, an icon of the Amsterdam militia brought to life as "a little commonwealth . . . a microcosm, not just of the militia, but of the whole teeming city".[30] The corporate group becomes the vehicle for capital accumulation: the burgers continually reinvest their money in the company which, crucially, not only transcends the sum of its individual members, but exists, like the Church, for eternity.

The Church – as the body of Christ – was eternal. It was only through participation and membership of this body that the individual could hope to achieve salvation – that is, remission of sins and eternal life. The structure was secularized without changing its essential character: the corporate body – the craft guild, the urban corporation, and eventually the trading company with transferable shares – retained its 'eternal' character. Unlike the Church it could not guarantee eternal life for the individual – but it did the next best thing. By creating a human institution that transcended an individual's life span, it provided a mechanism for the accumulation of capital powerful enough to create the conditions necessary for capitalist takeoff. Jesus Christ was the first president of General Motors: the original model for the modern business corporation is the *corpus mysticum* invented by the Catholic Church.

In the secular world corporate growth, driving overseas expansion, becomes a goal in itself. The schizophrenic division of personality between the corporate male and family man and now, increasingly, between corporate female and family woman, with the inevitable personal tensions such a division engenders, are the contemporary forms of Max Weber's "this-worldly asceticism". It is not just the individual monk who came out of the monastic closet to trade his divine calling for a worldly career: the whole monastery secularized itself along with its mystique of the divine body. Secularization involved not a "rejection of religion" (at least, not in the first instance) but rather the appropriation and dissemination of divine authority and spiritual power (as bestowed, for example, by the patron saints of guilds). The corporative patterns thus created were well suited to post-Meiji Japan, whose feudal structures resembled those of late medieval Europe. In modern times, the corporative ethos has been adopted in Japan with a vengeance. In the Islamic heartlands, if not the periphery (like Malaysia and Indonesia, which are in any case within the Japanese economic if not cultural orbit), the culture of corporate intitutions has generally fallen on much stonier ground.[31]

Capitalism, generated by what Marxists call the "bourgeois revolution", was the midwife of modernity. As I have tried to demonstrate, its cultural roots lie deep in the legal structures of pre-Reformation Western Christianity. Corporate power is the motor of technological development, and because eternity has been programmed into it, it is goalless and nonteleological. The corporation's *raison d'être* is expansion for its own sake. The technological revolution driven by it is relentless and perpetual. As Jaques Ellul observed:

> Technology never advances toward anything because it is pushed from behind. The technician does not know why he is working, and generally he does not much care . . . There is no call towards a goal; there is constraint by an engine placed in the back and not tolerating any halt for the machine . . . The interdependence of technological elements makes possible a very large number of "solutions" for which there are not problems.[32]

Many Muslim polemicists decry the immorality and "materialism" of the postindustrial West, which they see as attacking or undermining the certainties of faith essential for the preservation of decency and order. The charge of materialism, as I have already suggested, is naïve and parochial: the spiritual resources of an unbelieving West are neither greater nor less than those to be found in believing societies; but, being modern, they have become specialized, subdivided, redistributed and stored in cultural pockets outside the hegemonic control of established religion.

In "civilized" Europe, religious observance flourishes in inverse ratio with artistic appreciation. The churches may be almost empty, but the galleries and concert halls are full. In London on Sundays, many of the chairs in St Paul's Cathedral remain vacant; the Tate Modern, the art gallery recently created in a converted power station, just across the river, is jammed with people from every walk of life. The Bauhaus, the studio of architecture and design founded in Berlin in the 1920s, was one of the revolutionary fountainheads of modernity. It was also a temple peopled by mystics and spiritual visionaries, including two of the great modern Sufi fellow travellers, Wassily Kandinsky and Piet Mondrian. Just as modernity distributes spiritual feeling away from organized religion and into a pantheon of separate activities ranging from the high arts to sport, so it redirects the faith that formerly adhered to the pre-Kantian deity. Modern spiritual feeling gravitates towards the God within (which Jung identified with the collective unconscious) and outwardly toward the complex interconnected systems that sustain the fabric of modernity. In modern societies, Luther's early-modern "priesthood of the believers" who held to the doctrine of "justification by faith" has yielded to the priesthood of specialized knowledge and faith in the esoteric systems that modernity generates and services. In Giddens's formulation, "the nature of modern institutions is deeply bound up with the mechanisms of trust in abstract systems, especially trust in expert systems".[33]

Money is the most obvious example of an abstract system of trust: its value lies in a web of immense complexity underpinned by the millions of faceless transactions that keep a currency afloat. When trust in the integrity of these transactions is withdrawn, the currency may collapse, producing empty stomachs and violence, as happened recently in Argentina. There is nothing "materialistic" about money, or about shares whose tradable values are determined either by bullish expectations built on the intangible and sometimes self-fulfilling quality of hope, or, conversely, by the bear market's gloomy predictions, which are equally self-fulfilling. The heaven and hell, salvation and punishment so graphically described in the Quran's Meccan passages have not been abolished; like everything else pertaining to the divinity they have been actualized, appropriated and redrawn in the tones of the present. The oscillations of hope and despair that informed a medieval reading of scripture are experienced in the here and now, in the financial pages of the press.

We now entrust our lives to faith in an "abstract" or impersonal system of nuanced and sophisticated operations by a dedicated priesthood of experts when we board a train or an aircraft. It is not just the train driver, or the pilot, in whom we place our trust, but also the complex chains of finely calibrated and synchronized operations by individuals, personally unknown to us, who work in finance, engineering, maintenance, signals and air traffic control. The hijacking of an aircraft in the name of Allah may appear at first sight as an attack on the civilization that manufactures and runs it, but on further reflection it is more than that: it is an attack not so much on *civilization*, as on *modernity* itself, the faith in the "system" that makes airplanes fly.

This universe of depersonalized human interactions, or "abstract systems", is the soulless soul of modernity, the condition of a kind of freedom that is distinctively "Western" in its individualism. It excels at providing convenience at the expense of human comfort – the comfort that is not about upholstery, but about the sense of belonging essential to personal well-being and personal identity. At the level of social interaction its manners are crude and formulaic. The "Have a nice day" of the waiter or cabin stew-ard conveys no sense of the real hospitality, esteem and affection one experiences as a guest in the Middle East. In Islamic cultures, one is often told, personal interactions count for more than they do in the West, they are given due weight. The visitor to Cairo's crowded Gamaliyya district does not experience the indifference accorded the foreigner in London or Manhattan.

Indeed the depersonalized abstractions of modernity find their perfect architectural expression in the impersonal aesthetic of modern downtown city areas, which seem to dwarf humanity. Old Islamic cities such as Aleppo (the subject of Mohammed Atta's dissertation), with its warren of covered *suqs* too narrow for motor traffic, its open booths where small merchants display their wares, are at the opposite "civilizational" pole to Oxford Street or Madison Avenue, just as the brusque and perfunctory attitude of the "Western" shop assistant or checkout person (who is as likely as not a non-Westerner) contrasts unfavourably with the tea-dispensing courtesy one finds in the Arab or Persian bazaar. According to *Newsweek* magazine, the wall of Atta's otherwise austere apartment in Hamburg displayed a poster of the black-and-white photograph taken by Lewis Hine in 1930 of construction workers perched on a beam of the Empire State Building. Former teachers and classmates told the magazine that Atta believed that high-rise buildings had desecrated his homeland.

In the ancient cities of the Middle East, the time-honored mode of construction was to build one- and two-story houses with private courtyards. The construction of towering, imper-sonal and usually ugly apartment blocks in the 1960s and '70s, Atta believed, had ruined the old neighborhoods, rob-bing their inhabitants of privacy and dignity. It may have been particularly galling to Atta that his own family had moved into an 11th-floor apartment in just such a hulking monstrosity in 1990, as he was graduating with an engineer-ing degree from Cairo University. To Atta, the boxy building was a shabby symbol of Egypt's haphazard attempts to modernize and its shameless embrace of the West.[34]

The high-rise tower block which stacks people vertically may have come to suit societies where freedom is experienced as personal privacy (freedom from being observed by one's neighbours, freedom not to make conversation in the elevators). But in societies conditioned by centuries of "horizontal" living, where the rules of extended family living, including sexual segregation, were maintained less by draconian restrictions than by the customary zoning of male and female areas, living in a skyscraper becomes a kind of tyranny, in which males and females are imprisoned vertically into the discretely separated nuclear families that prevail in Western societies.

If "civilizations" could be reduced to or defined in terms of such differences in styles of living, not only I would find myself in substantial agreement with Huntington, but I would cheer him for the compliment he pays to the "other" of Islamic "civilization". He would recognize its distinctive character, by according it equality of status, even when he fails to mention the particular qualities it promotes of courtesy, dignity and charm.

Curiously, however, that is not the way Huntington approaches "civilization", the abstracted "cultural entity" in which human identities supposedly reside. To do so would be to open his flank to an obvious line of criticism. However enticing it seems to compare Aleppo and Manhattan (or Isfahan and Paris) as cities that exemplify the cultural distinctiveness of the "Islamic" and "Western" civilizations, both are now part of a modernity which has spread itself throughout the world. Thanks to globalization, the same, or similar goods – manufactured in Taiwan, Malaysia, China or Vietnam – can be bought in Muhammad Sa'id's store in Aleppo or in Bloomingdale's. With rare exceptions (such as the late unlamented Taliban regime in Afghanistan), the limits on availability are imposed not by cultural choice, but by the strength of a country's currency and its import controls. Even the shacks in the poorest of "traditional" markets I visited nearly two decades ago – that of Ouagadougou, capital of Burkina Faso – were stocked to their palm-fronded ceilings with Japanese electronics; even then, bright but tacky textiles made on industrial looms in South-East Asia were displacing the painstakingly beautiful work of local handlooms. Would that the religious and social tensions existing along the "fault lines" between "civilizations" were indeed the underlying structural reasons for the conflicts Huntington describes in Africa, Europe and Asia. An equally plausible analysis, however, views the same set of data through a different lens, one that (unlike Huntington) does not accord some notional equality of status to the combatants as members of rival "civilizations". That is the scenario sketched out by Benjamin Barber in his expressively titled book *Jihad versus McWorld*.

For Barber, Jihad, a term he borrows from Islam but does not apply exclusively to it, is inextricably bound up with the McWorld of consumer capitalism which it resists in the name of a pre-existing religious or "partisan identity that is metaphysically defined and fanatically defended".[35] It is "a rabid response to colonialism and imperialism and their economic children, capitalism and modernity; it is diversity run amok, multiculturalism turned cancerous so that the cells keep dividing long after their division has ceased to serve the healthy corpus".[36] It is a response to the revolution in communications which dictates that nations or peoples, however much unified internally, "must nonetheless operate in an increasingly multicultural global environment".[37] As I myself have argued elsewhere, "far from being a bland, homogeneous audio-visual utopia", the global village predicted by Marshall McLuhan in the 1960s "resounds to a cacophony of warring clans".[38]

The jihads or religious movements of cultural authenticity that are erupting throughout the world in most of the major religious traditions are the struggles that produce such a cacophony. For Barber, Jihad and McWorld are bound up together because "the integrating forces of interdependence associated with globalism actually reinforce the fragmenting tendencies of Jihad they seek to combat".[39] As the world gets smaller, so more people become aware of the differences between their own inherited values and those of the West, with its pagan cultures of celebrity, sybaritic hedonism, commercialism and instant self-gratification, exemplified by the fast-food chain McDonald's. "Infantilism is a state of mind dear to McWorld, for it is defined by 'I want, I want, I want' and 'gimme, gimme, gimme' favorites from the Consumers Book of Nursery Rhymes."[40] McWorld's "front parlor" is Walt Disney World,[41] its storyteller is Hollywood, the means by which "the abstraction of language is superseded by the literalness of pictures" whose transgressive, seductive images created in hundreds of studio complexes are transmitted nightly to Muslim countries including Iran and Saudi Arabia whose aniconic cultural traditions may make them more, not less, susceptible to the blandishments of the image.

Hollywood, according to Barber, "inculcates secularism, passivity, consumerism, vicariousness, impulse buying, and an accelerated pace of life, not as a result of its overt themes and explicit storylines but by virtue of what Hollywood is and how its products are consumed". Marketed by Hollywood, McWorld becomes "an entertainment shopping experience that brings together malls, multiplex movie theaters, theme parks, spectator sports arenas, fast-food chains (with their endless movie tie-ins) and television (with its burgeoning shopping networks) into a single vast enterprise that, on the way to maximizing its profits, transforms human beings".[42]

"What I have called the forces of Jihad," Barber concludes, "may seem then to be a throwback to premodern times: an attempt to recapture a world that existed prior to cosmopolitan capitalism and was defined by religious mysteries, hierarchical communities, spellbinding traditions and historical torpor. As such, they may appear directly adversarial to the forces of McWorld. Yet Jihad stands not so much in stark opposition as in subtle counterpoint to McWorld and is itself a dialectical response to modernity whose features both reflect and reinforce the modern world's virtues and vices – Jihad *via* McWorld rather than Jihad *versus* McWorld. The forces of Jihad are not only remembered and retrieved by the enemies of McWorld but imagined and contrived by its friends and components."[43] As I suggested in Chapter 1, there is a disturbing complicity, discernible yet unacknowledged, between the scriptwriters of *Executive Decision* and the "reel bad Arabs" who planned and participated in the September 11th attacks.

Barber's critique of the unholy alliance between the infantilism of popular culture, consumer capitalism and American commercial power is a helpful antidote to Huntington because of the different context in which he places his jihadist revolts. A "clash of civilizations" conveys an implicit idea of parity, of a contest between equals, of a struggle between ancient, even honourable foes, like the mythical encounter between Saladin and King Richard the Lionheart in Sir Walter Scott's *The Talisman*. A true "clash of civilisations" would serve the Islamist cause by allowing the Muslim world to redefine itself and to consolidate its forces behind the "bloody borders" Huntington so controversially details.[44] Barber reminds us that Jihad's resistance, epitomized by September 11th, is not to "civilization" but to its opposite, the McWorld of junk food and junk culture disseminated for profit by three contemporary monstrosities – Rupert Murdoch, McDonald's and Madonna. Or as one Pakistani religious scholar put it, Michael Jackson – another McWorld creation – and Madonna are "torch-bearers of American society with their cultural and social values . . . that are destroying humanity. They are ruining the lives of thousands of Muslims and leading them to destruction, away from their religion, ethics and morality."[45]

On the days following September 11th, George W. Bush and Tony Blair told the world that the assault was an attack on "civilization" itself. Barber suggests a rather different perspective. The terrorists did not attack the Metropolitan or Guggenheim museums, the Frick Collection or Carnegie Hall. The symbolic target they chose, the towers which had dominated the Manhattan skyline for thirty years, represented the financial power that fuels the corrosive culture of "McWorld" and MTV – a far cry from the distilled products of human genius and imagination we associate with the word "civilization" in ordinary usage.

But is Barber right in seeing the Jihads erupting in various parts of the world as manifestations (albeit co-opted and recycled in typically postmodern fashion) of the *Weltanschauung* rich in magic and mystery that preceded what Weber called "the disenchantment of the world" – a return to what the great sociologist, building on the work of Ferdinand Toennies, called *Gemeinschaft* (community) as distinct from *Gesellschaft* (association)?[46] The Islamists share important features with many of the nationalist and separatist movements Barber places in the box he labels Jihad, which include Serbs, Flems, Quebec separatists, Tutsis and Catalans, all of whom seek to reinvent themselves as 'imagined communities". One theme they share in common is nostalgia for a mythical or mythicized past. Where Serbs look back to medieval Kosovo, scene of an early triumph against the Ottomans, Muslims idealize the era of the "rightly guided" caliphs and their contemporaries, the "pious companions" (*al-salaf al-salih*) who led the Muslims during the era of triumph and conquest before internecine disputes tore the leadership of the Umma apart in the Shi'a–Sunni conflict that has yet to be resolved. Even the American Protestant Jihadists, disciples of Jerry Falwell and Pat Robertson, share a nostalgia for an innocent, pre-1960s, mainly "white" and "Christian" America, before homosexuality, drugs, divorce, teenage pregnancies, "strong language" on television, civil rights, affirmative action, multiculturalism and publicly funded works by gay artists such as Robert Mapplethorpe had begun to disturb the philistine complacency of the public culture.

Another feature common to all Jihadist or fundamentalist groups is the Manichaean division of the world between insiders and outsiders, saved and sinners, "true" Muslims and idolators, "us" and "them". Jihadism confers identity on the individual by granting her or him a group membership card, an entrée into the club of born-agains who identify themselves, and each other, by the outward symbols of social conduct, dress and physical appearance ("Christian" haircuts – that is, short back and sides – for men in Falwell's Liberty University, bushy Pushtun beards for the now defunct Taliban, midi-length skirts for women at Liberty, burqas

for *Muslimat* – female Muslims – in Kabul). Jihad in Barber's sense
is the antidote to social anomie and confused identities, a panacea
for the loneliness, indecision, cultural dislocation and social fragmentation that accompany globalization and accelerating
economic change.

There is, however, an important dimension that Barber, a political scientist, fails to fully address or comprehend, and that is
religion itself. In likening modern Jihad to a "yearning for a recon-
structed and remystified community",[47] he conflates the modern
Islamists (if not the other groups he mentions) with two other
forces to which, in theology and theory, they have historically been
opposed: mysticism and nationalism. In his definition, "Jihad is a
metaphor for anti-Western anti-universalist struggle"[48] in which
the local and parochial resists the corrosive, atomizing forces of
McWorld. But to judge by their propaganda, the Islamists are anything but anti-universalist. Their version of nostalgia may be
rooted in the impulse to recover the sacred, to restore the sense of
Gemeinschaft and to desecularize a world "disenchanted" by
modernity. At first glance, however, their aspirations appear to be
anything but parochial.

We saw from Maududi that Islamism aims to complete the project, left unfinished by the caliphs, of spreading the message of
Islam throughout the world. Nor would most Islamists recognize
their project as being linked to the "yearning for a . . . remystified
community" if one associates mystification with mysticism and
its Islamic current in Sufism. With the onslaught of Saudi- and
Gulf-funded religious imperialism, which anathematizes what
might be called the Islamic *bakhti* (devotional) tradition once dominated by the Sufi tariqas, the local and parochial structures by
means of which Islam acquired its variegated regional colourings
have been bleached into a rigorous, puritanical conformity that is
strongly opposed to "innovative" religious practices. The leaders of
the Sunni reformist tradition in Islam, from Ibn Hanbal to Ibn
Taymiyya to Ibn 'Abd al-Wahhab, had a violent disdain for idolatry,
which they mostly equated with Sufi religious practices. In their
own way they were "protestants", like Luther and Calvin. Their

assaults on current religious practices in the name of the "pious ancestors" may be regarded as a premodern, or non-Western, version of the theology of disenchantment proclaimed by the German and French reformers.

Barber is also on thin ground when he states, much too categorically, that while "religion may represent a more profound force in the human psyche . . . as politics it finds its vessel in nationalism".[49] The discourse of modern Islamism is formally anti-nationalist. Maududi regarded nationalism as tantamount to idolatry, the worship of false gods. For him the parochial allegiances it engendered ran directly counter to the interests of the Umma. The jihadist disciples of Sayyid Qutb who made their first attempt to murder the Egyptian president in 1974, were committed to restoring the universal Caliphate abolished by the Turks in 1924. Although several modern Islamist intellectuals have begun to change their tune, and to adopt a more nuanced attitude towards the modern national state, most Islamists agree that secular nationalism, whether Nasserist, Ba'thist or simply "statist" as in Turkey or Tunisia, is a form of "man worship" to be despised. Ideologically, Islamists are internationalists or, rather, supranationalists, by definition. For them the secular national state is an alien implant in their culture which lacks legitimacy. Just as the early Bolsheviks insisted that the "proletariat has no country", the disciples of Qutb and Shaikh Nabahani are committed, at least in theory, to restoring Islamic universalism.

It is the universalist aspiration, coupled with local grievances, that makes the phenomenon of al-Qa'ida both formidable and menacing. It is formidable because its appeal runs deep into the Muslim psyche, in the figure of the Prophet as hero who took on, and defeated, the forces of injustice and idolatry. The figure of Muhammad as a heroic archetype as well as a historical person is too vast a subject to be considered in this essay: suffice it to say that the life recorded in the biographical literature assembled from oral traditions up to two centuries after his death contains an abundance of material that fits the pattern of the "monomyth". The late Joseph Campbell discerned such myths in numerous other narratives, including the "vast, almost Oceanic images of the Orient, . . . the vigorous narratives of the Greeks, . . . the majestic legends of the Bible" in which the hero's adventure follows a consistent pattern: "separation from the world, a penetration to some source of power, and a life-enhancing return".⁵⁰

Anyone familiar with the Quran and the life of the Prophet will be able to discern his features in Campbell's composite portrait:

> The composite hero of monomyth is a personage of exceptional gifts. Frequently he is honoured by his society, frequently unrecognized or disdained. He and/or the world in which he finds himself suffers from a symbolical deficiency. In fairy tales this may be as slight as the lack of a certain gold ring, whereas in apocalyptic vision the physical and spiritual life of the whole earth can be represented as fallen, or on the point of falling, into ruin. Typically the hero of the fairy tale achieves a domestic, microcosmic triumph, and the hero of myth a world-historical macrocosmic triumph. Whereas the former – the youngest or despised child who becomes the master of extraordinary power – prevails over his personal oppressors, the latter brings back from his adventure the means for the regeneration of his society as a whole. Tribal or local heroes, such as the emperor Huang Ti, Moses, or the Aztec Tezcatlipoca, commit their boons to a single folk; universal heroes – Muhammad, Jesus, Guatama Buddha – bring a message for the entire world.⁵¹

Like other mythic heroes Muhammad's triumph consisted in restoring a sense of cosmic wholeness or *tawhid* (divine unicity) to a world fragmented by doubt, injustice, social vices, idolatry. He triumphs in battle over the pagan Quraish, his own kinsfolk: like Arjuna in the Bhagavad Gita (and unlike Christ, the divine–human chimera), his humanity requires him to work out his destiny on the field of battle. The transcendental imperative requires him to act on the plane of history. His battles are bloody, his actions sometimes ruthless: the Jews of the Banu Qainuqa are massacred; the poet Asma bint Marwan is slaughtered with a child at her breast. The Jews and the poets challenge the prophet's teachings – just as adulterers, homosexuals, thieves, idolators and apostates undermine the social order – because they treat with Muhammad's enemies, or cast doubt on the authenticity of his Message, or otherwise threaten a cosmic order established for eternity by God.

Faced with a prophetic model that penetrates so deeply into the tradition's psychic and cultural roots, the denunciations of terrorism by political leaders, by the official 'ulama who are seen as their appointees or even lackeys, by the moderate and liberal scholars favoured by Western media or by foreign statesmen, carry little weight. Whatever the outcome of the campaign in Afghanistan, the appeal of bin Laden and al-Qa'ida will persist.

One can argue, of course, that bin Laden is a cruel, vindictive man utterly unlike the Prophet, that he is a callous terrorist whose actions show no regard for human life, and that any parallels discerned between the figure he presents through his interview and videos and the Prophet Muhammad are *ipso facto* blasphemous. "The Prophet, peace and blessings be upon him, warned against extremism . . . [he] never returned an evil with an evil – he pardoned and forgave,"[52] states Shaikh Hamza Yousef Hanson, an imam favoured by Washington, who is described as making "monumental efforts" to return Islam to its "primordial course" by emphasizing the need to "reclaim the Islamic message of love, justice and relevancy".[53] Shaikh Yousef, an American convert to Islam who studied under traditional Islamic scholars in the Gulf, North Africa and Mauretania, is damning in his criticism of Muslims who displayed *shamatat al-'ada'i*, or *schadenfreude*, after September 11th, by burning American flags or otherwise "rejoicing at the calamities of one's enemies".[54] The shaikh concurs with Western scholars, who link the upsurge in religious militancy to the decline of traditional scholarship: "Traditionally, Muslims had an idea that to have an opinion about a certain subject meant that you really understood it. Now everybody voices their opinions without really having deliberated . . . We need to study our tradition so that we can recognise what legitimises real authority in Islam."[55] Shaikh Yousef is especially critical of the neo-Kharijites who "delude others by the deeply dyed religious exterior that they project", and who "use takfir and character assassination as a tool for marginalising any criticism directed at them". "The outward religious appearance and character of the *khawarij* deluded thousands in the past and continues to delude people today. The Muslims should be aware that despite the *khawarij* adherence to certain aspects of Islam, they are extremists of the worst type."[56]

The problem Shaikh Yousef puts his finger on is one I myself have identified elsewhere:

> The crisis of modern Islam – and few would deny that such a crisis exists – is not so much a "spiritual crisis" as a crisis of authority – political, intellectual, and legal as well as spiritual. The "best community" ordained by God for "enjoining what is right and forbidding what is wrong" – a community that successfully conducted its own affairs for centuries without external interference – demands leadership. Yet outside the Shi'ite minority tradition, a leadership commanding universal support is conspicuously absent.[57]

In the absence of a universally accepted religious authority, the Sunni tradition is vulnerable to religious extremism and to the appeal of fundamentalist leaders. As suggested earlier, petrodollars from Saudi Arabia and the Gulf have contributed to this tendency by promoting versions of Islam that verge on neo-Kharijism, even when they hold back from pronouncing *takfir* on other Muslims with whom they disagree. In certain respects the configuration of the majority tradition in Islam resembles the Protestant tradition in the United States, where democratic forms of church governance, anti-intellectualism and the constitutional separation of church and state conspire to foster religious extremism. In Arabia, petrodollars have enabled a significant number of Muslims to enjoy the fruits of modernity without undergoing the painful moral and mental adjustments required elsewhere: for example individual Saudis are able by virtue of their wealth to treat foreign workers as slaves rather than citizens, to sexually abuse female workers and to torture and mutilate foreigners (including Britons) without much more than whispers of protest from their governments. In America the followers of Jerry Falwell and Pat Robertson are restricted in the political agendas they pursue by the constitutional limitations placed on churches by the separation of church and state. The anathemas they pronounce on gays, for example, are largely rhetorical. In Saudi Arabia or under the Taliban in Afghanistan, gays face execution. Though neutralized by church–state separation, the activities of American fundamentalist are nevertheless encouraged by the state through the hidden subsidy they enjoy by virtue of their tax-exempt status. Their power, sustained as it were by default from the public purse, is far from being without political effects.

To take but one example, highly significant in the context of the present discussion: many American evangelicals, and nearly all those described as Christian fundamentalists, subscribe to the premillennial belief, based on literalistic readings of the Bible, that the foundation of Israel in 1948 and its acquisition of the Old City of Jerusalem, containing the al-Aqsa mosque and the Western Wall of the Second Temple, are part of a divine scenario. This was, they believe, prefigured in the Book of Revelation, and will lead to the return of Christ and the conversion of the Jews to Christianity. Not all Evangelicals are premillennialists, but a majority certainly subscribe to such beliefs when it comes to the significance of Israel. According to a survey published in 1989 62 per cent of Americans have "no doubt" that Jesus will return to earth "one day", including 93 per cent of Evangelical Protestants.[58]

Of course, this does not necessarily translate into political support for Israel. Among white Evangelical Protestants, however, 37 per cent were described by George Gallup Jr and Jim Castelli as "strong supporters" of the Jewish state (compared to non-Evangelical Protestants and Roman Catholics, where a small majority of both groups are described as "weak supporters"). Gallup and Castelli attribute these differences in the levels of support for Israel to the-ological rather than political factors (such as concern for Jewish safety or American strategic interests):

> The importance of Israel in Evangelical theology appears to be responsible for these differences in views. At one level Evangelicals believe that God's promise to Abraham in the Book of Genesis – "I will bless those who bless you and curse those who curse you" – is still in effect. At another level, many believe that events leading to the Second Coming of Christ – the Battle of Armageddon – will take place in the Middle East and that the creation of the State of Israel in 1948 is the clearest signal that the thousand-year earthly reign of Christ is imminent.[59]

Any withdrawal by Israel from the territories it occupied in 1967 and the Jewish settlements it established in defiance of interna-tional law would, in the view of many Evangelicals, contradict the stated purpose and intentions of God.

While Israelis understandably balk at the theological denoue-ment anticipated in the premillennialist scenario – the conversion of the "righteous" Jews to Christianity, and the destruction of the unrighteous ones, along with Muslims, Hindus, Confucians and all the rest of humanity who have failed to take Jesus Christ as their "personal saviour" – Israeli politicians opposed to any withdrawal from "biblical" Israel have not always balked at using the funda-mentalists to bolster their cause inside the United States.

Though widely seen in the Arab world as pro-Israeli, the Clinton administration succeeded in presiding over the first phase of the Oslo accords which brought the PLO leader Yasser Arafat and the Israeli premier Yitzhak Rabin to their famous handshake on the White House lawn (a gesture for which Rabin would pay with his life). In January 1998 Rabin's successor, the Likud premier Benyamin Netanyahu who opposed the Oslo accords, infuriated the Clinton administration by holding a private meeting with Falwell during which the latter agreed to mobilize evangelical opposition to any territorial concessions by Israel.

"There are about 200,000 evangelical pastors in America," Falwell told reporters, "and we're asking them all through e-mail, faxes, letters, telephone, to go into their pulpits and use their influence in support of the state of Israel and the prime minister." At a conservative estimate, each pastor would have had at least 100 congregants: simple arithmetic suggests that through Falwell's network Netanyahu's message would reach 20 million Americans, more than three times the Jewish population. According to Larry Goodstein, who reported the meeting, Netanyahu deliberately set up the meeting with Falwell and other evangelical leaders to counter the influence not only of the Clinton administration, which was pressurizing him into making territorial concessions, but of liberal elements in the Jewish lobby as well. After Clinton's departure from office in 2001, the Palestinian negotiators accused the US team of prevarication and interference, and not delivering on its promises. There is no certainty that if Al Gore had succeeded Clinton as president, US efforts at mediation would have been more fruitful. Nevertheless there can be no doubt where the fundamentalist lobby stood on the issue: in the 2000 election Falwell was unequivocal in his support for George W. Bush. On 30 November, during the judicial proceeding following the contested Florida vote, he circulated a petition to 162,000 evangelical pastors belonging to the "Jerry Falwell Support Circle" instructing them to send e-mails to the Vice President urging him to step down.[60]

Fifteen months into the Bush administration, the consequences seem clear: whereas former Yugoslav president Slobodan Milosevic is tried, with US support, as a war criminal, the Israeli prime minister Ariel Sharon, whose complicity in the massacres of Palestinians in Beirut in 1982 bears comparison with the crimes of which Milošović has been accused, is treated as a statesman. At the time of writing this, in the spring of 2002, his government is engaged in the final destruction of what remains of the Palestinian Authority without protest from the US government, an act of international sabotage that will fatally undermine President Bush's "war on terror" by making it impossible for any

Arab government, including Saudi Arabia, to lend its support for an attack on Iraq. Meanwhile, the Arab states, including Iraq, have made an unprecedented offer of full recognition of Israel and normalization of relations, including diplomatic links, trade and tourism, in exchange for a full withdrawal by Israel to its 1967 frontiers in accordance with United Nations resolutions. A settlement along these lines is obviously in the US interest. But it is far from clear if the Bush administration has the political will to enforce such a settlement, which would involve a direct confrontation beween the forces of reason and modernity and the fundamentalists in the Jewish, Christian and Islamic communities who insist that God has commanded them to fight for all the land.

Religious extremism is far from being limited to the Islamic tradition. In recent years the world has seen numerous examples of violence in the local and mainstream traditions. Sikh extremists fought a terrorist campaign against the Indian government during the 1970s. After Indian troops stormed the heavily defended Golden Temple in Amritsar in 1984, the prime minister, Indira Gandhi, was assassinated by her Sikh bodyguards. Thousands of Sikhs were killed in the ensuing riots. Similar eruptions, with equally severe loss of life, occurred in the communal riots between Hindus and Muslims in the winter of 1992–93 after Hindu militants of the RSS and BJP stormed and destroyed the Babri Masjid, a thirteenth-century mosque at Ayodhya which Hindus regard as the birthplace of Lord Rama, the hero–deity of the Hindu epic, the *Ramayana*. In early 2002 the dispute again erupted, causing hundreds of deaths in communal rioting. In Sri Lanka, Tamil separatists at war with the Sinhalese majority government have dedicated their lives to Shiva before undertaking suicide missions. In February 1994 in Hebron in occupied Palestine, Baruch Goldstein – a middle-class Brooklyn physician, "an otherwise decent man"[61] – shot more than thirty Muslims at prayer before being overcome and killed by survivors. To the embarrassment of the Israeli authorities, his tomb has become a shrine. To some young Israelis Yigal Amir, the religious student who assassinated the Israeli prime minister Yitzhak Rabin in 1995, is a hero.

Religious violence appears to be on the increase everywhere. Many religious believers object to the labelling of violence as being in any way "religious", pointing out that religion itself is often just a convenient badge tagged onto conflicts that are really about power, ethnicity and identity. As the American humourist P.J. O'Rourke observed regarding Bosnia, the three parties to the conflict "are of the same race, speak the same language and are distinguished only by their religion – in which none of them believe".[62] In Northern Ireland, British newspapers (in contrast to American ones) tend to avoid using the labels "Catholic" and "Protestant" when referring to acts of violence or paramilitary organizations, preferring the more political labels "republican" and "loyalist", though everyone knows that virtually all republicans are Catholic, and all loyalists are Protestant. The nomenclature may reflect the fact that the conflict, despite its sectarian underpinnings, is also secular. The churches on both sides have never ceased to condemn violence, yet they have been powerless to intervene. Progress has been achieved very largely by political measures aided by external pressures from the Irish and British governments. The issues are about allegiance and identity, not theology: very few parties to the Irish conflict show the slightest interest in ritual matters such as the "Real Presence" of Christ at the Catholic Mass, or the Low-Church Protestant custom of sitting, instead of kneeling, during prayers.

Much of the religious violence erupting in the world today is less about religion than about conflicts over purely mundane matters, such as power, land and resources. The religious dimension emerges when group identities are buttressed by religious differences. The rise in the power and popularity of Hamas and Islamic Jihad in the Israeli-occupied territories during the 1990s at the expense of the more moderate PLO is the consequence of the PLO's failure to deliver on the possibly unrealistic expectations most Palestinians had of the Oslo accords – a complete Israeli withdrawal to the 1967 borders, the dismantling of the illegal Jewish settlements, the creation of a Palestinian state with Jerusalem as its capital.

Despite the Islamist movement's maximalist claims – that the whole of Palestine (including land occupied by Israel after 1948) is a *waqf*, or religious trust, that cannot be ceded to "the Jews" – it can be argued that if the basic Palestinian demands were satisfied, support for the maximalist positions would evaporate, and Hamas would eventually change its tune, just as the PLO did in 1988 when it accepted the "two-state" solution, including Israel's right to exist behind the 1948 borders. According to this view, Hamas is more political than religious, though its support and underpinning are based on an Islamic identity brought into focus by a conflict that has a religious dimension, while its most efficacious tactic, suicide bombing, clearly demands an overpowering religious commitment. The symmetry between Jewish and Islamic fundamentalisms may be less than absolute. The demands of the Jewish settlers whose very presence has impeded, if not completely sabotaged, the peace process are non-negotiable: unlike most Palestinians the settlers cannot back down on their demands – the right to settle in all parts of "biblical" Israel – without abandoning their religious outlook altogether. This is similar to that of their Christian fundamentalist supporters. Holding on to all the Promised Land is a necessary stage in the process of redemption: if they give up an inch of the territories, Messiah may never come.

Religion can mediate conflicts, as occurred recently in South Africa, where the pervasiveness of Christian culture, aided by changes in the doctrine of the Dutch Reformed Church and the charismatic leadership of the Anglican archbishop Desmond Tutu, is widely credited with helping the peaceful transition of power from the European minority to the African majority. There seems very little prospect that religion can play a similar role in the Palestine–Israel conflict, because in that context religion "ups the ante", buttressing a local (and theoretically negotiable) conflict over the occupation of land and the use of water, with the absolutism of chiliastic expectations.

The modern state of Israel was built from what I have called "actualized eschatology". The founder of modern Zionism, Theodor Herzl, was a secularized Jewish nationalist who became convinced of the necessity for a Jewish state. The founding fathers of modern Israel, Chaim Weizman and David Ben Gurion, were likewise secular men, who believed like Herzl that Israel should be as "Jewish as England is English" with modern, progressive, secular institutions. Like the Indian republic created one year before Israel, the state was committed to a social democratic ideology strongly influenced by the English Fabianism of writers such as Kingsley Martin and George Bernard Shaw.

At the beginning of the Zionist project the Jewish rabbinate was overwhelmingly hostile. For them Jewish eschatology – the coming of the Messiah – was entirely symbolic. To create or "restore" the "kingdom" – albeit in republican form – was blasphemy, and impious appropriation of the Messiah's role. It was only during the 1930s, when the Nazi persecutions were gathering momentum, that the orthodox line began to change. The Chief Rabbi of Palestine, Avraham Kook, took a step towards the religious legitimation of the Jewish state by arguing that, unbeknownst to themselves, the secular Zionists were actually participating in God's final plan, by unwittingly preparing a stage on the path of redemption. It was left to his son, Rabbi Zvi Yehuda Kook, the patron of the main settler movement, Gush Emunim, to complete the theological accommodation by arguing (like the Christian premillennialists) that Israel's victory in the 1967 war, which brought the whole of Jerusalem and the West Bank under its control was also foreordained, bringing the coming of the Messiah even nearer. Not all orthodox Jews support Zvi Yehuda's line: a substantial part of the religious community accepted the principle of trading "land for peace" with the Arabs, while a small minority of the ultra-orthodox Haredim still formally "reject" Israeli sovereignty on religious grounds. Some of their rabbis have actually taken part in demonstrations against the appropriation of Palestinian lands and the building of Jewish settlements.

For a majority of Israelis, however, believers and non-believers, "redemption" in the form of the state's existence has either occurred, or is in the process of unfolding on the physical plane of real-time terrestrial existence. As Juergensmeyer explains, the persistence of religion in the political realm "has much to do with the nature of the religious imagination, which always has had the propensity to absolutize and to project images of cosmic war".[63] For fundamentalists in both camps, "the cosmic struggle" which forms the content of so many religious narratives "is understood to be occurring in this world rather than in a mythical setting. Believers identify personally with the struggle. The struggle is [seen to be] at a point of crisis in which individual action can make all the difference."[64] For Palestinians, too, the conflict has acquired "Manichaean proportions". A Hamas communiqué written after US troops were sent to Saudi Arabia in 1991 describes the operation as "another episode in the fight between good and evil" and as "a hateful Christian plot against our religion, our civilization and our land".[65]

Karen Armstrong has explained the this-worldly actualization of the myths to be found in scriptures as a form of secularization. In premodern times, she argues, people "evolved two ways of thinking, speaking and acquiring knowledge, which scholars have called *mythos* and *logos*. Both were essential; they were regarded as complementary ways of arriving at truth, and each had its separate area of competence."[66] Instead of maintaining complementarity, modern religious ideologues have assimilated *mythos* to *logos*, rationalizing and secularizing, as it were, ideas that premoderns had safely kept confined to the realm of myth. Thus she condemns 'Abd al-Salam al-Farag (the engineer who planned the assassination of Anwar Sadat, the Egyptian president, in 1981) for reading "the words of scripture as though they were factually true in every detail . . . [which] showed yet another danger of using the *mythos* of scripture as a blueprint for practical action. The old ideal had been to keep *mythos* and *logos* separate: political action was the preserve of reason."[67] The implication of this analysis, of course, is that people in premodern societies were less prone to take action on the basis of "mythical" ideas than they are in modern times. Her argument overlooks the historical evidence that plenty of premoderns (howsoever defined) enacted their myths in rational terms: the early conquests of Islam and the development of Islamic law, not to mention the numerous eschatologically oriented movements throughout Islamic history, or similar movements in Jewish and Christian history, from Sabbatai Sevi to the Fifth Monarchy men, are the most obvious examples.[68]

While I question Armstrong's assumption that premoderns somehow kept *mythos* and *logos* in balance, her point about the literalism with which modern ideologues treat scripture is well taken. As I suggested earlier, part of the problem is caused by the way fundamentalist ideologues trained in technical subjects such as engineering treat religious texts as operational manuals. Abd al-Wahhab el-Affendi, the Sudanese Islamist writer, makes a direct link between the textualism of the Islamists and the lack of functioning democracies. Chastened, one suspects, by the bitter experience of Islamist rule in his country, he writes:

We have seen Islamists and venerable *'ulama* backing despotic regimes which murder and torture innocent people, but ban alcohol and mixed dancing! I am not alone in inviting Muslims to have a sense of perspective on these issues ... The root cause of this lack of proportion is due to the "textualism" I have pointed to earlier. It so happens there are clear references to alcohol and dress [in the Quran] but none to political organisation.[69]

A leading anthropologist, the late Ernest Gellner, argued that in the Muslim world "civil society", meaning market-regulated, privately controlled or voluntary institutions outside government control, was conspicuous by its absence: "Muslim polities," says Gellner, "are pervaded by clientelism. There is government-by-network. Law governs daily life, but not the institutions of power".[70] El-Affendi, however, refuses to blame the absence of civil society or the lack of democracy to be found in most Muslim states, on religion as such. "The whole history of Islam has been of a vibrant civil society which defied state control, especially in the intellectual

sphere."[71] El-Affendi's analysis focuses rather on the utopian trend
in Islamic thought: "There is some truth in the claim that the
Muslim ummah, as a self-contained religious community, is one
that is, in theory at least, committed to an 'uncompromising devotion to virtue'."[72] Olivier Roy sees the weakness in Islamist thought
in its reliance on personal virtue. As he argues in *The Failure of
Political Islam*, because the Islamist model is predicated on a belief
in government by morally impeccable individuals who can be
counted on to resist temptation, it does not generate institutions
capable of functioning autonomously. Political institutions function
only as a result of the virtue of those who run them, but virtue can
become widespread only if society is already Islamic. The Islamists
are therefore trapped in a kind of "virtuous circle" or logical cul-
de-sac, the consequence of utopian thinking. The rage of the
Islamists who attacked New York and Washington on September
11th may be a reflection less of utopian aspirations than of utopian
despair at the continued failure of their project, for which they
blame the United States which backs the Saudi and Egyptian
regimes they want to overthrow.

Ultimately there exists a theological dimension to this most
singular and spectacular act of terrorism. The West *is* "Christian"
(though mercifully also pagan and *jahili* in its exuberance and
diversity) to the extent that its functioning democracies are
predicated, not just on the secularized eternities embedded in its
corporations, but on the Christian doctrine of human fall.
Because human nature is deemed to be corrupt and unperfectable
in this world, the institutions that make up Western democracies
are provided with checks and balances that help to insulate
them from tyranny. Modern democracy is predicated on the
assumption that human nature is fallible, that all power corrupts,
as Lord Acton famously put it, and that "absolute power corrupts
absolutely".

The recent experience of the Muslim world points in the same
direction. The Islamists and the dictatorships they oppose are
locked into a logic of complicity between power and corruption.
The Islamists attack the state as an illicit manifestation of *jahiliyya*

without cultural or religious authenticity within the Islamic tradition. They propose to replace it instead with a state of their own making, based on the myth of Muhammad and his "rightly guided" successors when the rule of virtue is presumed to have prevailed. Because they are taught, by the religious leaders they choose to follow, to believe that Islam is perfect and self-consistent, they refuse to learn from the Western experience that the idea of virtue as a political principle inevitably leads to tyranny. The names of Robespierre and Saint-Just, the classic exemplars of virtue and terrorism in the Western political tradition, do not loom large in their discourses.

The Islamist attacks against the tyrannical state and its supposed protector, the United States, provide the self-fulfilling justifications for their critique. A majority of Muslim states are able to justify their repressive and dictatorial methods because their governments face armed opposition from the Islamists.

There is no easy way out of the vicious cycle of violence and repression that has become the major impediment to the development of Muslim societies. Economically, Muslim countries are growing at a slower rate than other developing countries, including most African countries south of the Sahara. As well as the cultural factors inhibiting growth (which include the interference of religion in the teaching of science),[73] Muslim countries are experiencing a massive population bulge, which is in the process of detonating a demographic time bomb. If present trends continue, the proportion of Muslims in the world population will increase from 18 per cent (under one fifth of humanity) to nearly one third (30 per cent) by 2025.[74]

Compared to the rest of the developing world, Muslim countries suffer from a severe democratic deficit. The continuing presence of tyrannical or repressive regimes, including the oil-rich regimes, which are unable to provide their young people (especially young men) with the job opportunities that would enable them to marry and create families converts the demographic time bomb into something much more menacing. The al-Qa'ida network has been damaged, but not dismantled, by the war in Afghanistan. Bin

Laden, if not dead, is still at large. The chances are that the network is being reconstituted in one of the areas where the writ of the government and the security forces is weak – in Yemen, Somalia, Pakistan or even again in Afghanistan, if the Karzai government fails, or in a collapsing Saudi Arabia.

The challenge posed to the international status quo by the al-Qaʻida network and its affiliates bears some resemblance to the patterns of revolt and renewal as described in the Khaldunian scenario. Although in Muslim countries the writ of government over civil society and especially over marginal areas has been hugely reinforced by military and bureaucratic power, including the ubiquitous presence of the *mukhabarat* (intelligence or internal security services) with their ruthless police methods, "lands of insolence" persist under the nominal control of failing or failed states such as Sudan, Somalia and Afghanistan.

At the time of writing, the United States had largely succeeded by aerial bombardment in enabling the Northern Alliance to overthrow the Taliban regime in Afghanistan, although months later pockets of resistance remain. With diplomatic help from its European allies it had established a new interim government under Hamid Karzai, a kinsman of the former King, which should provide a less hospitable environment for the al-Qaʻida network in the coming years. Bin Laden had apparently escaped the bombardment of the al-Qaʻida headquarters at Tora Bora, north of Qandahar. The Taliban leader, Mullah Omar, had also disappeared. Most of the prisoners held at the US military base at Guatanamo Bay in Cuba were described as low-level members of the organization.

Although the Taliban had been decisively defeated, with support for it melting away, the hold of the incoming government on power still looked precarious. There was no guarantee that, despite the pro-Western policy of Pakistan's military ruler, General Musharraf, the war had finally been won, or that al-Qaʻida would fail to reconstitute itself. With cells or sympathizers in some sixty countries, there was every possibility that al-Qaʻida would continue to threaten United States interests and governments considered hostile to the Islamist movements.

With globalization, what might be called a transnational "Zone of Insolence" has also come into being, comprising some "born-again" Muslims from migrant communities living in the West and the radical Islamists influenced by the teachings of charismatic intellectuals and religious leaders. A majority of terrorists, writes Paul Pillar of the Brookings Institute, are "worldwise young adult males, unemployed or underemployed (except by terrorist groups), with weak social and familial family support and with poor prospects for economic improvement and advancement through legitimate work".[75] The anger and rage of such "worldwise" young men, sexually frustrated because of the restrictions imposed on them by cultural values that limit sexual activity to marriage and marriage to economic conditions such as housing and family support that can no longer be satisfied, is indeed terrifying, especially when the "satanic" Western culture they love to hate and hate to love ceaselessly plays on their desires, arousing feelings that cannot legitimately be assuaged.

Although there are no obvious or quick solutions to the dangers posed by international Islamist terrorism, there are certain prerequisites. The attacks on New York and Washington may have been planned during a hopeful phase of the Middle East peace process, when the government of Ehud Barak, under pressure from the Clinton administration, was poised to accept a deal that would have returned 22 per cent of Palestine to its original inhabitants. But the failure of the Oslo process to produce a solution acceptable to the Arab majority is a festering sore on which Islamist resentments must continue to feed. The outlines for a settlement acceptable to reasonable people on both sides, based on the long-standing principle of trading peace for territory, with Palestinian sovereignty over what remains of their homeland, including East Jerusalem, has recently been revived by the Saudi monarch-in-waiting, Crown Prince 'Abdullah. Low oil prices, the parlous state of the Saudi economy and Saudi embarrassment at the extent of its citizens' involvement in September 11th should make it possible for the Americans to force the Israelis and Palestinians back to the table. A resolution of the Palestinian problem will not by any means remove the threat to US and Western interests posed by al-Qa'ida. But it would be a vital step in the right direction.

In April 2002 the Bush administration was beginning to see its "war on terrorism" unravel as the Sharon government in Israel, in ironic collusion with the Islamist extremists, used the campaign of suicide bombings to destroy what was left of Arafat's reputation and that of the Palestinian Authority. Lacking a coherent Middle East policy, the administration appeared to be vacillating between trying to appease both the Israelis and the moderate Arab leaders whose support it needed for the campaign against al-Qa'ida. The reality had finally dawned in Washington that the whole anti-terrorist campaign, against both the remnants of al-Qa'ida and Iraq, would be doomed to failure so long as Israeli tanks were deployed in Palestinian areas to root out those who threatened Jewish settlers and murdered Israeli civilians. Yet it was not at all clear if the administration had the will to impose a settlement along the lines proposed by Crown Prince Abdullah for fear of offending the powerful domestic alliance of the Jews and fundamentalist Christians who were vociferously opposed to substantive Israeli concessions. Paul Wolfowitz, the hawkish deputy defence secretary, was heckled and booed at a pro-Israeli rally in Washington when he dared to mention Palestinian sufferings. Yet the Sharon government's policy of halting Palestinian resistance to the occupation and settlements by purely military methods had failed. The more the Israelis piled military pressure on Yasser Arafat to halt the shootings and suicide bombings that were killing Israeli citizens, the more the Islamist extremists were able to demonstrate that it was they, rather than the emasculated and discredited regime of Arafat, who retained the initiative.

Needless to add, the real beneficiary of the escalating crisis had been Saddam Hussein: as Crown Prince 'Abdullah is reported to have warned the Bush administration, the United States would "never again get the use of any military base against Iraq" if it failed to stop the fighting on the West Bank.[76] At the time of writing the United States and Britain are still engaged in preparations for war against Iraq on the ground that Saddam Hussein is stockpiling weapons of mass destruction in violation of UN resolutions.

Similar charges have been made against Iran, which President Bush pointedly included in his reference to the "axis of evil" in his State of the Union address in January 2002. A war with Iraq, however, appears to be the more likely event. The *casus belli* may be Saddam's refusal to allow the return of UN weapons inspectors.

Such a war would in any event be a high-risk venture. Unless there is vital intelligence unknown to any but government leaders and their intelligence services, it is difficult to see how the forcible removal of Saddam Hussein can be achieved without the dismemberment of Iraq. The first Bush administration held back from attacking Baghdad in 1991 for precisely this reason. The same considerations apply today. Saddam's power is severely restricted by the imposition of no-fly zones, which effectively guarantee the autonomy of the Kurdish areas in the north. The removal of Saddam could easily lead to another Shi'ite rebellion in the south, or even an Iranian invasion, which, if successful, might lead to the creation of an Iranian-backed state on the borders of Kuwait – hardly a prospect to be relished by the Sunni rulers of Kuwait, Saudi Arabia, Bahrein and the United Arab Emirates. According to Robert Baer, a former CIA agent, a plan to topple Saddam Hussein by means of a Kurdish insurrection combined with a "classic" military coup using an armoured corps to surround Saddam's palace in his home town of Takrit was "scuppered" by the Clinton administration in 1995 – less than thirty-six hours before it was due to be launched. With three armies – those of Turkey, Iran and Iraq – on full alert, the White House decided that the danger of a major conflagration far outweighed the benefit of Saddam's removal. The chances of a similar coup succeeding today, said Baer, were "zero to none". The Sunni Arabs, who make up 20 per cent of the Iraqi population, still preferred Saddam to the prospects of being ruled by non-Sunnis.[77]

By any sober reckoning, another Gulf war will do far more harm than good. The sensible policy, as Jessica Mathews, president of the Carnegie Endowment for International Peace, has argued, is not to pursue the removal of Saddam Hussein, unpleasant though he may be, but to try to thwart his drive towards acquiring weapons of mass destruction by working through the United Nations and the rest of the international community. There is no guarantee that even in the unlikely event of a successful coup against Saddam Hussein that his successor would be more amenable to weapons inspections than he is. Equal pressure must be applied on Iran and Iraq, both of whom are acquiring nuclear and other weapons in order to counter the threat of the other. The pressure must come, not only from the United States, but from the 186 other nations which have signed the non-proliferation treaty and "share an interest in its integrity". Even-handedness aimed at stopping nuclear proliferation on the part of both countries would produce a better and fairer outcome for US policy in the region than the potentially destabilizing effects of an attempted coup in Iraq. A prerequisite, however, must be a resolution of the war between Israel and the Palestinians.

Here it seems obvious that the long-established principle of trading land for peace between Israel and the Palestinian Arabs, along the lines suggested by Saudi Arabia and endorsed by the Arab League in March 2002, is the only basis for a possible solution. As the commentator Thomas Friedman, citing the opinion of Middle East analyst Stephen Cohen, has argued, an Israeli withdrawal will require the stationing of NATO or US troops to supervise the emergence of a Palestinian state, in order to prevent it from becoming a base for renewed attacks against Israel. The other side of the equation is obvious to any reasonable observer: the Israelis must give up their illegal settlements. Friedman lays out the issue with admirable bluntness: after condemning Arab leaders for their failure to "decry the utterly corrupt and inept Palestinian leadership, or the depravity of the suicide bombers" Friedman turns his pen on "the feckless American Jewish leaders, fundamentalist Christians and neoconservatives who together have helped make it impossible for anyone in the US administration to talk seriously about Israeli settlement-building without being accused of being anti-Israel. Their collaboration has helped prolong a colonial Israeli occupation that now threatens the entire Zionist enterprise."[78]

There are some hopeful signs that this message is getting

through. In a surprisingly even-handed statement on 4 April 2002 President Bush commended the Saudi initiative as "promising" and "hopeful" because it involved recognition by the whole of the Arab League of Israel's right to exist along with the hope of "sustained, constructive Arab involvement in the search for peace". As well as reaffirming his previous commitment to a Palestinian state, the President stated that "Israeli settlement activities in the occupied territories must stop" and that the occupation must end through an Israeli withdrawal to "secure and recognized boundaries" consistent with United Nations resolutions.[79]

There is no certainty, of course, that the President's initiative will succeed. Conspicuous by its absence in his statement was any reference to the status of Jerusalem – the sticking point in the previous round of negotiations between Arafat and the Barak government. The problem was delicate, but not insuperable. In allowing the Palestinians a symbolic presence in Jerusalem, and urging a full withdrawal of Israel from the occupied territories, the administration may have to brush aside the objections of the fundamentalist Jewish and Christian lobbies – just as the American people ignored the pernicious statements of Falwell and Robertson, who implicitly justified the attack on New York as an "act of divine punishment" on a sinful city where homosexuality is tolerated.

In due course the US will have to move towards disengaging its troops from Saudi Arabia in order to allow democratic forces to take hold, even if that means a period of instability and hard-line Islamist rule. The Algerian example, when France tolerated military intervention to suppress democracy on the specious pretext of saving it is not a precedent to be emulated. That disastrous mistake not only cost 100,000 Algerian lives in the civil war between the Islamists and the government; it was an act of catastrophic hypocrisy that hardened Islamist sentiment by reinforcing the anti-democratic tendencies within the movement. There are examples of what might be called "good practice" in dealing with Islamists democratically, for example in Jordan and Kuwait, where Islamists have been permitted to win seats in national parliaments. The best way of deflating their utopian fantasies is to subject them to the disciplines of practical action and informed political debate.

The road to democracy in Saudi Arabia will be long and difficult. But the experience of Iran since 1979 has shown that the forces of progress are better served when people are permitted to work out their own destinies, without the external pressures exercised by oil companies and arms manufacturers supported by Western governments. Iran is moving slowly towards secularism and democracy under its own momentum. The corrupt religious *nomenklatura* that blocks reform will self-destruct when enough people are sufficiently well educated to see through its pretensions. As Jessica Mathews has argued, "Eventually (not soon) the mullah's conservatism, venality and economic incompetence will undo them."[80]

Islamism depends for its following on the paranoid perception that the "West" is virulently anti-Islamic. That perception is reinforced when Western governments give their backing to regimes that systemically violate the rights of their subjects. At the same time, public opinion rallies behind regimes deemed to be under Western attack, however repressive they are. Islamic solidarity always operates negatively, rarely positively. Given the manner in which present territorial arrangements are buttressed by the international system, pan-Islamism and a restored caliphate have no more chance of success as a political movement than the pan-Arabism that dominated Arab politics in the 1950s and 1960s. If the price of disengagement from Saudi Arabia is turbulence in the oil markets and a temporary hike in prices, that will prove a minor inconvenience compared with the long-term consequences of complicity in sustaining a tribal despotism. A policy which attacks systemic human rights violations in Iraq whilst implicitly defending them (by arming the government and by not condemning violations) in the Israeli-occupied territories and Saudi Arabia is certain to fail in the long term.

At the risk of courting charges of "cultural imperialism", Western countries must export liberalism more assertively, as has been suggested by Roy Mottahedeh, professor of Islamic studies at Harvard, who argues that Western arts and humanities should be taught in vernacular languages, and not just to the anglophone

Westernised elites whose lack of cultural legitimacy is a major source of Islamist resentment.[81] As things stand, Muslim countries are exposed to nightly barrages of "Western cultural imperialism" in the shape of soap operas and transgressive sexual imagery. What is lacking in the "image" Western societies project to non-Western consumers is any sense of cultural depth and spiritual resonance.

Having made these rather obvious points, there are no short-term solutions to the problems posed by the Islamists and their terrorist offshoots. The people who make up the leadership of the movement from which al-Qa'ida has drawn its most able recruits are the victims of a peculiarly modern dilemma, a "clash of cultures" occurring, not so much *between* civilizations, as Huntington maintains, but rather within the individual. The movement's spearhead, its "tungsten tip" as it were, has been forged in a furnace in which uneducated religiosity combines with rage, utopianism, social anomie and technical sophistication. But the shaft of the weapons which so devastated New York and Washington on 11 September 2001 were made from more traditional stuff. Of the nineteen hijackers led by Mohammed Atta, fifteen were Saudi citizens from the mountainous province of Asir, a formerly semi-independent sultanate conquered by Faisal ibn 'Abd al-'Aziz bin Sa'ud (later King Faisal) in the 1920s and annexed by the Kingdom in 1930. Here the *Sunday Times* researchers found that a "disproportionate number of families" were able to trace their origins to the Yemeni tribes defeated by the Al Sa'ud.[82]

The menace posed to the "satanic" countries of the US and Western Europe by angry young Islamists is indeed a formidable one. "Deployed assets," write Simon and Benjamin, two academic experts on terrorism, using the jargon of their trade, "have proved to be technologically savvy, confident about operating in enemy territory, resourceful, highly motivated and able to act on their own initiative." "The looseness of these networks," they conclude, "and the way in which the cells within them coalesce, makes identification, penetration and disruption of the groups extremely difficult, particularly for Western intelligence agencies with expertise mainly in recruiting foreign government officials as sources."[83] Peter

Bergen, CNN's terrorist analyst, argues along similar lines that the failure of US intelligence to anticipate and prepare for the September 11th attacks may in part be attributed to over-dependence on electronic sources of intelligence, and too little stress on old-fashioned "humint" – human intelligence – which depends on personal intuition, personal interaction and personal engagement on the part of agents with groups suspecting of harbouring terrorists.

Changing the culture of intelligence (for example, by employing Muslims loyal to their adopted Western homelands and who have a more sophisticated understanding of the subcultures in which Islamist terrorists operate than their occidental counterparts) is a matter of the greatest urgency. The culture of separation between church and state which prevails in the United States will have to be modified if mosques (like the Nazi-worshipping church in Idaho which inspired Timothy McVeigh and his associates) are not to become malignant cells in the American body politic. Time is not on the side of the authorities in the West. Bin Laden has on several occasions expressed interest in securing weapons of mass destruction (WMD), such as "dirty" bombs that spread levels of nuclear radiation sufficient to kill hundreds of thousands of people. According to Simon and Benjamin, the mathematical probability of such a bomb being detonated in a major Western city by a terrorist group is very high indeed. "If 20 groups are separately trying to get WMD over a ten-year period and each has a 1% chance of success in any given year, then the chance that one of the group succeeds during the ten-year period is over 70%; if the assumptions are changed such that each group has a 2% chance, the probability of a group obtaining WMD is approximately 90%".[84]

The parochialism of the intelligence community is a scandal in societies supposedly committed to the values of "multiculturalism". Human intelligence requires engagement at the level of cultural discourse: people loyal to the state in which they live will have to persuade disaffected youngsters that their interests lie in rejecting festering resentments and adopting the better values of the countries in which they reside.

Contrary to the Huntington thesis and the Islamist discourses it reflects, as in a mirror-image, there are areas of genuine ideological compatibility which need to be explored more fully. Many "born-again Muslims" have become militant Islamists; but there are also increasing numbers of former Islamist intellectuals such as Rashid Ghanoushi, the Tunisian leader, and Abd al-Wahhab el-Affendi, the well-known Sudanese Islamist writer now based in London, who have come by bitter experience to recognize that the Islamist dream of restoring the Shari'a "from above" by political action is a recipe for tyranny and violence:

> The reconstruction of Muslim society must start from the unwavering commitment to democratisation and respect for freedom, especially the freedom of association. And when I say democracy I mean exactly that: democracy, the self-rule of the people through their freely chosen institutions and representatives. Not the rule of God, nor *shura* [a Quranic term meaning consultation] nor "Islamic democracy". Just democracy. Give the Muslim people the right to decide how they want to be ruled, and the power to hold their rulers accountable. It goes without saying that the Muslim people would want to rule themselves according to the values of Islam, according to one understanding of these. But it is the people who decide what these values are. The moment we start saying that the authority in a polity is for God and not for the Muslims, or allow a class of people to determine for others what the values of Islam are, this means that someone, other than the community (and above it) must decide what the will of God is. *Experience has shown that this is a recipe for bringing to power despots for whom the will of God is the last thing on their minds.*[85] (emphasis added)

NOTES

Chapter I: September 11th

1   Jenny Baxter and Malcolm Downing (eds.), *The Day That Shook the World: Understanding September 11th* (London, 2001), p. 14.

2   Ibid., pp. 15–16.

3   *Guardian*, 11 December 2001.

4   Baxter and Downing (eds.), *The Day That Shook the World*, p. 2.

5   John K. Cooley, *Unholy Wars: Afghanistan, America and International Terrorism* (London/Sterling, Virginia, 2000), p. 246.

6   Minoru Yamasaki, *A Life in Architecture* (New York, 1979), p. 116.

7   Ibid., p. 118.

8   Ibid., p. 116.

9   *International Herald Tribune*, 23 February 2002.

10   Joan Smith, *Moralities*, revised edn (London, 2002). I am grateful to Ms Smith for letting me see her appendix on September 11th prior to publication.

11   *Guardian*, 14 September 2001.

12   Paula Hawkins, "Why the Twin Towers Collapsed", an article on the Channel Four website to accompany the documentary feature broadcast on 13 December 2001; Smith, *Moralities*; John Seabrook, "The Fall Guy", *Sunday Telegraph Magazine*, 30 December 2001.

13   Smith, *Moralities*.

14   Peter L. Bergen, *Holy War Inc.: Inside the Secret World of Osama bin Laden* (London, 2001), p. 148.

15   Details from Baxter and Downing (eds.), *The Day That Shook the World*, p. 25.

16   *Sunday Times*, 28 October 2001, section 1, p. 11; *Sunday Times*, 27 January 2002, section 5, p. 6.

17   *Sunday Times*, 3 February 2002, section 5, p. 8.

18   *Guardian*, 14 September 2001, p. 2.

19   *Sunday Times*, 3 February 2002, section 5, p. 8; *Newsweek*, 7 January 2002.

20   *Newsweek*, 7 January 2002.

21   *Sunday Times*, 3 February 2002, section 5, p. 8.

22   *Independent*, 11 December 2001, p. 13.

23   *Sunday Times*, 3 February 2002.

24   *Guardian*, 17 October 2001, p. 7.

25   Ibid.

26   Baxter and Downing (eds.), *The Day That Shook the World*, p. 25.

27   Brian Keenan, *An Evil Cradling* (London, 1993), p. 133.

28   Jack G. Shaheen, *Reel Bad Arabs: How Hollywood Vilifies a People* (New York/Northampton, 2001), p. 1.

29   Ibid., p. 13.

30   Ibid., p. 14.

31   The Runnymede Trust, *Islamophobia: A Challenge for Us All* (London, 1997), p. 1.

32   Ibid., p. 27.

33   Shaheen, *Reel Bad Arabs*, pp. 187–8.

34   *Guardian*, 2 March 2002

35   Mark Juergensmeyer, *Terror in the Mind of God: The Global Rise of Religious Violence* (Berkeley, 2001), p. 69.

36   *Guardian*, 2 February 2002.

37   *Guardian*, 15 December 2001.

38   Ibid.

39   *Independent*, 14 December 2001.

40   Mark Lawson, *Guardian*, 15 December 2001.

41   Martin Kramer, "Hizbullah: The Calculus of Jihad", in Martin E. Marty and R. Scott Appleby (eds.), *Fundamentalisms and the State* (Chicago, 1993), p. 550.

42   Juergensmeyer, *Terror in the Mind of God*, pp. 70–71.

43 *New York Times*, 23 February 2002.

44 Paul R. Pillar, *Terrorism and US Foreign Policy* (Washington, DC, 2001), p. 32.

45 Juergensmeyer, *Terror in the Mind of God*, p. 127.

46 Orlanda Ruthven, personal communication.

47 Cited in Juergensmeyer, *Terror in the Mind of God*, p. 141.

48 See W.M. Watt Bell's *Introduction to the Quran* (Edinburgh, 1974), pp. 127–35.

49 CNN News, 14 September 2001.

50 *Houston Chronicle*, 14 September 2001.

51 Pillar, *Terrorism and US Foreign Policy*, p. 171.

52 Herman Melville, *White-Jacket* (1850), Ch. 36

53 Paul Boyer, *When Time Shall Be No More: Prophesy Belief in Modern American Culture* (Cambridge, MA, 1992), p. 2.

54 Ibid., p. 101.

55 Ibid.

56 Cf. Grace Halsell, *Prophecy and Politics* (Westpoint, Connecticut, 1986).

57 Kanan Makiya and Hassan Mneimneh, "Manual for a 'Raid'", *New York Review of Books*, 17 January 2002, pp. 18–21.

58 Quran 3:160.

59 Quran 9:46–7.

60 Quran 3:143.

61 Makiya and Mneimneh, "Manual for a 'Raid'", p. 21.

62 Nasr Hamid Abu Zaid, "Divine Attributes in the Qur'an – Some Perspectives", in John Cooper et al. (eds.), *Islam and Modernity* (London, 1998), p. 144.

63 Nasr Hamid Abu Zaid, *Naqd al-khitab al-dini* (Cairo, 1992).

64 Ralph Bodenstein, telephone conversation with author, 23 October 2001.

65 Malise Ruthven, *A Satanic Affair: Salman Rushdie and the Wrath of Islam* (London, 1991), p. 141.

Chapter 2: Jihad

1 Letter book of 'Abd al-Rahman al-Nujumi. MS SOAS 101492, cited in P.M. Holt, *The Mahdist State in the Sudan* (Oxford, 1958), p. 34.

2 The full text of the fatwa declaring jihad against Jews and Crusaders is printed in Yonah Alexander and Michael S. Swetnam (eds.), *Usama bin Laden's al-Qaida: Profile of a Terrorist Network* (Ardsley, NY, 2001), appendix 1B, p. 103.

3 www.fatwa-online.com.

4 Conference proceedings: al-Khoei Centre, London, 19 October 2001.

5 Ibid.

6 Quran 16:125.

7 Quran 29:46.

8 Quran 2:256.

9 Quran 22:39–40.

10 Muhammad Asad, *The Message of the Quran* (Gibraltar, 1984), p. 512.

11 Quran 2:194.

12 Asad, *The Message of the Quran*, p. 42.

13 Quran 9:5.

14 Quran 2:106.

15 Asad, *The Message of the Quran*, pp. 22–3.

16 Quran 87:6–7.

17 *Encyclopedia of Islam*, new edn (Leiden, 1960–), hereafter *EI*, s.v. *naskh*.

18 Reuven Firestone, *Jihad: The Origin of Holy War in Islam* (New York, 1999), pp. 59–60.

19 *EI*, s.v. *naskh*.

20 Firestone, *Jihad*, p. 50.

21 Ibid., p. 91.

22 Ibid., p. 125.

23 Ibn Khaldun, *The Muqaddimah*, trans. F. Rosenthal, 3 vols. (Princeton, 1967).

24 Albert Hourani, *A History of the Arab Peoples* (London, 1991), p. 128.

25 Majid Khadduri, *War and Peace in the Law of Islam* (Baltimore, 1955), p. 51.

26 Ibid., p. 52.

27 Ibid., p. 53.

28 Tilman Nagel, *The History of Islamic Theology from Muhammad to the Present*, trans. Thomas Thornton (Princeton, NJ, 2000), pp. 215–33.

29   Bat Ye'or, *The Dhimmi Jews and Christians under Islam* (Cranbury, NJ, 1985), p. 56; Fuad I. Khuri, *Imams and Emirs: State, Religions and Sects in Islam* (London, 1990), pp. 84–5.

30   Khadduri, *War and Peace in the Law of Islam*, p. 61.

31   Rudolph Peters, *Islam and Colonialism: The Doctrine of Jihad in Modern History* (The Hague/New York 1979), p. 16.

32   Ibid., p. 17.

33   Ibid., p. 18.

34   Ibid.

35   Ibid., p. 19.

36   Ibid., p. 20.

37   Ibid.

38   Ibid., p. 21.

39   Ibid., p. 22.

40   Firestone, *Jihad*, p. 100.

41   Ibid.

42   Ibid.

43   Khadduri, *War and Peace in the Law of Islam*, p. 61.

44   Ibid.

45   A. Guillaume, *The Life of Muhammad: A Translation of Ishaq's Sirat Rasul Allah* (Karachi, 1987), p. 300.

46   Khadduri, *War and Peace in the Law of Islam*, p. 61, with citations.

47   Ibid.

48   Peters, *Islam and Colonialism*, p. 118.

49   Cited in Khadduri, *War and Peace in the Law of Islam*, p. 13.

50   Cf. Quran 2:187; 214.

51   Cited in Khadduri, *War and Peace in the Law of Islam*, p. 13

52   *EI*, s.v. *kafir*.

53   *EI*, s.v. *takfir*.

54   Ibid.; cf. Malise Ruthven, *Islam in the World* (London, 2000), p. 264.

55   *EI*, s.v. *djaysh*.

56   Moshe Gammer, *Muslim Resistance to the Tsar: Shamil and the Conquest of Chechnia and Dagestan* (London, 1994); Akbar S. Ahmed, *Millennium and Charisma among Pathans: A Critical Essay in Social Anthropology* (London, 1976).

57   Ibid., p. 105.

58   Ibid.

59   Peters, *Islam and Colonialis—*, p. 162.

60   Ibid., p. 107.

61   Ibid., pp. 118–19.

62   Ibid., p. 119.

63   Olivier Roy, *The Failure of Political Islam* (London, 1994), pp. x, 27.

64   Sayyid Abu 'Ala Maududi, *The Religion of Truth* (Lahore, 1967), pp. 3–4.

65   Yousef Choueiri, *Islamic Fundamentalism* (Boston, MA, 1990), p. 111.

66   Wilfred Cantwell Smith, *Islam in Modern History* (Princeton, 1957), p. 234.

67   Maududi, *al-jihad fi sabil Allah*, trans. from Urdu (Beirut, n.d.), cited in Peters, *Islam and Colonialism*, p. 130.

Chapter 3: The Aesthetics of Martyrdom

1   Richard Mitchell, *The Society of Muslim Brothers* (London, 1969), p. 29.

2   Pierre Cachia, "The Critics", in M.M. Badawi (ed.), *Modern Arabic Literature* (Cambridge, 1992), p. 434.

3   Gilles Kepel, *The Prophet and the Pharaoh: Muslim Fundamentalism in Egypt*, trans. John Rothschild (London, 1985), p. 40.

4   John Calvert, "'The World is an Undutiful Boy!': Sayyid Qutb's American Experience", *Islam and Christian–Muslim Relations*, Vol. 11, No. 1, 2000, pp. 87–103: 98. I am grateful to Dr Calvert for providing me with an offprint of his article.

5   Ibid., p. 91.

6   Quran 2:164.

7   Calvert, "'The World is an Undutiful Boy!': Sayyid Qutb's American Experience", p. 93.

8   Ibid., p. 98.

9   Ibid., p. 96.

10   Ibid., p. 97 and passim. The following quotes are all from this article.

11   Leonard Binder, *Islamic Liberalism: A Critique of Development Ideologies* (Chicago, 1988), p. 193.

12   Ibid., p. 194.

13   Ibid., p. 204.

14   Ibid.

15   Ibid., p. 195.

16   Kepel, *The Prophet and the Pharaoh*, p. 41.

17   Sayyid Qutb, *Milestones on the Road: A Translation of Ma'alim fi'l-tariq* (Plainfield, IN, 1990), p. 5.

18   Ibid., pp. 7–8.

19   Ibid., p. 8.

20   Ibid., p. 15.

21   Ibid., p. 9.

22   Kepel, *The Prophet and the Pharaoh*, pp. 53–4, citing *Ma'alim fi'l-tariq*, pp. 129–30.

23   Qutb, *Milestones on the Road*, p. 13.

24   Ibid., p. 50.

25   Ibid.

26   Ibid., p. 51.

27   Ibid., pp. 51–62.

28   Ibid., p. 51.

29   Binder, *Islamic Liberalism*, pp. 125–6.

30   Don Cupitt, *After God: The Future of Religion* (London, 1997), p. 58.

31   Ibid., p. xii.

32   For example, W. Ivanow, Introduction to *On the Recognition of the Imam (Fasl dar Bayan-i Shinakht-i Imam)*, trans. W. Ivanow, second revised edn (Bombay, 1947), p. 47.

33   *Ma'alim fi'l-tariq*, p. 303, cited in Azza M. Karam, "Islamisms and the Decivilising Processes of Globalisation", in Alberto Arce and Norman Long, *Anthropology and Development: Exploring Discourses, Counter-tendencies and Violence* (London/New York, 2000), p. 69. I am grateful to Orlanda Ruthven for drawing my attention to this article.

34   Paper delivered at North-South Conference, Oslo, November 1995.

35   Kepel, *The Prophet and the Pharaoh*, p. 42.

36   Ibid.

37   Ibid., p. 201.

38   Ibid.

39   Ibid.

Chapter 4: A Fury for God

1   *Guardian*, 15 September 2001.

2   Quran 4:29.

3   *EI*, s.v. *intihar*.

4   Mark Juergensmeyer, *Terror in the Mind of God: The Global Rise of Religious Violence* (Berkeley, 2001), p. 77.

5   See Chapter 1, n. 43.

6   Abu Hamid al-Ghazali, *ihya ulum al-din* (Cairo, n.d.), cited in Fatima Mernissi, *Beyond the Veil: Male–Female Dynamics in Modern Muslim Society* (London, 1985), p. 29.

7   See Madelain Farah (trans.), *Marriage and Sexuality in Islam* (Salt Lake City, 1984).

8   Suha Taji-Farouki, *A Fundamental Quest: Hizb al-Tahrir and the Search for the Islamic Caliphate* (London, 1996), pp. 67–71, 195–6.

9   *Sunday Telegraph*, 7 August 1994, cited in ibid., p. 76.

10   Gilles Kepel, *The Prophet and Pharaoh: Muslim Extremism in Egypt*, trans. John Rothschild (London, 1985), p. 94. On the links between Sirriyya and Hizb al-Tahrir, see Taji-Farouki, *A Fundamental Quest*, pp. 167–8.

11   *Al-Sharq al-Awsat*, 2 December 2001.

12   Ibid.

13   Kepel, *The Prophet and Pharaoh*, p. 75.

14   Ibid., p. 89.

15   Ibid.

16   Ibid.

17   Ibid., p. 97.

18   Ibid., p. 80.

19   Ibid., p. 84.

20   Ibid., p. 85.

21   Ibid., p. 86.

22   Ibid., p. 98.

23   Sa'd al-din Ibrahim, "Egypt's Islamic Militants" (1977), in Sa'd al-din Ibrahim and Nicholas S. Hopkins (eds.), *Arab Society: Social Science Perspectives* (Cairo, 1985), pp. 494–507.

24   Kepel, *The Prophet and Pharaoh*, p. 99.

25   Ibrahim, "Egypt's Islamic Militants", p. 503.

26   Ibid.

27 Valerie J. Hoffman, "Muslim Fundamentalists: Psychosocial Profiles", in Martin E. Marty and R. Scott Appleby (eds.), *Fundamentalisms Comprehended* (Chicago, 1995), p. 204.

28 Ibid., p. 205.

29 Ibid., p. 206.

30 Ibrahim, "Egypt's Islamic Militants", p. 499.

31 Francis Robinson, "Technology and Religious Change: Islam and the Impact of Print", *Modern Asian Studies*, Vol. 27, No. 1, 1993, p. 230ff.

32 Martha Mundy, "The Family, Inheritance and Islam", in Aziz al-Azmeh (ed.), *Islamic Law: Social and Historical Contexts* (London, 1988), pp. 21, 22.

33 Ibid.

34 James Rupert, "Tunisia: Testing America's Third World Diplomacy", *World Policy Journal*, Vol. 4, Winter 1986–7, p. 24, cited in Hoffman, "Muslim Fundamentalists: Psychosocial Profiles", p. 208.

35 Nazih Ayubi, *Political Islam: Religion and Politics in the Arab World* (London, 1991), pp. 176–7, cited in Hoffman, "Muslim Fundamentalists: Psychosocial Profiles", p. 208.

36 Ibid., p. 210.

37 Ibid.

38 Susan Waltz, "Islamist Appeal in Tunisia", *Middle East Journal*, Vol. 40, 1986, pp. 651–70; Hoffman, "Muslim Fundamentalists: Psychosocial Profiles", p. 210.

39 Ibid., p. 210.

40 Ibid., p. 218.

41 Cited ibid.

42 Cited ibid.

43 Mernissi, *Beyond the Veil*, pp. 160–64, cited in Hoffman, "Muslim Fundamentalists: Psychosocial Profiles", p. 212.

44 Cited in Martin Riesebrodt, *Pious Passion: The Emergence of Modern Fundamentalism in the United States and Iran* (Berkeley, 1993), p. 64.

45 Ibid., pp. 127–8.

46 Ibid., p. 196.

47 Ibid., p. 198ff.

48 Daniel Easterman, *New Jerusalems: Reflections on Islam, Fundamentalism and the Rushdie Affair* (London, 1993), p. 37.

49 Pervez Hoodbhoy, *Islam and Science: Religious Orthodoxy and the Battle for Rationality* (Kuala Lumpur, 1992), p. 68; Maurice Bucaille, *The Bible, the Quran and Science*, trans. A.D. Pannel and the author (Indianapolis, 1979).

50 Details of what follows are taken from Jillian Becker, *Hitler's Children: The Story of the Baader-Meinhof Gang* (London, 1978); *Encylopedia of World Terrorism* (Armonk, NY, 1997), s.v. Red Army Faction.

51 Becker, *Hitler's Children*, pp. 330–31.

52 Quoted in Adam Robinson, *Bin Laden: Behind the Mask of the Terrorist* (Edinburgh, 2001), p. 233.

53 Ibid., p. 234.

Chapter 5: Cultural Schizophrenia

1 Aziz Al-Azmeh, *Islams and Modernities*, second edn (London, 1996), p. 145.

2 Muhammad 'Umar Memon, *Ibn Taymiyya's Struggle against Popular Religion*, with an annotated translation of *Kitab Iqtida . . .* (The Hague, 1976), p. 78.

3 Ibid., p. 210.

4 Ibid., p. 144.

5 John L. Esposito (ed.), *Oxford Encyclopedia of the Modern Islamic World*, 4 vols. (New York, 1995), hereafter *OEMIW*, s.v. Wahhabiya.

6 Robert Lacey, *The Kingdom* (London, 1981), p. 145.

7 Hafiz Wahba, *Arabian Days* (London, 1964), p. 129.

8 Leslie McLoughlin, *Ibn Saud: Founder of a Kingdom* (London, 1993), p. 43.

9 Fred McGraw Donner, *The Early Islamic Conquests* (Princeton, 1981), pp. 256–7.

10 Ibid., p. 268.

11 Soraya Altorki and Donald P. Cole, "Change in Saudi Arabia: A View from 'Paris of Najd'", in Sa'd al-din Ibrahim and Nicholas S. Hopkins (eds.), *Arab Society: Class, Gender, Power and Development* (Cairo, 2001), p. 31.

12 Al-Azmeh, *Islams and Modernities*, p. 148.

13 Lacey, *The Kingdom*, pp. 212–14.

14   James Buchan in David Holden and Richard Johns, *The House of Saud* (London, 1981), p. 515.

15   Al-Azmeh, *Islams and Modernities*, p. 150.

16   Dilip Hiro, *Desert Shield to Desert Storm: The Second Gulf War*, (London, 1992), p. 290.

17   Jean P. Sasson, *Princess* (London, 1997), pp. 215–16.

18   Geoff Simons, *Saudi Arabia: The Shape of Client Feudalism* (London, 2001), p. 39.

19   Ibid.

20   US Department of State, *Country Reports on Human Rights Practices for 1996*, p. 1,375.

21   http://www.hrw.org/reports/1997/Saudi.

22   Amnesty International *Behind Closed Doors: Unfair Trials in Saudi Arabia* (November 1997), cited in Simons, *Saudi Arabia*, p. 39.

23   Al-Azmeh, *Islams and Modernities*, pp. 151–2.

24   Ibid., p. 151.

25   Pervez Hoodbhoy, *Islam and Science: Religious Orthodoxy and the Battle for Rationality* (Kuala Lumpur, 1992), p. 48.

26   Simons, *Saudi Arabia*, p. 21.

27   Ibid.

28   Ibid., p. 22.

29   Ibid., p. 29.

30   Sa'd al-din Ibrahim, *The New Arab Social Order: A Study of the Social Impact of Oil Wealth* (Boulder, 1982), p. 11ff.

31   Ibid., p. 9ff.

32   Ibid., p. 9ff.

33   Simons, *Saudi Arabia*, p. 205.

34   Ibid., p. 304.

35   "A Dangerous Addiction", *The Economist*, 15 December 2001.

36   Gawdat Bahgat, "Managing Dependence: American-Saudi Oil Relations", *Arab Studies Quarterly*, Vol. 23, No. 1, Winter 2001, pp. 1–14.

37   "A Dangerous Addiction", *The Economist*, 15 December 2001.

38   Ibrahim, *The New Arab Social Order*, p. 98.

39   *The Middle East and North Africa 1999* (London, 2000), pp. 933–4.

40   Bahgat, "Managing Dependence: American-Saudi Oil Relations", p. 8.

41   Simons, *Saudi Arabia*, p. 213.

42 "A Dangerous Addiction", *The Economist*, 15 December 2001.

43 The above is based largely on F. Gregory Gause III, "Saudi Arabia over a Barrel", *Foreign Affairs*, Vol. 79, No. 3, May/June 2000, pp. 80–94.

44 Ibid., p. 87.

45 "A Dangerous Addiction", *The Economist*, 15 December 2001.

46 Ibid.

47 Anthony H. Cordesman, *The Gulf and the West: Strategic Relations and Military Realities* (Boulder 1998), pp. 265–6, cited in Simons, Saudi Arabia, p. 247.

48 Ibid., p. 31.

49 Ibrahim, *The New Arab Social Order*, pp. 7–8.

50 Simons, *Saudi Arabia*, p. 241, citing Congressional hearings on arms controls.

51 Buchan in Holden and Johns, *The House of Saud*, p. 515.

52 Jean-Charles Brisard and Guillaume Dasquié, *Ben Laden: La Vérité Interdite* (Paris, 2001), p. 147.

Chapter 6: The Seeds of Terror

1 John K. Cooley, *Unholy Wars: Afghanistan, America and International Terrorism* (London/Sterling, Virginia, 2000), p. 2.

2 Ibid., pp. 2–3.

3 Michael Griffin, *Reaping the Whirlwind: The Taliban Movement in Afghanistan* (London, 2001), p. 147.

4 Peter L. Bergen, *Holy War Inc.: Inside the Secret World of Osama bin Laden* (London, 2001), p. 70.

5 John K. Cooley, *Unholy Wars: Afghanistan, America and International Terrorism* (London/Sterling, Virginia, 2000), pp. 4–5.

6 Ibid., p. 3.

7 "Flawed Justice: The Execution of 'Abd al-Karim Mara'i al-Naqshbandi", *Human Rights Watch*, Vol. 9, No. 9 (E), October 1997. http://www.hrw.org/reports/1997/Saudi.

8 Geoff Simons, *Saudi Arabia: The Shape of Client Feudalism* (London, 2001), p. 271.

9 From an account by an anonymous local authority RE adviser cited by Philip Lewis in "Depictions of 'Christianity' within British Islamic Institutions", in Lloyd Ridgeon (ed.), *Islamic Interpretations of Christianity* (London, 2000), pp. 212–13.

10 John L. Esposito (ed.), *OEMIW*, 4 vols. (New York, 1995), s.v. *Wahhabiyya*.

11 Philip Lewis in Ridgeon (ed.), *Islamic Interpretations of Christianity*, p. 226.

12 Elisabeth Sirriyeh, *Sufis and Anti-Sufis: The Defence, Rethinking and Rejection of Sufism in the Modern World* (London, 1999), pp. 158–9.

13 Annemarie Schimmel, *And Muhammad Is His Messenger: The Veneration of the Prophet in Islamic Piety* (Chapel Hill, North Carolina, 1985), p. 148.

14 Philip Lewis, *Islamic Britain* (London, 1994), p. 85, citing my original report for the BBC World Service; Sirriyeh, *Sufis and Anti-Sufis*, p. 159.

15 Zeeshan 'Ali is quoted in Stephen Schwartz, "Ground Zero and the Saudi Connection", *Spectator*, 22 September 2001, p. 13.

16 Ibid.

17 Meeting with Shaikh Hamza Yousef Hanson, "Open Democracy", London, 17 January.

18 "Flawed Justice", details in note 7 above.

19 Dilip Hiro, *Desert Shield to Desert Storm* (London, 1992), p. 122.

20 Ibid., p. 109.

21 Ibid., p. 121.

22 Ibid., p. 401.

23 Cooley, *Unholy Wars*, p. 31.

24 Ibid., pp. 32–3.

25 Ibid., p. 41.

26 Ibid., p. 44.

27 *Crescent International*, April 16–30 1983, cited in Kalim Siddiqui (ed.), *Issues in the Islamic Movement 1982–83 (1402–3)* (London, 1984), p. 294.

28 Cooley, *Unholy Wars*, p. 82.

29 Ibid., p. 88.

30 Ibid., p. 89.

31 Ibid., p. 23.

32 Ibid., p. 53.

33 Ahmed Rashid, *Taliban: Islam, Oil and the New Great Game in Central Asia* (London, 2001), p. 195.

34 Barnett Rubin, *The Search for Peace in Afghanistan* (New Haven, 1995), p. 198.

35 Ibid., p. 199; Rashid, *Talilban*, p. 19.

36 Griffin, *Reaping the Whirlwind*, p. 20.

37 Cooley, *Unholy Wars*, p. 108.

38 Ibid., p. 107.

39 Rubin, *The Search for Peace in Afghanistan*, p. 199.

40 Vo Nguyen Giap, *People's War, People's Army*, cited in Geoffrey Fairbairn, *Revolutionary Guerrilla Warfare* (Harmondsworth, 1974), p. 336.

41 Bergen, *Holy War Inc.*, p. 80.

42 Ibid.

43 Griffin, *Reaping the Whirlwind*, p. 158.

44 Cooley, *Unholy Wars*, p. 101.

45 Ibid., p. 111.

46 Ibid., p. 163.

47 Griffin, *Reaping the Whirlwind*, p. 131.

48 Cooley, *Unholy Wars*, p. 232.

49 Ibid., pp. 131–2.

50 Ibid., p. 83.

51 Mumtaz Ahmed, *OEMIW*, s.v. Tablighi Jama'at.

52 Lewis, *Islamic Britain*, p. 90.

53 Ahmad, *OEMIW*, s.v. Tablighi Jama'at.

54 Ibid., p. 168.

55 Ibid.

56 John King, "Tablighi Jama'at and the Deobandi Mosques in Britain", in Peter B. Clarke (ed.), *New Trends and Developments in the World of Islam* (London, 1998), pp. 75–103: 85.

57 Ibid., p. 169.

58 Cooley, *Unholy Wars*, p. 85.

59 Bergen, *Holy War Inc.*, p. 143, citing incorporation paper from office of New York Secretary of State.

60 Ibid., citing *New York Times*, 21 March 1993.

61 Cooley, *Unholy Wars*, p. 87.

62 Ibid., p. 118.

63 Adam Robinson, *Bin Laden: Behind the Mask of the Terrorist* (Edinburgh, 2001), p. 39.

64 Ibid., p. 70.

65 Ibid.

66 Simon Reeve, *The New Jackals: Ramzi Yousef, Osama bin Laden and the Future of Terrorism* (London, 1999), p. 160.

67　Robinson, *Bin Laden*, pp. 77–9.

68　Reeve, *The New Jackals*, p. 160.

69　Shaikh Muhammad Qutb, *The Future Is for Islam*, an excerpt from *Hal nahnu Muslimun* ("Are We Not Muslims?", 1995), available at www.msapubli.com.

70　Robinson, *Bin Laden*, p. 86.

Chapter 7: Jihad in America

1　Robert Lacey, *The Kingdom* (London, 1981), p. 514.

2　Geoff Simons, *Saudi Arabia: The Shape of Client Feudalism* (London, 2001), p. 28.

3　Ibid.

4　Adam Robinson, *Bin Laden: Behind the Mask of the Terrorist* (Edinburgh, 2001), p. 91.

5　Peter L. Bergen, *Holy War Inc.: Inside the Secret World of Osama bin Laden* (London, 2001), pp. 56–7; Yossef Bodansky, *Bin Laden The Man Who Declared War on America* (Roseville, CA, 1999, 2001), pp. 11–12.

6　John K. Cooley, *Unholy Wars: Afghanistan, America and International Terrorism* (London/Sterling, Virginia, 2000), p. 88.

7　Adapted from Shaikh 'Abdullah Yousef 'Azzam, "Martyrs: The Building Block of Nations", www.Azam.com; cf. Bergen, *Holy War Inc.*, p. 59.

8　Ibid.

9　See 'Ali Shari'ati, *Marxism and Other Western Fallacies*, trans. H. Algar (Berkeley, 1980).

10　Mark Neocleous, *Fascism* (Buckingham, 1997), p. 11.

11　Benito Mussolini, "The Doctrine of Fascism" (1932), in Adrian Lyttleton, *Italian Fascisms: From Pareto to Gentile* (London, 1973), pp. 59–67, in Neoceous, *Fascism*, p. 14.

12　Ibid, p. 15.

13　Ibid., p. 11.

14　Bodansky, *Bin Laden*, p. 11.

15　Text and translation kindly provided by Professor Fawwaz Gerges.

16　Ahmed Rashid, *Taliban: Islam, Oil and the New Great Game in Central Asia* (London, 2001), p. 129.

17 Bodansky, *Bin Laden*, p. 25.

18 Ibid.

19 Ibid., p. 26.

20 Cooley, *Unholy Wars*, p. 87.

21 Bodansky, *Bin Laden*, p. 26.

22 Rashid, *Taliban*, p. 129.

23 Cited ibid., p. 130.

24 Robinson, *Bin Laden*, p. 124.

25 Nawaf Obeid, quoting a Saudi official, in Bodansky, *Bin Laden*, p. 30.

26 Ibid.

27 Robinson, *Bin Laden*, p. 132; Bodansky, *Bin Laden*, p. 30.

28 Bergen, *Holy War Inc.*, p. 72; Laurie Mylroie, *The War Against America* (New York, 2001), p. 89.

29 Simon Reeve, *The New Jackals: Ramzi Yousef, Osama bin Laden and the Future of Terrorism* (London, 1999), p. 60.

30 Ibid.

31 Mylroie, *The War Against America*, p. 16; Reeve, *The New Jackals*, pp. 142–3.

32 Ibid., p. 112.

33 Ibid., p. 77.

34 Ibid., p. 117.

35 Ibid., p. 119.

36 Reeve, *The New Jackals*, pp. 120–21; a photocopy of the LHR stamp is shown in Mylroie, *The War Against America*, Appendix A, p. 267.

37 Reeve, *The New Jackals*, p. 121.

38 Mylroie, *The War Against America*, p. 84ff.

39 Reeve, *The New Jackals*, p. 246.

40 Ibid., p. 251f.

41 Mylroie, *The War Against America*, p. 244, citing Reeve, *The New Jackals*, pp. 63, 66, 83, 246.

42 Mylroie, *The War Against America*, p. 245.

43 Reeve, *The New Jackals*, p. 118.

44 Mylroie, *The War Against America*, p. 60.

45 Ibid., p. 55.

46 Reeve, *The New Jackals*, p. 251.

47 Mylroie, *The War Against America*, p. 5.

48 Ibid., pp. 62–4.

49 Ibid., p. 29.

50   Ibid., pp. 81–2.

51   Ibid., p. 79.

52   Ibid., p. 81.

53   Ibid., pp. 82–3.

54   Ibid., p. 83.

55   Ibid., pp. 40–41.

56   Reeve, *The New Jackals*, p. 62.

57   Mylroie, *The War Against* America, p. 183.

58   Ibid.

59   Ibid., p. 187.

60   Ibid.

61   *New York Times*, 28 August 1993; Mylroie, *The War Against America*, p. 185.

62   Ibid., p. 189, citing pre-trial documents.

63   Ibid.

64   Ibid., p. 188.

65   Ibid., p. 191.

66   *New York Times*, 28 June 1993; Mylroie, *The War Against America*, p. 192.

67   Ibid., p. 4.

68   Ibid., p. 192.

69   Ibid., p. xvi.

70   Ibid.

71   Ibid., p. 193.

72   Ibid., pp. xiii, xiv, xv.

73   Ibid., pp. 251–3.

74   Fred Halliday, *Two Hours That Shook the World: 11 September 2001: Causes and Consequences* (London, 2002), p. 42.

75   Bodansky, *Bin Laden*, pp. 75–91.

76   Ibid., pp. 129–31.

77   *International Herald Tribune*, 19 March 2002.

78   Jeffrey Goldberg, "The Great Terror", *New Yorker*, 25 March 2002, pp. 52–75.

79   Bergen, *Holy War Inc.*, p. 39.

80   Jim Muir, *Middle East International*, 11 February 2002.

81   *International Herald Tribune*, 25 February 2002.

82   *Guardian*, 14 February 2002.

83   Sir Michael Howard, "Mistake to Declare This a War", *Royal United Services Institute Journal*, December 2001, p. 1.

84 Bodansky, *Bin Laden*, p. x

85 Bodansky's political bias may be inferred from his reference to 'Abdullah 'Azzam's birthplace in 1941 as being near "Jenin in Samaria" (p. 11), a term for what is now the West Bank of the Jordan employed only by the right in Israel.

Chapter 8: A Clash of Civilizations?

1 *The Nation*, 22 October 2001, p. 12.

2 Ibid., p. 11.

3 Samuel Huntington, *The Clash of Civilizations* (London, 1996), p. 183.

4 *The Nation*, 22 October 2001, p. 12.

5 I am grateful to Neil Belton for help in clarifying this argument.

6 Huntington, *The Clash of Civilizations*, p. 210.

7 Ibid., p. 211.

8 Ibid., p. 212.

9 Ibid., p. 311.

10 Ibid., p. 174ff.

11 Ibid., p. 130.

12 Harold Bloom, *The American Religion: The Emergence of the Post-Christian Nation* (New York, 1992), p. 29.

13 Mark Juergensmeyer, *Terror in the Mind of God: The Global Rise of Religious Violence* (Berkeley and Los Angeles, 2001), p. 158.

14 Ibid., p. 159.

15 Malise Ruthven, *Islam in the World* (London and New York, 2000), p. 284.

16 Rodney Stark, *The Rise of Christianity* (San Francisco, 1997), p. 211.

17 Ibid.

18 Peter Brown, *The Making of Late Antiquity* (Cambridge, MA., 1978), pp. 55–7.

19 Jack Goody, *The Development of the Family and Marriage in Europe* (Cambridge, 1983), pp. 56–9.

20 Jean Lambert, *Le Dieu distribué: une anthropologie comparée des monothéismes* (Paris, 1995), p. 251.

21 Marshall G.S. Hodgson, *The Venture of Islam: Conscience and*

History in a World Civilization (Chicago, 1975), Vol. 1, *The Classical Age of Islam*, p. 124.

22 Cf. Malise Ruthven, *Torture: the Grand Conspiracy* (London, 1978), pp. 183–217.

23 Lawrence Rosen, *The Anthropology of Justice: Law as Culture in Islamic Society* (Cambridge, 1989), pp. 17, 49.

24 Ernest Gellner, *Muslim Society* (Cambridge, 1981), pp. 196, 197, 211.

25 Quran 3:110; see also 4:41 and 16:89.

26 Ernst Kantorowics, *The King's Two Bodies : A Study in Mediaeval Political Theology* (Princeton, 1957), pp. 194–206.

27 Ibid., p. 206.

28 F.W. Maitland, Introduction to Otto Gierke, *Political Theories of the Middle Age*, trans. F.W. Maitland (Cambridge, 1900), p. xi.

29 Ibid., p. xxvii.

30 Simon Schama, *Rembrandt's Eyes* (London, 1999), pp. 494–5.

31 Hodgson, *The Venture of Islam*, Vol. 2, *The Expansion of Islam in the Middle Periods*, pp. 340–62 passim; A.H. Hourani and S.M. Stern (eds.), *The Islamic City* (Oxford and Philadelphia, 1970).

32 Quoted in Anthony Giddens, *The Consequences of Modernity* (Cambridge, 1990), p. 169.

33 Ibid., p. 83.

34 *Newsweek*, 7 January 2001.

35 Benjamin R. Barber, *Jihad vs McWorld* (New York, 1996), p. 9.

36 Ibid., p. 11.

37 Ibid.

38 Malise Ruthven, "Religious Strife in the Global Village", unpublished paper, 1994.

39 Barber, *Jihad vs McWorld*, p. 43.

40 Ibid., p. 93.

41 Ibid., p. 134.

42 Ibid., p. 97.

43 Ibid., p. 157.

44 Huntington, *The Clash of Civilizations*, p. 258.

45 Paul R. Pillar, *Terrorism and US Foreign Policy* (Washington, DC, 2001), p. 64.

46 Barber, *Jihad vs McWorld*, p. 161.

47 Ibid.

48 Ibid., p. 207.

49 Ibid., p. 165.

50 Joseph Campbell, *The Hero with a Thousand Faces* (London, 1988 [1949]), p. 35.

51 Ibid., p. 38.

52 *Q-News*, November 2001, p. 20.

53 Ibid., pp. 18, 19.

54 *Q-News*, October 2001, p. 14.

55 *Q-News*, November 2001, p. 20.

56 *Q-News*, October 2001, p. 14.

57 Malise Ruthven, *Islam: A Very Short Introduction* (Oxford, 2000), p. 8.

58 George Gallup Jr and Jim Castelli, *The People's Religion: American Faith in the 90s* (New York, 1989), p. 66.

59 Ibid., p. 210.

60 Laurie Goodstein, "Falwell Offers to Mobilize Churches to Oppose Israeli Pull Back", www.ishipress.com/falwell.htm.

61 Juergensmeyer, *Terror in the Mind of God*, p. 9.

62 Quoted by Peter Berger, "Secularism in Retreat", in John L. Esposito and Azzam Tamimi (eds.), *Islam and Secularism in the Middle East* (London, 2000), p. 49.

63 Juergensmeyer, *Terror in the Mind of God*, p. 242.

64 Ibid., p. 161.

65 Ibid., p. 193.

66 Karen Armstrong, *The Battle for God: Fundamentalism in Judaism, Christianity and Islam* (London, 2000), p. xiii.

67 Ibid., p. 337.

68 See numerous studies by Norman Cohn, including his classic *The Pursuit of the Millennium* (New York, 1961) and *Chaos, Cosmos and the World to Come* (Newhaven, 1993); major studies of Islamic eschatological movements include Marshall G.S. Hodgson, *The Order of Assassins* (New York, 1980). For Sabbatai Sevi see Gershom Scholem, *Sabbatai Sevi: The Mystical Messiah* trans. R.J. Zwi Werblowsky (Princeton, 1973).

69 Abdelwahab el-Affendi, "Rationality of Politics and Politics of Rationality", in Esposito and Tamimi (eds.), *Islam and Secularism in the Middle East*, p. 166.

70 Ernest Gellner, *Conditions of Liberty: Civil Society and Its Rivals* (London, 1996), p. 26; Esposito and Tamimi (eds.), *Islam and Secularism in the Middle East*, p. 151.

71   Ibid., pp. 165–6.

72   Ibid., p. 167.

73   Pervez Hoodbhoy, *Islam and Science: Religious Orthodoxy and the Battle for Rationality* (Kuala Lumpur, 1992), pp. 37ff., 47.

74   Steven Simon and Daniel Benjamin, "The Terror", *Survival* (London Institute of Strategic Studies), Vol. 43, No. 4, Winter 2001, pp. 5–17.

75   Pillar, *Terrorism and US Foreign Policy*, p. 31.

76   *Los Angeles Times*, 5 April 2002.

77   *Today*, BBC Radio 4, 28 February 2002.

78   *New York Times*, 3 April 2002, p. A 21.

79   Full text in *New York Times*, 5 April 2002, p. A 21.

80   Jessica Mathews, "Not Saddam but His Weapons", *International Herald Tribune*, 5 March 2002, p. 6.

81   *International Herald Tribune*, 13 February 2002.

82   *Sunday Times*, 27 January 2002, News Review, p. 6.

83   Simon and Benjamin, "The Terror", p. 9.

84   Ibid., pp. 10–11.

85   Esposito and Tamimi (eds.), *Islam and Secularism in the Middle East*, p. 168.

INDEX

Note: Since most Arabic names appear in western documents and newspapers in journalistic rather than academic transliterations (eg Gamal 'Abdul Nasser for the Egyptian leader Jamal 'Abd al-Nasir) I have used the most recognisable forms where this seems appropriate. The names of Muslim authors writing in English appear as on their books and not as sometimes corrected in library catalogues.

'Abd al-'Aziz b 'Abd al-Rahman al-Sa'ud – see Ibn Saud

'Abd al-'Aziz b Fahd, Prince 156-7,

'Abd al-Basit, Karim 3, 4, 216-223, 228 (see also Yousef, Ramzi)

'Abd al-Ghafur, Akhund 65

'Abd al-Qadir 65

'Abd al-Rahman b 'Abd al-'Aziz, Prince 156

'Abd al-Rahman, Shaikh 'Umar 184-5, 202, 214, 215, 220, 223, 225, 226, 227, 228

'Abd al-Wahhab, Muhammad b 111, 134, 135, 136, 137, 148, 174, 266

'Abduh, Muhammad 66, 74

'Abdullah b 'Abd al-'Aziz, Crown Prince 283 [and more] 284,

'Abdullah b Hussein, King of Jordan 67, 138

'Abdullah, Sulayman b 136

Abu Bakr, caliph 92, 139, 204,

Abu Daud 59

Abu Halima, Mahmud 19-20, 215, 217, 220, 222, 225

Abu Sufyan, 248

Abu Zaid, Nasr 39, 40, 82, 103,
    109,

Acton, Lord 280

Adham, Kamal 183,

el-Affendi, Abd al-Wahhab
    279–80, 291

al-Afghani, Jamal al-Din 66, 75

Ahl-i Hadith 176

Ahmad b 'Abd al-'Aziz, Prince
    156

Ahmad Khan, Sir Sayyid 66

Ahmed, Akbar 65

Ahmed, Mumtaz 193

Aidid, General Muhammad 232

AIPAC (American Israel Public
    Affairs Committee) 164

Al al-Shaikh 148

Al al-Shaikh, 'Abd al-'Aziz b
    'Abdullah 46

Al Sa'ud (dynasty) 64, 136, 141,
    146, 147, 148, 151,
    158–160, 166–8, 178, 213,
    289,

Alexander the Great 54

'Ali b Abi Talib, caliph 178

'Ali, Zeeshan 177

Amir, Yigal 274

Amnesty International 144

al-Ani, Ahmad Khalil 233–4

al-Ansari, Talal 105

al-'Aqqad, 'Abbas 75, 82

al-Aqsa Martyrs Brigade 101

Aquinas, St. Thomas 118

Arab League, 67, 68, 286,

Arafat, Yasser 22, 29, 272, 284,
    287,

Aramco 157–8

'Arif, 'Abd al-Salam, Iraqi
    President 84

Armstrong, Karen 278, 279

Asad, Muhammad (Leopold
    Weiss) 49, 50

al-Ash'ari 62, 207,

Atef, Mohammed 10

Atta, Muhammad 8, 10, 11, 12,
    13, 18, 21, 35, 39, 41, 43,
    103, 120, 131, 233, 234,
    260, 289,

Augustine, St. 247

Averroes (see Ibn Rushd)

Ayyubi, Nazih 119

'Azzam, 'Abdullah 202–14
    passim.

al-Azhar, university 39, 112,

el-Azmeh, 'Aziz 140, 142, 145,

Baader, Andreas 128–30

Baader-Meinhof gang – see Red
    Army Faction

Baer, Robert 285f

al-Bahi, Muhammad 121

Bakri, Mahir 111

Bakri, Omar – see Muhammad,
    Omar Bakri

Bandar b Sultan, Prince 156,
    182,

al-Banna, Hasan 73, 74, 78, 117

Banu Qainuqa 269

Barak, Ehud 283, 287,

Barber, Benjamin 262–267
  passim

Barbouti, Ihsan 218

Barelwi, Ahmad Riza Khan 176,
  177

Barks, Coleman 178

al-Bashir, General 'Umar 112,
  227

Baudrillard, Jean 31

Baz, Sheikh 'Abdullah b 143,
  148–9, 167, 176, 192, 213,

Beamer, Todd 14

Becker, Ernest 245

Becker, Jillian 130

Ben Gurion, David 277

Benjamin, Daniel 289

Bergen, Peter 8, 234, 289–90,

Berlusconi, Silvio 240, 241

Bhutto, Banazir 210, 219

Bhutto, Zulfikar 'Ali 210

Bin 'Ali, Zin al-Abidin, President
  194

Binder, Leonard 82, 83, 93, 94, 97

Bingham, Mark 14

Bin Laden, Mahrus 167–8

Bin Laden, Muhammad 168, 196

Bin Laden, Osama 10, 21, 23,
  30, 43, 45, 46, 150, 170,
  185, 195–200, 202, 208,
  209, 210, 212, 213, 217,
  220, 230–233, 236, 237,
  238, 269, 282

Bin Laden, Salim 197, 212,

BJP (Bharatiya Janata Party) 22

Bloom, Harold 245

Bodansky, Yossef 210, 232, 233,
  237, 238,

Bojinka plot 218

Bonaparte, Napoleon 95

Bourguiba, President Habib 68,
  194,

Boyer, Paul 33

Bremer, Paul 29

Brezhnev, Leonid

Brisard, Jean-Charles 167

Brown, Peter 247

Brzezinski, Zbigniew 169

Bucaille, Maurice 126

al-Bukhari 59

Bultmann, Rudolph 93

Burckhardt, Jacob 136

Burnett, Thomas 14

Bush, George H, President
  170–1, 181, 182

Bush, George W, President 7, 21,
  32, 34, 169, 172, 219, 234,
  235, 273, 285, 287,

Cairo university 41

Calvert, John 76, 77, 81

Calvin, Jean 266

Campbell, Joseph 267

Cannistrano, Vincent 227

Cantor FitzGerald 3

Carrell, Alexis 69, 116

Carter, Jimmy President 164,
  184

Castelli, Jim 271

Cheney, Richard 182, 213
Childers, Gil 228
Choueiri, Youssef 70
Christ, Jesus 18, 38, 42, 56, 174,
    245, 246, 256, 268, 271,
    272, 275,
CIA (Central Intelligence
    Agency) 24, 25, 169, 170,
    171, 172, 186, 188, 205,
    211, 214, 215, 227, 237
Clifton, Charles 6
Clinton, Bill President
    (administration) 229–30,
    272–3,
Cohen, Stephen 286
Coleridge, Samuel Taylor 75, 82
Constantine, emperor 247, 248
Conway, Gordon 17
Cooley, John 169, 171, 192,
    194, 211
Copernicus 148
Cordesman, Anthony 164
Cupitt, Don 93

Dan Fodio, Usumanu 63
Dasquié, Guillaume 167
Dawkins, Richard 99, 100, 102
Deedat, Ahmed 173
Deobandi sect 171, 176, 193,
Descartes, René 93
al-Dhahabi, Sheikh Muhammad
    109, 111
Dickens, Charles 80
Donner, Fred 139

Durkheim, Emile 28

Easterman, Daniel (Dennis
    McEoin) 125
Ellul, Jaques 257
Engels, Friedrich 85, 187,
Ensslin, Gudrun 128, 130

Fadlallah, Muhammad Hussein
    27
Fahd b 'Abd al-'Aziz, Saudi King
    19, 155, 179, 181,
Faisal, b 'Abd al-'Aziz, Saudi
    King 143, 154, 155, 183,
    196, 289,
Faisal b Hussein, King of Iraq
    67, 138
Falun Gong sect 22
Falwell, Jerry 31, 265, 271,
    272–3, 287
Fanon, Franz 116
al-Farag, 'Abd al-Salam 185, 278
FBI (Federal Bureau of
    Investigation) 9, 12, 35,
    214, 217, 219, 224, 225,
Feda'i guerrillas (Iran) 114, 115,
Fedayan-I Islam (Iran) 123
Firestone, Reuven 48, 50,
Foda, Farrag 39
Ford, Gerald, President 161
Foucault, Michel 83
Fox, James (FBI) 216, 226
Franklin, Benjamin 187

Friedman, Milton 187
Friedman, Thomas 286
Fyfield-Shayler, Brian 196

Gabriel, Archangel 57, 197,
Galileo 148
Gallup, George Jr 271
Gandhi, Indira, 274
Gandhi, Rajiv 26
Gellner, Ernest 279
George, Harry 11
Ghanoushi, Rashid 291
al-Ghazali, Imam 63, 102, 124
al-Ghazali, Zaynab 96
Ghumuqi, Jamal al-Din al-Ghazi
    65
Giap, General Vo Nguyen 189,
    190
Giddens, Anthony 125, 258
Glick, Jeremy 14
Goldberg, Jeffrey 234
Goldstein, Baruch 274
Goodstein, Larry 273
Gordon, General 45
Gore, Al 273
Gran, Peter 253
Griffin, Michael 171
Gul, General Hamid 24, 210, 211
Gush Emunim 277

al-Hakim, Tewfiq 78
Halliday, Fred 232
Hamas 27, 101, 211, 276, 278,

Hamoud b 'Abd al-'Aziz, Prince
    156
al-Hamzi, Nawaq 10
Hanjur, Hani 13
Hanson, Sheikh Hamza Yousef
    269–70
al-Haq, General Zia 112, 169,
    187, 193, 209,
Harith, 'Auf bin 60
El-Hassan b Talal, Prince 47
Hawkins, Paula 7
Hazlitt, William 75
al-Haznawi, Ahmad 12
Hermassi, Elbaki 114
Herzl, Theodor 277
Hicks Pasha 45
Hikmatyar, Gulbuddin 188
Hilton, Isabel 22
Hine, Lewis 260
Hitler, Adolf 33, 83, 192, 207,
Hizb al-Tahrir (Islamic
    Liberation Party) 103
Hizbollah, 26, 27, 101, 232,
Hodgson, Marshall 249
Hoffman, Valerie 114, 115, 120,
    121,
Hoodbhoy, Parvez 126
Hourani, Albert 53
House of Saud – see Al Sa'ud
Howard, Sir Michael 236–7,
al-Hudaibi, Hasan 84
Huffman Aviation 10, 11
Huntington, Samuel 212,
    240–243, 255, 260, 261,
    262, 264, 289, 290

Husayn, Taha 81
Hussein b 'Ali, Shi'a Imam 121, 178, 246
Hussein b Ali, Sharif of Mecca 67, 138
Hussein, Qusay b Saddam 232
Hussein, Saddam President 102, 162, 181, 182, 212, 213, 228, 232, 235–6, 284, 285, 286,
Hussein b Talal, King of Jordan 47, 156, 187,

Ibn Hanbal, Ahmad 40, 204, 207, 266
Ibn Hazm 59
Ibn Jama'a 62
Ibn Khaldun 52–3, 249, 2 50
Ibn Qayyim 91
Ibn Rushd (Averroes) 117
Ibn Saud, King 107, 136, 137, 138, 139, 141, 142, 150, 154,
Ibn Taymiyya 106, 111, 135, 174, 266
Ibrahim Pasha 136
Ibrahim, Qutb b 72
Ibrahim, Sa'd al-din Eddin 112, 113, 115, 119, 127, 151, 152, 153, 166,
Ikhwan (Brethren) Arabia 138, 141, 142, 167
Ilyas, Muhammad 193,

IRA (Irish Republican Army) 228–9
ISI (Interservices Intelligence Pakistan) 24, 169, 170, 186, 187, 188, 194, 205, 210, 211, 237
al-Islambouli, Khalid 184
Islamic Jihad 27, 41
Isma'il, Khedive 46

Jackson, Michael 264
Jacobins 91
Jalal, Sheikh Su'ad ("Sheikh Stella") 110
bin Jaluwi family 178
al-Jama'at al-Islamiya (Egypt) 42, 122,
Jama'at-i-Islami (Afghanistan) 188
Jama'at-i-Islami (Pakistan) 68, 69, 114, 176, 187,
Jarrah, Ziad 10, 11, 12, 13,
Jefferson, Thomas 187, 254
Jesus of Nazareth – see Christ, Jesus
Johnson, Lyndon President 210
Jones, Terry 24
Juergensmeyer, Mark 19, 28, 30, 245, 278,
Jung, Carl Gustav 93, 258

al-Kabbani, Hisham 177
Kahane, Rabbi Meir 215, 226

Kamil, Mustafa 72

Kandinsky, Wassily 258

Kant, Immanuel 82, 93

Kantorowics, Ernst 254,

Karzai, Hamid 22, 235, 282

Keenan, Brian 15

Kepel, Gilles 107, 108, 110, 111,
    112,

Kepler, 148

KGB (Soviet intelligence) 211

Khadduri, Majid 53, 59, 60,

Khalid b 'Abd al-'Aziz, King of
    Saudi Arabia 155

Khamenei, Ayatollah 235

Kharijites, neo-Kharijites 63,
    109, 126, 198, 270

Khashoggi, Adnan 165

al-Khifa Center 194, 215,

Khomeini, Ruhallah (Ayatollah)
    180, 181

Kirkegaard, Soren 93

Kissinger, Henry 161

Kitchener, General Lord 45

Kook, Avraham rabbi 277

Kook, Zvi Yehuda rabbi 277

Koresh, David 109

Kreisky, Bruno, Chancellor 128

Lacey, Robert 201

Lambert, Jean 248

Lampson, Sir Miles 76

Late Great Planet Earth 32

Lenin (Vladimir Ilych Ulyanov)
    85, 187,

Levine, Eric 2

Liebnecht, carl 129

Lindsay, Hal 32

Luther, Martin 93, 258, 266

Luxemburg, Rosa 129

Madonna (singer) 264

Mahdi as messiah 244

al-Mahdi, 'Abd al-Rahman 45

Mahdi, Muhamad Ahmad 45

al-Mahdi, Sayyid Sadiq 46

Maher, 'Ali 76

Mahfouz, Khalid b 195

Mahmud, 'Abd al-Halim 183

Maitland, FW 255

Makhluf, General Muhammad
    'Abd al-Halim 111, 112

Makiya, Kanan 35 37

MAK ("office of services") 202,
    209

al-Ma'mun, caliph 39, 40, 116

Mapplethorpe, Robert 265

Martin, Kingsley 277

Marwan, Asma bint 269

Marx, Karl 85, 116, 187, 207

Mash'al b Sa'ud, Prince 179

Massignon, Louis 116

Massoud, Ahmad Shah 188,
    190,

Masterton, Gordon 5

Mathews, Jessica 285, 288

Maududi, Sayyid Abu Ala 68, 69,
    70, 71, 75, 95, 111, 114,
    116, 176, 184, 266, 267

al-Mawardi 63

Mayblum, Adam 2

McCarthy, Andrew 228

McCarthy, John 15

McDonalds (fast food chain)
263

McEoin, Dennis (see Easterman)

McLuhan, Marshall 262

McVeigh, Timothy 290

Mehmet 'Ali dynasty 95, 136

Mehmet V, Sultan 67

Meinhof, Ulrike 128–133

Melville, Herman 33

Mernissi, Fatima 122

al-Midhar, Khalid 10

Milani, Dr S F 47

Military Academy group – see
Technical Military
Academy

Milosevic, Slobodan 273

Minh, Ho Chi 189

Mneinmeh, Hassan 35, 37

Mondrian, Piet 258

Morgan Stanley 2

Mossad (Israeli intelligence) 24,
211,

Mottahedeh, Roy 288 [CK sp]

Moussaoui, Zacarias 12

MTI (Movement de la Tendence
Islamique) 114

Mu'awiya b Abi Sufyan 248

Mubarak, Husni President 233

Muhammad, Ahmed Yousef 227

Muhammad b 'Abd al-'Aziz,
Prince

Muhammad the Prophet 36, 42,
49, 50, 51, 53, 54, 55, 57,
58, 59, 60, 61, 64, 65, 80,
86, 90, 91, 100, 107,
134–136, 138, 139, 150,
159, 206, 208, 244, 247–8,
267, 268, 269, 282, 291

Muhammad b Fahd, Prince 156

Muhammad, Omar Bakri 104

Mugabe, Robert 23

Mujahedin-e Khalq 114, 115

Mundy, Martha 117, 118,

Murad, 'Abd al-Hakim 175

Murdoch, Rupert 264

Musharraf, General Pervez 112

Muslim Brotherhood, Brothers
41, 68, 73, 74, 78, 84, 95,
96, 97, 106, 176, 183, 198,
220,

Muslim League (Pakistan)
187

Mussolini, Benito 207

Mustafa, Shukri 105–111 passim
117,

Mu'tazilites 39, 40, 41, 62, 116,
118, 207,

Mylroie, Laura 216–231 *passim*,
237

al-Nabahani, Sheikh Taqi al-Din
103, 104, 267

Nacke, Louis 14

Nahas Pasha 76, 83

Naif b 'Abd al-'Aziz, Prince

al-Naqshabandi, 'Abd al-Karim
178, 179,
Nasser, President Gamal 'Abdul,
84, 95, 110, 115, 154, 184,
Nazis, Nazism 20
Neguib, General Muhammad 84
Nehru, President Jahawarlal
Netanyahu, Benyamin 272–3,
Nichols, Terry 219
Nietzsche, Friedrich 83, 126, 207,
Nkrumah, President Kwameh 95
Nosair, El Sayyid 215
Nuqrashi Pasha 78

OPEC (Organisation of
Petroleum Exporting
Countries) 161–2, 181
O'Rourke, P J 275

Pahlavi dynasty 158
Pahlavi, Mohammed Reza, Shah
169, 180
Patten, Chris 235
Parker, Ishtiaq 219
Pentagon, 14
Peters, Rudolph 57, 60
PFLP (Popular Front for the
Liberation of Palestine)
101, 128,
Philby, H St. John 140,
Pillar, Paul 283
Plato 93
PLO (Palestine Liberation
Organisation) 187, 275

Powell, Colin 182, 235
Putin, Vladimir 22

al-Qadhafy, Mu'ammar Libyan
leader 129
al-Qahtani, 'Abdallah 167, 244
al-Qa'ida 8, 11, 21, 2419, 20,
109, 120, 169, 183, 205,
211, 232, 233, 234, 236,
267, 269, 281, 282, 284,
289
Quran 18
Qutb, Muhammad 198–200
Qutb, Sayyid 69, 71, 72–98
passim, 103, 105, 106,
109, 110, 111, 117, 118,
120, 124, 184, 198, 202,
206, 216, 220, 267

Raban, Jonathan 19, 20
Rabin, Yitzhak 272, 275
RAF – see Red Army Faction
RAF – see Royal Air Force
Rashid, Ahmed 171, 211
Rashid dynasty 136, 140, 141,
Raspe, Jan-Carl 129
Reagan, Ronald President 165,
170
Red Army Faction ("Baader-
Meinhof gang") 91,
127–133
Reeve, Simon 198, 216–222
passim,

Reich, Wilhelm 122
Rembrandt van Rijn 256
Reno, Janet 227
Ressam, Ahmad 12
Riesebrodt, Martin 122
Robertson, Leslie 6
Robertson, Pat 31, 265, 271,
    287,
Robespierre, Maximilien 281
Robinson, Adam 132, 197, 208,
    209
Rodinson, Maxime 253
Rosen, Lawrency 249
Rosenberg, Alfred 207
Rosenthal, Franz 100
Ross, Dr William 79
Roy, Olivier 69, 280,
Royal Air Force 138, 250
RSS (Rashtriya Swamyamsevak
    Sangh- National Voluntary
    Service, India) 274
Rumi, Jalal al-Din 178
Rumsfeld, Donald 8
Rupert, James 118
Rushdie, Salman 42, 173,
Russell, Kurt 17

al-Sadat, President Anwar 103,
    127, 183, 214, 278,
Said, Edward 240
Saint-Just, Louis de 281
Salameh, Muhammad 223, 224,
    226
Salem, Emad 225, 226,

Salman b 'Abd al-'Aziz, Prince
    156, 179
Salman b Sa'ud, Prince 178–9
Sanchez, Carlos Ilych ("The
    Jackal") 128
Sa'ud b 'Abd al-'Aziz, King 154
Sa'ud b Faisal, Prince 156
al-Sa'ud, 'Abd al-Rahman 142
al-Sa'ud, Muhammad 134
al-Sayyaf, 'Abd al-Rasul 185,
    188,
Schlesinger, Justice 215
Schleyer, Hanns-Martin 129, 130
Scott, Sir Walter 264
Sevi, Sabbatai 279
Shah of Iran (see Pahlavi,
    Mohammed Reza)
Shah, Pir Maroof Hussein 176
Shaheen, Jack 16, 18
Shalabi, Mustafa 214
Shaltut, Mahmud 110
Shariati, 'Ali 206
Sharon, Ariel 22, 273, 284,
Shaw, George Bernard 277
al-Shehi, Marwan 10, 11, 13, 60
al-Shibh, Ramzi bin 12
Siddig 'Ali, Ibrahim 225, 226,
    227,
Simon, Steven 289
Sirriyya, Salih 102–105, 112,
    127, 130,
Smith, Joseph 109
Society of Muslims – see Takfir
    wa-l-Hijra
Sorel, Georges 207

Springer, Axel 128
Ssangyong Oil 158
Stalinists 20
Stark, Rodney 236, 247
Stockhausen, Karlheinz 31
Straton, John R 122
Suchet, David 17
al-Sudairi, Hassa 156
Sukarno, President 95
Sultan b 'Abd al-'Aziz, Prince
    156, 182,
Sultan b Salman b 'Abd al-'Aziz,
    Prince 149
Sun Yang Moon, 109

Tablighi Jama'at (Preaching
    Association) – see also
    Jama'at-i Tabligh) 176,
    192–4, 195,
al-Takfir wa-l-Hijra group
    (TwH) 96, 106–113
    passim, 126, 184, 198,
Taliban 8, 21, 171- 2, 190, 271
Technical Military Academy
    group, 103, 113, 127, 133
Thatcher, Mark 165
Thomas, Dylan 217
Tillich, Paul 132
al-Tilmisani, 'Umar 198
Tipping, Steve 165
al-Tirmidhi 59, 205
Tito, President Joseph Bros 95
Toennies, Ferdinand 265
Torrey, Reuben 33

Truman, President Harry S 76
al-Turabi, Hasan 46, 112, 184,
    213, 227, 232
Turki b 'Abd al-'Aziz, Prince
    156
Turki b Faisal, Prince 201, 202,
    211
Tutu, Desmond archbishop
    276

al-Udah, Sheikh Salman b Fahd
    233
'Umar, caliph 92, 139, 140, 173,
al-'Umari, 'Abd al-'Aziz 13
al-Utaibi, Juhaiman 167, 244
'Uthman, caliph 92

VHP 251 (Vishwa Hindu
    Parishad – World Hindu
    Council)

Wahba, Hafiz 137
Waltz, Susan 120
Washington, George 187
Watt, W Montgomery 51
Weber, Max 123, 253, 257,
Weizman, Chaim 277
Wilkerson, David 32
Wilson, Rep Charles 191
Wolfowitz, Paul 219, 284,
Woolsey, James 219, 229,
    230,

World Islamic League 175, 176,
177, 192, 194

Yamani, Ahmad Zaki 129
Yamasaki, Minoru 4, 5
Yasin, 'Abd al-Rahman
224
Yazid b Abi Sufyan 248 [CK]
Yousaf, Brigadier 188

Yousef, Siraj 227
Yousef, Ramzi (see also 'Abd al-
Basit) 3, 4, 216–223,
228

Zahir, ex-King 235
Al-Zawahiri, Ayman 105, 120,
206,
Zedong, Mao 25, 115, 187, 190